LETTERS FROM WALES

Other books by the same author:-

The Art Galleries of Britain and Ireland
John Ruskin, the Passionate Moralist
My LSE (ed.)
The Music Lover's Literary Companion (with Dannie Abse)
Voices in the Gallery (with Dannie Abse)

2 OCT 07

LETTERS
FROM
WALES

♦

EDITED BY
JOAN ABSE

seren

seren is the book imprint of
Poetry Wales Press Ltd
Wyndham Street, Bridgend, CF31 1EF, Wales

ISBN 1-85411-270-8

A CIP record for this title is available from
the British Library

*The publisher works with the financial assistance of the
Arts Council of Wales*

Printed in Plantin by CPD Wales, Ebbw Vale

CONTENTS

INTRODUCTION

When I began, some years ago, to gather material for this collection of letters from Wales I had little idea where my search would lead me and only a vague notion as to how it should be shaped. As time went on, however, and my vast ignorance diminished somewhat, I began to see a kind of history of Wales appearing through the vivid disclosures of the letters I had already discovered. A patchy history, no doubt, and I was reluctant to endow what I saw emerging with that name: after all, other sources which might reinforce or supplement the evidence of letters were denied to me, leaving certain events or people ignored or but sketchily delineated.

My reluctance was all the more appropriate as I feared my ignorance of the Welsh language might restrict or distort my view. I had already imposed on myself what I felt must be a necessary restriction: that the letters must all come *from* Wales – no interlopers from over the border, however tempting or possibly relevant. Despite these doubts a perceptible picture, a narrative even, seemed to be urging itself upon me through the abundance of letters and journals from Wales, written in English or translated (from Latin or French as well as Welsh).

It is a long while now since I encountered Thomas Carlyle's dictum – he makes a lively appearance in this book – that history is the essence of innumerable biographies. Whether one agrees that this is so or not, it gradually occurred to me that what I had been doing was putting together a kind of biography – with all the limitations the biographer has of never knowing enough – of Wales. After all, what do biographers long for most when starting their task but a supply of letters or intimate journals which may, they hope, provide some insight into their subject, give the sensation of intimacy with what was happening or how someone was feeling or behaving on certain occasions.

In letters, and certainly, I hope, among those in this book, is often to be found eloquent evidence of a situation immediately confronted. Let me instance but a few in these pages: in 1245, an English knight in the army of Henry III, fighting the Welsh, writes from North Wales with news of brutal, horrific happenings and describes himself 'oppressed by cold and nakedness and without winter clothing'; Owain Glyndwr appeals for help from the King of Scotland against the English in 1401, writing, "I and my ancestors and all my said people have been and still are, under the tyranny and bondage of mine and your mortal enemies, the Saxons..."; a Royalist commander during the Civil War writes in exasperation to Prince Rupert of his inability to recruit Welshmen "...if your Highness shall be pleased to command me to the Turk, or Jew, or Gentile, I will go on my bare feet to serve you; but from the Welsh, good Lord deliver me..."; Lewis Morris announces to a friend Evan Evans's discovery of *Y Gododdin*, "Who do you think I have at my elbow, as happy as ever Alexander thought himself after a conquest?"; Shelley sends the following desperate note to a friend: "I have just escaped an atrocious assassination. Oh, send £20 if you have it! You will perhaps hear of me no more!"; Dic Penderyn, awaiting hanging, instructs his sister: "I wish you to come at once to fetch my body..."; John Evans to Lady Charlotte Guest, "We have had twenty-one deaths since Saturday and the disease [cholera] is spreading..."; etc. etc.

Of course, letters do not always depend on the dramatic; they can be invaluable sources of more considered information and points of view and many of these are to be found in the following pages whether dealing with social, religious, political or other matters. They may not give the whole story, and details of the story will sometimes perhaps escape them altogether, but as they were written – people are not always so obliging to posterity – their witness is irreplaceable.

Another resource for the biographer is the journal or the diary, often providing invaluable information and stimulation. Frequently they seem like letters written to the self, records for the future. Indeed, it was interesting to discover that Michael Faraday, whose journal is of the greatest interest, found it uncomfortable to be, as it were, only addressing himself, and began to pretend he was writing a letter addressed to his sister. While Beatrix Potter, determined to be only communicating with herself, made up a secret language which has, nevertheless, since been decoded.

Often I was loth to curtail some journals for reasons of space, so vivid and individual were their observations of the country and its people. In the eighteenth century the preachers of a revived religion told not only of the enthusiasm or rejection they encountered but also wrote about the hardships of their itineraries; while visitors from England like Daniel Defoe and Jonathan Swift provided idiosyncratic and often amusing accounts of their travels. With the onset of Romanticism and the search for the Picturesque in Nature at the end of the eighteenth century the flow of visitors into Wales accelerated and along with it a flood of travellers' descriptions and reminiscences, many of these decidedly designed for publication. These latter, mostly written after the event, I have tried to avoid.

The urge to visit Wales spread widely as the nineteenth century progressed. Charles Fulke Greville in 1841 may have commented, "I have never travelled in any country which appeared more foreign"; but little more than a decade later, the American, Nathaniel Hawthorne, was complaining of the tourists "vulgarising the place" – though he had the grace to admit that this view might include him! From such writings, in a century prolific in their production, I have culled what seemed to me to show the most vivid experience of Wales and the Welsh.

It would seem that the age of letter writing and journal keeping has almost passed. Nevertheless the twentieth century is represented here by a host of rewarding pieces illustrating close observation and feeling for Wales – from, for example, John Cowper Powys's relating of individual experiences to Caradoc Evans's wry journal and Graham Sutherland's powerful description of the influence of Pembrokeshire on his art. Alongside such writings, as always in this book, I have tried to keep to the fore the feeling of the actual life being vividly lived in Wales, the essential history, the struggles, the suffering and indomitability of the people.

Joan Abse

The Thirteenth Century

My purpose in choosing the following selection of letters (originally in Latin) for the most part is to provide glimpses of the intense struggles for domination pervading medieval Wales – struggles of the Welsh not only with successive Anglo-Norman and English kings but between the Welsh princes, avid for territorial acquisitions themselves. As with most attempts at conquest and colonisation the subjugation of religious organisations and their appurtenances played a part. The Normans, having in recent times reformed their own Church, disdained the ecclesiastical structure they encountered in Wales with its well-established practice of such things as clerical marriage and clerical dynasties and its own collection of 'unknown' local saints. They were, of course, not averse to seizing the lands and wealth of the Church where possible but the object of policy rapidly became to exercise ecclesiastical as well as political control: to establish their own religious orders in Wales and to place the Welsh church firmly under the authority of the Archbishop of Canterbury. Opposition to this was centred in the church of St. David's, as the contender for religious authority in Wales, and eventually was waged chiefly by Giraldus Cambrensis – Gerald of Wales – scholar, cleric and descendant of Princes, whose attempt to gain the Bishopric of St. David's, defeated by the King in 1176, was revived in 1198 when the see again became vacant and pursued for some years with great persistence. The following letters were written during the time of this struggle. The first, in support of Giraldus, comes from the CHAPTER OF MYNYW (ST. DAVID'S) and is addressed to Pope Innocent III:

To the most revered Lord and Father, Innocent, by the Grace of God, High Pontiff, the Chapter of Mynyw, greeting and homage and fidelity. If perchance it shall have come to your hearing that the Prior of Llantony has been consecrated Bishop and set over our Church by the Archbishop of Canterbury, know well that this has assuredly been done contrary to our election and our will. For from the beginning when our See was vacant we have demanded and to this day demand of your fatherly love that Master Giraldus, our Archdeacon, should be consecrated, whom we have already canonically elected in our Church, being willing, by the Grace of God and of yourself, to agree to no other. Moreover, as at the outset, so continually and constantly we have appealed to your protection, that no man may presume to do anything to the prejudice of our Church and of this election canonically made with the assent both of the clergy and people of this country. May your Paternity fare well always and be a blessing to the whole world of the faithful.

The Autobiography of Giraldus Cambrensis, ed. and trans. H.E. Butler (London: Jonathan Cape, 1937).

The second letter, written in either 1200 or 1201, and also addressed to the Pope, comes from a group of temporarily united Welsh princes: Llywelyn, Prince of Gwynedd, known as Llywelyn Fawr (the Great); Gwenwynwyn and Madoc, Princes of Powys; Gruffydd, Maelgwn, Rhys and Meredith, sons of Rhys, Prince of South Wales. It has been suggested that Giraldus wrote it for them as it encapsulates views which he expressed elsewhere. Whatever the case the letter is a precursor of the complaints reiterated throughout the following centuries about English misrule and disregard of the Welsh language particularly in the sphere of religion:

WELSH PRINCES to Pope Innocent III.

And first, the Archbishop of Canterbury, as a matter of course, sends us English bishops, ignorant of the manners and language of our land, who cannot preach the Word of God to the people, nor receive their confessions but through interpreters.

And besides these bishops that they send us from England, as they neither love us nor our land, but rather persecute and oppress us with an innate and deep-rooted hatred, seek not the welfare of our souls; their ambition is to rule over us, and not to benefit us; and on this account they do not but very rarely fulfil the duties of their pastoral office among us.

And whatever they can lay their hands upon or get from us, whether by right or wrong, they carry into England, and waste and consume the whole of the profits obtained from us, in abbeys and lands given them by the king of England. And like the Parthians, who shoot backwards from afar as they retreat, so do they from England excommunicate us as often as they are ordered so to do....

Besides these things, when the Saxons [English] rush into Wales, the Archbishop of Canterbury puts the whole land under an interdict, and because we and our people defend our country against the Saxons and other enemies, he places us and our people under judgment of excommunication, and causes those bishops whom he sent among us to proclaim this judgment, which they are ready to do on all occasions. The consequence is, that every one of our people who falls on the field of blood, in defence of the liberty of his country, dies under the curse of excommunication.

We therefore with sighs and tears, beseech your Holiness, to whom belongs the government of the Universal Church, to give us effectual relief from these grievances and others which will be communicated to you by the mouth of the Canons of St. David's, and Giraldus, their Bishop elect, who is a discreet and reverent man.... For before the time of the three last Bishops, St. David's was the seat of an Archbishop of all Wales who, as Archbishop, was subject to none except to the Mother Church of Rome.

Essay on the Causes which have produced Dissent from the Established Church in the Principality of Wales, Arthur Johnes (Llanidloes: 1870).

The early years of the thirteenth century saw the rise of the power of Llywelyn, the Prince of Gwynedd, who came to be known as Llywelyn the Great. Llywelyn's prime objective was to extend his authority from his domain, Gwynedd, over the greater part of Wales, an ambition in which he was largely successful. The English King John who succeeded to the throne in 1199 became variously his opponent and ally: in 1205 Llywelyn married the King's illegitimate daughter, Joan, and in the following years succeeded in extending his power in Wales. But in 1211 John, whose attentions had been much engaged elsewhere, perceived the danger of Llywelyn's growing supremacy and made a successful attack on Llywelyn's lands in North Wales and laid plans for further devastation. But the situation which seemed disastrous for Llywelyn in 1211-1212 soon changed. John's attention to Wales was again withdrawn because of threats elsewhere, Llywelyn regained his losses, made an alliance with France, (see the following letter), gained concessions for the Welsh from the king at the signing of Magna Carta and by 1218 had become the effective leader and Prince of Wales, a situation which he more or less maintained for the rest of his life.

In 1212, Pope Innocent III called upon Philip Augustus, King of France, to make war upon King John, excommunicated because of disputation over the appointment of an Archbishop of Canterbury, to bring him back into "subjection of the Holy Church". At the same time the Pope absolved the Welsh princes from their oath of allegiance to King John. Llywelyn then allied the Welsh with Philip Augustus.

LLYWELYN FAWR to Philip Augustus.

To our most excellent lord Philip, by the Grace of God, the illustrious King of the French, Llywelyn, Prince of North Wales, his friend, sends greeting and such devotion as the debt of fealty and respectful service which I will repay the excellency of your nobility, on account of the singular and priceless gifts which you, King of the French, even prince of that country of kings, outstripping me, your friend, not more munificently than magnificently, have sent me by your knight, your letters, impressed by your golden seal in witness of the alliance of the kingdom of the French and the principality of North Wales, which I, before an assembly of clergy, even upon the sacrosanct relics swear to observe as they will be a perpetual memorial and inviolable testimony, that I and my heirs, cleaving separably to you and your heirs shall be to your friends friends, to your enemies enemies. This itself therefore stipulating, I expect and ask from your kingly dignity to be royally observed in every manner towards me and towards my friends, and in order that it may be inviolably observed, having called together a council of my chieftains, and with the common consent of all the princes of Wales, I have joined with you in the friendship of this treaty. I promise you, under witness of my seal, fidelity in perpetuity, and as I this faithfully promise I will carry out my promise the more faithfully. Moreover, since I received letters of your excellency, I have made neither truce, nor peace, nor any negotiation whatever with the English. But, by the grace of God, I and all the princes of Wales, unitedly confederated, will manfully resist our enemies, even yours, and by the help of God and with a strong hand, we will recover from the yoke of the tyrants themselves the great part of the land and the strongly fortified castles, which they by fraud and guile have occupied....

Welsh Records in Paris, ed. T. Matthews (Carmarthen: 1910).

The following sharp letter is from Llywelyn to the young King Henry III who had, as a boy of nine, succeeded his father, King John, in 1216. It was probably written in July 1224. Falkes de Bréauté, whom it concerns, was an adventurer who had been bailiff to John and was now in revolt against his son.

From LLYWELYN, PRINCE OF NORTH WALES to King Henry.

Has received the king's letter announcing the transgression of Falkes de Bréauté, for which the king laid siege to Falkes's castle of Bedford, and forbidding Llywelyn to receive Falkes or to give him aid or counsel. He informs the king that Falkes had visited him and complained that he was unjustly treated by the king's council but he left Llywelyn's territory on the same day as he arrived. Llywelyn informs the king of this, not because he is bound to offer any excuse for receiving Falkes, for he has no less liberty than the King of Scotland who receives outlaws from England with impunity. Llywelyn has not heard that Falkes has ever done the king any harm, and knows that he has done the king great services. Nor must the king feel vexed that Falkes should betake himself to Llywelyn since they both have reason for complaint against the king's council. As for the fact that Falkes has been excommunicated as a disturber of the realm, Llywelyn is of opinion that those who counsel the king to disinherit great men without cause are much greater disturbers of the realm....

Calendar of Ancient Correspondence concerning Wales, J. Goronwy Edwards (Board of Celtic Studies, *History and Law Series*, No. II University Press Board: Cardiff, 1915).

Llywelyn's wife, Joan, had, according to the chronicles, been a consider-able helpmeet to him in various negotiations and otherwise. In 1230, however, Llywelyn discovered that William de Braose, one of the Lords of the Marches whom he had captured in 1228 during a conflict with the king and with whom he had recently made peace, was Joan's lover – as Llywelyn informed the Earl of Pembroke, 'treacherously entering his chamber and bringing upon him opprobrium beyond measure.' The following letter tells what happened to William. Joan was imprisoned but released the following year, resuming her former position.

NICHOLAS, ABBOT OF VAUDEY, to Ralph, Bishop of Chichester, Chancellor.
Soon after May 18, 1230.

...As for William de Braose, he was undoubtedly hanged from a tree in a certain manor called Crokein on the morrow of the feast of Philip and James [May 2, 1230], in the presence of more than eight hundred persons, called together for the lamentable spectacle, especially those who were enemies of William de Braose senior and his sons.

Llywelyn was evidently determined not to let the matter alter previous arrangements to make peace, for he wrote to the wife of William de Braose in the following manner:

LLYWELYN, PRINCE OF ABERFFRAW, LORD OF SNOWDON, to Eva de Braose.
Soon after May 2, 1230.

Wishes to know whether she desires the alliance made between his son Dafydd and her daughter Isabel to stand, because it will not be Llywelyn's doing if the alliance does not stand. Informs her that he could in no way prevent the magnates of the land from making the judgement which they made, taking vengeance for the opprobrium and injury done to Llywelyn.

Calendar of Ancient Correspondence concerning Wales, J. Goronwy Edwards.

After the death of Llywelyn Fawr the stable conditions he had achieved soon were wrecked. His son and heir, Dafydd, imprisoned his illegitimate elder stepbrother, Gruffudd, whom their father had disinherited but, threatened by Henry III, he was soon to surrender his father's gains and in August 1241 abased himself in the following terms:

DAFYDD, SON OF LLYWELYN to followers.

To all the faithful followers of Christ to whom the presents shall come, David, son of Llewellyn, greeting. – Know that I have given my consent to my lord the illustrious Henry, King of England, son of King John, that I will release my brother Griffin, whom I hold imprisoned, together with his eldest son and others, who, by reason of the aforesaid Griffin, are detained in prison by me, and will give them up to my lord the king. And I will afterwards abide by the decision of his court, both as to whether the said Griffin ought to be detained in prison, as well as with respect to the portion of the territory late of my father, the aforesaid Llewellyn, if any ought to belong to the said Griffin, according to the Welsh custom... also that I will restore to Roger de Monthaut, seneschal of Chester, his territory of Monthaut, with its appurtenances, and will restore to him, and to the other barons and faithful subjects of the king, the seisins of the lands which have been occupied since the commencement of the war between his majesty King John and my father, the aforesaid Llewellyn... and I will repay to my lord the king all the expenses

18

which he and his have incurred by reason of that war, and that I will, according to the decision of the said court, satisfy him and his for the losses and injuries suffered by them, or will give up all malefactors to the king. And that I will also pay to my lord the king all the homage which King John, his father, received, and which the said king ought to have; and especially the homage of all the Welsh nobles.... And for the faithful observance for ever of all and singular the above articles, to the king and his heirs, I will give security for myself and my heirs by hostages or pledges, or in any other way that the king may choose to dictate, and in these and in all other things I will abide by the will and command of my lord the king, and obey the decision of his court in all things.... Done at Alnet, near the river Elvey; in the diocese of St. Asaph, on the feast of the Decollation of St. John the Baptist, in the twentyfifth year of the reign of our said lord the king.

Matthew Paris, *English History from 1235-1273,* trans. from Latin by Rev. J.A. Giles (1847).

Gruffydd, imprisoned by Henry in the Tower of London, in 1244 fell to his death in attempting to escape. Soon after Dafydd, allied with other princes, was in open revolt again; conscious that the king's aim was to take away their independence, in July 1244 Dafydd also appealed to the Pope to assume the overlordship of Gwynedd in return for an annual tribute. For a time the rebellion had its successes but Dafydd died in February 1246. A graphic account of the situation in North Wales in 1245 is to be found in the following letter to his friends by an English knight in the army of the king, written on September 24th of that year.

ENGLISH KNIGHT to friends.

His majesty the king is staying with his army at Gannock, for the purpose of fortifying a castle which is now built in a most strong position there; and we are dwelling round it in tents, employed in watchings, fastings, and prayers, and amidst cold and nakedness. In watchings, through fear of the Welsh suddenly attacking us by night; in fastings, on account of a deficiency of provisions, for a farthing loaf now costs fivepence; in prayers, that we may soon return home safe and uninjured; and we are oppressed by cold and nakedness, because our houses are of canvass, and we are without winter clothing. There is a small arm of the sea which flows and ebbs under the aforesaid castle, where we are staying, and forming a sort of harbour, into which, during our stay here, ships have often come from Ireland and from Chester, bringing provisions. This arm of the sea lies between us and Snowdon, where the Welsh quarter themselves, and is, at high tide, about a crossbow-shot wide. On the Monday next before Michaelmas, in the afternoon, a ship from Ireland, bringing provisions to us for sale, was coming up towards the entrance of the harbour, but being incautiously steered, as the sea receded, it remained aground under our aforesaid castle, but on the opposite bank, towards the Welsh, who immediately rushed down and made an attack on it as it lay on dry ground. We therefore, seeing this proceeding from the bank on this side, sent three hundred Welsh, our borderers from Cheshire and Shropshire, across the water in boats, together with some crossbowmen, to defend the said ship; on seeing which the Welsh hurriedly retreated to their accustomed and well-known hiding-places in the mountains and woods. Our knights, attended by their followers, pursued them for a distance of two leagues, and although they were on foot (for they had not brought their horses across the water with them), they wounded and slew many of the Welsh. Our people then returned after defeating their enemies and, like greedy and needy men, indulged in plunder, and spread fire and rapine through the country on the other side of the water, and amongst other profane proceedings, they irreverently pillaged a convent of the Cistercians called Aberconway, of all its property, and even of the chalices and books, and burnt the buildings belonging to it. The Welsh, in the mean time, having assembled a large host of their countrymen, suddenly rushed with noisy shouts on our men, who were laden with booty acquired by the most wicked means, and impeded by their sins, and put them to flight, wounding and slaying many as they retreated towards the ship; some of our people, choosing rather to trust to the billows, and to perish by drowning, than to be slain at will by their enemies, threw themselves of their own accord into the waves, there to perish. Some of our knights they took alive, to imprison them; but hearing that we had slain some of their nobles, and above all, Naveth son of Odo, a handsome and brave youth, they also hung these knights of ours, afterwards decapitating and mangling them dreadfully: finally, they tore their miserable corpses limb from limb, and threw them into the water, in detestation of their wicked greediness in not sparing the church, especially one belonging to religious....

In the mean time Walter Bissett, who was on board the ship with his followers, bravely defended it, and was engaged till about midnight in continued fight with the Welsh, who fiercely attacked him on all sides, and if our men had not had the sides of the ship for a wall, they would have altogether fallen into the hands of the enemy.

At length, as the sea rose, the ship began to roll, and it being now inaccessible, the Welsh withdrew, lamenting that our people had been snatched out of their hands....

Whilst we have continued here with the army, being in need of many things, we have often sallied forth armed, and exposed ourselves to many and great dangers, in order to procure necessaries, encountering many and various ambuscades and attacks from the Welsh, suffering much and often, by the fortuitous chances of war, doing damage to them. After one conflict, we brought back in triumph to our camp the heads of nearly a hundred decapitated Welsh. At that time there was such a scarcity of all provisions, and such want of all necessaries, that we incurred an irremediable loss both of men and horses. There was a time, indeed, when there was no wine in the king's house, and, indeed, not amongst the whole army, except one cask only; a measure of corn cost twenty shillings, a pasture ox three or four marks, and a hen was sold for eightpence. Men and horses consequently pined away, and numbers perished from want.

Matthew Paris, *English History from 1235-1273.*

Dafydd left no sons but Gruffydd left three, one of whom, Llywelyn ap Gruffydd (c.1225-1282) was destined to emulate his grandfather, Llywelyn Fawr, in endeavouring to break the power of the English. This power strengthened in the decade after Dafydd's death but in 1255 Llywelyn, having overcome his contentious brothers, attacked the English strongholds in Wales and overcame many recalcitrant Welsh lords. In 1257 he inflicted crushing defeats on the English and he assumed the title of Prince of Wales in 1258, confirmed for him by Simon de Montfort in June 1265, and confirmed for him and his heirs by Henry III at the Treaty of Montgomery in 1267. He himself agreed to pay homage to the English Crown. This agreement was not sustained when Edward I succeeded to the throne (the following letters bear witness to Llywelyn's grievances) and in 1276 Edward attacked Llywelyn, defeating him in 1277 and depriving him of many of the possessions he had acquired in Wales. A disturbed peace seems to have prevailed until towards the end of 1282 war broke out again in which Llywelyn, subsequently known as The Last Prince, was killed. This marked the collapse of hopes for a Welsh state and the event was lamented in Welsh literature as a national disaster. Edward I proceeded to consolidate his grip on Wales by the building of a series of castles and walled towns. The following letters give some idea of the story.

From JOHN DE GREY to King Henry (III).
Shortly after March 3, 1263.

When he arrived in the parts of Hereford, whither the king had sent him for the defence of those parts, he found that all the men of Humphrey de Bohun the younger in the land of Brecon, of Reginald Fitz Peter in Talegard, Egglesseil and Blenleveny, of Robert de Turbeville in Crikhoel, of Robert Wafre in Talelond, of Roger Pichard in Straddewy, of Roger de Tony in Elveil, of Matilda Lungespe in Cantrescelif, and of other marchers in those parts, had withdrawn from the king's fealty and had adhered to the king's Welsh enemies by all appearance in order to devastate and destroy the lands of the king and of those faithful to him; and from all of them Llywelyn ap Gruffydd, the capital enemy of the king's crown, had taken homage and fealty. Wherefore having immediately taken counsel with those faithful to the king, that is Maurice de Berkl., Roger de Sampford, and certain other knights of the king who had come to Grey to those parts, so that they numbered in all 12 knights together with sergeants, horsemen and footmen at the king's wages, together with Reginald Fitz Peter, Humphrey de Bohun and other loyal marchers, they invaded the land of the aforesaid king's enemies who had withdrawn from the king's lordship, until for the most part they had returned to the king's peace. The aforesaid Llywelyn, having learned of the arrival of Grey, sent into those parts against Grey the greater men of his council together with a great force from North Wales, West Wales, and South Wales, for the defence of the aforesaid districts which he had drawn to himself from the king's fealty; so that when Grey had reached Brecon, the aforesaid enemies had assembled, and they had about 180 barded horses, as well as unarmoured horses, and more than ten thousand foot. Grey and his party waited there for two days, but could have no engagement with them, nor they with Grey. And these enemies turned to the parts of Bergeveny [Abergavenny] burning and destroying the lands of those loyal to the king in these regions. Whereupon Peter de Montfort sent asking Grey to go thither in all haste to his aid. So he immediately went to the assistance of those districts, together with Roger de Mortimer, who has manfully and faithfully served the king. On the first Saturday in March [March 3, 1263] they arrived at Bergaveny, where the enemy awaited them, drawn up for attack. And when Grey and his force crossed the ford of Bergaveny ready to attack them, they suddenly fled to the hills for safety, and as Grey could not pursue them, he turned to other places, that is the woods and glens, where many of the enemy were slain or captured. He then returned to Brecon, because he had heard that Llywelyn was not far from its borders, investigating how he could most easily attack Grey. And Grey heard by good report that Llywelyn had caused a great army to be collected from all directions in order to devastate and occupy the lands of the king and of those loyal to the king. And on Grey's return from those parts he had received the king's letters saying that if Grey and Roger de Mortimer and others who had suffered damage from the aforesaid should think fit, Grey might assign to Llywelyn a day after easter to amend the aggressions committed by him and his men against the truce. Grey has therefore sent to Roger Mortimer and others of the March asking them to meet Grey to discuss this matter and other matters contained in the king's letters. Grey needs money and help for the defence of these parts; he is sending to the king William de Axmouth and Walter de Wernun, who will inform the king of the state of affairs.

Calendar of Ancient Correspondence concerning Wales, J. Goronwy Edwards.

LLYWELYN, PRINCE OF WALES, LORD OF SNOWDON, to King Edward (I).
Probably Feb 26, 1274 (possibly 1273). Criccieth.

Informs the king that the money which Llywelyn is bound to pay to the king for the making of peace between the late King Henry on the one part, and Llywelyn on the other, is ready to be paid to the king's attorneys, provided that the king performs to Llywelyn what he ought to perform according to the terms of the said peace. Therefore requests the king to compel the Earl of Gloucester, Humphrey de Bohun, and the rest of the Marchers to restore to Llywelyn the lands by them unjustly occupied and more unjustly detained, and Llywelyn will immediately pay the aforesaid money to the king.

Calendar of Ancient Correspondence concerning Wales, J. Goronwy Edwards.

HYWEL AP MEURIG to Lady Maud de Mortimer.
Possibly March, 1274.

Informs her that he hears that Llywelyn, Prince of Wales, will come on the following Tuesday to Kedeuhing [Cydewain] to see his new castle. It is stocked for his stay for three weeks at his own cost, and in addition all the bailiffs of Wales will supply him with provisions each for two days at his own cost. The writer also hears that Llywelyn will go into the forest of Cloune *(Clun)* to arrange a place for a new castle, and it is rumoured that a party of the great men of England are coming thither to speak with Llywelyn. The writer does not know whether this will be for good or for evil. He advises Lady Maud that she send all this news to his lord, and that she cause watch to be kept at Cloune and everywhere, so that they may be well prepared.

Calendar of Ancient Correspondence concerning Wales, J. Goronwy Edwards.

ANIAN, BISHOP OF ST. ASAPH, to King Edward (I).
Probably soon after Sept, 1275. *Anian was a bitter enemy of Llywelyn.*

Informs the king that on the king's recent withdrawal from the March, Llywelyn, Prince of Wales, caused it to be published throughout his dominion that peace had been made between Llywelyn and the king, and that the king had withdrawn: and on this pretext, the prince had imposed on the people a heavy tribute of threepence on each head of cattle, and on other animals at his pleasure, which money he pretends he will pay to the king. Wherefore some people are astonished and afraid, and suggest to Anian that he should report the matter to the king. Requests the king to signify by the bearer of this letter his wishes about Anian's coming to him.

Calendar of Ancient Correspondence concerning Wales, J. Goronwy Edwards.

To Pope Gregory X from the ABBOTS of Whitland, Strata Florida, Cwm-hir, Strata Marcella, Aberconwy, Cymer, Valle Crucis.

[Llywelyn] has been a vigorous and special protector of our Order and of all ecclesiastical Orders and persons in Wales in times of peace and in war. So we humbly beg you, Holy Father, on our knees, that, inspired by divine love, you will not believe such references as the bishop of St. Asaph has made concerning the said prince.

Councils and Ecclesiastical Documents relating to Great Britain and Ireland, Vol. I, (Oxford University Press).

From LLYWELYN, PRINCE OF WALES AND LORD OF SNOWDON, *suus devotus,* to King Edward (I).
Feb 2, 1282 (or possibly 1281). Nefyn.

The king had by the messengers signified to Llywelyn, concerning certain business about which Llywelyn has frequently informed the king, i.e. concerning Llywelyn's honey and horses detained at Chester by reason of a certain wreck which happened in Llywelyn's land before the war, that he would instruct the Justice of Chester to communicate his answer to Llywelyn. And when Llywelyn believed that he would have a remedy in this matter, behold on another day when Llywelyn sent his messengers to Chester to buy necessaries, they were attached there by order of the aforesaid Justice, and honey belonging to Llywelyn, to the value of four pounds sterling, was taken from them. This greatly surprises Llywelyn: if the Justice did this on his own authority he seems to Llywelyn to have acted unjustly, and if it has been done at somebody's instigation with the king's assent, Llywelyn is no less surprised, since he had understood from the king's letters and the king's answers that the king would not allow him to be aggrieved in this business or in others. He therefore requests the king to instruct the Justice to release the detained goods. If he on whose account they are detained says that he has been wronged in Llywelyn's land, let him come to Llywelyn whenever he will, and Llywelyn will cause justice to be done according to the customs of his land....

Calendar of Ancient Correspondence concerning Wales, J. Goronwy Edwards.

The following letter is from Eleanor, the wife of Llywelyn. She was the daughter of Simon de Montfort, the King's enemy, and had herself been held prisoner by King Edward before she was able to marry Llywelyn.

ELEANOR, PRINCESS OF WALES, LADY OF SNOWDON to Edward (I).
Feb 2, (probably 1282). Nefyn.

Desires to have news of the king, and requests that he will send her some news of himself. She is surprised that the king allows her husband, the prince, to be vexed by certain merchants... for since the prince is ready to show all justice, according to the customs of his land, in those matters which are done or which happen in his land, it seems strange that credence should be given to anybody who complains of the prince, before the matter has been thoroughly discussed in the prince's own land. Wherefore she prays the king to give a competent remedy in this matter. Moreover, she has heard that some of her men, and one whom the king knows well, i.e. John de Becard, who was captured with her, have through the prayers of certain persons been restored to the king's peace, and she has often petitioned the king on their behalf, and has not been heard: she did not believe that she was so estranged from the king that he would not more speedily receive them to his peace for her sake than for the sake of others. Nevertheless she prays the king to receive into his peace Hugh de Punfred, Hugh Cook, and Philip Tailor, for since they are poor, and are of English origin, they can make a living in England better than elsewhere, and it would be harsh to exile them from their own land.

Calendar of Ancient Correspondence concerning Wales, J. Goronwy Edwards.

The following letter was written in November 1282 by LLYWELYN *to the Archbishop of Canterbury, John Peckham, who had undertaken negotiations between Llywelyn and Edward I. It seems that secret proposals were afoot to give land in England to Llywelyn worth £1000 provided he would give up Snowdonia to Edward.*

With regard to the proposal that the prince should place the lord king in absolute possession of Snowdonia forever and in peace let it be known that since Snowdonia is something which pertains to the principality of Wales, which he and his ancestors have held since the time of Brutus ... his council does not permit him to renounce that land and take in its place a land in England to which he has less claim. Also the people of Snowdonia say that, even if the prince might wish to convey them to the king's possession, they are unwilling to do homage to a stranger with whose language, customs and laws they are unfamiliar. For if that were to happen to them they might be made captive forever and be cruelly treated, as other cantreds on every side have been treated by the king's officers and other rulers, more cruel than Saracens, as is revealed in the rolls which they sent you holy father.

C.T. Martin, *Registrum Epistolarum fratris Johannis Peckham, Archiepiscopi Cantuariensis*, Rolls Series, II. Quoted in *Edward I and Wales*, ed. by Trevor Herbert and Gareth Elwyn Jones (Cardiff: University of Wales Press, 1988.)

Immediately after December 11, 1282, the disaster is reported in an official dispatch by Roger l'Estrange to Edward I.

ROGER L'ESTRANGE to Edward (I).

To his very noble lord Edward by the grace of God King of England, Lord of Ireland, and Duke of Guyenne, Roger l'Estrange, if you please, sends honour and reverence. Know, sire, that the stout men whom you assigned to my command fought against Llywelyn ap Gruffudd in the region of Builth on the Friday next after the feast of St. Nicholas and that Llywelyn ap Gruffudd is dead, his army vanquished and the whole flower of his army killed, as the bearer of this letter will tell you and believe what he will tell you from me.

J.E. Morris, 'Two Documents relating to the Conquest of Wales,' *English Historical Review*, XIV (July 1899).

After the death of Llywelyn, Edward I set about consolidating the annexation of Wales, adding considerably to the number of castles and walled towns which had already been built. Archbishop Peckham was sent on a visitation to Wales to advise the King on what was to be done with the intractable Welsh. On July 8th 1284 he wrote thus to Edward I.

ARCHBISHOP PECKHAM to Edward (I).

...Sire, it seems to me that the people of Wales are too savage and wicked... and a lost people without profit to the world. And if it pleases you I would counsel you in this way if one cannot find a better. First, Sire, their bloody and other customs arise because they do not live together but keep themselves distant from one another. And if you wish to reform them, Sire, to be of benefit to God and the world and prevent bloodshed command that they live together in towns. The wickedness of the Welsh derives from their idleness; because they are idle they think up their wicked deeds... the clergy know no more of letters then the laymen....

Councils and Ecclesiastical Documents relating to Great Britain and Ireland, ed. Haddan and Stubbs (Oxford: Clarendon Press, 1869-78).

The following letter is on a lighter note. Another, dated 1345, indicates that there was still violent hostility to the English occupation. A decree of c.1295 had ordered that the Welsh could not purchase land nor be burgesses in the English walled boroughs and towns within Wales.

From KING EDWARD (I) to William de Hamilton.
Mar 16, 1295. Conway.

Order to summon immediately all the brewers of the town of Chester, and that Hamilton with the mayor and bailiffs of the town command them on the king's behalf to brew good beer for the king and his host, as much as they can; and that Hamilton arrange that the beer be speedily brought to the king by all the vessels which he can find in those parts. Also that the said brewsters have sufficient of the said beer ready brewed when the king sends thither his boats when he shall be in Anglesay, so that the king have no shortage, for the king does not will that his men take corn for his use, whereby the brewsters be hindered from brewing and the king be short of beer, because he has oats and wheat at Conway sufficient for himself and his host for the present.

Calendar of Ancient Correspondence concerning Wales, J. Goronwy Edwards.

The Fourteenth Century

From THE BURGESSES OF THE TOWN OF CARNARVON to The Prince of Wales and his Council.
Shortly after Feb 14, 1345.

  The burgesses have often shown to the council of the king, the prince's father, the great damages and destruction that they have suffered in the past and still suffer daily from the malevolence and enmity of the Welsh, who seek to destroy the prince's English ministers and burgesses. Thus when John de Huntingdon, the prince's sheriff of Merioneth, was holding his court in the king's name, he was, by the assent and compassing of the leading Welshmen of the country, feloniously slain and robbed of the rolls of the king, and of all his goods and chattels; and many other English bailiffs and burgesses have been feloniously slain, and no remedy has been given: whereby the Welsh have become so proud and cruel and malicious towards the English in the said land, that they dare not go anywhere for fear of death. And now their malice is growing, and when Henry de Shaldeforde, the prince's attorney in these parts, was journeying towards Carnarvon on Monday, St. Valentine's day last past (Feb 14, 1345) to perform his office, there came Tudor ap Goronwy with a great number of Welshmen by the compassing of his brother Hywel ap Goronwy and several others, and they slew the said Henry and his men feloniously and against the peace. The burgesses pray that the prince will ordain a speedy remedy, otherwise they will have to desert his towns and castles and leave the country. And as the said Tudor and Hywel and the other Welshmen have become so powerful that no Welshman dare indict them of the death of the said Henry or of other trespasses which they commit daily against the peace, the burgesses pray that the prince will send letters to his justice or his lieutenant, to make inquests through Englishmen, and they will state the truth concerning the above matters.

Calendar of Ancient Correspondence concerning Wales, J. Goronwy Edwards.

THE ABBOT AND CANONS OF BARDSEY to The Justice's
Lieutenant and the Chamberlain or their Viceregents.
Immediately after May 6, 1346.

The abbot and canons announce that a certain robber called J. [?]
Bannebury landed at Bardsey at dawn on Saturday the feast of St.
John *ante portam Latinam* in the present year with two boats containing thirty well-armed men, wherefore the writers are passing on the
information in order that the lieutenant and chamberlain may warn
the maritime districts through the bailiffs as they think best, lest
worse danger befall. The abbots and canons were shut up while the
visitors remained in Bardsey, and they have taken away everything
that was prepared for food and drink and much other goods, and
have done the abbot and canons much damage.

Calendar of Ancient Correspondence concerning Wales, J. Goronwy Edwards.

The Fifteenth Century

1401 ff.

OWAIN GLYNDWR (c.1354-c.1416), *was a distant descendant of Llywelyn ap Gruffudd and thus, with his undoubtedly charismatic character, seems to have represented a beacon of promise to the oppressed and disaffected Welsh – witness the poems written about him even before the uprising. Though he spent his early years on sufficiently cooperative terms with the English (for a time he attended the Inns of Court) the unlawful seizure of his land in 1400 by Lord Grey of Ruthin and Grey's further treacherous behaviour prompted him to ally himself in September 1400 with a widespread outbreak of rebellion in Wales. A chronicle in the British Library compiled by one of Henry V's chaplains speaks of the rising of the Welsh and their subsequent choice of Glyndwr as their leader. The rebellion was defeated and was followed by a tour of North Wales by Henry IV, the recent usurper of the English throne, demanding submission, followed by confiscation of the estates of the leaders, notably 'Owinus de Glyndordy.' But whatever Henry may have thought he had achieved rebellion soon reappeared. On Good Friday, 1401, a gang of Welsh rebels, led by Gwilym and Rhys Tudor captured the castle of Conway. It was an astounding blow to Hotspur (Henry Percy), then in command in North Wales at Denbigh Castle, even more so because the rebels could not be quickly dislodged. From Caernarvon where he was accompanied by Prince Henry, the Prince of Wales, Hotspur wrote, as follows, to the Privy Council at the beginning of May in an attempt to reassure the King that the Welsh rebellion was all but under control.*

HOTSPUR (HENRY PERCY) to Privy Council.

...excepting those rebels who are in the castles of Conway and Rees which is in the mountains, and whom I hope will be well chastised, if God pleases, by the forces and authorities which my redoubtable brother the Prince has sent there, as well of his counsel as of his retinue, to hold the siege before the rebels in the said castles; which siege if it can be continued until the said rebels are taken, will be a great ease and comfort to the governance of this country in time to come. And also Reverend Fathers in God and very dear Brethren, the peasantry of the said country of North Wales, that is to say the counties of Caernarvon and Merioneth, have just presented themselves before me and humbly thanked my redoubtable brother, the Prince, for his very great kindness in supplicating our lord the King for his gracious pardon, and they humbly beg for the confirmation of this under his seal, offering to give him of their own will (beside the usual dues) and without any other request, as great a sum as they gave to King Richard when he was King and Prince, as the bearer will fully declare to you....

Proceedings and Ordinances of the Privy Council, Vol. I, ed. Sir Harris Nicolas, (1834).

A deal was made with the rebels at Conway and the castle probably surrendered on May 28th. Hotspur, already intent on quitting Wales and returning to his lands on the Scottish borders, wrote news of Owain Glyndwr on June 4th in a letter to the Privy Council.

HOTSPUR to Privy Council.

I see such pillage and mischief in the country, that good and hasty measures ought to be immediately adopted by sea as well as by land. All the country is without doubt in great peril of being destroyed by the rebels if I should leave before the arrival of my successor, the which will be an affair of necessity... please to know that news has reached me this day from the Sieur of Powis, as to his combat with Owen de Glyndyfrdwy, whom he hath discomfited, and wounded many of his men on his way to my much honoured uncle and myself as he certified, for which I thank God.

Proceedings and Ordinances of the Privy Council, ed. Sir Harris Nicolas.

Despite this setback, during the following months Glyndwr and his forces roamed widely in Wales doing damage to many English strongholds and Henry IV's campaign against him had little success. Towards the end of 1401 Owain Glyndwr decided to seek help from other enemies of Henry IV, i.e. the King of Scotland and the chieftains of Ireland. The contents of the letters Owain wrote to them, dealing with genealogies and prophecies, were recorded by the chronicler, Adam of Usk, but the letters never reached their destinations, the messengers being seized and beheaded. Both were written on November 29th 1401.

OWAIN GLYNDWR to The King of Scotland.

Most high and Mighty and redoubted Lord and Cousin, I commend me to your most High and Royal Majesty, humbly as it beseemeth me with all honour and reverence. Most redoubted Lord and Sovereign Cousin, please it you and your most high Majesty to know that Brutus, your most noble ancestor and mine, was the first crowned King who dwelt in this realm of England, which of old times was called Great Britain. The which Brutus begat three sons: to wit, Albanact, Locrine, and Camber, from which the same Albanact you are descended in direct line. And the issue of that same Camber reigned loyally down to Cadwalladar, who was the last crowned King of the people, and from whom I, your simple Cousin am descended in direct line; and after whose decease, I and my ancestors and all my said people have been and still are, under the tyranny and bondage of mine and your mortal enemies, the Saxons; whereof you most redoubted Lord and very Sovereign Cousin, have good knowledge. And from this tyranny and bondage the prophecy saith that I shall be delivered by the help and succour of your Royal Majesty. But most redoubted Lord and Sovereign Cousin, I make a grievous plaint to your Royal Majesty, and most Sovereign Cousinship that it faileth me much in soldiers, therefore most redoubted Lord and very Sovereign Cousin, I humbly beseech you kneeling upon my knees, that it may please your Royal Majesty to send me a certain number of soldiers, who may aid me and withstand, with God's help, mine and your enemies, having regard most redoubted Lord and very Sovereign Cousin to the chastisement of this mischief and of all the many past mischiefs which I and my ancestors of Wales have suffered at the hands of mine and your mortal enemies. And be it understood most redoubted Lord and very Sovereign Cousin that I shall not fail all the days of my life to be bounden to do your service and to repay you. And in that I cannot send unto you all my business in writing, I send these present bearers fully informed in all things, to whom be pleased to give faith and belief in what they shall say to you by word of mouth. From my Court, most redoubted Lord and very Sovereign Cousin, may the Almighty Lord have you in his keeping.

The letter to Ireland, less fulsome but also appealing to prophecy, contained the same message:

OWAIN GLYNDWR to the Irish Chieftain.

Health and fulness of love, most dread Lord and most trusty

Cousin. Be it known unto you that a great discord or war hath arisen between us and our deadly enemies, the Saxons; which war we have manfully waged now for nearly two years past, and henceforth mean and hope to wage and carry out to a good and effectual end, by the grace of God our Saviour and by your help and countenance. But seeing that it is commonly reported by the prophecy, that before we can have the upper hand in this behalf, you and yours, our well beloved Cousins in Ireland must stretch forth thereto a helping hand, therefore most dread Lord and trusty Cousin, with heart and soul we pray you that of your horse and foot soldiers, for the succour of us and our people who now this long while are oppressed by our enemies and yours, as well as to oppose the treacherous and deceitful will of those same enemies, you despatch to us as many as you shall be able with convenience and honour, saving in all things your honourable State, as quickly as may seem good to you. Delay not to do this by the love we bear you and as we put our trust in you, although we be unknown to you, seeing that, most dread Lord and Cousin, so long as we shall be able to manfully wage this war in our borders, as doubtless is dear to you, you and all the other Chiefs of your land of Ireland will in the meantime have welcome peace and calm repose.... Dread Lord and Cousin, may the Almighty preserve your reverence and Lordship in long life and good fortune.

Written in North Wales, on the twenty-ninth day of November.

Welsh Records in Paris, Thomas Matthews (Carmarthen: 1910).

In the spring of 1402 Glyndwr, in the course of many successful ventures, captured his old enemy Reginald Grey in battle near Ruthin and held him for many months for a ruinous ransom. In June at the battle of Bryn Glas, Sir Edmund Mortimer was captured. The king had ambivalent feelings towards him and his ransom was not paid and eventually Mortimer threw in his lot with Glyndwr and married his daughter. Mortimer had extensive possessions in Wales and wrote as follows 'to all the gentles and commons of Radnor and Presteigne' from Machynlleth on December 13th, 1402:

SIR EDMUND MORTIMER to 'gentles'.

I greet you much and make known to you that Oweyn Glyndwr has raised a quarrel of which the object is, if King Richard be alive, to restore him to his crown; and if not that, my honoured nephew,* who is the right heir to the said crown, shall be king of England, and that

34

the said Oweyn will assert his right in Wales. And I, seeing and considering that the said quarrel is good and reasonable, have consented to join in it, and to aid and maintain it, and by the grace of God to a good end, Amen. I ardently hope, and from my heart, that you will support and enable me to bring this struggle of mine to a successful issue. I have moreover to inform you that the lordships of Melenyth, Gwerthrynion, Rhayader, Commote of Udor, Arwystli, Cyfeiliog, and Caereinion are lately come into our possession: wherefore I moreover entreat you that you will forbear making inroad into my said lands, or doing any damage to the said tenantry, and that you furnish them with provisions at a certain reasonable price, as you would wish that I should treat you: and upon this point be pleased to send me answer. Very dear and well beloved, God give you grace to prosper in your beginnings and to arrive at a happy issue.

* *Also named Edmund Mortimer, afterwards 5th Earl of March, who was lineal heir to the crown.*

Original Letters Illustrative of English History, ed. Henry Ellis, Second series, Vol. I.

Henry IV's efforts to suppress the rising had but intermittent success and in early 1403 Henry Percy and his father, Earl of Northumberland, never convinced adherents of the king, began negotiations with Owain Glyndwr for whom, it appears, they had considerable respect. By July 1403 the rebel army was sweeping through South Wales causing great alarm and distress to the English occupiers, witness the following two letters from Jenkin Hanard, the Constable of Dynevor Castle and John Skydmore from Carreg Cennen to John Faireford, the King's Receiver in Brecon.

JENKIN HANARD to John Faireford.

Dear Friend,

Oweyn Glyndour, Henry Don, Rhys Ddu, Rhys ap Griffiths ap Llewellyn, Rhys Gethin have won the town of Carmarthen and Wygmor, Constable of the Castle, has yielded up the castle to Oweyn who has burned the town and slain of men of the town more than fifty men and they are in purpose to be in Kidwelly and a siege has been ordered of the castle that I keep and that is a great peril for me and all that are here with me; for they have made a vow that they will kill us all; therefore I pray you that you will not boggle us but send us a warning within a short time whether we shall have any help or not;

or if there be no help coming that we may steal away by night to Brecon cause that we faileth victuals and men, and namely men. Also Jenkin ap Llywelyn have yielded up the castle of Emlyn with free will, and also William Gwyn, Thomas ap David ap Gruff and many gentils been in person with Owain. Warning hereof I pray that ye send me by the bearer of this letter. Fareth well in the name of the Trinity. I write at Dynevor in haste and in dread, in the feast of St. Thomas the Martyr.

Jenkin Hanard.

A Source Book of Welsh History, Mary Salmon (Oxford University Press: 1927).

JOHN SKYDMORE to John Faireford, Receiver of Brecknock.

Worshipful sir, I recommend me to you, and for as much as I may not spare no man from this place away from me, to certify neither the King nor my lord the Prince of the mischiefs of these countries about, nor can no man pass by any way hence, I pray you and require you that you certify them how all Kermerdynschire, Kedewely, Carnwaltham, and Yskenyn were sworn to Oweyn yesterday, and he lay at night in the Castle of Drosselan, with Rees ap Gruffuth; and I was there and spoke with him upon truce, and prayed for a safe conduct under his seal to send home my wife and her mother and their company, but he would not grant me it; and on this day he is about the town of Kermerdyn, and there thinks to stay till he may have the town and the Castle; and his purpose is from thence into Pembrokeshire; he holds himself sure of all the Castles and Towns in Kedewelly, Gowerslonde, and Glamorgan, for the same countries have undertaken the siege of them till they are won. Wherefore write to Sir Hugh Waterton, and to all those that you suppose will take this matter to heart, that they excite the King here in all haste to revenge himself on some of his false traitors whom he has overmuch cherished, and to rescue the towns and castles in these countries for I dread full sore there be too few men in them. I can do no more as now; but pray God help you and us that think to be true. Written at the Castle of Carreckenen the v. day of July.

Yours

John Skydmore.

Original Letters, ed. Henry Ellis.

Soon after, John Faireford wrote in great alarm to the King himself.

JOHN FAIREFORD to Henry IV.

My most noble and dread Lord,... I have received at Brecon certain letters addressed to me by John Skidmore, the which enclosed within this letter, I present unto your high person by the bearer of these, that it may please your most gracious lordship to consider the mischief and perils comprised in them, and to ordain thereon speedy remedy for the destruction and resistance of the rebels in those parts of South Wales, who are treacherously raised against you and your Majesty; so that your castles and towns and the faithful men in them be not thus ruined and destroyed for lack of aid and succour.

And besides, may it please your lordship to know that the rebels of this your lordship of Brecon, together with their adherents, are lying near the town of Brecon doing all the mischief that they can to its neighbourhood; and they of Cantreff Selyff and Builth on Wednesday last did burn certain houses within your manor of Bryn-Llys, and they purpose, all of them together, to burn and destroy all pertaining to the English in these same parts if they be not resisted in haste. Considering also, my most noble Lord, if you please, that the whole of the Welsh nation are by all these said parties confirmed in this rebellion, and with good will consent together, as only appears from day to day, by their governance, and also of their support against you and all your faithful ones, may it please your royal Majesty to ordain a final destruction of all the false nation aforesaid, or otherwise all your faithful ones in these parts are in great peril....
Written at Brecon, the 7th day of July

Your humble Clerk and Orator,

John Faireford

Receiver of Brecon.

Lett. Henry IV. Royal and Historical Letters during the reign of Henry the Fourth, ed. F.C. Hingeston for the Rolls Series (London: 1860).

However, Henry IV had better success with the rebellion of Henry Percy which broke out later in July for he defeated and killed Hotspur at the Battle of Shrewsbury on July 21st though his father, Northumberland remained a threat in the North of England. By now an alliance between Glyndwr and Charles VI of France must already have been contemplated for in September there were reports of French forces in Wales.

The CONSTABLE OF KIDWELLY to Henry IV.

Most high and most excellent Lord – We commend us to your most royal Majesty, so far as we know and are able. And, most excellent Lord, may it please you to know that Henry Don, and all the rebels of South Wales, with the men from France and Bretagne, were coming towards the Castle and town of Kidwelly, with all their array, and there have destroyed all the grain belonging to your poor lieges, on every side around your said Castle and the town; and that the greater part of your poor commons there have taken their departure and gone into England, with their wives and young children, and the rest are within your said Castle, in uncertainty about their lives. Concerning which may it please your most royal Majesty to ordain in this matter aid, rescue and succour, for the preservation of your said Castle, and your poor lieges within it, in a short time; or otherwise, your said Castle and all we your lieges there, are destroyed and undone for ever, as the bearers of these presents will more fully certify to you by mouth....

Written at Kidwelly, in very great haste, the Wednesday next after the feast of St. Michael the Archangel....

Royal and Historical Letters during the reign of Henry the Fourth, ed. F.C. Hingeston.

In 1404 Owain Glyndwr, having captured Harlech Castle, established his own court there as Prince of Wales and, according to Adam of Usk assembled a parliament at Machynlleth. He now held sway over a considerable part of Wales. In 1405 a letter to Henry speaks of Glyndwr summoning a Parliament at Harlech and rumours that, provided his strength is reinforced by the French, he will seek for peace. Yet his domination remained precarious and it seems he continually sought to strengthen the alliance with France; thus in July an agreement was signed in Paris by his envoys binding Owain and Charles in league against their mutual enemy, Henry of Lancaster. But though the forces sent by France were certainly in evidence harassing the English in Wales, they never proved decisive in the attacks and battles that continued over the next two years. Nevertheless the alliance with France provoked two documents of great interest. Owain's rebellion occurred at the time of the Papal schism when there were two Popes, one in Rome and the other, Benedict XIII in Avignon. Charles VI gave allegiance to Benedict and in 1406, pressed Glyndwr to take the same position.

An assembly was held to discuss this at Pennal, near Machynlleth from whence Glyndwr sent the following letter and manifesto to Charles. Echoes of Llywelyn Fawr's complaints against the English Church appear again which were, indeed, to echo over the centuries and his request for the setting up of two universities in Wales evidence his concern for Welsh learning and language.

OWAIN GLYNDWR to Charles VI, King of France.

Most Serene Prince,
    You have deemed it worthy on the humble recommendation sent, to learn how my nation for many years now elapsed has been oppressed by the fury of the barbarous Saxons; whence because they had the government over us and indeed, on account of that fact itself, it seemed reasonable with them to trample upon us. But now, most serene prince you have in many ways, from your innate goodness informed me and my subjects very clearly and graciously concerning the recognition of the True Vicar of Christ. I, in truth, rejoice with a full heart on account of that information of your excellency and because, inasmuch from this information I understand that the Lord Benedict, the supreme pontifex, intends to work for the promotion of a union in the Church of God with all his possible strength. Confident indeed of his right, and intending to agree with you as far as is possible for me I recognise him as the True Vicar of Christ, on my own behalf and on behalf of my subjects by these letters patent, forseeing them by the bearer of their communications in your Majesty's presence.
    And because most excellent prince the Metropolitan Church of St. David's was, as it appears, violently compelled by the barbarous fury of those reigning in this country, to obey the Church of Canterbury and *de facto* still remains in this subjection. Many other disabilities are known to have been suffered by the Church of Wales through these barbarians which for the greater part are set forth fully in the letters patent accompanying. I pray and sincerely beseech your majesty to have these letters sent to my Lord the Supreme Pontifex, that as you deemed worthy to raise us out of darkness into light, similarly you will wish to extirpate and remove violence and oppression from the church and from my subjects as you are well able to. And may the son of the glorious virgin long preserve your majesty in the promised prosperity.
    Dated at Pennal the last day of March in the year of our Lord 1406 and the sixth of our reign.

    Owain, Prince of Wales.

THE PENNAL MANIFESTO. Written to Charles VI, from Pennal, a village near Machynlleth, on March 31, 1406.

(Extracts) Whereas most illustrious prince the underwritten articles especially concern our state and the reformation and usefulness of the Church in Wales, we humbly pray that you will graciously consider it worthy to advance their object even in the Court of the said Lord Benedict....

Again that the Church of St. David's shall be restored to its original dignity which from the time of St. David, Archbishop and Confessor, was a metropolitan church....

Again that the same Lord Benedict shall provide for the metropolitan church of St. David's and the other cathedral church of our Principality, prelates, dignitaries and beneficed clergy and curates who know our language.

Again that the Lord Benedict shall revoke and annul all incorporations, unions, connections, appropriations and parochial churches of our Principality made so far, by any authority whatsoever with English monasteries and colleges. That the true patrons of these churches shall have the power to present to the ordinaries of these places suitable persons to the same or appoint others.

Again that the said Lord Benedict shall concede to us and our heirs, the Princes of Wales, that our chapels etc shall be free and shall rejoice in the privileges, exemptions and immunities in which they rejoiced in the times of our forefathers, the princes of Wales.

Again that we shall have two universities or places of general study, namely one in North Wales and the other in South Wales, in cities, towns or places to be hereafter decided and determined by our nuncios and ambassadors for that purpose.

Again that the Lord Benedict shall brand as heretics and cause to be tortured in the usual manner, Henry of Lancaster, the intruder of the kingdom of England, and the usurper of the crown of the same kingdom, and his adherents, in that of their own free will they have burnt or have caused to be burnt so many cathedrals, convents and parish churches; that they have savagely hung, beheaded and quartered archbishops, bishops, prelates, priests, religious men, as madmen or beggars, or caused the same to be done....

Finally Owain Glyndwr asks for the remission of the sins of his adherents '...of whatever nation they may be' who wage war against the intruder Henry and his heirs.

T. Matthews, *Welsh Records in Paris*, (Carmarthen: 1910).

Owain's hold on Wales gradually declined over the next few years under the repeated attacks of Prince Henry. After a major defeat at Welshpool in 1410 sporadic guerilla activity continued for some while but when and where Owain finally died remains a matter for speculation.

The Sixteenth Century

1523-4

The following letter is of some interest, revealing as it does the perennial objection to an influx of strangers. It was written by Richard Gruffithe, who seems to have been a person of power in Pembrokeshire, to Cardinal Wolsey, Henry VIII's Minister. Were the Irish mentioned here refugees from conflict in Ireland or, to use the modern term, 'economic migrants'? Sir Henry Ellis comments: 'From the mention of the Earl of Desmond in it, as in open rebellion, it may be taken for granted that the date must have been in 1523 or 1524...'. He subsequently records that from a Ms. in the Harleian Collection entitled The First Booke of the Description of Pembrokshire in General, *1603, the 4th chapter has the following title:* 'That the Countye is nowe inhabited by three severall nations: as Welshmen the remnant of the Ancient Brittains and first Inhabitants of the Countrey; Englishmen brought thither at the Conquest thereof; and by Irishmen which doe dailye ferrye over thither out of Ireland; and of the language spoken by these three severall nacions'. *No mention is made of the Flemings who settled in Dyfed about 1100; presumably they had been largely assimilated by this time.*

RICHARD GRUFFITHE to Cardinal Wolsey.

Pleasith it youre most noble Grace, my dutie of most humble recommendacions hadde unto your Grace, as apperteynyth, sygnyfyinge unto the same your most noble Grace that there is so gret aboundance of Irisshemen latelye comyn within these xii monthes into Pembrokeshire, the Lordship of Haverforde West, and so alongst the see syde to Saynt Davyes, and within the townes of Haverforde West, Pembroke and Tenbye, with such that be comyn thither before and inhabited there, that by estymacion to amounte at the leste to the nombre of twentye thousande persons and above, of all manner sorte, and the most part of the same Raskells be out of the domynyons of the Kings Rebellyon the erle of Desmonde; and verye fewe of theym out of the Englisshe pale of Irelande. And the Kings Towne of

42

Tenbye is almost cleane Irisshe, as well the hedde men and ruelers and the comyns of the said Towne; and of their highe and presumptuous myndes doo dissobey all maner the Kings processe that comythe to theym out of the Kings Eschequyer of Pembroke; supposying that their Charter woll bere theym therein, where of truthe their Charter is no thyng like so large of liberties as they do clayme it to be.... And the last yere I herde of a grete nombre of the same Irisshemen that were cast over lande upon the cost with in the said Shire, whereupon I made a preveye watche, and in two little parisshes in one nyght I gadered of theym above two hunderde that were newe comyn, besids as monye that were comyn there before; and all the same new Company I did sende to See agayne. Albeit, sythyn, they be comyn agen with manye mor: and every on that comythe doth clayme kyndred to one or other of the same shire, townes, and countre foresaid. And ever sythyn that I expulsed the said new comyn Irisshemen out of the countre as before, the rest do grudge agaynst me. And of truethe in all the said circuete there be four Iryshe agaynst one Englisshe or Welshe: and therfore, after my poore mynd, it were expedyent and necessarye that the Kings Highenes with his most honorable Counsaill shulde ponder the same, and devise some order to be takyn, as wel for th'avoiding of the most parte of theym, as alsoe that noo man within that parties shall reteigne any that shall come out of Irlande thider, at any tyme Hereafter into their service, upon a certaine penaltye; and ells they shall never be woren out but increas more and more. And furder sygnyfying unto your most noble Grace that the mayor and Towne of Tenby have commytted and don many great ryots, rowtes, and unlawfull assembles agaynst the Kings lawes, his peax, crowne, and dignyte, with diverse extorcions, as shall appere by divers indictaments, remaynynge agaynst theym in the Kings Records of Pembroke. And also it shal be duely proved that they have ayded and vittailed the Kyngs enymyes at sundrye tymes, and that as shalle pleas the Kyngs Highenes and your most noble Grace to commaunde me to do, concernyng any order that shal be takyn concernying the premyssis, shal be accomplisshed with all diligence to the uttremost of my little power; as knoweth God who ever preserve your most noble Grace in felicitie.

From Carmarden the viijth daye of this July,

Your humble servaunt R. Gruffithe.

Original Letters, ed. Henry Ellis, Vol. I, First series.

BISHOP ROWLAND LEE (d.1543) was one of Henry VIII's chaplains. He married Henry to Anne Boleyn in 1533 and was rewarded by being created Bishop of Coventry and Lichfield. In 1535 he was appointed Lord President of the Marches; he discovered much violence and disorder there which he ruthlessly quelled. He reported frequently to Thomas Cromwell, Henry VIII's chief adviser, the following letter being dated January 19th 1536.

BISHOP ROWLAND LEE to Thomas Cromwell.

After my most hearty recommendations this shall be to advise you that we have received from you the two outlaws, named David Lloide or Place, and Johan ap Richard Hockilton, with Richard ap Howell alias Somner, the murderer at Monmouth, for the which we heartily thank you. And the said two outlaws we have sent to their trial, according to justice, which tomorrow they shall receive (God pardon their souls). And farther within two days after the receiving of the said thieves, were brought to us iiij other outlaws as great or greater than the aforesaid David and Johan were, and two of the first of them had been outlawed these xvj years; whereof iij were alive, and one slain brought in a sack trussed upon a horse, whom we have caused to be hanged upon the gallows here for a sign. Would God you had seen the fashion thereof. It chanced the same day to be market day here by reason whereof iijc (300) people followed to see the said carriage of the said thief in the sack.... What shall we say farther: all the thieves in Wales quake for fear.... So that now you may boldly affirm that Wales is reduced to that state that one thief takes another and one cow keeps another for the most part....

The History of Ludlow, Thomas Wright (1852).

Rowland Lee refers in the following letter to provisions under the first Act of Union 1536 under which the Marcher Lordships were to be divided into shires – seven new counties (Denbigh, Montgomery, Radnor, Brecknock, Pembroke, Glamorgan and Monmouth) added to the existing six counties.

BISHOP ROWLAND LEE to Thomas Cromwell. March 19, 1536.

I was lately informed that the King wished to make Wales shire ground, and have justices of the peace and gaol delivery as in

England. I cannot do less than declare my mind in one point, especially as in trial of felons; for if they may come to their trials at home, where one thief shall try another, as before the last statute in that party provided they did, then that as we here have begun is foredone. You cannot do the Welshmen more pleasure than to break that statute. I would I had an hour to speak my mind to you. I think it not expedient to have justices of the peace and gaol delivery in Wales, for there are very few Welsh in Wales above Brecknock who have 10 li. land, and their discretion is less than their land. As there is yet some bearing of thieves by gentlemen, if this statute go forward, you will have no other but bearing and little justice, as you may judge by the demeanour of Merionethshire and Cardiganshire; for though they are shire ground they are as ill as the worst part of Wales. I trust you will keep the former statute provided for Wales, as for bearing of weapons, by which you will be assured of the good rule which is now begun.

Calendar of Letters and Papers, Foreign and Domestic, ed. J. Gairdner (London: 1868-1932).

1538

The following letters are concerned with the suppression, after Henry VIII's split with Rome, of ancient observations and superstitions associated with the Catholic Church. The first letter is from Bishop William Barlow, Bishop of St. David's from 1536, to Thomas Cromwell, Henry VIII's powerful Minister of State. Bishop Barlow, an ardent Protestant, was responsible for putting into effect some of the first stages of the Reformation in his diocese of St. David's.

BISHOP WILLIAM BARLOW to Thomas Cromwell.

...Concerning your lordship's letters addressed for the taper of Haverford West, ere the receipt of them I had done reformation and openly detected the abuse thereof, all parties which before time repugned penitently reconciled. But since then I chanced upon another taper of much greater credit and of more shameful detestation, called our lady's taper of Cardigan, which I have sent here to your lordship with convenient instructions of that devilish delusion. Furthermore, when I admonished the canons of Saint David's according to the king's instructions in no wise to set forth feigned relics for to allure people to superstition, neither to advance the vain observation of unnecessary holy days abrogated by the king's supreme authority, on Saint David's day the people wilfully solemnising the feast, certain relics were set forth which I caused to be sequestered and taken away, detaining them in my custody until I may be advised of your lordship's pleasure. The parcels of the relics are these: two heads of silver plate enclosing two rotten skulls stuffed with putrified clowtes; Item, two arm bones, and a worm eaten book covered with silver plate. Of the canons slumbering negligence toward the preferment of God's word, and what an ungodly disguised sermon was preached in the cathedral church in the feast of Innocents last passed, they being present with an audience of three or four hundred persons, this bearer, a minister of the same church, shall further declare, having part of the said sermon in writing apparent to be shown....

...From Carmarthen, the last day of March.

Letters relating to the Suppression of the Monasteries, ed. T. Wright (Camden Society: 1843), Letter XCIII.

In North Wales, the image of Derfel Gadarn, supposedly of a 6th century soldier, killed in the Battle of Camlan where Arthur was killed, was preserved and worshipped at Llanderfel in Merioneth. The wooden image showed him mounted on a horse and extraordinary protective and prophetic powers were attributed to him. The following letters concerning the image are from Dr Ellis Price, the monastic commissioner of the diocese of St. Asaph, to Thomas Cromwell. The image was burnt at Smithfield in May 1538.

DR ELLIS PRICE to Thomas Cromwell.

Right honourable and my singular good lord and master, all circumstances and thanks set aside, pleaseth it your good lordship to be advised that where I was constitute and made by your honourable desire and commandment commissary general of the diocese of Saint Asaph, I have done my diligence and duty for the expelling and taking away of certain abuses, superstitions and hypocrisies used within the said diocese of Saint Asaph, according to the King's honourable acts and injunctions therein made. That notwithstanding, there is an image of Darvellgadarn within the said diocese, in whom the people have so great confidence, hope and trust, that they come daily a pilgrimage unto him, some with kine, others with oxen or horses, and the rest with money, insomuch that there was five or six hundred pilgrims to a man's estimation that offered to the said image the fifth day of this present month of April. The innocent people have been sore allured and enticed to worship the said image, insomuch that there is a common saying as yet amongst them that whosoever will offer anything to the said image of Darvellgadarn, he hath power to fetch him or them that so offers out of hell when they be damned. Therefore, for the reformation and amendment of the premises, I would gladly know by this bearer your honourable pleasure and will, as knoweth God, who ever preserve your lordship long in wealth and honour. Written in North Wales, the vj day of this present April. [1538]

Your bedman and daily orator by duty,
Ellis Price.

ELLIS PRICE to Thomas Cromwell.

Right honourable and my singular good Lord and Master, pleaseth it your good lordship that I have repaired to the place whereas the Image of Darvel Gadarn stood, and have taken the same down according to the King's most honourable commandment and yours, which shall be carried to your Lordship with all diligence and expedition. The parson and the parishioners of the Church wherein the said Image of Darvel stood proffered me forty pounds that the said Image should not be conveyed to London and because that I nothing inclinable to their proffers and petitions, the said parson himself with others are coming to your Lordship not only to make suit and labour on the premises, but also to make feigned surmise and complaints on me. Therefore I purpose, God willing, to come and to give attendance upon your Lordship within this fortnight that I may answer to such things that they shall lay to my charge....

Written in North Wales the xxviij day of April.
Your daily orator by duty,
Ellis Price.

Original Letters, ed. H. Ellis, Vol. III, Third series.

1540

*The Mayor and Aldermen of Carmarthen to the Lord Privy Seal, asking
for the dissolved House of the Gray Friars there, that they might establish
a Grammar School in it. (The Grammar School does not seem to have
been established then, presumably they are writing around 1540, but later
under Queen Elizabeth.)*

MAYOR AND ALDERMEN OF CARMARTHEN to the Lord
Privy Seal.

To the right honourable Lord Privy Seal,

Pleaseth it your Honour to be advertised that the Site and Mansion
of the Gray Friars in the King's town of Carmarthen, in South Wales,
was of late surrendered in to the King's hands and is, and hath ever
since been void and desolate, running daily in continual ruin and
decay: for there is no foot of lead upon any part thereof, and it were
pity that such building in such a barren country, should not be
conveyed to some lawful and convenient use, for the maintenance of
the common wealth. Wherefore it may please your Lordship to be a
mean to the King's Majesty that the Mayor and Aldermen of the said
town may have and enjoy for ever, to them and their successors, the
same Site and Mansion with three meadows of pasture ground, with
a garden and orchard at the backside, to the same belonging, being
of the annual rent of xviij in the whole, so that they may have a
Grammar School at the cost and charge of Master Thomas Lloyd,
chanter of Saint David's there maintained, and otherwise the same to
bestow for the common wealth and commodity of the same towne;
the said Mayor and Aldermen now there, for the time being, will give
his Majesty xlii sterling for the same Site and Mansion, with the
appurtenances as is aforesaid, and to your good Lordship xxii for
your good mediation and travail taken to bring it to pass, over and
besides the continual prayer and service not only of the said Mayor
and Aldermen now being, but also of all the whole inhabitants of the
same town and all the whole country thereabout. As knows our Lord
God, who preserve your honour long to his pleasure. Amen.

By your Lordship's bedesmen the Mayor and Aldermen of the
King's Town of Carmarthen in South Wales.

Original Letters Illustrative of English History, ed. H. Ellis.

In 1563 an Act was passed ordaining the translation of the Bible into Welsh. It stated: Because the English tongue is not understood of the most and greatest number of all her majesty's most loving and obedient subjects inhabiting within her Highness Dominion and Country of Wales, being no small part of this realm.... Be it therefore enacted.... That the whole Bible containing the New Testament and the Old, with the Book of Common Prayer, and Administration of the Sacraments... be truly and exactly translated into the British or Welsh tongue....

It was ordained that at least one of these translated Bible and Prayer Books were to be in every church in Wales by March 1st. 1566. The Welsh Bishops were made responsible for all this on pain of a fine of £40 each. Bishop Richard Davies (1501?-1581), who had been in exile in Frankfurt during the reign of Mary but was now Bishop of St. David's, was the only one of them capable of doing a translation. He shared the task of translating the New Testament with the scholar and linguist William Salesbury. This appeared in 1567 with a preface in the form of a letter to the Welsh people (written in Welsh) by Bishop Davies. It begins as follows:

BISHOP RICHARD DAVIES to the Welsh people.

Richard by the Grace of God Bishop of Menevia, wishing the renewal of the old Catholic Faith and the light of the Gospel of Christ to all the Welsh people, especially to every living soul within his diocese.

Forasmuch as I know for certain what I have not seen with my own eyes, that every country from Russia to this place, as the German States and Prussia, Poland, England and Britain, France, Brittany, Ireland and some in the hinterland of the enemy in Italy and Spain, yea, and in islands, bordering countries, and other neighbourhoods and districts, are anxious and would with great welcome receive the word of God through a second blossoming of the Gospel of our Lord Jesus Christ, it grieves me to see thee, Wales, which was at one time foremost, but now the last in such a glorious triumph as this: awake thou now lovely Wales, my dear and fond brother in Christ Jesus: do not denationalize thyself, do not be indifferent, do not look down, but gaze upwards to the place thou dost belong: do not add to my grief. Remember the times of old, enquire of thy forefathers, search their history, thou who hast been formerly honourable and of great privileges. I will not speak of the dignity, esteem, and the worldly honour of the old Britons: I will be silent respecting the bravery, courage, heroism and ventures of the Welsh of old times. I will pass by their arts, mental powers, learning, wisdom and supreme genius... I will not delay on any of these. I will recall one excellent virtue which is an equivalent to all the above, which adorned thee of old, and gave thee a privilege and a pre-eminence, namely, undefiled religion, pure Christianity, and an effective fruitful faith. For... in the thirtieth year after the Ascension of Christ, the honourable Senator Joseph of Arimathea, a disciple of Christ, and with him other learned Christian disciples, came to this Kingdom: these men as they had received the faith and religion and Christianity from Christ Himself and from his Apostles, so they preached and taught in this Kingdom....

Bishop Davies goes on to tell of the invasion of Britain by the pagan Saxons, the Britons being driven west into Wales and Cornwall, and then the subsequent conversion of the Saxons by Augustine (the monk) to the false version of Christianity held by the Roman church. Then through conquest –

...the Christianity of the Britons was mixed up with the impure religion of the Saxons. Next to this recall the loss which the Welsh sustained in whatever books they had, in their art, their histories, and their pedigrees, and their Holy Scriptures: for the whole of Wales was entirely despoilt of them... In this way it happened that never was there a nation so badly off for books and knowledge in their own language as the Welsh. Great is the light which has come into the world, and great is the development and extension of every art and spiritual and physical knowledge in every language and in every country, and in every Kingdom since the art of printing was invented. But so despised the Welshman's language used to be, and so far neglected, that the printing press was unable to bring forth fruit to the credit of the Welshman in his own language until today.... Perchance it may be strange for thee to hear that thy old faith has its source and history in the Testament and in the word of God: for thou hast never seen the Bible nor the Testament in Welsh, neither in manuscript nor in print. Truly, I was never fortunate to see the Bible in Welsh: but when I was a lad I remember that I saw the five books of Moses in Welsh, in the house of an uncle of mine who was a learned man: but no one had any conception of the book, neither valued it. It is doubtful (as far as I know) whether it is possible in the whole of Wales to see one old Bible in Welsh since the Welsh were robbed and spoilt of all their books.... But I have no doubt that before that the Bible was common enough in Welsh....

Bishop Davies goes on to lament the present condition of society:

Look at the way of the world and thou wilt obtain proof. There is so much covetousness of the world today for land and possessions, gold and silver and wealth that only unfrequently thou wilt find one who trusts in God and his promises. Violence and theft, perjury, deceit, hypocrisy and arrogance: and these as if with rakes every condition of men gather and drag to themselves. God will not again drown the world again with the waters of a flood; but the lust of the world's goods has drowned Wales today, and impoverished every special quality and good virtue. For what is office in Wales today but a hook for a man to draw to himself the wool and the crops of a neighbour? What are legal learning, knowledge, and wisdom but thorns in the sides of neighbours, to cause them to flee away? Often in Wales, though the law marks it not, the mansion of the nobleman is a refuge for thieves.... Therefore I will say that but for the help and protection of the nobleman there would be little thieving in Wales. I know that there are noblemen who are virtuous men and hate thieving, and put down thieves: I do not say a word against these. Time will not permit now to unfold the harm which the lust of this world's goods has wrought, and the disbelief of the promises of God among all conditions of men in Wales by the lack of teaching of the Holy Scripture....

And Richard Davies concludes by asking the potential readers to forgive any possible errors they may discover for it is the first printed Testament in Welsh and the printers did not understand the language so may, at times, have misunderstood the copy. In 1588 the scholar and linguist, William Morgan, later to be Bishop of St. Asaph, produced his translation of the whole Bible.

A.O. Evans, *A Memorandum on the Legality of the Welsh Bible* (1925).
William Hughes, *Life and Times of Bishop William Morgan* S.P.C.K. (1891).

1567

Though the effort had been made by the government to make the Bible available to the people in their own language, the problem of the majority of the priesthood being ignorant of Welsh and thus unable to preach to their congregants in their own language, remained. Evidently some of the people made up for this lack by continuing to cling to their former habits and superstitions as the following letter makes clear.

DR ROBINSON, BISHOP OF BANGOR to Sir William Cecil, afterwards Lord Burleigh.

In Christo Jesu salutem, pacem, etc.

Righte honorable, I thought it some part of my dewtie, to certifie your honour touching the state of these shierres wherein I was borne, and where I now live by the Queene's maiesties singular goodnes towardes me. Yt in these three shierres called Caernarvon, Anglesey, and Merioneth, through the wisdome and carefull diligence of Mr George Bromley, Chefe Justice, the people live in much obedience, fredome, and quiet, so that toward their prince they are like to continew faithful subjects, and among themselves peacable neighbours.

But, touching the Welsh peoples receaving of the gospell, I find by my small experience among them here that ignorance contineweth many in the dreggs of superstition, which did grow chiefly upon the blindness of the clergie, joined with the greediness of getting in so bare a country, and also upon the closing up of God's worde from them in an unknown tongue, of the which harmes though the one be remedied by the great benefite of our graciouse Queene and Parlement, yet the other remayneth without hope of redresse: for the most part of the priestes are too olde (they saye) to be put to schole. Upon this inabilitie to teache God's worde (for there are not six yt can preache in ye three shierres) I have found since I came to this countrey images and aulters standing in churches undefaced, lewde and indecent vigils and watches observed, much pilgrimage goyng, many candels sett up to the honour of saintes, some reliques yet carried about and all the countries full of bedes and knotts, besides diverse other monuments of wilfull serving of God. Of the which abuses some (I thank God) are reformed and other, my hope is, wyll dayly decaye by the helpe of the worshipfull of the countries who show some better countenance to the Gospel by the godly parte of the Chefe Justice, whose counsell and code I have in such matters; all which (I trust) Almightie God will turne to his owne glorie and the salvation of his people.

Fare you well in Christe. From my house at
Bangor ye 7 of Octob., An.Dom. 1567
Your honour's most assured
Nicholas Bangor.

Letter quoted in *Vol. I, Civil War in Wales,* J.R. Phillips (Longmans, Green & Co.: 1874).

The Council of the Marches, disturbed by the proliferation of vagabond minstrels and bards, set up a Commission, authorised by Queen Elizabeth, to officiate at the second Caerwys Eisteddfod, 1568, in North Wales and determine who could be named a worthy bard and those deemed not worthy admonished to take up some honest labour. Here the Council writes to the appointed Commissioners.

COUNCIL OF THE MARCHES to Commissioners.

Whereas it is come to the knowledge of the Lord President and other of our said Council in our Marches of Wales that vagrant and idle persons naming themselves Minstrels, Rithmers and Bards are lately grown into such an intolerable multitude within the Principality of North Wales, that not only gentlemen and others by their shameless disorders are often times disquieted in their habitations.

But also the expert minstrels and musicians in tongue and cunning are thereby much discouraged to travel in the exercise and practice of their knowledge and also not a little hindered in their livings and preferments.

The reformation whereof and the putting of those in order the said Lord President and Council have thought very necessary and knowing you to be men both of wisdom and upright dealing and also of experience and good knowledge in the science, have appointed and authorised you to be Commissioners for that purpose. And forasmuch as our said Council of late, travelling in some part of the Principality, had perfect understanding by credible report that the accustomed place for the execution of the like commission hath been heretofore at Caerwys in our county of Flint, and that William Mostyn, Esquire, and his ancestors have had the gift and bestowing of the silver harp appertaining to the Chief of that faculty, and that a year's warning at the least hath been accustomed to be given of the assembly and execution of the like commission. Our said Council have therefore appointed the execution of this Commission to be at the said town of Caerwys the Monday next after the Feast of the Blessed Trinity which shall be in the year of our Lord God 1568. And therefore we require and command you by the authority of these presents not only to cause open proclamations to be made in all fairs, markets, towns and other places of assembly within our counties of Anglesey, Caernarfon, Merioneth, Denbigh and Flint that all and every person and persons that intend to maintain their livings by name or colour of minstrels, rithmers or bards within Talaith of Aberffraw comprehending the five shires, shall be and appear before you the said day and place to show forth their learnings accordingly... whereof you Sir Richard Bulkeley, Sir Rhys Gruffudd, Ellis Price and William Mostyn, Esquires or iii or ii of you to be of the number to repair to the said place the day aforesaid and calling to you such expert men in the said faculty of the Welsh music as to you shall be thought convenient to proceed to the execution of the premises and to admit such and so many as by your wisdoms and knowledges you shall find worthy into and under the degrees, heretofore in semblable sort to use, exercise or follow the sciences and faculties to their professions in such decent orders as shall appertain to each of their degrees; and as your discretions and wisdoms shall prescribe unto them giving straight monition and commandment in our name, and on our behalf to the rest not worthy that they return to some honest labour and due exercise, such as they be most apt unto for maintenance of their livings upon pain to be taken as sturdy and idle vagabonds and to be used according to the laws and statutes provided in that behalf....

...Signed: her Highness's Council
in the Marches of Wales.

J.G. Evans (ed.), *Report on Manuscripts in the Welsh Language* (1898).

1575

A letter concerning extortion and corruption among officials of the State, particularly abuse of the ancient custom of comortha, *and repeating the continual complaint of the lack of Welsh-speaking preachers.*

RICHARD PRISE OF BRECKNOCK to Lord Burghley, Minister of State.

My singular good Lorde, the great and most provident care which (as the world knoweth) your Honour hath always had of the whole state of this realm and the good government thereof, dothe give me present boldness to signify unto you some great disorders which do very grievously annoy the commonwealth of this poore Country of Wales and the good subjects of the same....

First, whereof ancient time it hath been accustomed in Wales, with a kinde of free benevolence called comortha, to relieve such as by some great misfortune were decayed and fallen into poverty, the same proceeding (no doubt) of a charitable and good meaning at the first, is nowe, in the generall corruption of all good things, grown to so great abuse, that it is no more a free giving unto the poor decayed but more than half a constrained exacting of lewd officers, as Under-Sheriffs, Bailiffs of Hundreds and their deputies; Bailiffs of Lordships and their deputies, with such like; and of unruly gentlemen, such as having consumed their own riotously and in maintaining of light and disordered persons, will seek to redress their fall and maintain their riot by this colourable spoil of the poore true subjects; yea and of murderers and arrant thieves also which, having by some means escaped the law, do return immediately (as unto a last refuge) unto these outrageous comorthas. And of all these the poore true man dare in no wise devise anie end. Indeed I must confess there is already a good law made to meet herewith, and the punishment thereof referred unto her Majesty's honourable Council in the Marches of Wales; but I fear me their honours are often abused by false suggestions whereupon they grant licences to comortha, and besides that, of so great a number as doth yearly comortha without any licence at all. If haply some few of them be accused for the same by the said Council they escape with so easy fines that they care little to incur the like again; much less is it any terror unto others. Yea I know that gentlemen of good living and calling have obtained licences (but I know not by what means) to gather a general comortha, having no other colour or cause but the marrying of a daughter; and such are commonly of such calling, kindred and friendship in the country that they will have, not according to the will and power of the givers, but to their own liking.

For redresse whereof (in my poore opinion) it were well that no person at all by colour of his office, nor any other, without very good cause and the same well known and tried, be licensed thereunto; and that such as shall presume otherwise to comortha be punished by such fine as shall surmount the value of his comortha (as near as may be) or otherwise, very sharply, to the terror of others....

There resteth yet one matter amisse, of as great or more importance than anie of the rest, which God grant may be as soon amended as it is most to be wished. That is, an extreme wante of learned and godly Preachers to instruct the people in knowledge and fear of God: for in this whole shire of Brecknock there are scarce ij learned and sufficient Pastors, and for a great parte some one slender Chaplain, which can but read the divine service, doth serve ij, some iij parishes, and these two or three miles asunder at the least. Whereby the common people are so rude and ignorant in the most necessary pointes of the Christian faith, that over many of them cannot as muche say the Lordes Prayer and Articles of the Belief in anie Language that they understand. And therefore it is no mervell that they are very injurious one to another, and live in contempt both of the Laws of God and man; as in keeping one his brother's wife, another his wife's daughter, and living and dwelling with them (as manie doth most abominably) seeing they are not instructed in the fear of God....

From Brecknock, the last of January 1575
Most humbly ever at your
Lordships commandment
Rich. Prise.

Original Letters, ed. Henry Ellis, Vol. III, Second series, (1827).

1577

Disorder in sixteenth Century Wales plagued the coast as well as inland. This is a letter to the Privy Council from Fabian Phillips, member of the Council in the Marches and Judge of Assize and Thomas Lewis, Justice of the Peace, concerning their appointment to control pirates in the Bristol Channel.

FABIAN PHILLIPS AND THOMAS LEWIS to Privy Council.

Our duties to your good Lordships humbly remembered.... And being appointed to begin the service the xviiith of March last, we the said day, repaired to Cardiff.... We have taken the examinations of three score persons at the least, by the which we find a great number of names of pirates discovered that have been received and lodged in this town and from whom many spoils have been had, but such is the forwardness of the inhabitants that whatsoever is set down by the schedule sent from your honours or otherwise objected by common report, they have taken a general rule that they will neither accuse one another nor yet answer to any matter that toucheth themselves upon their oaths. Although they all confess that the most part of the inhabitants by this their harbouring and receiving of the pirates, have felt such smart and sustain thereby such discredit with foreign nations and countries that they that travel to other places to maintain their living by trade of merchandise dare not well be known or to avow the place of their dwelling is Cardiff. This we find partly to grow by the great fear they have of some of note... and for that cause (as it seemeth chiefly) they dare not disclose their knowledge. In this our travel one William Chick, one of these pirates, a great doer and chief champion amongst them, is haply fallen into our hands. We find but little saving that he can yield no account of this last year's travel: we doubt not but he can tell all, howbeit, such is his jollity that he will answer but what he listeth; and therefore order is taken that he and others shall presently be had to the Council where the manicles may make them speak....

The comptroller of Cardiff... and other chief offenders in receiving the pirates and their spoils have and do absent themselves from their dwelling place sithence our coming to town, and cannot be found.

From Cardiff the third of April 1577.

J. Gwynfor Jones, *Wales and the Tudor State* (Cardiff: University of Wales Press, 1989).

1585

DR DAVID POWEL (1552-98), *scholar and antiquary, known for his* Historie of Cambria, *now called* Wales (1584). *Sir Philip Sidney, poet, literary patron, son of Sir Henry Sidney who some years before was Lord President of the Marches in Wales, was appointed Governor of Flushing in 1585.*

DR DAVID POWEL'S letter-dedicatory to Sir Philip Sidney.

To Philip Sidney, gilded Knight, honourable and eminently famous on account of all the glory of his virtues and learning: the address of David Powel.

Right honourable Sir! There are three things which bring man to perfection and make him a true and renowned gentleman. The first is founded on acquiring knowledge of ancestral achievements; the second on directing present events for the good of all; and the third on caring for the interests of those who are to follow him. For what is more suitable for a gentleman than for him to keep in his mind the memory of the old times that have gone by; meditating with himself upon the exceptional feats of very prominent men; keeping in his sight the structure, origin, progress and condition of states; noticing the causes and effects of events; guarding eminent historical writings and bringing them to light from darkness, extracting from them those things which are virtuous and adapting them in order that life can be properly organised? Furthermore, what more appropriate service can a good man offer than to present himself entirely in the interests of the state, considering any personal gain to be secondary; applying all labour, all care and all thought to promote the prosperity of the people generally; and concentrating entirely on that one thing only by which the soul rests after achieving it, desiring nothing further? Lastly, what is more appropriate for true gentility than to earn the gratitude of people to come, to provide for the next generation and to be a benefactor to those who are, as yet, unborn? For it is from this that comes the glory of a name which is everlasting; from this fame associated with eternal glory derived; from this begotten in posterity a praiseworthy impression and memory. Those who are endorsed and decorated with these virtues are to be considered wholly good men but also true gentlemen; men who, truly, deserve to be advisers of princes in their councils and placed in offices of government and honoured with the highest titles.

You have, most honourable Philip Sidney, at home and inherited by you, all this in your most gentle father as if they are shown to you in a mirror so that they can be imitated....

Progress, therefore, in virtue, most honourable Philip, by reading and studying the ancient authors and by keeping an eye on the general welfare of the state, and follow in your father's footsteps by caring for the welfare of the future.

J. Gwynfor Jones, *Wales and the Tudor State* (Cardiff: University of Wales Press, 1989).

1592

The Stradling family were living at St. Donat's Castle, Glamorgan from the late thirteenth century. The following letter was addressed to Sir Edward Stradling (1529-1609), scholar and antiquary and shows Sir Edward as patron. The writer, Sion Dafydd Rhys, (c.1534-1619), known as John Davies, scholar and doctor of medicine, among numerous other works published a Welsh grammar in 1592, Cymraecae Linguae Institutiones, *and dedicated the book to Sir Edward Stradling whom he called his Maecenas.*

SION DAFYDD RHYS (JOHN DAVIES) to Sir Edward Stradling.

To the r. wor. Sr Edwarde Stradlinge, Knighte,
My dutye remembered you youre wor. You shall understande that

I am come home.... The cause of my longe tarynge in London was for the sure setlinge and placinge of the bookes, and perusinge every one of them, sheete by sheete, that noe imperfection mighte be found in them; which sheetes in xii hundreth and odd bookes growe to a great number and a tedious perusall. Of these bookes the Queenes Matie hadd one, my Lorde Tresorer an other, and my L. of Essex the thirde, for that these three hadd just cause to have a consideracion of this excellent language. From the Queene I knowe not what answere was hadd for that I came awaye before I spake with Mr Skudamore who did deliver the book; but at the cominge of Mr Scudamore to Holm Lacy I shall knowe. There is more worshipful speeches concerninge youre selfe about the setting forthe of that booke then about anye one thinge that ever you dyd in all youre life. And thus, with my humble dutye to yor selfe and to my singular good ladye, and hartye comendacon to Mr John Stradlinge, I beseeche God to blesse and save you all.

Brecknocke, this xii of Julye 1592
Yor wor to comaunde
during liffe
John Dawys.

Stradling Correspondence A Series of Letters written in the Reign of Queen Elizabeth, ed. Rev. John Montgomery Traherne (Orme, Brown, Green, Longmans and William Bird: Cardiff, 1840).

1592

In 1588 appeared the Bible translated by Bishop William Morgan (1545-1604); the Old Testament being done by him alone and his revised version of the New. It has been said of him that 'His work was the foundation and example for all the literature written in Welsh after the end of the sixteenth century and it helped to create a consciousness of national identity over the centuries which followed.'

The following letter from justices of the peace with instructions about the suppression of a superstition indicates that despite the authorities' commands and the advent of a Welsh Bible, old superstitions, at least in some parts, were unabated.

GEORGE OWEN, ALBANE STEPNETH and JOHN AP REES to Robert Vaughan, John Garnons and Owen Phillipes of Penbedo,

Gentlemen, Thomas ap Richard, Clerk, Parson of Penbedo, Jevan David, Clerk, Parson of Bridell, and George Owen, clerk, parson of Whitchurche.
July 4, 1592. Haverfordwest.

Whereas we have received letters from the lords and others of Her Majesty's most honourable privy council to us and others directed whereby we are willed and required to inform ourselves of all places within this county of Pembroke where in times past there have been pilgrimages, images or offerings whereunto (as their lordships are informed) divers sorts of people do use to repair as well in the night season as other times of day, and that in great numbers, and that we should cause those idolatrous and superstitious monuments to be pulled down, broken and quite defaced, so as there be no monument, token or memory remaining of the same, and likewise to take order that thereafter there be no such unlawful resort to these superstitious places, but to appoint some discreet and well affected persons to have an eye and regard to those that, notwithstanding this inhibition, shall repair to those places and to see them apprehended and brought before us to be severally punished for their disobedience and lewd behaviour.

These are therefore by virtue and authority of the said honourable letters and commission to will and require you, being gentlemen to us known to be well affected and forward in Her Majesty's service and good of the country, forthwith with all convenient speed to repair to the place called St. Meygans, where sometimes offerings and supplicatious pilgrimages have been used, and there cause to be pulled down and utterly defaced all relics and monuments of that chapel, not leaving one stone thereof upon another, and from time to time to cause to be apprehended all such person and persons of whatever sex, kind or sort whatsoever, that shall presume...to repair either by night or day to the said chapel or well in supplicatious manner and them to bring or send before us or any one of us to be used and dealt withal according to their deserts....

Pembrokeshire Life: 1572-1843, ed. B.E. and K.A. Howells (Pembrokeshire Record Society 1972).

Citizens from Carmarthen writing to Lord Burghley etc. in the reign of Queen Elizabeth indicate a continued anxiety about the threat of invasion despite the defeat of the Spanish Armada in 1588.

ANTHONY MENEVENSIS, JOHN WOGAN, GEORGE OWEN, FRANCES MEYRIKE AND ALBANE STEPNETH to Sir John Puckering, Lord Keeper, Lord Burghley, Lord Treasurer, The Earl of Essex, Lord Buckhurst, and The Earl of Pembroke. November 8, 1595.

The bounden duty we owe to Her Majesty, the conscience we have for the safeguard of the whole realm, and the care that in nature and reason we carry of this our country have emboldened us to offer this discourse unto your honour concerning the safety of them and us all.

It becomes us not to fear, neither do we doubt of the wise and grave consideration that your lordship and the rest of the lords of Her Majesty's most honourable privy council have had and still have for the preservation of Her Majesty and the realm, but yet fearing your want of due information touching the estate of Milford Haven and the adjoining parts, it may please you to understand that the haven itself, being neither barred to hinder entry nor to be embayed by any winds to let issuing forth, is a sufficient harbour for an infinite number of ships, which haven being once got by the enemy may draw on such fortification at Pembroke town and castle, standing upon a main rock and upon a creek of the Haven, and the town and castle of Tynby with other places near unto them, as infinite numbers of men and great expense of treasure will hardly in a long time remove the enemy, during which time Her Majesty shall lose a fertile country which yields Her Majesty £1,200 by year and more in revenue paid to Her Majesty's receiver besides all other receipts both temporal and ecclesiastical, as tenths and subsidies etc.

Also it is to be remembered that the soil near the said haven yields corn in such abundance as would suffice to maintain a great army and the sea coasts near about it yield great plenty of fish. The haven also stands very commodiously to receive victuals from France, Brittany or Spain, all which things may be an occasion to move the enemy to attack that place before others.

Also there are in Pembrokeshire eighteen castles of which though there be but two or three in repair, yet are the rest places of great strength and easily to be fortified by the enemy, some of which are so seated for strength as they seem impregnable. Also there are in that shire to be seen in sundry parts thereof divers sconces or forts of earth raised in great height with great ramparts and ditches, to the number of 120 or 140, which in times past have been places of strength in time of wars, all which castles and forts would yield great advantage to the enemies to strengthen themselves in such sort that it would be an infinite charge to remove them from thence.

Again, the same is situate within seven hours' sailing to Waterford and Wexford in Ireland, so as if the enemy have an intention to invade Ireland (as by report we have heard he has) his harbour in this haven may serve him to great purpose.

Furthermore, being lord as it were of these seas by possessing the haven, what spoil he may make along Seaverne in both sides even to Bristowe may be easily conjectured. And if he, which God forbid, should enjoy Brittany withal, our English merchants can have no trade, which will decrease her Highness's customs and decay the navy.

If it be thought that he may be kept from landing, neither the force of men nor furniture here will serve the turn, considering here be many places where he may easily land and he may come upon us within half a day's sailing, we having no ships at sea to descry him sooner, and how then our small forces may be in readiness to withstand him we refer to your honour's judgement.

If it be thought that Her Majesty's navy royal be able to conquer them being once in this haven, and that by them fortified, it would be found very hard by reason that upon a very little storm for want of any other harbour or bay to abide in they should be in great danger of wreck, and no land forces are able to expel them. Whereupon we humbly pray your lordship to consider whether it be not expedient for the withstanding of the enemy that he obtain not this harbour, to have a convenient number of ships of war and fortifications to defend the same, which preparation if the enemy might perceive we believe verily it would alter his mind from adventuring his navy upon this coast.

And whereas of late Mr Pawl Ivy was sent hither to survey the haven and to consider of fit places for fortifications, what report he has made of his opinion we know not, but sure we are that his abode about that service was very short and his survey very speedily dispatched, so that because none of us were privy to his intent or conceit we do yet retain some hope that if some other men of experience were sent down hither to consider of all the said circumstances, some such report would 'happily' be made unto your honour and the rest as some better event might ensue for the safety of this poor country and the whole realm than for aught we know has been determined upon, especially if the party shall have instruction to view the town and castle of Tynbye, being a place which may easily be made of exceeding strength and was not seen by Mr Ivy nearer than two miles distance for aught we can learn.

Thus having, we hope, discharged the duties of true and faithful subjects we humbly commit your good lordship and all your grave 'consayles' to the blessed protection and direction of Almighty God.

Subscribed: Four several letters verbatim were sent to the Lord Keeper, the Lord Treasurer, the Earl of Essex, the Lord Buckhurst, and a copy hereof enclosed in a letter to my lord of Benbrocke, all sent by Mr Robert Davy, esquire, Receiver of South Wales to be delivered to their lordships.

Pembrokeshire Life.

The Seventeenth Century

Reign of James I *(no date)*.

Instructions by WILLIAM WYNN of Glyn, Merioneth to his son, Cadwalader, a student at Oxford.

The recipient will receive by the bearer a suit of apparel and 40/- which he is to deliver to his tutor. He is to write how he profits from his studies, what authors his tutor reads to him, and what he spends weekly. He is to have care to serve God and to live as sparingly as he can. He is to consider his parents' means and great charge of children, insomuch that the writer cannot maintain any of the recipients brothers at the university. 'Therefore prayse God that thou hast careful parents to place thee in Oxenford, a famous university, the fountayne and wellhead of all learning. Keep company with honest students who aphore evill courses as drinking and takeing toebacko, to their own loss and discredit of their friends and parents who sent them to University for better purposes' ...Wishes to know whether his son has received Owen's *Epigrams* by Edward ap William and what has become of his russet coat?... 'I will allow you noe servitor. You may serve yourself and spare 6d a weeke. Take heed lest you be gulde by the butler that he set down in his booke more for bread and beer than you call for. Speak no Welsh to any that can speak English, no not to your bedfellowes, and therby you may freely speak English tongue perfectly. I had rather that you should keep companie with studious, honest Englishmen than with many of your own country-men who are more prone to be idle and riotous than the English.

Calendar of the Clenennau Letters and Papers in the Brogyntyn Collection, transcribed by T. Jones Pierce (ed.) (National Library of Wales Journal, Supplementary Series IV, pt.1, 1947).

1620 ff.

The following letters, of considerable interest, are from Dr John Davies (c.1567-1644) to members of the Wynn of Gwydir family regarding the progress and publication of a Welsh-Latin Dictionary. First, however, comes a sad, somewhat irascible letter from Dr Thomas Williams (Wiliems) (1545/6-1622) whose Latin-Welsh dictionary was subsequently edited and incorporated in his own by Dr Davies.

Letter from DR THOMAS WILLIAMS to Sir John Wynn of Gwydir rejecting terms for publishing his dictionary.
October 21, 1620.

For the Latin and Cambrian Dictionarie, which with greate laboure and travayle, as God knoweth, I have congested and digested these fiftie yeares, I see very small surtie or consideration for my paynes, and therefore I mean not in haste, God reward you for your permission, to deliver the same to any of these men, whose great promises I have tried to small effect, in things done for them, and imparting certaine collections unto them, never receiving quid pro quo for any of them. God doth know that in the four years while I did write the Dictionaries, I was so instant to the work that often when I came from the book, I did not know many time what day of the weeke it was, and soe lost my practis that might have been a hundred pounds unto me or some great matter, and during that time I have pined for hunger, if it had not been for God and your worship's good considerations and not to these illiberal men's liberalities.

Dr John Davies of Mallwyd (he spells it variously in the following letters) was a great Welsh scholar who not only produced the Welsh-Latin dictionary referred to in the letters but also a Welsh grammar in Latin and numerous other works.

DR JOHN DAVIES to Sir John Wynn of Gwydir.
Aug 26, 1623. Malloyd.

Has been long desirous of seeing his old friend Sir Thomas ap William's dictionary, not so much for any excellent perfection in the work as for the great pains the author has taken therein. Cousin Robert Vaughan tells the writer that he is to have the book on condition that he sees it printed and that he dedicates it to Sir John Wynn and ascribes all the glory to Sir Thomas ap William. If the work proves fit for the press the writer will set it out without expectation of glory or gain; the printing thereof to be at Sir John's cost.

DR JOHN DAVIES to Owen Wynn at Gwydir.
Jan 23, 1627/28. Malloid.

Upon his good father's desire he undertook the reviewing of the Welsh dictionary of Sir Thomas ap William, but his dwelling so far from Gwydir, as well as troubles occasioned by Mr Pigott, hindered him. Began it in April last and made an end on Saturday last. Has much abridged it in some places, and enlarged it in others. Is only beginning to make a fair copy of his own dictionary, which he began in 1593. Hopes it will be ready by the beginning of summer. Sir Thomas William's has the Latin first and Welsh following, and his has the Welsh first and Latin after, and both will not exceed the bulk of Sir Thomas's dictionary as written by himself [Sir Thomas]. As for the charge of printing, it will come to £140, whereof Sir John paid but £10, but understands fron Owen Wynn's letter that his brother (Sir Richard) will pay more. The charge of the corrector to attend the printing will come to some £60 or £70 more. If Sir Richard will see what may be had towards that charge the writer will endeavour to have it fully ready by midsummer....

DR JOHN DAVIES to Sir Richard Wynne.
October 2, 1628. Malloyd.

Worthie good Sir, Your brother, Mr Owen Wyn, hath written to me, as by your appointment, to know how forward I was with the Welsh Dictionarie, and with all to shewe me of your forwardnesse to helpe the printing. Wherefore I make bould to acquaynte you, that is now ready; and request to know, per bearer, what further you are pleased to shewe in the setting fourthe of it. So, in haste, with remembraunce of my best service, I pray God blesse bothe you and yours; and ever rest, at your com'aunde.

DR JOHN DAVIES to Owen Wynne.
May 1, 1629. Mallwyd.

Good Sir, I rec'd your l're by the way, as I returned from our quarter-sessions at Bala; wherby I understand what greate behouldingnesse I owe your self and your noble brother Sir Richard, for your care and labour about the Welshe Dictionarie. I rec'd from you a note of the printer's names; besides which, there is one Mr Beale, a little with out Aldersgate. Some of them are but poore men, and not able to deale with it themselves. Robert Vaughan, of Wengraig, told me that Mr Jones, of Whitecrosse-streete, was desirous to move his presse to the Marches of Wales, and intended so to doe. If he will doe it shortly, I had rather deale with him than with others; because I might be neere my home: otherwise I would be glad to deale with such of them as would beare half the charge, and take half the book. The same l're will serve as *Rider* is printed in, by Adam Islip, 1617; and the same volume, but that this will not be so bigge. The l'res must be Romane and Italique, and now and then among some Hebrewe and Greek l'res, and a few English l'res. Yf none will beare half the charge, the way to treate with them will be, to agree with them by the sheete, for 500 or 600 copies, they bearing all the charge; and so I hope they may take XIIs a sheete, or somewhat more, if paper be dearer than ordinarie. I would have the paper to be good pott paper, and not the paper that *Rider* is in of a^o 1617. Seeing you have begonne to take the paines, I shall request you to continewe to some end, and to let me heare from you, as soon as conveniently you can; for the time of the yeare passeth, and I grow ould and heavie. I beseeche you remember my service and present my heartie thanks to Sir Richard Wynn; and with my com'endac'ons unto you, I com'end us all to God, and rest, your ever truly assured, and much bounden.

(P.S.) You may tell them, that my copie is faire and certaine, all written with my owne hand, much fairer than this l're.

DR JOHN DAVIES to Owen Wynne.
September 5, 1629. Mallwyd.

Good Sir, Your paynes about my Dictionarie hathe been so greate, that I shall be able to requite you only with my prayers. I knowe Mr Beale, and have bene at his house. Yf he will advanture £100, I knowe he would expecte but his share of the printed copies according to that charge: but it is no purpose for us to make him beleeve that every P'ishe in Wales will buy a booke; for I, for my parte, doe not like that course: but let them be bought as they deserve, without compulsion. As for the estimate of the printing, I have sent you the printed leafe enclosed; whereby I have cast over the wholle booke, and do guesse it will amount to 245 sheetes a booke, of the letter that this leafe is printed in. The fashion of it he may see by this leafe; and so shall not neede to see the written copie it selfe, excepte he doubte of the fairnesse of the hand; and for that, you may assure him, it is all written with my owne hand, fairer than this I're, and without many interlynings. I pray you resolve with him, and let me heare from you, as soone as may be, whether he will undertake a share of the worke; and if he will undertake the halfe, or the 1-4th part.

So with my verie heartiest com'endac'ons, and my daylie prayers for my good ladie your mother, and all at Gwedir, I ever rest, your much bounden and assured.

DR JOHN DAVIES to Owen Wynne.
October 20, 1629. Mallwydd.

Good Sir, My service remembred to your worthie brother, Sir Richard, and your good selfe, I make bould to salute you, and to put you in minde to conferre with the printers, and to let me heare from you as soone as you can. Mr Charles Jones tould me, he had acquayntance with some printers with whom yf you please to conferre, I persuade my self he will put to his helping hand, if you have not allready settled that businesse. So, in haste, I pray God belesse you and yours, and rest, your truely assured.

LEWES BAYLY, Bishop of Bangor, to Mr John Beale, Printer in Aldersgate Street.
October 28, 1629. Bangor.

Good Mr Beale, I heartily commend me unto you. I understand that Mr. Doctor Davies hath perfected a worthy and necessary piece of work which all our Welsh preachers do much want; I mean a Welsh dictionary. I do much desire to see it printed, and if you will undertake the work, I am persuaded it will sell very well, for it is a work that hath long been desired; and to encourage you to so necessary a work, I will undertake to put off a hundred of them and to return you money within six months for them. And if I can help to sell more of them, I will do the best that lieth in me; but for one hundred I will procure you good payment; and I persuade myself that this edition will not long stand on your hands.

Calendar of the Wynn Papers 1515-1690, ed. J. Ballinger (Cardiff: 1926).

1643 ff.

CIVIL WAR

The forces of Parliament made some gains in the North of Wales early in the war while the Royalists, supporters of the king, Charles I, were largely in control of the South. Late in 1643, however, a Royalist army, withdrawn from Ireland because of a truce with rebels there, challenged the Parliamentarians in the North. Here are some exchanges of letters between the two sides during the besieging of Hawarden Castle by the Royalists.

From the Royalist, LT.COL. MARROW.

Gentlemen. It is not for to hear you preach that I am sent here, but in his majestie's name to demand the castle for his majestie's use: as your allegiance binds you to be true to him, and not to inveigle those innocent souls that are within with you; so I desire your resolution, whether you will deliver the castle or no?

From the commanders of the Parliamentary forces, JOHN WARREN AND ALEXANDER ELLIOT.

Sir, We have cause to suspect your disaffection to preaching, in regard we find you thus employed. If there be innocent souls here, God will require their blood of them that shed it. We can keep the castle and our allegiance too; and therefore you may take your answer, as it was in *English* plain enough before: we can say no more but God's will be done.

Reply by Captain of Firelocks, THOMAS SANDFORD, Royalist.

Gentlemen, I presume you very well know, or have heard of, my condition and disposition; and that I neither give nor take quarter. I am now with my Firelocks (who never yet neglected opportunity to correct rebels) ready to use you as I have done the Irish: but loth am I to spill my countrymen's blood; wherefore, by these I advise you to your feilty and obedience to his majesty; and show yourselves faithful subjects by delivering the castle into my hands for his majesty's use; in so doing you shall be received into mercy, etc. otherwise if you put me to the least trouble or loss of blood to force you, expect no quarter for man, woman or child. I hear you have some of our late Irish army in your company: they very well know me; and that my Firelocks use not to parley. Be not unadvised; but think of your liberty; for I vow all hopes of relief are taken from you; and our intents are not to starve you, but to batter and storm you, and then hang you all, and follow the rest of that rebellious crew. I am no bread-and-cheese rogue, but, as ever, a loyalist, and will ever be, while I can write or name

Thomas Sandford.
Captain of Firelocks.
November 28, 1643.

Thomas Pennant, *Tours in Wales, Vol. I* (1810).

Another Royalist wrote as follows about destruction done by the Puritans (to what they saw as idolatrous signs) in the church at Hawarden.

Now if you desire to know what I find by my little experience in Britain of the behaviour of our zealots, [i.e. the Puritans] I can do no less, (if no more) than confirm what you have often heard. I myself coming into the Church of Hawarden the morning after they were there, found the Common prayer-book scattered up and down the Chancel; and some well-read man without doubt, conceiving that the Common-prayers had been in the beginning of a poor innocent old Church Bible, tore out almost all Genesis for failing, it stood so dangerously it was suspected to be malignant. In windows where there was oriental glass they broke in pieces only the faces; to be as frugal as they could; they left sometimes the whole bodies of painted Bishops, though in their rochets. But if there was anything in the language of the beast, though it was but an *hoc fecit*, or at worst *orate* etc (and I but guess for I could not read it when it was gone) which had stood for many years, and might many more without idolatry, that was dashed out. They had pulled down the rails about the table, and very honestly reared them to the wall: (it was well they were in a coal Country where fewel was plentiful) and brought down the table into the midst of the Church. Some of our soldiers came and swore it stood not right, (alas! that we have no better reformation), and set it close to the East wall again. At Wrexham they say (I was not there) they did the like villainy almost in all points, and broke in pieces one of the best pair of organs in the King's dominions: which Sir Thomas Middleton took for his proper pillage to make bullets of.

A Collection of Original Letters and Papers Concerning the Affairs of England, ed. Thomas Carte (1739). Quoted in *Protestant Dissenters in Wales 1639-1689*, Geraint H. Jenkins (Cardiff: University of Wales Press, 1992).

As will be seen from the following letters, support for the two sides Parliament or the King wavered in parts of Wales during the Civil War, in some cases the participants prevaricating or changing sides. The conventional view seems to be that the Welsh were essentially Royalist but the first letter following would seem to dispute that notion. No doubt the majority of the population favoured peace above all.

From THOMAS DABRIDGECOURT to Prince Rupert (complaining of the lukewarmness of the people of Monmouthshire towards the cause of the King).
March 11th, 1644. St. Pere.

May it please your Highness,
I am very sorry I should be so unfortunate, these being the first commands you were pleased to honour me withal, as not to be able to perform them with that speed you expected; if your Highness shall be pleased to command me to the Turk, or Jew, or Gentile, I will go on my bare feet to serve you; but from the Welsh, good Lord deliver me. And I shall beseech you to send me no more into this country, if you intend I shall do you service, without a strong party to compel them, not to entreat them. And then I will give them cause to put me into their Litany, as they have now given me cause to put them into mine. The ammunition hath been here these seven days for want of carriages, and I fear shall stay seven more unless I have some power to force the people. They value neither Sir John Winter, his warrants, nor mine, nor any. Some say they will not come; the rest come not and say nothing. All generally disaffected, and the force that is in Chepstow not able to compel them. I have sent to Colonel Holbye for what horse he hath; if they come to me I will try what may be done. Here be two or three constables deserve hanging, and I had done it ere this if I had but a party to defend me from their Welsh bills. I beseech you let me receive your commands that you may have no occasion to blame him who is, and ever will be,
  Your Highness's humble servant,
  Thomas Dabridgecourt.

P.S. Colonel Kirke writes on the 10th from Bridgenorth that Tuesday, the 14th is a day on which cattle are usually driven out from Wales into the enemy's garrisons into Staffordshire, which he shall stop until he has command from the Prince.

By 1647 King Charles was in the hands of the Commissioners of Parliament. A group of Royalists in Glamorganshire, however, began a fresh revolt, ostensibly against the Committee of Usk, but really somewhat deviously in support of the King in that they pretended to believe that Sir Thomas Fairfax, Commander-in-Chief of the Parliamentary army, had joined forces with him. Among the letters which follow are those sent by the group to Major-General Laugharne, in command of the Parliamentary forces in South Wales where he had conducted many campaigns during the last few years. Included also are his letters about the development to the Speaker of the House of Commons and to Sir Thomas Fairfax. Subsequently Laugharne, in dispute with the Parliamentary forces himself over pay etc., abandoned the Parliamentarians and declared for the King. After Cromwell's victories in South Wales he and other apostate officers were sent to the Tower and sentenced to death as traitors to Parliament. A kind of mercy was shown to them in that they had to draw lots to choose just one of them to die. Colonel Poyer was the unlucky one. After the Restoration Laugharne became M.P. for Pembroke.

ROWLAND LAUGHARNE to the Speaker of the Honourable House of Commons.
17th June, 1647. Carmarthen.

Mr Speaker,
   The first rumour of his Majesty's departure with the army hath put the delinquents in Glamorganshire to their old frenzy: the enclosed papers will express their present posture, and shorten my relation. The leaders of them are of the principal delinquents engaged in the former revolt of that county, and whom the Parliament's clemency for offences past hath occasioned to this ungrateful relapse. Divers of the well-affected gentry of that county disfavour their courses, and cast about for their own security. Some of them are come hither to me, and I am drawing up my forces thitherward to suppress the Insolency; and find my soldiers, I thank God, very cheerful and inoffensive when they came, not capitulating for any conditions. I shall (God willing) never desert my first principles for the Parliament of England. The issue of this insurrection, probably, will occasion speedy and frequent records of this address by him, who is, Sir,
   The State's and your loyal servant,
   ROWLAND LAUGHARNE.

[Enclosures Laugharne mentions follow.]

To the Honourable Major-General Laugharne.

SIR,

It hath pleased God to make Sir Thomas Fairfax's army a miraculous means of the King's restitution (in appearances.) These counties, very apprehensive of their long-desired liberty and present sufferings, have already declared for the King and Sir Thomas Fairfax. Now that there might be nothing untimely done to your prejudice, we thought it fit to communicate so much of our business as can be no way prejudicial to yours. We should be very glad to hear how you look upon our proceedings and unfeignedly rest

Your humble servants,
THO. NOT, RICH. BASSET,
EDWARD THOMAS, JO. STRADLING,
THO. THOMAS.

To the High Constable of the Hundred of Miskin.

SIR,

We require you forthwith to direct your Warrants to the petty constables of the several parishes within your hundred, that they summon all able men from sixteen to sixty to appear before us at Cowbridge tomorrow by nine o'clock in the morning with all horses fit for service, or dragoons, and all such arms as are defensive or offensive, as they have, or can come by, for the use of the King's Majesty and Sir Thomas Fairfax, General, for the preservation of the peace and safety of this county. Hereof fail not, as you owe your allegiance to his Majesty. Dated 13th Junii, 1647

EDW. THOMAS, THO. NOT,
RICHARD BASSET, GRENVILE WEEKS.

To the Honourable Major-General Laugharne.
June 14, 1647. Cowbridge.

SIR,

There hath happened a business in Cowbridge which may (except you be pleased to interpret it in a fair sense) be liable to misconstruction. The truth is, the Committee, as is known, had an intent to seize on the persons of divers gentlemen, some whereof, for their security, betook themselves to Cowbridge, and there made bold with the magazine, without any the least meaning of opposition or disrespect to you; to whom, by many civilities, they are much obliged. And being certain of his Majesty's conjunction with Sir Thomas Fairfax's forces, they conceived they had been wanting to themselves, in not providing so well for their safety as they could. And they more than hope you will be so far from being any way displeased with it, as to receive assistance from you in their first and necessary defence; whereby you shall eternally oblige the whole country, and more particularly

Your most humble servants,
Jo. Stradling, Will. Basset,
Tho. Stradling, Robert Thomas,
Jo. Vanne, Thomas Basset,
Rich. Gwyn, Jo. Walter,
William Merrick, Miles Watkins,
Edward Seis, Jo. Powel,
George Gibbon, Rich. Wilcocke,
William Fleming, John Stradling,
Theodore Basset, John Jones,
Richard Basset, Rice Merrick,
Henry Stradling, Robert Coroche.

ROWLAND LAUGHARNE to his Excellency Sir Thomas Fairfax, General of the Parliament's Forces.
June 17, 1647. Carmarthen.

May it please your Excellency,

These last days there appeared a sudden and violent distraction in Glamorganshire. I shall use all power and diligence to allay it, and expect your Excellency's orders for my proceedings and the rather, in that the turbulent party, as I am informed, pretend your Excellency's authority for what they do. The enclosed copies of some expresses I received out of these parts, and of one of the delinquents' Warrants, will supply what I here omit. The chief actors are ancient malignants of a deep stain, and can pretend no grievance, but the just and conscientious proceedings of the Committee according to the Ordinances of Parliament. Other gentlemen well-affected and of good quality in the county are not engaged with them, but stand upon their guard. This is all I can at present in that affair, present to your Excellency, with my humble service and readiness to obey what commands you will please to impose on

Your Excellency's most humble servant,
Rowland Laugharne.

ROWLAND LAUGHARNE to Fairfax.
June 21, 1647. Cardiff.

May it please your excellency,
  My letter of the 17th inst. informed your Excellency of a violent distraction in Glamorganshire, which I have been diligent to allay without the effusion of innocent blood. The country hearing of my approach deserted the chief actors, who, to the number of fifty, all well mounted, are fled the country. The names of them are subscribed to the letters I sent to your Excellency, only some few added. They had convened 1,500 to 2,000, pretending authority for so doing; but the country are made sensible how they were seduced; and I shall neglect no diligence to settle quietness, and remove the disturbers of it. This account in duty I conceived myself bound to give your Excellency, and remain
  Youe humble servant,
  Rowland Laugharne.

In April 1648 Colonel Poyer, the castellan of Pembroke Castle and a moderate Parliamentarian, fearful of the extreme elements who wanted to 'turn the world upside down', declared for the King. He joined forces with the castellan of Tenby and together they marched through South Wales to Cardiff where they were now joined by forces led by Rowland Laugharne. On May 8 this apostate army was defeated by the Roundheads at the battle of St. Fagan's. The following letters find Cromwell besieging Pembroke Castle to which Poyer had retreated. With the capture of this castle Cromwell virtually broke the back of resistance in Wales.

OLIVER CROMWELL to the Speaker of the House of Commons.
Leaguer before Pembroke, June 14, 1648.

SIR,
  All that you can expect from hence is a relation of the state of this garrison of Pembroke, which is briefly thus:
  They begin to be in extreme want of provisions, so as in all probability they cannot live a fortnight without being starved. But we hear that they mutinied about three days since; cried out 'Shall we be ruined for two or three men's pleasure? Better it were we should throw them over the walls.' It's certainly reported to us that within four or six days they'll cut Poyer's throat, and come away to us. Poyer told them Saturday last, that if relief did not come by Monday night, they should no more believe him, nay, they should hang him.

We have not got our guns and ammunition from Wallingford as yet; but, however, we have scraped up a few which stand us in very good stead. Last night we got two little guns planted, which in twenty-four hours will take away their Mills; and then, as Poyer himself confesses, they are all undone. We made an attempt to storm him about ten days since; but our ladders were too short, and the breach so as men could not get over. We lost a few men, but I am confident the enemy lost more. Captain Flower of Colonel Dean's regiment, was wounded; and Major Grigg's lieutenant and ensign slain. Captain Burges lies wounded and very sick. I question not but within a fortnight we shall have the town; and Poyer hath engaged himself to the officers of the town not to keep the castle longer than the town can hold out; neither indeed can he, for we can take away his water in two days by beating down a staircase, which goes into a cellar where he hath a well. They allow the men half a pound of beef, and as much bread a day, but it is almost spent.

We much rejoice at what the Lord hath done for you in Kent. Upon our thanksgiving for that victory, which was both from sea and leaguer, Poyer told his men it was the Prince, Prince Charles and his revolted ships coming with relief. The other night they mutinied in the town. Last night we fired divers houses, which 'fire' runs up the town still; it much frights them. Confident I am we shall have it in fourteen days, by starving.

I am, Sir, your servant,
Oliver Cromwell.

CROMWELL to Richard Herbert (successor of the Lord Herbert of Cherbury) residing at St. Julian's, Monmouthshire.
Leaguer before Pembroke, June 18, 1648.

SIR,

I would have you to be informed that I have good report of your secret practice against the public advantage; by means whereof that arch-traitor, Sir Nicholas Kemeys, with his horse, did surprise the Castle of Chepstow; but we have notable discovery from the papers taken by Colonel Ewer on recovering the castle that Sir Trevor Williams of Llangibby was the malignant who set on foot the plot.

Now I give you this plain warning by Captain Nicholas and Captain Burges, that if you do harbour or conceal either of the parties, or abet their misdoings, I will cause your treasonable nest to be burnt about your ears.
Oliver Cromwell.

CROMWELL's last letter to Col. Poyer.

SIR,

I have (together with my Council of War) renewed my propositions. I thought fit to send them to you with these alterations, which if submitted unto I shall make good. I have considered your condition, and my own duty; and (without threatening) must tell you that if (for the sake of some) this offer be refused, and thereby misery and ruin befall the poor soldiers and people with you, I know where to charge the spill. I expect your answer within these two hours. In case this offer be refused, send no more to me about this subject.

I rest your servant,
OL. Cromwell.
July 10, at 4 a'clock
this afternoon, 1648.

Pembroke (Town and Castle) surrendered to Parliament; OLIVER CROMWELL *writes to the Speaker of the House of Commons.*
July 11, 1648. Pembroke.

SIR,

The Town and Castle of Pembroke were surrendered to me this day, being the eleventh of July, upon the propositions which I send you here enclosed. What arms, ammunitions, victuals, ordnance, or other necessaries of war are in [the] town I have not to certify you the Commissioners I sent in to receive the same not yet being returned, nor like suddenly to be; and I was unwilling to defer the giving you an account of this mercy for a day.

The persons excepted are such as have formerly served you in a very good Cause; but being now apostatised I did rather make election of them than of those who had always been for the King; judging their iniquity double, because they have sinned against so much light and against so many evidences of Divine Providence going along with and prospering a just Cause, in the management of which they themselves had a share.

I rest your humble servant,
Oliver Cromwell.

Memoirs of the Civil War in Wales, ed. J.R. Phillips (1874).

As in England, the Puritan Revolution in Wales engendered an atmosphere of spiritual excitement which expressed itself in various sects attached to particular dogmas. Prominent among these new convictions was Millenarianism, a belief in an imminent paradisal period of a thousand years after the Second Coming of Christ, and, for a time, a widespread force among Puritan radicals. The Fifth Monarchists were an extreme group who believed that Charles I embodied the Anti-Christ and the revolution heralded the fulfilment of prophecy, i.e.the Second Coming of Christ, the Fifth Monarchy, (succeeding, so they believed, the previous empires of Babylon, Assyria, Greece and Rome) when he would rule on earth with his chosen saints – by that, it seems, they meant those who espoused their views.

In 1650 an Act for the Better Propagation and Preaching of the Gospel in Wales was passed by Parliament. It reflected the anxiety of Welsh Puritans about the ignorance of the Welsh people because of the failure of Anglican preachers to communicate with them in their own language. Of the existing Anglican clergymen 278 were deprived of their livings (Thomas Vaughan, brother of the poet, among them) and approved new Puritan preachers were sent all over Wales. A grant was also made from the state to establish a rudimentary form of elementary education for the first time in Wales. But the new measure failed for several reasons: the lack of suitable personnel, the hardship inflicted on the poor on whom were levied extra tithes in order to pay the preachers and evidence of corruption in the collecting of the tithes. The Act was not renewed in 1653.

William Erbury, a former minister appointed as one of the preachers and a rigid Puritan, movingly portrays the situation in a letter to one of the Commissioners in South Wales, April 19, 1652.

WILLIAM ERBURY to Commissioner.

Then the oppression of Tithes came to my ears, and the cry of the oppressed filled my heart, telling me, That I and my children fed on their flesh, that we drunk their blood, and lived softly on their hard labour and sweat.

All the Petitions against Tithes were presently presented and spread before me by God, who asked, Is it not the gain of oppression that thou and thine live on?

Truly Sir, there was never a day went over my head, but I heard something of him from God, and from men also, who, not knowing the working and wrath that was within, did continually hit me in the teeth with something of Tithes.

One came to my Chamber, a worthy Gentleman from England, complaining of the Commissioners of Monmouth-shire, who (as he came along) had a meeting at Christ-Church, to take a more strict account of each man's Tithes, and that he met with many poor Country-men in the way crying out their oppression, and that (as they said) by the people of God.

Another day an honest man of our Country, comes in and tells me, he had formerly taken a good bargain of Tithes, from the Commissioners of Glamorgan-shire, but he had no rest in his Spirit from the time he farmed it from them, but was continually tormented till he delivered it up, which he did (as he said) very quickly, else he thought in his heart he had run stark mad out of his wits.

And truly Sir, 'twas so with me in this, though I have been afflicted from my youth, and suffered the terrors of the Lord to distraction; yet (for the time) I was never so distracted, confounded, and filled with fears in all my former temptations, as in this of Tithes.

And yet this trouble was not like those legal terrors I suffer of old; but it was like fire in my bones which I believe is the eternal Spirit, and everlasting burnings, which will shortly break forth upon all the oppressors of the land to burn up their flesh, fulness, and those fair buildings which they have raised on the ruines of others, enriching themselves in the Nation's poverty.

Geraint H. Jenkins, *Protestant Dissenters in Wales*, (Cardiff: University of Wales Press, 1992).

One of those who was an Approver under the 1650 Act was Morgan Llwyd (1619-59) who had already served as a minister in Wrexham and as a chaplain in the Parliamentary army. He counted himself one of saints who, in this time of change, believed in the imminent coming of Christ but his inclinations were mystical rather than political (unlike his onetime friend Vavasor Powell) and his reputation as a fine writer in the Welsh language seems undoubted. The following letter, at the time of the Commonwealth, is to 'his loving cozen Mr John Price'.

MORGAN LLWYD to Mr John Price.

A few words from you are more to me than many lines from some others, because there are (I hope) more than ordinarie affections endearments and suitable atomes of the minde between us, yt doe glew our hearts together in a conscientious adherence to those best things yt are eternall occult mistaken matters of true glory. I am persuaded yt (though my earthly bodily tabernacle be shaken dayly with natural distempers) you may probably live to see more blessedness than ever our fathers thought any of their posterity should be made to understand. In yor letter, you mention the oven and the sunne yt Malachy speaks of, That day is now dawned, what is life to some is burning to the rest. The oven signifieth an unavoydable inneffable intolerable consumption to all proud flesh. Therefore be we humble for God resisteth the proud and giveth more grace to the lowly. Now that SUNNE of RIGHTEOUSNESSE shall bring with him (and that shortly) light, life justice healing liberty and growth, knowledge shall cover this darke earth, life shall enter into dead bones yt are without the marrow of the spiritual word of God.... And... you would enquire of present affaires in all Europe then heare the news out of Revel. 11. 13. 15. 17. 18. You have all the sacred scriptures before you let them be yor companions, counsellors, fountaines, wings, wisdome and learning. For want of yt knowledge the land of our nativitie is asleepe and the people dreame and talke through their sleepe, and shall we then lay to heart what they say of us? I have beene in an agony there, least I should imprison the truth of God in silence. Sorrow is to us for their sakes and they are drawing a woe upon themselves even as many of them as by following lying vanityes forsake their owne mercyes and spin out their webbs of false hopes frothy witt and humane reason. Notwithstanding (as sure as Jesus is king) the good beginning in Merion will quickly conquer their greatness and learning, falsely so called. Hath God begun (victoriously) to build in the land, and will he not finish his worke? Surely he will, for his works are (like himselfe) perfect.... I hope and desire we may meet together with God in the inheritance of the saints in light.... I have you in my thoughts and when the iron is hott we may strike for it and for the good of our countrey....

Yor cozen and servant

Mor. lloyd.

Wrexham 1651. Ye 25th of ye 11th month cold January.

Gweithiau Morgan Llwyd o Wynedd, Vol. I, ed. T.E. Ellis (Jarvis & Foster: Bangor and Dent: London, 1899).

A letter, written in 1653, expressing exasperation and despair at his fellow countrymen's ignorance and the religious teaching afforded them comes frorn the fierce Puritan COLONEL JOHN JONES who was one of the signatories to Charles I's death warrant.

...how many are there in poore Wales that thincke sufficiently served by their going once a week to heare a hudle of Prayers delivered many times by a poore creature whose mind is in his alehouse, or rather in hell (for that indeed is here upon earth) even at the instant of time when he seems to be speaking to God as the mouth of the people and them to return to their carnall sports and licentious pleasure never minding to sett their hearts and affections above all earthly comforts.... The Lord knoweth I judge no man but speake the many yeares experience I have learned in my own heart.

J. Gwyn Williams, 'The Quakers of Merioneth during the Seventeenth Century', *Journal of the Merioneth History and Records Society* 8 (1978-9).

From Vavasor Powell (1617-70), the most militant millenarian and evangelist, comes a letter to Oliver Cromwell denouncing his abandonment of the millenial cause in which he had formerly believed and his assumption of the role of Lord Protector. After the restoration of the monarchy Powell suffered persecution and died in prison. The letter formed the preface of his A Word for God *(1655).*

VAVASOR POWELL to Oliver Cromwell.

Sir, For as much you have caused great searching of heart, and divisions among many of God's people by a sudden, strange, and unexpected alteration of government, and other actions, to the great astonishment of those, who knew your former publick resolutions and declarations; considering also, how (contrary to foregoing acts and engagements) you have taken upon you a power, by which you are utterly disinabled (if there were in you a heart) to prosecute the good things covenanted and contended for, with so many great hazards, and the effusion of so much blood; and by reason whereof you are become justly suspected in your ends in time past, and actions for future, to the very many of those, of whose affections and faithful services you have enjoyed no small share, in all the difficult passages, and enterprizes of the late war. These things considered by us, (as we know they are by many churches and saints) and there being a deep sense upon our spirits of the odium under which the name of Christ, his cause, people, and ways do lie (as it were) buried; and also of the exceeding contempt, which the wonderful and excellent operations of God are brought into, even those eminent wonders, which the nations have been spectators and witnesses of, and wherein your hands have been partly engaged; we cannot, after much serious consideration and seeking of the Lord, many of us, both together and apart, but present to your hands the ensuing testimony, which (however you may look thereon) is no more than necessity exacts from us, for the clearing of our own souls from guilt, and discharging of our duty to God and men. Therefore we earnestly wish you to peruse and weigh it, as in the sight of God, with a calm and Christian-like spirit; and harden not your neck against the truth, as you will answer it to their great judge, before whose impartial tribunal you (as well as we) shall be very shortly cited to give an account of the things done in the body, whether good or evil. Where the true motives and ends of all your actions will be evident, where no apology will be accepted of your slighting and blaspheming of the spirit of God, nor for the hard measure you give his people, by reproaches, imprisonment, and other oppressions; and where pride, luxury, lasciviousness, changing of principles, and forsaking of good ways, justice and holiness will not have the smallest rag of pretence to hide them from the eyes of the judge, which things (whatsoever you say for your self) are (even at present) to be read in your forehead, and have produced most sad effects everywhere. Especially first, the filling of the saints' hearts and faces with inexpressible grief and shame. And secondly, the stopping (at least) of the strong current of their prayers, which was once for you, if not the turning thereof directly against you. To these we might add (thirdly) the hardening of wicked men, yea the refreshing and justifying of them in their evil doings, and speaking against the gospel, name and spirit of our Lord Jesus Christ. And lastly, God's signal withdrawing from you his designs. Oh then! that you would lie down in the dust, and acknowledge your iniquity, and return unto the Lord by unfeigned repentance, doing your first works; and that you would make haste to do so, lest God's fury break forth like fire upon you, and there be no quenching of it. This would rejoice us much, as being real well wishers to your soul's everlasting happiness, though we must declare with equal piety and detestation against your designs and way.

Geraint H. Jenkins, *Protestant Dissenters in Wales.*

1652

These two letters vividly depict one of the afflictions of the people and the responsibilities faced by those in authority locally.

(THE COMMON COUNCIL) to The Worshipful Thomas Davids, Esq., (Mayor of Haverfordwest) in London.
April 26, 1652. Haverfordwest.

We have received your letter from Hereford whereby we understand that you are driven to go to London. We pray to God to send you well there. You have left a sad town behind you without government, yet we hope that will be for the good of the town. You being there yourself may with God's assistance do some good. We know that Mr Herbert Perrot will join you.

The sickness doth increase. There died since your departure from us the number of seventeen, the one of them was a servant maid of William Johnes, the high constable, Thomas Bowen the carpenter's wife, Philip Andrewes and Richard Web, labourer, who dwelt in Cowky Street, whose houses are now infected, and there is a great many of them sent to the pesthouse out of their houses and others, which causes the charge to be heavy upon this town and more like to be unless the Lord turn his judgement from us. There is now locked up within the gates in Castle town of number of three score which will expect to be relieved by the town, the Lord comfort them, besides many more which will want unless the Lord out [of] his infinite mercy do look upon them....

The people go daily out of the town: here will be none left to maintain the poor. We pray you hasten home as soon as possibly you can.

WILLIAM BOWEN to Thomas Davids, Mayor of Haverfordwest, in London.
May 24, 1652. Haverfordwest.

The Lord be blessed there have not many died of the sickness since our last letter sent you, but it is entered into St. Thomas's parish. Lawrens Butler is dead there and one of his children and another poor child there and a daughter of the widow Thomas in St. Martin's, there died but four all since: the Lord be praised they are all well in the Bridge Streete and Mr Bateman and his son are well, but Richard Luntley's house is still infected. The woman that tended upon him is infected and gone into the pest house, but he is so stubborn we cannot have him to remove but is in the house by himself: the doors be chained up upon him. The sickness is much dispersed in the county. It is at the Ford in the hundred of Dewsland and in other places there. The Lord withdraw his judgement from them and us!

As for the government of the town I do what possible in me lies. I can have no assistance at all, for they are all gone out of the town. John Edowe, being one of the high constables, is gone, and Mr William Davids, whom you appointed treasurer for the poor to receive the weekly rate, is gone presently after your departure. Were it not for William Jones and James Griffith we should have nothing done here. Mr. William Browne is somewhat stiff and high. I can have but small service from him. I wish that your business were ended that you might come here yourself, which I hope will be shortly, and I pray to God to send you well....

Pembrokeshire Life.

1657 ff.

GEORGE FOX (1624-91), *founder of the Society of Friends or Quakers, here recounts in his journal some of the incidents which occurred during his eventful tour of Wales in 1657 when he was accompanied by his devoted Welsh supporter and fellow preacher, John ap John.*

...And so we passed up into Wales through Montgomeryshire and up into Radnorshire, where there was a meeting like a leaguer for multitude. And I walked a little off from the meeting whilst the people were a-gathering, and there came John ap John to me, a Welshman: and I bid him go up to the people, and if he had anything upon him from the Lord to speak to the people in Welsh he might (and thereby gather them more together).

Then there came Morgan Watkins to me who was loving to Friends and, says he 'The people lie like a leaguer and the gentry of the country are come in.' So I bid him go up to the meeting, for I had a great travail upon me for the salvation of the people. And so I passed up to the meeting and stood a-top of a chair about three hours and sometimes leaned my hand of a man's head, and stood a pretty while before I began to speak, and many people sat a-horseback. And at last I felt the power of the Lord went over them all and the Lord's everlasting life and truth shined over all....

And so I passed through Wales and had several meetings till I came to Tenby, and when I came up the street a justice of peace came out of his house and desires me to alight and stay at his house, and I did so.

And on the First-day the mayor and his wife and several other heads of the town came in about the tenth hour and stayed all the meeting, and a glorious meeting it was. And John ap John was with me, and he went to the steeplehouse; and the governor cast him into prison. And on the Second-day morning the governor sent one of his officers to the justice's house for me, and it grieved the mayor and the justice for they both were with me in the justice's house. So the mayor and the justice went up to the governor before me; and after, I went up with the officer; and the governor had got another justice of peace with him. And when I came in I said, 'Peace be unto this house', and before he could examine me I was moved to ask him why he did cast my friend into prison, and he said, 'For standing with his hat on his head in the church.'

I said, 'Had not the priest two caps on his head, a black one and a white, and cut off the brims of his hat and my friend would have but one; and the brims of the hat were only to save the rain from his neck.'

'These are frivolous things,' said he.

Said I, 'Then why dost thou cast my friend into prison for such frivolous things?'

So then he began to ask me whether I owned election and reprobation. 'Yes,' said I; 'and thou art in the reprobation.' Then he was up in a rage and said he would send me to prison till I proved it, and then I told him I would prove it quickly, if he would confess truth. Then I asked him whether wrath, fury and rage, and persecution were not in the reprobation, for he that was born of the flesh persecuted him that was born of the spirit. For Christ and his disciples never persecuted nor imprisoned any.

And so he fairly confessed that he had too much of wrath haste and passion in him; so I told him Esau was up in him, the first birth, and not Jacob, the second birth. So the Lord's power so reached the man, and came over him that he confessed to Truth: and the other justice came and took me by the hand. And as I was passing away I was moved to speak to the governor again, and he invited me to dinner with him and set my friend at liberty....

Journal of George Fox (1694).

In the following pathetic letter, written from Brecon prison in 1668, a young woman Quaker, BRIDGET BERROW, *confesses her sin of adultery to her fellow Quakers and her fear that she has brought dishonour on their faith. Presumably she was in prison because she was suffering persecution, like many other Quakers.*

Dear friends it is layd upon me from ye Lord to let you understand yt I have sinned against ye Lord God of Heaven & Earth, & his people in yt I have given you great offences, & greived their tender Consciences, & burthened ye pure seed of God in them by letting my minde run forth toward Edmond Williams not knowing but yt his wife had been dead for I was pswaded in my heart yt she was out of ye body because he sd he had not heard from her in soe long a time as sevean years wch caused me to erre, & hearken to ye subtilty of ye serpent which wrought in ye missery of iniiquity, & begot in me a false birth which seemed to me to be of God, & ye leadings of his spirit but it was of ye Devill wch is a lyar from ye beginning, & ye Spirit of Erroe wch darkned my understanding, & caused me to follow ye outgoeings of my minde wch was gone a wandring from ye pure light of God in my Conscience; therefore dear friends I doe here with greife of heart, & shame, & confusion to my face owne my condemnation from ye Lord God & his people & deny, judge & condemne all such disoerderly carriage to be of God or ye leading of this spirit but of ye spirit of error & darknes & ye fruits of this world soe from whence it came thither I doe return it with shame to my face for ever, & woe is me for ever yt I have done this deed against ye Lord my God & ye sheep of his pasture for I have opened ye mouthes of ye wicked, & caused ye Heathen to rejoyce, & brought a reproach upon ye everlasting truth for wch I am a sufferer; oh! woe is me for it, or yt ever I was borne to do this wickedness; Oh! wt shall I doe where wth shall I appease the wrath of my God, & make satisfaction to his saints, & tender lambs for ye Truth is unreprovable who can lay any thing to ye charge of Gods elected ones. Oh! Woe is me for ever for shame & confusion doth cover my face as a vayle, & how shall I appear before ye Lord, & his people for our God is A consumeing fire, & who can dwell with everlasting burnings but he, yt hath clean hands, & a pure heart; And soe dear friends for your better satisfaction I doe here in ye feare of ye Lord God deny, judge, and condemne and abhorre to have any more to doe with him then wth another faithfull friend yt walketh spiritually as long as his wife is in ye body; And dear friends in ye fear of ye Lord God I shall desire you to be mindfull of me in your prayers yt my faith faile not for ye Judgmt of ye Lord I must bear untill he hath executedd judgmt in ye Earth, and brought it to victory and speaketh peace unto my soule for my tryall is verry great, and A wounded conscience who can bear & I have not one friend yt is near me.

Given forth ye 7th day of ye 5th month 1668 by Bridget Berrow from ye Common goale in Brecon

Geraint H. Jenkins, *Protestant Dissenters in Wales.*

This letter to William Penn, dated July 7 1684, is from RICHARD DAVIES, *a feltmaker from Cloddiau Cochion, near Welshpool, who was first an adherent of Vavasor Powell but later found his true home with the Quakers. It reveals, that though Davies himself is remaining in Wales, many Welsh Quakers were seeking refuge from persecution in a promised haven in America.*

Deare – will its not nether seas nether danger of siprack keeps me from thee; for I am often with thee in sperit and glad would I be if I in truth be servisable to thee or aney as belongs to thy contrey: I have freely left my self to the disposing of my god in whose fear I stand, by whose councel I desier to be guided. Deare William keep noe place or placis for me to the prediguce of the people for if I com thow shall see if it pleace god soe to be that we shall Imbrace one another in that contrey that it shall not be for honor or profit: for if those things had bin in my Eye I might have snapt at them when thy love Extend soe largely to mee as I see it doth continue; the feeling and seeing by letters of thy cordial continued kindness to me and mine still oblige me more and more to love thee thow art noe buble nor mussroom. thow art born of that stock and seeds that the blessing is unto that we with thee and all the familes that beleves in him coms to be blesed....

Dear will the formoest of this was written before and now Charls Lloyd John ap John and my self being together in meryonith shire, taking our leave of friends that are boun[d] for thy contrey:seeing maney letters that came from thence to ther friends here, speack wel of thee, the contrey and Governmt and allsoe that thow hast granted us 4000 acker of land together which is great content to them they be hastning to it as fast as they can, that I think this contrey will be shortly with but few frinds in. Som grumbls that soe maney should goe away but it is to little purpose. the god of my life continue thy health and life among them.

Geraint H. Jenkins, *Protestant Dissenters in Wales.*

HENRY HYDE, 2nd EARL OF CLARENDON (1638-1709) was appointed Lord-Lieutenant of Ireland in 1685. These letters to the Earl of Rochester tell of the difficulties he encountered on his journey to take up his appointment.

Dec 30, 1685. Conway.
Wednesday, nine at night.

I left this place at two of the clock in the afternoon and came to the foot of the Penman (Mawr) by four, and stayed there till five, when it should have been dead low water; but the guides and others on horseback found it impassable; and the skilful say the ebb was not so low as it useth to be in these seasons, by forty yards; which they can give no reason for but the weather; for I must confess it has been as great a storm all this day of hail, rain, and wind, as ever I knew in all my life; the people in the place say the ebbs have been very little since August. This being the case, we came back hither again, and the resolution I have taken, upon the advice with the most skilful upon the place, is this to be tomorrow, at six of the morning, at the foot of the Penman again, and if the tides will not suffer the coach to go under the rocks, then my wife shall go into a litter, which a gentleman has lent me, and I will ride, and so shall her women over the Penman: and so to Bangor, and thence to Beaumaris, where, God willing, we shall be at noon, and will rest there the rest of that day and night; and on Friday we propose to borrow my Lord Bulkeley's coach to carry us to Holyhead.

To the Earl of Rochester.
New Year's Day, 1685-6. Beaumaris.

We left Conway yesterday at six in the morning and pursued the method for our journey, which I mentioned in my last from thence; my wife in a litter, and the rest of us on horseback, (though, I confess, for my own particular, I went on foot) passed over Penman Mawr, at the foot of which, on this side, I met my Lord Bulkeley's coach and servants, but they told us they had escaped very narrowly being cast away on coming over the ferry, and that the winds were so very high that it was not fit for us to attempt going that way; so the coach carried us to Bangor, where we ferried over into Anglesey, and then put my wife in the litter again; for never was, or can come a coach into that part of the country; and thus we came safe hither about three in the afternoon, God be praised, without any mischance to any of our company; and here we are lodged at my Lord Bulkeley's who makes very much of us, and entertains us most nobly... we are now ready to embark as soon as the wind is fair, but it is now full in our teeth.

Sunday, Jan 3, 1685-6. Holyhead.

...at present the winds are contrary: however we are now ready when the Captain calls upon us, and you will believe this is not a place to invite one to stay in longer than is absolutely necessary. My Lord Bulkeley has been most extraordinary kind to me, and by his care in sending pioneers before, the way from Beaumaris hither was made as good as possible, though still it was worse than I ever yet went...

Jan 7, 1685-6. Holyhead.

This will show you that we are still here, though the Dogger, which went out on Tuesday morning, be not yet heard of, and therefore we hope she has got safe over; yet the weather has been so very foul and tempestuous ever since, that Captain Wright would not go out with the yacht....

They finally got to Ireland after another 2 days and a seasick crossing.

From *Hyde Correspondence,* between Henry, Earl of Clarendon and his brother, Laurence Hyde, Earl of Rochester, ed. S.W. Singer (London: 1828).

HENRY VAUGHAN (1621-95), *devotional poet who was born and lived much of his life in the vale of Usk. He was a fierce supporter of the Royalist cause and the Established Church during the Civil War and the Interregnum. Here he is writing to his cousin, John Aubrey, the author of* Brief Lives, *on October 9th, 1694.*

HENRY VAUGHAN to John Aubrey.

Honoured Cousin.

I received yours & should gladly have served you, had it bene in my power, butt all my search & consultations with those few that I could suspect to have any knowledge of Antiquitie, came to nothing; for the antient Bards (though by the testimonie of their Enemies, the Romans;) a very learned societie: yet (like the Druids) they communicated nothing of their knowledge, butt by way of tradition wch I suppose to be the reason that we have no account left us: nor any sort of remains, or other monuments of their learning, or way of living.

As to the later Bards, who were no such men, butt had a societie & some rules & orders among themselves & several sorts of measures & a kind of Lyric poetrie: wch are all sett down exactly In the learned John David Rhees, or Rhesus his welch or British grammer: you shall have there (in the later end of his book) a most curious Account of them. This vein of poetrie they called Awen, which in their language signifies as much as Raptus, or a poetic furor; & (in truth) as many of them as I have conversed with are (as I may say) gifted or inspired with it. I was told by a very sober & knowing person (now dead) that in his time, there was a young lad father & motherless, & soe very poor that he was forced to beg; butt att last was taken up by a rich man, that kept a great stock of sheep upon the mountains not far from the place where I now dwell, who cloathed him & sent him into the mountains to keep his sheep. There in Summer time following the sheep & looking to their lambs, he fell into a deep sleep; In wch he dreamt, that he saw a beautifull young man with a garland of green leafs upon his head, & a hawk upon his fist: with a quiver full of Arrows att his back, coming towards him (whistling several measures or tunes all the way) & at last lett the hawk fly att him, w^{ch} (he dreamt) gott into his mouth & inward parts, & suddenly awaked in a great fear & consternation: butt possessed with such a vein, or gift of poetrie, that he left the sheep & went about the Countrey, making songs upon all occasions, and came to be the most famous Bard in all the Countrey in his time.

Dear Cousin I should & would be very ready to serve you in any thing wherein I may be usefull, or qualified to doe it, & I give you my heartie thanks for yr continued affections & kind remembrances of

Sr

Yr most obliged & faithfull

Servant,

Hen: Vaughan.

The Works of Henry Vaughan, ed. by L.C. Martin (O.U.P: 1957).

CELIA FIENNES (1662-?), *the daughter of a Roundhead Colonel, travelled round various parts of England on horseback and just managed to visit North Wales briefly. Her visit to Holywell shows she was a matter-of-fact, sceptical, but observant traveller.*

...St. Winifreds Well is built over with stone on pillars like a tryumphall arch or tower on the gates of a Church; there is a pavement of stone within ground 3 sides of the Well which is joyn'd on the fourth side by a great arch of stone which lies over the water that runs off from the Well, its many springs which bubbles up very fast and lookes cleane in a compass which is 8 square walled in with stone; in the bottom which you see as clear as Chrystall are 9 stones layd in an oval on which are dropps of red coullour some almost quite covering the top of the stone, which is pretended to be the blood of this holy saint whose head was struck off here, and so where her body laid this spring burst forth and remaines till now, a very rapid current, which runs off from this Well under a barre by which there are stone stepps for the persons to descend which will bathe themselves in the Well; and so they walke along the streame to the other end and then come out, but there is nothing to shelter them but are exposed to all the Company that are walking about the Well and to the little houses and part of the streete which runs along by it; but the Religeuse are not to mind that; it seemes the Saint they do honour in this place must beare them out in all things, they tell of many lameness's and aches and distempers which are cured by it; its a cold water and cleare and runs off very quick so that it would be a pleas-ant refreshment in the sumer to washe ones self in it, but its shallow not up to the waste so its not easye to dive and washe in; but I thinke I could not have been persuaded to have gone in unless I might have had curtains to have drawn about some part of it to have shelter'd from the streete, for the wet garments are no covering to the body; but there I saw abundance of the devout papists on their knees all round the Well; poor people are deluded into an ignorant blind zeale and to be pity'd by us that have the advantage of knowing better and ought to be better; there is some small stones of a reddish coullour in the Well said to be some of St. Winifreds blood also, which the poore people take out and bring to the strangers for curiosity and relicts, and also moss about the bancks full of great virtue for every thing but its a certaine gaine to the poore people, every one gives them something for bringing them moss and the stones, but least they should in length of tyme be quite gather'd up, they take care to replenish it dayle from some mossy hill and so stick it along the sides of the Well there is good streames runs down from it and by meanes of steepe descent runs down and turns mills; they come also to drinke of the water which they take up in the first square which is walled round and where the springs rise, and they say its of wonder full operation; the taste to me was like good spring water which with wine and sugar and lemons might make a pleasant draught after walking amongst those shady trees of which there is a great many and some straight and tall like a grove but not very uniforme, but a sort of irregular rows.

From thence I went back to Harding which is 8 very long miles; at Holly Well they speake Welsh, the inhabitants go barefoote and bare leg'd a nasty sort of people, their meate is very small here, mutton is noe bigger than little lamb, what of it there is was sweete; their wine good being neare the sea side and are well provided with fish, very good salmon and eeles and other fish I had at Harding.

The Journeys of Celia Fiennes, ed. Christopher Morris (Cresset Press: 1949).

1697 ff.

EDWARD LHUYD (1660?-1709), *was a brilliant and many-sided scholar: botany, geology, philology, archaeology were his principal interests. While still an undergraduate at Oxford, he demonstrated a piece of incombustible paper, at a meeting of the Philosophical Society, made from specimens of the mineral asbestos from Anglesey which he had ground up and mixed with water – a discovery which has recently been found to have mixed blessings. He was one of the first assistants at the Ashmolean Museum when it opened in 1683 and was appointed keeper in 1691. In 1707 he published his* Archaeologia Britannica, *a philological, archaeological and geological survey of the Celtic countries, the result of many years travel and research. The following extracts from letters after he had begun research in Wales in 1696, are but a sample of his vast correspondence.*

EDWARD LHUYD to Dr Tancred Robinson, F.R.S.
June 15, 1697. Usk in Monmouthshire.

Sir,

The most considerable discoveries, since my last, were some new species of *Glossopetrae* and *Siliquastra* (the first *Ichthyodontes*, I suppose that ever were observ'd in Wales) on the top of a high mountain called Blorens near Aber Gavenni....

Advancing about 3 miles further into Brecknockshire, at a place call'd Lhan Elhi we searched some coal and iron mines. Their coalworks were not pits sunk like draw-wells; but great inroads made into the side of the hill, so that three or four horsemen might ride in abreast... close by the pit we found a valuable curiosity, viz. a stone for substance like those we make lime of; of a compress'd cylinder form; and as it were cut off even at each end: About 8 inches long, and 3 in breadth: Its superficies adorn'd with equidistant dimples, like Dr Plot's *Lepidotes*... and in each dimple a small circle; and in the center of each circle a little stud like a pins head. This is the only curiosity of the kind I have seen; and is not referrable to anything I can think of, either in the animal or vegetable kingdom. Among the Iron Oars of the same hills we found some new spars, and several specimens of oars shot into a constant and regular figure, tho' not reducible to any animal or vegetable bodies....

To Dr. Tancred Robinson, F.R.S.
Sept 22, 1697. Lhan Dyvodog, Glamorganshire.

Sir,

I had no sooner received your last, but was forced to retire in a hurry to the mountainous parts of this County, in order to copy out a large Welsh MS, which the owner was not willing to spare above two or three days, and that in his neighbourhood. It was writ on vellom, about 300 years since; and contained a collection of most of the oldest writers mentioned by Dr Davies at the end of the *Welsh Dictionary*: So I thought it better trespassing on the gentleman's patience that lent it, than lose such an opportunity as perhaps will not occur again in my travels. This is the occasion of my long silence – the transcribing of that book taking up two months of our time.

I sent Mr Ray an account of some plants we met with, with three or four figures, which perhaps you have seen....

In a steep rock called Craig y park, and others in the parish of Ystrad Dyvodog, we observed divers veins of Coal, exposed to sight as naked as the rock; and found a Flint axe, somewhat like those used by the Americans.

At Goldcliff in Monmouthshire we had some variety of form'd stones: But what pleased me most was an *Asteria*, or Column Star-Stone, beset with sprigs the whole length of it, issuing from the commissures of the plates.

This County abounds with *Entrochi*; one whereof I saw in a rock at the Isle of Barry, above 15 inches in length; and an other about 10 inches long, but as thick as a cane. We took their figures and dimensions, but could not get off the stones without breaking....

R.T. Gunther, *The Life and Letters of Edward Lhuyd* (1945).

To Dr Richard Richardson.
18 April, 1699. Gogerdhan in Cardiganshire.

Dear Sir,
...I have here sent you ye draught of a remarkable sea plant which we met with adredging for oysters near Lhan Danwg in Meirionydshire. The whole plant is of a straw colour, and much of ye bignesse the figure represent. The stems are hollow, and fill'd with a kind of thick reddish liquor, as much like bloud (or goar) as the juyce of plants, insomuch that it seems referrable to the Zoophyts. If you presse these stems at ye bottom betwixt your fingers the red liq'r is foarc'd up and causes the drooping flowers (or seed vessels) to mount erect. We have lately discover'd a sort of marble in yt county which when polish'd represents a number of small oranges cut acrosse, ye reason whereof is an infinite quantity of *Porus* (or Alcyonium) stuck through ye stone. This might serve very well for inlaying work, as tables, windows, cabinets, closets etc. and would make curious salt sellers. If you are acquainted with any gentlemen that deal in alone (alum) or coppras you may please to acquaint 'm yt Wales affords good quantity of each, if they judge it worth their while to put up any works there, particularly Pembr'shire and Carmardhinshire for the former, and Meirionydshire for copras where we saw a great vein of (iron pyri)tes strongly impregnated. My next removal is to Mr Griff. Jones's, vicar of Lhan Rwst in Denbighshire....

To Dr Richard Richardson.
July 3, 1699. Denbigh.

Having left ye neighbourhood of Lhan Rwst before your letter came it did but lately find me out at Mostyn in Flintshire....
At Holywell they assur'd me that about twenty years since some miners had found a living toad in a solid lump of oar, and a few miles farther a Derbyshire man, who knew nothing of this, gave me the like relation of one found in his countrey. There was a small cavity of water in ye cavity of that in Flintshire, and it liv'd but a very short time after it came to the air; but I have one relation of the like nature to communicate which is, for ought I know unparallel'd in history. Some workmen on the twentyseventh of May last, digging ye foundation of a buylding at two-foot depth, met with some muscles (mussels) which were not only exactly agreable to those of the sea as to colour etc., but being open'd they found them full of liquor, and the animals alive and fresh in them. The place they were found was

an ordinary dry gravel near Mould in Flintshire, a small town distant from ye sea about six miles. Having heard of it, I made what speed I could to ye place, and dug about a foot deeper, but could discover no such thing; so that all I could doe was onely to get the three workmen present to attest ye relation by subscribing their marks, etc., and they are very willing to make oath of it, if requir'd. This being allow'd, I know not but my hypothesis may stand as fayr as any other; and I must confesse that one or two such other instances would make me very tenacious of that opinion, because no man I suppose will contend that they might have lived in this grave since the Deluge, and tho' it be possible that some one might lately have buryed them there, yet there being none in the neighbourhood anything curious about enquiries of this nature, and the workmen having no suspicion yt the ground had ever been mov'd, nothing seems more likely than that they were bred here, as they are at sea.... I have observed immense quantity of coppras-stone near Dol Gelhey in Meirionydshire, and no lesse of it near Lhan Rwst in Caernarvonshire, and enough of alum slat in Caermarthenshire and Pembrokeshire, but none here understanding them there's no use made of them. The limestone above ye lead-oar in Flintshire affording greate quantities of *entrochi* amongst which I pick'd up one afternoon about a dozen specimens perfectly converted into spar, tho' retaining their figures so far as to be easily distinguish'd and known for *entrochi*, and in all probability such might be found on diligent search at Clattering Syke. This transmutation of ye matter of stones seems very surprizing and remarkable; and I must desire you to recommend it to Dr Leigh's examination when you write to him, or discourse with him, as well as to consider of it your self; for I am as fully satisfy'd of the matter of fact as I can be of any thing, and I would gladly have you as thoroughly satisfy'd your self (as occasion is offer'd) from your own observations....

Catalogue of Welsh Manuscripts in the British Museum.

The Eighteenth Century

1719/20

The following letter graphically describes a problem of fishing rights and the destruction of stocks such as persists today.

WILLIAM LLOYD, Deputy Vice-Admiral for the County of Pembroke, to the Water Bailiffs in the County, the Masters of Ships within the Harbours of Milford and, if occasion requires, to Hugh Fowler and William Bowen, Esquires, Justices of the Peace. March 3, 1719/20.

...Whereas complaint has been made to me by several of the principal gentry and other inhabitants within the said county that several foreign ships of great burden have lately with their crew not only fished and dredged for oysters upon the coasts of this county, but are now actually come within the harbour of Milford and up into the branches thereof, and don't only fish and dredge for the private use while in harbour but employ many other fishing boats to dredge for the said oysters, whereby to lade their several ships therewith and the same to export out of His Majesty's dominion, to the great and unspeakable prejudice of His Majesty's subjects of this county, as well as by the said foreigners engrossing into their ships and possessions such immense quantities of oyster fish before the same are brought into a market to the benefit especially of the poor inhabitants of this county, whereby the price of this commodity is greatly enhanced and sometimes not to be had for money in the next adjoining markets to the said harbour, as by such extravagant fishing to take away and totally destroy all or most of the oyster beds within the said harbour and the rivers thereof, not only to the entire destruction of this beneficial produce and commodity to the people of this county in particular but to the general impoverishment of the very many poor families of other counties that support wholly by carrying... oysters into the more inland parts of His Majesty's own dominion....
(*Draft Letter*)

Pembrokeshire Life.

DANIEL DEFOE (1660-1731), *prolific writer of books, pamphlets and journals, among them* Robinson Crusoe *and* Moll Flanders. *The following letters, in which his astonished aversion to Wales's high mountains becomes somewhat amusing, were written in 1724 during his tour of Great Britain.*

LETTER VI.

...I am now at the utmost extent of England west, and here I must mount the Alps, traverse the mountains of Wales, (and indeed, they are well compar'd to the Alps in the inmost provinces); But with this exception, that in abundance of places you have the most pleasant and beautiful valleys imaginable, and some of them, of very great extent, far exceeding the valleys so fam'd among the mountains of Savoy, and Piedmont....

We now entered South Wales; The provinces which bear the name of South Wales are these, Glamorgan, Brecknock, Radnor, Caermarthen, Pembroke, and Cardigan. We began with Brecknock, being willing to see the highest of the mountains, which are said to be hereabouts; and indeed, except I had still an idea of the height of the Alps, and of those mighty mountains of America, the Andes, which we see very often in the South Seas, 20 leagues from the shore: I say except that I had still an idea of these countries on my mind, I should have been surprized at the sight of these hills; nay, (as it was) the Andes and the Alps, tho' immensely high, yet they stand together, and they are as mountains, pil'd upon mountains, and hills upon hills; whereas sometimes we see these mountains rising up at once, from the lowest valleys to the highest summits which makes the height look horrid and frightful, even worse than those mountains abroad; which tho' much higher, rise as it were, one behind the other: So that the ascent seems gradual, and consequently less surprising....

Tho' this county be so mountainous, provisions are exceeding plentiful, and also very good all over the county; nor are these mountains useless, even to the city of London, as I have noted of other counties; for from hence they send yearly, great herds of black cattle to England, and which are known to fill our fairs and markets, even that of Smithfield it self.

The yellow mountains of Radnorshire are the same and their product of cattle is the same; nor did I meet with any thing new, and worth noticing, except monuments of antiquity, which are not the subject of my enquiry... so we made it our north boundary for this part of our journey, and turn'd away to Glamorganshire.

Entering this shire from Radnor and Brecknock, we were saluted with Monuchdenny-Hill on our left, and the Black Mountain on the right, and all a ridge of horrid rocks and precipices between, over which, if we had not had trusty guides, we should never have found our way; and indeed, we began to repent our curiosity, as not having met with any thing worth the trouble; and a country looking so full of horror, that we thought to have given over the enterprise, and have left Wales out of our circuit: But after a day and a night conversing thus with rocks and mountains, our guide brought us down into a most agreeable vale, opening to the south, and a pleasant river running through it, call'd the Taaffe; and following the course of this river, we came in the evening to the antient city of Llandaff, and Caerdiff, standing almost together.

Llandaff is the seat of the episcopal see, and a city; but Caerdiff which is lower on the river, is the port and town of trade; and has a very good harbour opening into the Severn Sea, about 4 miles below the town. The cathedral is a neat building, but very antient; they boast that this church was a house of religious worship many years before any church was founded in England, and that the Christian religion flourish'd here in its primitive purity, from the year 186, till the Pelagian heresy overspread this country....

The south part of this country is a pleasant and agreeable place, and is very populous; 'tis also a very good, fertile, and rich soil.... The chief sea port is Swanzey, a very considerable town for trade, and has a very good harbour: Here is also a very great trade for coals, and culmn [anthracite] which they export to all the ports of Sommerset, Devon, and Cornwal, and also to Ireland itself; so that one sometimes sees a hundred sail of ships at a time loading coals here; which greatly enriches the country, and particularly this town of Swanzey, which is really a very thriving place; it stands on the River Tawye, or Taw: 'Tis very remarkable, that most of the rivers in this county chime upon the letters T, and Y, as Taaf, Tawy, Tuy, Towy, Tyevy.

Neath is another port, where the coal trade is also considerable, tho' it stands farther within the land. Kynfig Castle, is now the seat and estate of the Lord Mansel, who has here also a very royal income from the collieries; I say royal, because equal to the revenues of some sovereign princes, and which formerly denominated Sir Edward Mansel, one of the richest commoners in Wales; the family was ennobled by Her late Majesty Queen Anne....

Before we quitted the coast, we saw Tenbigh, the most agreeable town on all the sea coast of South Wales, except Pembroke, being a very good road for shipping, and well frequented: Here is a great fishery for herring in its season, a great colliery, or rather export of coals, and they also drive a very considerable trade to Ireland.... We left Pembrokeshire, and after about 22 miles, came to the town of Cardigan.... It has a good trade with Ireland, and is enrich'd very much, as is all this part of the country, by the famous lead mines, formerly discover'd by Sir Carbery Price, which are the greatest, and perhaps the richest in England; and particularly as they require so little labour and charge to come at the oar, which in many places lyes within a fathom or two of the surface, and in some, even bare to the very top.

Going N. from the Tyvy about 25 miles, we came to Abrystwyth, that is to say, the town at the mouth of the River Ystwyth. This town is enrich'd by the coals and lead which is found in its neighbourhood, and is a populous, but a very dirty, black, smoaky place, and we fancy the people look'd as if they liv'd continually in the coal or lead mines. However, they are rich, and the place is very populous....

Now we enter'd N. Wales.... In passing Montgomery-shire, we were so tired with rocks and mountains, that we wish'd heartily we had kept close to the sea shore.... The vales and meadows upon the bank of the Severn, are the best of this county, I had almost said, the only good part of it... all the North and West part of the county is mountainous and stony. We saw a great many old monuments in this country, and Roman camps wherever we came, and especially if we met any person curious in such things, we found they had many Roman coins; but this was none of my enquiry, as I have said already.

Merionithshire, or Merionydshire, lyes west from Montgomery-shire.... The principal river is the Towy, which rises among the unpassable mountains, which range along the center of this part of Wales, and which we call unpassable, for that even the people themselves call'd them so; we look'd at them indeed with astonishment, for their rugged tops, and the immense height of them: Some particular hills have particular names, but otherwise we called them all the Black Mountains, and they well deserv'd the name; some think 'tis from the unpassable mountains of this county, that we have an old saying, that the devil lives in the middle of Wales, tho' I know there is another meaning given to it....

LETTER VII.
SIR, My last from West Chester, gave you a full account of my progress thro' Wales, and my coming to Chester, at the end of that really fatiguing journey: I must confess, I that have seen the Alps, on so many occasions, have gone under so many of the frightful passes in the country of the Grisons, and in the mountains of Tirol, never

believ'd there was any thing in the island of Britain that came near, much less that exceeded those hills, in the terror of their aspect, or in the difficulty of access to them; But certainly, if they are out done any where in the world, it is here: Even Hannibal himself wou'd have found it impossible to have march'd his army over Snowden, or over the rocks of Merioneth and Montgomery Shires; no, not with all the help that fire and vinegar could have yielded, to make way for him.

The only support we had in this heavy journey, was (1.) That we generally found their provisions very good and cheap, and very good accommodations in the inns. And (2.) That the Welsh gentlemen are very civil, hospitable, and kind; the people very obliging and conversible, and especially to strangers; but when we let them know we travell'd merely in curiosity to view the country, and be able to speak well of them to strangers, their civility was heightened to such a degree, that nothing could be more friendly, willing to tell us every thing that belong'd to their country, and to show us every thing that we desired to see.

They value themselves much upon the antiquity: the antient race of their houses and families, and the like; and, above all, upon their antient heroes: their King Caractacus, Owen ap Tudor, Prince Lewellin, and the like noblemen and princes of British extraction; and as they believe their country to be the pleasantest and most agreeable in the world, so you cannot oblige them more, than to make them think you believe so too.

A Tour Through the Whole Island of Great Britain, Volume 2.

1727

JONATHAN SWIFT (1667-1745). *In 1727, en route back to Dublin having visited London after an absence of twelve years, primarily to arrange for the publication of* Gulliver's Travels, *Swift was forced to remain in Holyhead for several days because of the inclemency of the weather. The enforced delay and inactivity combined with the anxiety he felt because of the serious illness of his dear friend, Stella, induced him to write a journal from which the following are extracts.*

Monday, Sepr. 25.
The Captain talks of sailing at 12. The talk goes off; the Wind is fair, but he says it is too fierce; I believe he wants more company. I had a raw chicken for dinner, and Brandy with water for my drink. I

walkt morning and afternoon among the rocks.... Not a soul is yet come to Holyhead, except a young fellow who smiles when he meets me, and would fain be my companion; but it is not come to that yet. I writ abundance of verses this day; and severall useful hints (tho' I say it). I went to bed at 10, and dreamt abundance of nonsense....

Sept. 26th. Thoughts upon being confin'd at Holyhead. If this were to be my settlement, during life, I could courage my self a while by forming some conveniencyes to be easy; and should not be frighted either by the solitude, or the meanness of lodging, eating or drinking... I cannot read at night, and I have no books to read in the day. I have no subject in my head at present to write on. I dare not send my Linnen to be washed, for fear of being called away at half an hour's warning, and then I must leave them behind me, which is a serious point; in the mean time I am in danger of being lowsy, which is a ticklish Point. I live at great expense without one comfortable bite or sup. I am afraid of joyning with passengers for fear of getting acquaintance with Irish. The Days are short, and I have five hours at night to spend by my self before I go to bed. I should be glad to converse with Farmers or shopkeepers, but none of them speak English. A Dog is better company than the Vicar, for I remember him of old. What can I do but write everything that comes into my head.... I confine myself to my narrow chamber in all unwalkable hours. The Master of the pacquet-boat, one Jones, hath not treated me with the least civility, altho' Watt gave him my name. In short I come from being used like an Emperor to be used worse than a Dog at Holyhead. Yet my hat is worn to pieces by answering the civilityes of the poor inhabitants as they pass by. The women might be safe enough, who all wear hats yet never pull them off, if the dirty streets did not foul their petticoats by courtsying so low. Look you; be not impatient, for I only wait till my watch marks 10, and then I will give you ease, and my self sleep, if I can. On my conscience you may know a Welch dog as well as a Welch man or woman by its peevish passionate way of barking....

Wednesday. ...The 3 Pacquet boats are now all on this side; and the weather grows worse, and so much rain that there is an end of my walking. I wish you would send me word how I shall dispose of my time. If the Vicar could but play at backgammon I were an Emperor; but I know him not. I am as insignificant here as parson Brooke is in Dublin; by my conscience, I believe Caesar would be the same without his army at his back. Well; the longer I stay here, the more you will murmur for want of packets. Whoever would wish to

101

live long should live here, for a day is longer than a week, and if the weather be foul, as long as a fortnight. Yet here I could live with two or three friends, in a warm house, and good wine – much better than being a Slave in Ireland. But my misery is, that I am in the worst part of Wales under the very worst circumstances; afraid of a relapse; in utmost solitude; impatient for the condition of our friend; not a soul to converse with, hindered from exercise by rain, cooped up in a room not half so large as one of the Deanery closets....

Thursday. 'Tis allowed that we learn patience by suffering. I have now not spirits enough left me to fret. I was so cunning these last 3 days, that whenever I began to rage and storm at the weather, I took special care to turn my face towards Ireland, in hopes by my breath to push the wind forward. But now I give up.... Well, it is now 3 afternoon. I have dined and invited the Master, the wind and tide serve, and I am just taking boat to go the Ship: so adieu till I see you at the Deanery....

The Holyhead Journal (1727).

1734

WILLIAM BULKELEY *of Brynddu was a member of one branch of the Anglesey Bulkeley family who gained their peerage during the Civil War. He was a wealthy squire who kept a diary of his activities in which the following account of the goings-on at an election – reflective, no doubt, of many other parts of the British Isles – occurs.*

April 30.
Mr John Bulkeley of Bwlchanau, Lord Bulkeley's agent, came here today to engage my vote and interest for Mr Baily. If it be against Hugh Williams I told him he should certainly have it; Mr Watkin Williams Wynn of Wynstay was then at Baron Hill and was to go to Denbighshire to-morrow to attend his own election which is to be on the 2nd of May next, from thence proceeding to the Bridgenorth Election, which is to be ye 4th and will probably last 2 or 3 days and from thence he is to come to our Election for this county which is to be on the 9th; he told me that there was an association or confederacy betwix 25 or 30 Greatmen, the Duke of Bolton, Earl of Chesterfield, Earl of Scarborough and several other Lords, Mr Watkin Wm. Wynn, Mr Sandys of Worcester, Mr Pulteney, Sir Wm.

Wyndham and others, to exert all their interest and power in all parts of the Kingdom to get a majority if possible against the villain Walpole, and they hoped to get amongst them 270 members to sit in the House of Commons whose knees had not bowed down to Baal. God send it may be so, Amen.

May 8.

I set out to Beaumaris to attend the county election which begins to-morrow about 12 in the forenoon; it began to rain again and I had rain all the way till I came to Maenaddwyn. I was sufficiently tired and wet by ye time I became to Beaumaris. Upon Red Wharf sands I met John Davies of Llandyfrydog who is one of the 24 capitall Burgesses of Beaumaris who gave me an account that he was then coming from Beaumaris Election, where Lord Bulkeley had been chosen without opposition; that they dined at Bull's Inn and that all the company after dinner had mounted their horses and gone in a body to meet Mr Baily as far as Cefn Coch, from whence they all came in a body to Town. I called at Bwlch Gwyn to give some drink to the voters that came along with me....

May 9.

About 9 o'clock in the morning all the Gentlemen from Carnarvonshire and this county met at the house of Mr David Williams the Attorney, son of William ap David ap Hugh ap Thomas of Llanfechell, where the candidate Mr Baily lay.... At half an hour past ten, when my Lord Bulkeley with several other Gentlemen came to the said house and joined them there; they proceeded to the County Hall and the King's writt being read and the act of Parliament against bribery and corruption read likewise, they proceeded to elect, when Lord Bulkeley polled for Mr Baily, Mr Meyrick, Mr Bodvel did the same, after which all ye house catched the word and there was nothing heard but Baily, Baily, Baily, without intermission, till they were tired reckoning the name, after which the Sheriffs declared him duly elected (proclamation being made before, that if anybody did demand a poll for anybody else, should appeal, but nobody did). The Elected member with all the Electors dined at the Bull's Head Inn where a grand entertainment was made; 3 Barrels of ale were given to the populace at the Cross to drink....

May 10.

All the gentlemen in town dined at Baron Hill; there were three tables set in the dining room, 11 or 12 at each table; the entertainment was handsome and elegant.... Everybody in the company drank ye horn which contained something above a quart, and afterwards full glasses till 7 o'clock, when the company broke up, some went to Town, others staid there.

Diary of William Bulkeley, Transactions of the Anglesey Antiquarian Society and Field Club (1931).

1739 ff.

HOWELL HARRIS (1714-1773) *was an outstanding and zealous leader of the Methodist Revival in Wales and a stalwart supporter of the Circulating Welch Charity Schools started by Gruffyd Jones. He was born in Trevecka, Breconshire and after some years he gathered together a community there. He remained a member of the Established Church though he was repeatedly refused ordination and denounced by the clergy. He wrote, 'I saw both from Scripture and the practice of the Church that the preaching of laymen was proper in times of necessity. In many churches there was no sermon for months together; in some places nothing but a learned English discourse to an illiterate Welsh congregation.' The following extracts give some glimpses into his evangelical life and of the relations between different sects.*

July 16, 1739. Mr Chapman's House, St. Clears.
   ...What a black account would it be should I write down all I hear of the laziness, negligence, doctrine, lies, pride, malice, drunkenness and immorality of the generality of the clergy. Here very crowded audience among whom was the vicar, a justice of the peace, and a young attorney. I am willing to be ordained or to go on thus, or to have my mouth stopped. Soul filled with pity to the country that sits in darkness, and have none to call them. This is what goes nearest to my heart, pity to the country lest I should not be further useful....

March 18, 1740. Hendre Einion in St. David's.
   Captain Davies and his wife attested to me that I had been owned vastly to do good in this county and parish. Discoursed to some scores to near 11. Towards Trefin, 4 miles. Discoursed about 3 hours (some thousands met) for universal love and against disputing. I hope it was a glorious day. With Mr Thomas of Longhouse to dine. Had my spirit much disturbed by him objecting against our Church, and despising for the vile lives of the clergy, none good in all this country. I took upon me to defend all its articles and forms. Shewed

the danger of leaving any Church but for conscience sake, that it was our duty to hear powerful sermons everywhere, but to communicate where we were before....

Dec 10, 1740. Maenclochog.

Discoursed with the woman of the house that had been born again, I hope, in hearing me about 9 months ago, when I was so sorely set upon by the Baptists. She never has that savour with John Powell as she had with me (though he has the light of all the scriptures). He has done great mischief in these parts, incensed poor people vastly, and brought poor children over to them that were very raw. He said of 6 errors I held. I find the Baptists had rather I should not come this way. I hope I come in the fear of God, and am owned and helped by him....

Feb 26, 1741. Cardigan Town.

...Came to Trehaidd past 3, where I was received with much welcome and love, and no opposition to about 7 or 8,000. Discoursed on the broken heart, most thundering and dreadful to the whole heart to near 6. I hear of a minister near the seaside that when the servants were gone out to sing Psalms, he brought the hounds to drown their voices. O! horrid....

HOWELL HARRIS to John Wesley.
Feb 28, 1741-2. Llanhithel near Pont y Pool.

Dear. Dr. Br:

I am perswaded you have fresh Discoveries of the base Ingratitude of your Nature to the best of Friends.... I believe he has a great work yet to do in us, and perhaps by us before we shall be brought to that Union with every one that feels the inward work in himself He longs for. In the meantime, I trust our Dear Lord will help us for his Glory's Sake and for the Church's Sake, so to behave to each other in Love, and forbearance that Shan't give the Enemy Room to blaspheme, or the Weak ones to take occasion to behave Spiteful, or angry, or Unbrotherly, towards each other. I trust we are of the same Seed, and shall at last stand before the same throne for ever, and who knows but we shall first be ty'd by the same Stakes, and ascend up in the same fiery Chariot; Let us not then quarrell, tho' we cant see alike. Let Love and Forbearance be your Topicks among the Lambs.... I bless God for this Power to write to you Sweetly and Brotherly & in Love. I have often felt Since I saw you some Coolnes to you, and for want of being enough in the Love of God, and of hearing from you, hearing Various Reports, have been Staggered; But still I feel there remains, I hope, a Spark of Solid Love in the Bottom I see more and more daily that there are Depths of unconceivable evils in our Natures, and incomprehensible Depths of the Riches of Grace in Christ.... I thank you tenderly for your Sermon, and I believe, when 'tis God's Time to bring us together, to ask one another what we mean in many Expressions which I believe one Speaks in this Wise and another in another Wise and so tis made the Root of Contention. I believe I say when we shall have more Simplicity, Tenderness, Love and Forbearance, with each other, to object and answer, and meet in Love with Simple minds, open to the truth, weighing fully what is said of both sides, and praying much, we shall be brought to see we aim at the same things but by Satan's Craft and the Prevalency of Self in all of us, we wont take the right way to come together....

But who am I to speak to you, I know all this you feel etc
  H H.

To Br: Whitefield
August 9th, 1742. Near Cerrig Howel in Breconshire.

Dr Dr Br:
  ...I have now been in all ye Greatest County Towns in So: Wales, but such is ye Power of the Devil and ye Prejudice that tis few of the Better sort come to hear, and they would come to hear you many of them: But in a more Particular Manner the Cause of the Lambs calls you down. Here are many precious Members of our Dear Lord toss'd and perplexed up and down, and it has been Set upon me that you are ye Person that Should be used to help them. The Clergy with us are so carnal and bitter against God's ways many of them, that there is no going near them as to their Doctrine, and many Scruple to go to ye Sacrament there, tho' God does as yet own that Ordinance by Giving his Presence alike there, as most I believe that go unprejudic'd and humbled there Testifie. The Dissenters again they do all they can to draw them over to them to make a Party, and when they go as there are a few of them that lead them on from Grace to Grace, and build them up but in Head knowledge, so most that go do visibly grow more Careless in their Walk, Selfish in their Spirit, Lukewarm as to the Power of Godliness, and become zealous for their party, losing their Love to those they dissent from, Disputing & c.... Most of the poor Lambs too being too far from Br:

Rowlands or Br: How. Davies or Mr Griffith Jones to go to their Communion and our Call being not clear to me to Seperate from the Church till we are turned out I am at a loss, Dr Dr. Br. Whitefield what to do....

Many here in Wales enquire earnestly for your Coming. O let us not be forgotten! Did not the Lord once Set Wales much upon your Heart, and does he now withdraw your Heart from us? Was not his Love free we might justly expect it, for we are a barren unfruitful People....

11 Sept. 1748. Longhouse.

Came to Dewisland, 5 or 8 miles through much rain. Kept a private society. The strength I now have in my body, I had not awhile. If it were not that I know Christ is the strength and life of my body as well as my soul, it would be presumptuous of me ever to go on a journey, for by the rules of nature, I am sure I have been a dead man this 12 years. Before I came here I was ready to faint and so began the work in public, and so again now in private, but I come to work in faith and you see how I am strengthened. Went hence in much hurry to Haverfordwest, and sure the Lord resides there. Discoursed on 2 Tim. 2:1 to a vast throng of people, the largest I ever saw here.

Howell Harris's visits to Pembrokeshire, transcribed by The Rev. Tom Beynon from the *Diaries of Howell Harris* (Aberystwyth: The Cambrian News Press, 1966).
Selected Trevecka Letters, ed. G. M. Roberts (Caernarfon: 1956).

1739 ff.

JOHN WESLEY (1703-1791). *Founder of Wesleyan Methodism was an indefatigable itinerant preacher who, however, never formally separated from the established Church. The following extracts from his journals comment on his visits to Wales and provide an interesting contrast to those of Howell Harris.*

Volume 2.

Mon. October 15th, 1739. Upon a pressing invitation, some time since received, I set out for Wales.

Wed. 17th Oct. When I came to Pontypool in the afternoon, being unable to procure any more convenient place, I stood in the street, and cried aloud to five or six hundred attentive hearers to 'believe in the Lord Jesus' that they might be 'saved.' In the evening I showed His willingness to save all who desire to come unto God through Him. Many were melted into tears. It may be that some will 'bring forth fruit with patience....'

Fri. 19th. I preached in the morning at Newport on "What must I do to be saved?" to the most insensible, ill-behaved people I have ever seen in Wales. One ancient man, during a great part of the sermon, cursed and swore almost incessantly; and, towards the conclusion, took up a great stone, which he many times attempted to throw. But that he could not do. Such the champions, such the arms, against field-preaching!

Sat. 20th. I returned to Bristol. I have seen no part of England so pleasant for sixty or seventy miles together as these parts of Wales I have been in. And most of the inhabitants are indeed ripe for the gospel. I mean (if the expression appear strange) that they are earnestly desirous of being instructed in it; and as utterly ignorant of it they are as any Creek or Cherokee Indians. I do not mean they are ignorant of the name of Christ. Many of them can say the Lord's Prayer and Belief. Nay, and some all the Catechism; but take them out of the road of what they have learned by rote, and they know no more (nine in ten of those with whom I conversed) either of gospel salvation or of the faith whereby alone we can be saved than Chicali or Tomo-chachi.

Volume 3.
Thur. May 5th, 1743. I rode over such rugged mountains as I never saw before, to Cardiff....

Fri. 6th. I preached at eleven in the new room, which the society had just built in the heart of the town; and our souls were sweetly comforted together. About two I preached at Llantrisant; and at Fonmon Castle in the evening, to a loving and serious congregation.

Sat. 7th. I was desired to preach at Cowbridge. We came into the town about eleven; and many people seemed very desirous to hear for themselves concerning the way which is everywhere spoken against. But it could not be: the sons of Belial gathered themselves together, headed by one or two wretches called gentlemen, and continued shouting, cursing, blaspheming, and throwing showers of stones, almost without intermission. So that after some time spent in prayer for them, I judged it best to dismiss the congregation.

Volume 4.

Fri. August 13th, 1756. Having hired horses for Chester, we set out about seven. Before one we reached Bangor, the situation of which is delightful beyond expression. Here we saw a large and handsome cathedral, but no trace of the good old monks of Bangor; so many hundreds of whom fell a sacrifice at once to cruelty and revenge. The country from here to Penmaenmawr is far pleasanter than any garden. Mountains of every shape and size, vales clothed with grass or corn, woods and smaller tufts of trees, were continually varying on the one hand as was the sea prospect on the other. Penmaenmawr itself rises almost perpendicular to an enormous height from the sea. The road runs along the side of it, so far above the beach that one could not venture to look down but that there is a wall built all along, about four foot high. Meantime, the ragged cliff hangs over one's head, as if it would fall every moment....

Volume 5.

Sun. August 21, 1763. ...We reached Tenby about eleven. The rain then ceased and I preached at the Cross to a congregation gathered from many miles round.... About five I preached to a far larger congregation at Pembroke. A few gay people behaved ill at the beginning; but in a short time they lost their gaiety, and were as serious as their neighbours....

Thurs. 25th. I was more convinced than ever that the preaching like an apostle, without joining together those that are awakened and training them up in the ways of God, is only begetting children for the murderer. How much preaching has there been for these twenty years all over Pembrokeshire! But no regular societies, no discipline, no order or connexion; and the consequence is that nine in ten of the once-awakened are now faster asleep than ever....

Sat. 27th. I preached (at Swansea) at seven to one or two hundred people, many of whom seemed full of good desires; but, as there is no society, I expect no deep or lasting work.

Mr Evans now gave me an account, from his own knowledge, of what has made a great noise in Wales: 'It is common in the congregations attended by Mr W.W. and one or two other clergymen, after the preaching is over, for any one that has a mind to give out a verse of a hymn. This they sing over and over with all their might, perhaps above thirty, yea, forty times. Meanwhile the bodies of two or three, sometimes ten or twelve, are violently agitated; and they leap up and down, in all manner of postures, frequently for hours together.' I think there needs no great penetration to understand this. They are honest, upright men who really feel the love of God in their hearts. But they have little experience either of the ways of God or the devices of Satan. So he serves himself of their simplicity in order to wear them out and to bring a discredit on the work of God.

About two I preached at Cowbridge, in the assembly room and then went in to Llandaff. The congregation was waiting, so I began without delay, explaining to them the righteousness of faith. A man has need to be all fire who comes into these parts, where almost every one is cold as ice. Yet God is able to warm their hearts, and make rivers run in the dry places.

Sun. 28. I preached once more in Wenvoe Church; but it was hard work. Mr H(odges) read the prayers (not as he did once with such fervour and solemnity as struck almost every hearer, but) like one reading an old song, in a cold, dry, careless manner; and there was no singing at all. Oh what life was here once! But now there is not one spark left.

Thence I rode to Cardiff, and found the society in as ruinous a condition as the Castle. The same poison of Mysticism has wellnigh extinguished the last spark of life here also. I preached in the town hall on 'Now God commandeth all men everywhere to repent'. There was a little shaking among the dry bones; possibly some of them may yet 'come together and live'.

The Journal of the Rev. John Wesley, ed. by Nehemiah Curnock (London: 1909).

ANONYMOUS LETTER-WRITER, Autumn 1746.

As I happened once to lodge of a Saturday night within ¼ mile of Mr Daniel Rowland, a Methodistical clergyman and a relation of mine, I went to his church ye Sunday following, where I own I heard a pretty good discourse (as far as I could hear) delivered to a very large congregation. While he was performing Divine Service, the people seemed to behave quietly and somewhat devoutly, but as they began to sing, I could hear a voice louder than all the rest crying out 'Rhowch Foliant', and by and by another hollowing 'Rhowch Glod', by this conduct... I concluded that these two persons might be seiz'd with a fit of the lunacy or frenzy. But as soon as this solemn part of the service was over Mr Rowland made a long extempore prayer before his sermon which prayer it seemed worked so upon most part of the audience that some cry'd out in one corner 'Rhowch Glod', others in different parts of ye church bawled out as loud as possibly they could, 'Bendigedig, rhowch foliant', and so on, that there was such a noise and confusion through the whole church that I had much ado, though I stood nigh the minister to make sense of anything he said. His preaching again flung almost the whole society into the greatest agitation and confusion possible, some cry'd, others laughed, ye women pulled one another by ye caps, embraced each other, caper'd like, where there was any room, but the perfectionists continued as before their huzzas. By this time poor me began to be uneasy too to see (I am sorry to say it) so much madness, so much irreverence, in the House of God.... Nay I never saw greater instances of madness, even in *Bedlam* itself.

Theophilus Evans, *The History of Modern Enthusiasm* (London: 1752).

1749 ff.

GRIFFITH JONES (1683-1761), *was the founder of the Welsh Circulating Schools designed to bring literacy to adults and children in their own language so enabling them to read the Welsh Bible and learn the Catechism. By the time of his death some 3000 of these schools had been established in Wales. In 1749, he published the following letter (in Welsh) on the 'Duty of Catechising Ignorant Children and People' in which he expressed his indignation at the deplorable conduct of some of the Welsh clergy:*

Peasantry cannot understand from sentences of deep learning in sermons the Articles of Faith without being catechised in them, which, at present, is more necessary, because there is among us such *monstrosity* and such evil and barefaced craft in some places, as the frequent preaching of *English* to the *Welsh* people, not one jot more edifying or less ridiculous than the Latin service of the Papists in France. One author states that he could not help rebuking such clergymen, in spite of the spleen and wrath it was likely to bring upon him, viz., the lazy vicars and rectors, who have led a careless life from their youth, and have set their mind on keeping company, and going unsteadily from tavern to tavern, and not minding their books; in consequence of which they are as ignorant of their mother tongue as they are of Greek and Hebrew, and therefore read the service and preach in English, without sense of shame, in the most purely Welsh assemblies throughout the country. Not much better, if any, are those who patch up a sermon of mixed language and jargon sounds, inconsonant, dark, and unintelligible, to the great scandal and disgrace of the ministry, and to the grief, damage, and weariness of the congregation.

Henry Richard, *Letters and Essays on Wales* (London: 1884).

The schools moved from place to place, spending a few months in each location. Jones published annual reports, Welch Piety, *in which he wrote to the benefactors describing the progress of the schools and printed a selection of letters of thanks and appreciation, of which the following are examples. It is notable that his correspondents almost invariably wished that the school could remain longer in their neighbourhood, they were so conscious of its benefits.*

Letter from BENJAMIN MORGANS, Vicar of Trelech, to Griffith Jones, March 14, 1754.

In a short Time after the School was opened, I went to visit it, and was agreeably surprised to see there an Old Man seventy one years of Age, with his Spectacles on his Nose, and the Church Catechism in his Hand, with five other poor People far advanced in Years, who came there with their little Children to be taught to read the Word of God... I could not help being much affected.

Griffith Jones, *Welch Piety* (London: 1755).

Letter from a Gentleman [WATKIN WATKINS] in or near Llandiffiliogogo in Cardiganshire, Feb 4, 1758.

Reverend Sir,
The Benefit that our Neighbourhood received this last Quarter from the Welch School, incites us to bless God, and to return you our hearty Thanks, praying God to reward all the Promoters of so needful a Charity. I make bold to acquaint you that M R the Schoolmaster at present in Llandissilio Parish has used his utmost Diligence in a very engaging and familiar Way, to draw People of all

Ages to be taught with Delight and Pleasure: in this manner the Young and the Old have reaped uncommon Benefit in so small a Time. When the Parents and other Labourers, and indeed many Farmers, saw the Children so well instructed in the Principles of the Christian Religion, then they, who were of riper Years flocked there by Night, with their Candles and Fuels, desiring with great Concern to be likewise instructed. And I own, we, who were Standers by, had no small Pleasure and Satisfaction in seeing the Willingness of the Master to teach them, together with the Willingness of the Neighbourhood to be taught by him. I therefore pray God to prosper and increase the Number of faithful Schoolmasters. I hope you will take Notice of him for the Encouragement of others, and leave him to continue some Time longer here which will oblige, etc. Watkin Watkins.

Letter from GEORGE PARRY, curate of Kelly-Gare in Glamorganshire, July 13, 1758.

Rev. Sir
...The Place where the School is at present is somewhat Mountainous, where there never was a school before... After the Master had instructed the Children for some time in the Principles of Religion which their Parents were ignorant of, both their Parents and others came to the School to hear them examined, who all admired the Master, and the Progress the children had made; counting it as a kind of Miracle. The Fame of this spread through the whole Neighbourhood insomuch that their Number increased immediately to Fifty Scholars; and now heartily pray for the Continuance of the School, and the same Teacher, and beg of me to interceed with you for them...

Griffith Jones, *Welsh Piety.*

1748 ff.

LEWIS MORRIS (1701-65). *Writer, scholar, antiquarian, cartographer, a dominant figure in the Welsh literary and antiquarian revival, Lewis Morris was the eldest of the four brothers, the Morrises of Anglesey who shared these intellectual interests.*

LEWIS MORRIS to William Jones.
January 1, 1748 or 9.

Sir,

It was a custom among the Ancient Britons (and still retained in Anglesey) for the most knowing among them in the descent of families to send their friends of the same stock or family, a dydd calan Ionawr a calennig, a present of their pedigree; which was in order, I presume, to keep up a friendship among relations, which these people preserved surprisingly, and do to this day among the meanest of them, to the sixth and seventh degree.

Some writers take notice that the Gauls also were noted for this affection and regard for their own people, though ever so distantly related. These things to be sure are trifles; but all other things in the world are trifles too.

I take men's bodies in the same sense as I take vegetables. Young trees propagated by seeds or grafts, from a good old tree, certainly owe some regard to their primitive stock, provided trees could act and think; and as for my part, the very thought of those brave people, who struggled so long with a superior power for their liberty, inspires me with such an idea of them, that I almost adore their memories.

Therefore, to keep up that old laudable custom, I herewith send you a calennig of the same kind as that above mentioned, which I desire you will accept of.

I have reason to know, it is founded on good authority; for both my father and mother were related to your mother, and came from the same stock mentioned in the inclosed, which is the reason I am so well acquainted with your mother's descent; and on the same account, till further enquiry, an utter stranger to your father's family....

LEWIS MORRIS to Edward Richard, poet and schoolmaster (1714-77). August 5th, 1758. Penbryn.

...Who do you think I have at my elbow, as happy as ever Alexander thought himself after a conquest? No less a man than Ieuan Fardd, who hath discovered some old MSS lately that no body of this age or the last ever as much as dreamed of. And this discovery is to him and me as great as that of America by Columbus. We have found an epic Poem in the British called Gododin, equal at least to the Iliad, Aeneid or Paradise Lost. Tudfwlch and Marchlew are heroes fiercer than Achilles and Satan. But as I suppose you will see the bard soon, he can tell you more than I can of these things; I am only an admirer and stander by, and fit for nothing but growing fat....

EDWARD RICHARD to Lewis Morris.
20th Octr, 1759. Ystradmeirig.

If I have said any thing disrespectfully of your *favourite Bards*, you must impute it to want of Judgement & skill in Poetry; I own Horace is liable to the same Censure as D. ap Gwilim and his fame suffers for it to this day, whilst the *Chaste Virgil* is admired by all the World: & particularly for describing a Captn and a Bunter in a Cave, without offending the nicest Ear. The Song I mean was one i ofyn Tarad, ar y Don Crimson Velfed, which I dont like, & have an Antipathy to two or three besides of our Welch Tunes; they are such doleful strains, that I think they were made soon after we had lost our Country & were expelled to this barren part of the Island. Indeed, most of the Welch Tunes have something mournful in them, as far as I can judge, the merry Catches were dropt upon our Defeat, as I fancy, and nothing would go down but what was in some measure expressive of our unhappy condition....

EDWARD RICHARD to Lewis Morris.
16 Nov, 1759. Ystrad Meuryg.

I am very glad to find you are all pretty well... David Jones I think has done wisely in inserting in his Book two or three things that are good, for those may make Amends for the rest. I long to see the Book, & hope to see a proper regard paid to Morfa Ryyddlan, yr hen Sion Green, of noble race was Siencin, or Triban & some other British Tunes. I have a very great opinion of Hugh Morris, though he has a hundred faults; & if I remember right I heard a Song lately of Humphrey Owen's, which I had rather be Author of than of all his Works. I have no Vote, or would give it against Dafydd ap Gwilym, for the Unconscionable Liberties he takes. I am sure he would be hanged for it at Parnassus; & I dont know what should save him at Cadair Idris. This I think I told you before but you warmly support him, & perhaps you are the best Friend he has. I dare not give myself Airs against so great an Authority, or I would tell you that his thoughts may corrupt our morals, & his Liberties spoil our poets.

LEWIS MORRIS to Edward Richard.

...When you see David Jones's book, you will say I suppose it is a very bad collection of mere jargon, worse than ever was done in any other language, some of it (and a great deal) wrote by people as ignorant of all learning and knowledge as Mathew Wirion or Angas'r Trawscoed. Good God what instruction this must afford. I suppose the good song attributed to Humphrey Owen (that you heard) was made by Hugh Morris, for I never saw anything of his that would not set my teeth on edge in the reading; want of language, want of thought, want of that great ingredient in song writing, a melodious easy cadence, which lulls the soul, while the contrary of it pulls sense by the hair of the head, is so often to be met with in almost all our song writers, but Hugh Morris, that I am in pain when I read any of them... David ap Gwilym should not be mentioned on the same sheet of paper with any of the song writers (not even Hugh Morris). He is in a higher sphere, and a spirit of a superior order. One line of his work is worth hundreds of their songs, in the same sense as we say of Horace or one of the great poets that a single verse of theirs would weigh down all the ballads of the kingdom. But I am far from defending David ap Gwilym's morals. He had none, he was as debauched as a wandering poet. He also wrote some poems in an extreme loose stile as to poetry, and they can hardly be called poems, for there is no poetry intended to be in this new way of writing, but in every other line. The other was a beauty-spot to set it off. He was such a master of poetry, that he was the first that had the confidence to introduce that loose way of writing in our language since the establishment of the new prosody, and he knew that nobody would dare to oppose him, nor has any poet ventured to write in that way after him, though he was followed in his Traeth Odlau (another kind of loose writing) by John Tudur. But there is no fear that those examples in poetry will ever gain ground, for the people in our age (except a few) write all bad lines, and not good and bad alternately; and as for immorality in his works, the common people will hardly ever see them, and the men of letters are too often taught immorality before they ever read D. ap Gwilym. He has never wrote anything against true Religion, and only to ridicule image worship and confession. The rest is merely heat of love-passion, which perhaps was in his constitution (being a bastard) and certainly was the taste of the age he lived in: the Popish religion and civil government allowing great lengths that way on payment of certain mulcts, &c. Has not Horace wrote some things which are concealed from vulgar eyes, and some that are published had better been suppressed, but what has that to do with the Poet? Look into Dr Davies's Dictionary and Grammar, a famous Divine of our reformed Church, and you will see D. ap Gwilym is his chief authority. I dont lay as much stress upon this as upon the general approbation of mankind for 350 years past, which have suffered this poet's works with all that we call their faults to live to this day, and probably some of them will live while the Welch language has a being. Those poems he had taken pains with are inimitable, his images full of life, his language pure and nervous, his prosody unexceptionable according to the new rules just then adopted, but he might have led the whole nation into what rules he pleased, his felicity of expression was such, that he never was at a loss to express his ideas in strong colours...

Additional Letters of the Morrises of Anglesey (1735-86), ed. Hugh Owen, Transactions of the Anglesey Antiquarian Society (Parts 1-2, 1947-9).

LEWIS to Richard Morris.
August 3, 1761. Penbryn.

   In regard to Mr Jones of Welwyn's ingenius observation on the designs of the Cymmrodorion Society, this is my opinion: that he considers that Society in a light too extensive, it being as yet but in its infancy, and begun by a Society of those Ancient Britains that reside in London, who are not to dictate to all Wales till their name is better established. And they think that if they can but raise a spirit of enquiry among their country men in Wales it will be a means to bring Arts and Sciences into vogue among them, and by degrees the improvements that Mr Jones mentions, which are certainly laudable and good. But by all means the bringing the people to love and caress their language and antiquities and to be masters of it is the first step of establishing national honour in their hearts as Cymmrodorion, notwithstanding what Mr Jones says of the Circulating Charity Welsh Schools which are in Wales, which should rather be called English Schools, it being the English language they teach, contrary to the original design, and against the true intent of that Charity. For this kind of education as matters now stand, only enables them, like the Irish, to crowd over in droves to England, to the utter ruin of their place of nativity, which by degrees must turn to a wilderness for want of hands: so that if these circulating Schools to teach the English tongue are continued, farewell public Welsh Academies that Mr Jones mentions, and farewell the public use of the ancient British tongue....

Letters of Lewis, Richard, William and John Morris of Anglesey (1728-65), 2 Vols ed. J.H. Davies (Aberystwyth: 1907-09).

EVAN EVANS (1731-38), *Welsh poet and scholar known as Ieuan Fardd (Evans the Poet), a pupil of Edward Richard and also instructed by Lewis Morris. He was ordained in 1754 but did not succeed in the church, moving from curacy to curacy – one of his problems seems to have been too great a fondness for drink. However he did become a great and scrupulous scholar, discovering and transcribing, among many others, the texts of Aneirin and Taliesin. The following letter, dated August 8th 1761, is to Rice Williams, a fellow scholar and friend of Thomas Percy, celebrated for his collection* Reliques of Ancient English Poetry, *with whom Evans corresponded.*

EVAN EVANS to Rice Williams.

...I need not expatiate on Poetry, as you have before you what I have spoke on that head to Mr Percy. You see how different the Language is, from what is spoke now in Wales. And if Mr Percy understood as much of the British as you do, he will not be surprized at what I tell him of the obscurity of some of our old bards of the sixth Century. I may modestly say there are not above 3 persons now in Wales, that understand the old British Language better than myself, yet after all I must own I do not absolutely understand above 3 parts in four of the Works of Aneurin Gwawdrydd, who wrote an Epic poem about the year 570. As far as I understand it, it is a noble and grand piece. The author lived either in Cumberland or Scotland, so that it is quite another Dialect, perhaps that of the picts, or Ystrad Clwyd Britons in the North. So that it is no wonder when we consider the distance of time and place, it should be so obscure to us, who have preserved but some few fragments of our once noble Language and its monuments. – As for the production of our modern poets, they are but mean and paltry....

EVANS to W. Griffith.
Llanvair, Talhaiarn (1762).

Revd Sir,
As I have been desired by Mr Rob: Wynn of Garthewyn to give your Oxford acquaintance some account of the British Bards, which in your letter you requested of him to procure of me, I am willing to give all the information I can, but for want of good copies of those venerable remains of our ancestors, I cannot give you that satisfac-

tory account I could wish.... I have by me a Collection of some of the works of Taliesin, Llywarch Hen, Aneirin Gwawdrydd, and Merddin Wyllt, who all lived in the time of Maelgwn Gwynedd King of Britain about the year 570 and are all mentioned by Nennius, the oldest British historian we have extant in Latin, excepting the railing Monk Gildas, who hardly deserves that name. But where is that great Apollo, who at this distance of time can understand any of their poems? The famous Dr Davies, author of the Dictionary, could not, as appears by the many obsolete words he has left without any interpretation. And indeed it is too great a task for any one man to undertake in a language so little cultivated, and so much neglected as our's has been for some centuries. It is so hard a task as for a modern Englishman to attempt to understand the oldest Saxon or Runic poetry extant without either dictionary, or glossary to help him, which I believe is next to impossible. I have with great reluctancy been forced by some of my English friends, who were desirous to know something of the nature of our poetry to attempt a translation of an ode of Taliesin, and I have of my own accord translated an Ode of Gwalchmai the son of Meilir, who flourished about the year 1157, who has wrote a very spirited one on one of the victories of prince Owain Gwynedd. This I thought might serve as a specimen of the poetic genius of our Bards, and of their manner of writing, which tho it be not as regular and methodical as the works of the refined genius of Greece and Rome, I think, does not want it's beauty. I have in my custody a collection of all the Bards that have wrote since the Norman Conquest to the death of Llywelyn last prince of Wales of the British line, which in my opinion are the most valuable of any we have in our language, though there are very good ones that wrote in Owain Glyndwr's time and even some as low as Queen Elizabeth, when the order was extinct.

The next letter is to Sir Watkin Williams Wynn, the great landowner, who was Evans's patron from 1771 to 1778, a time in which he was very active transcribing manuscripts and in trying to secure their publication in case they should be lost. Sir Watkin withdrew his pension when he discovered that Evans had begun the study of Hebrew and Arabic. Though his subsequent life seems to have been hard, he did have another patron, Paul Panton, who acquired his manuscripts when he died in 1788.

EVAN EVANS to Sir Watkin Williams Wynn.
Octr 15, 1776. Aber Ystwyth.

Worthy Sir,

The bearer is a person that I employ to distibute my sermons to the Subscribers, as well as to take the names of Subscribers to the Triades and Adagia Britannica. If you have received the printed proposals from Dr Percy, be so kind as to deliver him some of them. I have drawn a proposal in the subscription book which he brings along with him, before which I have apprized my countrymen of my undertaking. I have received the copy of Howel Dda's laws that I desired from Llan Fordaf library, for which I am much obliged to you. I have removed from my lodging at Towyn, which was a very damp unhealthy situation in the winter to Aber Ystwyth in Cardiganshire, and brought all your books and Manuscripts along with me. Upon second thoughts I thought it best not to return any as I am desirous of knowing what the Monkish historians say of our British laws, and of the Lawgiver Howel Dda. However depend upon it Sir that I will take particular care of every thing in print or Manuscripts in my custody. I should be glad to know whether Doctor Percy hath sent you the Manuscripts with the proposals. If you have received them, you may either send them me by the bearer, or leave them with a safe hand till I call for them at Wynnestay. I shall not begin to print them till I know what number of subscribers I shall have. It is now so late in the year, that it is very unseasonable for this poor old man to go about to gather Subscriptions in the winter. I therefore think it best to defer till the spring of the year. I thought it however advisable for him to wait on you for the printed proposals. It is with grief and concern that I observe how regardless of the interest of their Country our Country gentlemen are become, and how preposterous it is to see Clergymen read one part of divine service in English and the other in Welsh, and that not only in the Marches of Wales but in the very extremities of it. The Curate of Llan Badarn fawr last Sunday read the first lesson and the psalms in English to a Welsh Congregation, where [only] one in twenty did not know [knew] any thing of English.* The parishioners heavily complain of this popish usage. I wish Sir for the good of your country, and the interest of religion you would procure us a redress of this grievance all over the Principality in such places as are merely Welsh. The gentlemen who act thus are very much the enemies of their country and no friends to religion. It is in vain to complain to the Bishops, for as they are Englishmen, they will rather encourage the practice, however one thing I am sure of, God Almighty whose service is thus

120

unfaithfully performed will not be mocked. I think the Society of Cymmrodorion should put the laws into execution once more, and the Archbishop of Canterbury should be acquainted with this unchristian Custom. And if he hath any sense of his duty as Head of the English Church put an end to it. You will excuse my being an advocate for my injured country, and I wish I could direct you how to procure us a redress....

Your most obliged humble sert.

Evan Evans.

* *Words in brackets signify Evans's intended meaning as suggested by the editor, Aneirin Lewis.*

The Correspondence of Thomas Percy and Evan Evans, ed. Aneirin Lewis (1957).

1764 and 65

Two letters from David Lloyd, a dissenting minister and great preacher in Cardiganshire – an anti-Trinitarian and Arianist i.e. one who believed that Christ was created like other human beings and endowed with divinity by God. His dissent, as can be seen, took a very different path from that of the Methodists.

DAVID LLOYD to his brother the Rev. Posthumus Lloyd.
April 27, 1764. Brynllevrith.

...The Methodists after having kept quiet for several years have lately been very active. Their Number increases, and their wild Pranks are beyond Description. The worship of the Day being over, they have kept together in ye Place whole Nights, singing, capering, bawling, fainting, thumping and a variety of other Exercises. The whole Country for many Miles round have crowded to see such strange Sights....

From Brynllevrith, to the Rev. Posthumus Lloyd.
October 8th, 1765.

...Our Assembly at Carmarthen is without a Seer, a *truly Venerable* one. We have no Acts that deserve ye name of Synodal in ye odious sense of ye Word; No Decrees, No Anathemas, No Canons, No Domineering over Conscience in any Respect. Some sour ones no doubt we have yt wd. be meddling in things of this Nature, were they but supported, but we are happy in a great Majority of hearty Friends to Liberty. Dr Taylor says somewhere on ye Meeting at Salter's Hall in 1718... was ye only Synod yt asserted ye religious Rights of Xtians for so many hundred Years. One Philips yt lately wrote ye life of Cardinal Pole with a view to serve ye cause of Popery complains yt ye Synod of *Serinia* in *Poland* came to this *Wild* resolution of *allowing everyone to believe as he thought proper* and at ye last Day it wd. appear who had been in ye Right. Were not these very honest Souls? and was not this ye wisest Resolution yt. ever was formed since ye first meeting of Synods?

Lloyd Letters (1754-1796), ed. G. Eyre Evans (Aberystwyth: 1908).

1772

ARTHUR YOUNG (1741-1820). *Writer on agriculture and social matters. He wrote these critical letters when touring South Wales in 1772.*

Letter V.

About Cowbridge and Bridgend in Glamorganshire the husbandry is the most imperfect I ever met with; and totally contrary to the most common ideas in more informed counties. To give you some notion of their management, let me inform you that some farmers keep two, three and four hundred sheep, and yet never fold them; which is so extravagantly stupid that I was astonished at it: About Bridgend there are many farms which consist of a very light sand, especially near Cantillon, and yet no turnips are sown: one farmer from England, in the latter parish, sowed two acres, and was at great pains to hoe them well, and keep them clean; the neighbouring ones ridiculed him infinitely, and really thought him mad; but were surprised to see what a crop he gained, for it was very considerable, and he sold it by the sack to all the neighbouring towns to vast profit: This practice he has since continued; but strange to tell, he has never been copied!

...It is a great pity the Glamorganshire gentlemen do not on a large scale practise a better husbandry, that the force of numerous examples might influence the farmers to change their bad methods. Their soil is capable of as great improvement as any I ever saw, especially in the light parts. The great points they want to be well instructed in are these: First, The general management of their farms, in respect of draught cattle, to keep no more than necessary for their work; but if they will keep a larger number, to give a better idea of employing them proportionably to the improvement of their lands. Secondly, Folding of sheep, many of them have good flocks, but never fold them. Thirdly, The turnip and carrot husbandry: great quantities of their land being admirably adapted to both, but unknown, and when a few turnips are sown, they are never hoed. Fourthly, The growing of sainfoine, which grass would thrive finely upon their lime-stone lands; but they are unacquainted with it. Fifthly, Cropping their fields in a better course, and not continue in the vile custom of sowing a crop of barley, and two crops of oats after one of wheat, on the credit of a fallow and liming, which many of them do....

I should not omit to inform you that Cowbridge is a very neat, clean, well paved, well built town; much prettier than either Chepstow, Newport, Cardiff, or Bridgend, the latter of which places, and its environs, form the westermost point of my tour.

Six Weeks Tour through the Southern Counties of England and Wales (1772).

1774

SAMUEL JOHNSON (1709-1784). *Johnson visited Wales with his friends Mr and Mrs Thrale in 1774. Mrs Thrale was born in North Wales and had inherited a house at Bachycraig built by an ancestor, Sir Richard Clough. The following are extracts from a journal Johnson wrote during the tour.*

July 30... We went to Bachycraig where we found an old house built 1567 in an uncommon and incommodious form. My Mistress chattered about tiring, but I prevailed on her to go to the top. The floors have been stolen; the windows are stopped. The house was less than I seemed to expect. The River Clwyd is a brook with a bridge of one arch about one third of a mile. The woods have many trees generally young but some which seem to decay. They have been lopped.... The ground seems to be good. I wish it well.

July 31. We went to Church at St. Asaph. The Cathedral though not large has something of dignity and grandeur. The cross isle is very short. It has scarcely any monuments. The Quire has, I think, thirty two stalls, of antique workmanship.... The Bishop was very civil. We went to his palace, which is but mean....

August 1. We visited Denbigh and the remains of its Castle. The town consists of one main street, and some that cross it which I have not seen. The chief street ascends with a quick rise for a great length. The houses are built some with rough stone, some with brick, and a few are of timber. The Castle with its whole enclosure has been a prodigious pile....

In the chapel (St. Hilary's) on Sundays the service is read thrice, the second time only in English, the first and third in Welsh....

August 3. We went in the coach to Holywell. Talk with Mistress about flattery – Holywell is a Market town neither very small nor mean. The spring called Winifred's Well is very clear, and so copious that it yields one hundred tuns of water in a minute. It is all at once a very great stream which within perhaps thirty yards of its eruption turns a mill and in a course of two miles eighteen mills more. In descent it is very quick. It then falls into the sea. The Well is covered by a lofty circular arch supported by pillars, and over this arch is an old Chapel, now a school. The Chancel is separated by a wall. The Bath is completely and indecently open. A Woman bathed while we all looked on. In the Church, which makes a good appearance, and is surrounded by galleries to receive a numerous congregation, we were present while a child was christened in Welsh....

We went down by the stream to see a prospect in which I had no part. We then saw a brass work where the lapis calaminaris is gathered, broken, washed from the earth and the lead, though how the lead was separated I did not see, then calcined, afterwards ground fine, and then mixed by fire with the copper. We saw several strong fires with melting pots but the construction of the fireplaces I did not learn.

At a copper work, which receives its pigs of copper, I think, from Warrington, we saw a plate of copper put hot between steel rollers, and spread thin. I know not whether the copper roller was set to a certain distance, as I suppose, or acted only by its weight.

At an iron work I saw round bars formed by a notched hammer and anvil... I then saw wire drawn, and gave a shilling. I have enlarged my notions. Through not being able to see the movements, and having not time to peep closely, I know less than I might. I was less weary, and had better breath as I walked further.

August 5. ...I dined at Mr Middleton's of Gwaynynog. The house was a Gentleman's house below the second rate, perhaps below the third, built of stone roughly cut. The rooms were low, and the passage above stairs gloomy, but the furniture was good. The table was well supplied, except that the fruit was bad. It was truly the dinner of a country Gentleman. Two tables were filled with company not intelligent. After dinner the talk was of preserving the Welsh language. I offered them a scheme.... Middleton is the only man who in Wales has talked to me of literature. I wish he were truly zealous. I recommended the republication of David ap Rhees's *Welsh Grammar*.

August 14. At Botfarry (Bodfari) I heard the second lesson read, and the sermon preached in Welsh. The text was pronounced both in Welsh and English. The sound of the Welsh in a continued discourse is not unpleasant.

Aug. 19. We obtained a boat to convey us to Anglesea, and saw Lord Bulkeley's house and Beaumaris Castle.... The Castle is a mighty pile... corresponds with all the representations of romancing narratives. Here is not wanting the private passage, the dark cavity, the deep dungeon or the lofty tower.... This is the most complete view that I have yet had of an old castle.

Aug. 20. We went by water from Bangor to Caernarvon where we met Poali and Sir Thomas Wynne. Meeting by chance with one Troughton, an intelligent and loquacious wanderer, Mr T. invited him to dinner. He attended us to the Castle, an Edifice of stupendous magnitude and strength. It has in it all that we observed at Beaumaris, of much greater dimension.... We mounted the Eagle tower by 169 steps each of ten inches. We saw but a small part of this mighty ruin... I did not think there had been such buildings. It surpassed my ideas.

Welsh Diary, July 1774. From *Diaries, Prayers and Annals*, ed. by E.L. McAdam Jr. with Donald and Mary Hyde, *Works of Samuel Johnson Vol. I* (Yale and O.U.P: 1958).

1775

THOMAS JONES (1742-1803). *One of the finest of Welsh painters who was a pupil of Richard Wilson and, like his master, spent a number of years in Italy. Some of the paintings he did there are remarkable for their feeling of freshness and modernity. The following are entries from his journals before he left for Italy. He returned to Penkerrig on his father's death and took over the estate.*

August 26th. Sent my pictures and Baggage to my friend Woolett's to take care of for me and set off next Evening by the Coach for Brecon where I arrived on the morning of the 30th – Here I met my brother in law and Sister, Mr and Mrs Humphrey of Pennant in Montgomery-Shire, and my eldest Brother John who accompanied me to Penkerrig where we arrived on September 1st. 1775....

On the 8th about 10 o'clock at night as I was sitting alone reading in the hall, I was suddenly alarmed by the jarring of the windows, and the Doors flying open, which I at first took for the effect of some sudden gust of Wind – my brother Michael who was in bed at the time on the second floor, felt the Shock more violently, – so that he could plainly perceive it to be the Effect of an Earthquake – the papers afterward announced the Extent of the Shock, and how much People were terrified, particularly the Inhabitants of Bath and Bristol....

I had now, in a manner, taken leave of London, and was on a farewell visit, to my Parents, Relations, and friends in the Country, previous to my departure for Italy – a favourite project that had been in agitation for some Years, and on which my heart was fixed, but which, through some pecuniary Difficulties, was still postponed from time to time – There were Obstacles still remaining for I had contracted some little debts which I wished to discharge, and was determined to sit down and endeavour to extricate my Self, if possible – Accordingly in the Course of the time I continued at my father's, I painted pictures sufficient to clear all demands, and leave a few Guineas in my pocket. This made me easy in my mind as to that point, and I had only to gain my Father and Mother's consent to set out forthwith on my Travells and which was a circumstance, I knew, they were very much Averse to – But an Application being made to me about this time by Mr Stewart (the *Athenian*, as he was called) in the name of the Dilettanti Society to go out with Capt'n Cook in his next voyage, in the situation that Hodges was in his last – They preferr'd sending me to Italy than to the South Seas....

30th [November]. Went to Castlemadock, between this place & Brecon I spent my time till February 5th, 1776 when returning to Builth I found the Bridge carried away & so great a flood in the River, that I was obliged to stay there that night, and crossed the next day in a boat – arrived at Penkerrig where I found my poor father on the recovery from a sudden & violent fit of Illness – From this time to the beginning of September following I kept close to Painting with few intervals, and finished the Task I had imposed upon myself....

Memoirs, Walpole Society Vol. 32 (1951).

1781

THE LADIES OF LLANGOLLEN – *Lady Eleanor Butler (1745-1829) and Hon. Miss Sarah Ponsonby (1755-1831). These two ladies eloped together from Ireland and set up home at Plas Newydd in Llangollen where they lived happily for the rest of their lives, reading, taking pleasure in their surroundings, keeping up, at a distance, with society gossip and entertaining a stream of illustrious visitors. Here are a few extracts from Eleanor Butler's journals.*

Monday, October 31st.
...At seven we walked before our door and in the shrubbery to see the Bonfires, which as Commemoration of a Victory gained over the English are annually lighted up on this night upon every Eminence in North Wales. From the lawn on which we stood, saw nineteen Fires around us. One on the Eglwseg, Pen-y-coed, Pengwern, Llantysilio, the Hill of the Empty Well, one large Fire in the centre of Dinas Bran, three on the Berwyn, and an immense one on the summit of Moel Mawr.

Thursday, Nov. 10th.
...Our Landlord, Richard Griffiths, and the Clerk, ploughing, sowing, harrowing and limeing the Field before our Cottage. No Words can describe the Sweetness, the Festivity of the Scene, the Brilliancy of the Day, the Beauty of the Country. The field so animated. The number of workmen, the various implements of Husbandry, as Carts, Plough, Harrow and Sacks of Corn, altogether formed a Picture of Rural Content and Simplicity that monarchs might behold with envy.

Tuesday, November 22nd.
White glittering frost. Country magnificently beautiful. A Fair in the Village. What a picture might be drawn from the Parlour Window of the crowds descending the opposite mountain and passing through the Field before our Cottage. Some on horseback, many on Foot, all comfortably clad, each bringing their different commodity to the Fair,

as Cattle, Pigs, Poultry, Eggs, Cheese, Woolen Cloth, Baskets, Wooden ware, Spinning Wheels. The women knitting as they went along, the young people in their best apparel; health, content and Innocence illuminating every countenance, all speeding with heartfelt Joy to Llangollen.

The Harmwood Papers of the Ladies of Llangollen, ed. G.H. Bell (Macmillan & Co: 1930).

1793

Agrarian disturbances occurred sporadically in Wales throughout the eighteenth century, largely because of the low and uncertain standard of living of the population. In the last decade corn riots became increasingly frequent because of rising prices, perceived corruption in the corn trade coupled with the dependence of the working people for sustenance on bread. The following confused but expressive letter of protest to the magistrates, with its grim warning of recent happenings in France when the poor had cried for bread, comes from the time of the Swansea Corn Riots of February 1793.

To all and every of the Magistrates of the Town of Swansea & Towns Men.

Resolutions of all the poor who live by their daily Labour both in the Town & Country and a Sincere Caution to all the petty Merchants who has no dependancy, but makes a trade by imposing upon the Poor....

Resolved. The weights of bread Butter also Measures be Inspected to, there is 60 Public Houses in Town, what is the Brewery &c for? To consume our Bread, to get riders to go to Gower to Buy Corn (in the Sack) and ship it at Port Inon Newton Nottage Ogmore St. Donats Boverton Aberthaw Sully and Barry Island and then it is English Corn. This is their Plan, will soon be in agitation. Very fine Tongued Gentry. Very few Gent will be as good as his word. We must Inspect and keep some Inspectants if Mr Portrieve gets the best Salary, but if we take him to the – Salary wont pay tolls for him. Look at France.

Resolved that no Imposition be laid upon us, no buying Corn but in Market and at the usual reasonable price, no petty Merchandizing, no Sneaking underhand business, in buying at the Toll Gates. This is an old practice, but it is now we feel it. Robbing Peter to pay Paul, ay this is your way of Life. ...Peace or no Peace it lies at your adoption. No Imposition, no underhand Merchandizing every article to Market. Tell Mr Rose to put a little more weight to his *bread*.... But the Generality must peruse this, for fear, & rectify, no particular dealing in Country, we will set to rights.

The Patriots Deed.

Appendix II, *Before Rebecca*, David J.V. Jones (Allen Lane: 1973).

Riots, disturbances, and consequent intervention by the authorities and the military continued for several years, the chief enemies of the people often being the richer farmers who kept the price of food at impossibly high levels as is revealed in the following sympathetic letter.

DUDLEY ACKLAND ESQ., to Mr Campbell.
March 10, 1796. Pembroke.

My brother's account of the conduct of the troop and his own company is highly flattering to both, and I have no doubt that they would have supported the magistrates and their officers properly. However, I sincerely hope neither one nor the other will ever be brought to the disagreeable necessity of firing upon poor creatures who have certainly great reason to complain, for I am convinced, and so are all your friends here, that the scarcity at Pembroke is artificial and not real and that two thirds of the corn remains unthreshed, and that it is owing to the avarice of the farmers that our markets are so high.

I have the mortification to find on my return to Pembroke that mutton is at 5d. a pound (the same as I paid in London and Bath all the winter for the best), and here I have had some at nine months old. This is so glaring an imposition that we have come to a resolution of not buying it till the price falls. Annexed you have a copy of the resolution which is signed by all the principal people here, and we mean to send it to Haverfordwest for the same purpose. In this business the farmers alone are to blame, for the price of the sheep is so high to the butcher that he cannot get above a shilling or eighteen-pence for his trouble.

In short, every order of people here are dissatisfied with the attempt to impose upon them and do not allow that the farmers here have a right to charge as much as in England, where the price of labour is double and the rent of farms much higher, and, what is remarkable, there never was known any winter to be more grass in the country than the last....

Subscribed: We whose names are hereunto subscribed, inhabitants of Pembroke, taking into consideration the very unprecedented high price of provisions in the market, exorbitant beyond all former times or any just cause at the present for the same, do agree for the purpose of counteracting an injurious combination against the public, which appears to us to be the sole cause of the unreasonable price now subsisting, and which if submitted to longer will not only subject the inhabitants of this town in general to great inconvenience but will be the means of absolutely starving the lower order of industrious tradesmen and labourers, that we will not ourselves, nor suffer any person for us, to purchase from the date hereof any beef at a higher price than $4^{1}/_{2}$d per lb, any mutton at more than $4^{1}/_{2}$d, or fresh butter at a higher price than $9^{1}/_{2}$d per pound, prices that we are fully satisfied are fully equal to the value of lands, price of stock or wages of labour in this county, and ought not therefore to be exceeded. In confirmation of which agreement, we have hereunto set our hands this 10th day of March 1796.

Pembrokeshire Life 1572-1843, ed. by B.E. and K.A. Howells, (Pembrokeshire Record Society 1972).

Another trial which the Welsh agricultural population had to endure was the enclosure of common lands chiefly by the expansion of the great estates. The enclosure of 80,000 hectares of land in Wales was authorised by Parliament between the years 1793 and 1818 resulting in increased wealth on the one hand and dire poverty on the other. One consequence was increased emigration, either to the burgeoning industrial districts, to England, or to America. The following two letters are concerned with the latter choice.

WILLIAM RICHARDS (LYNN) to Dr Samuel Jones, Philadelphia. 22 March, 1796. St Clears.

Where is this new country which you are going to secure to the Welsh and how are the poor moneyless emigrants to get thither? ...I recommend the bearer of this, Theophilus Rees, a man with a competent share of property but with the disadvantage of knowing but little English. He and his family of eleven are leaving with many

Baptists... together with a number of Presbyterians and other serious people to the number of six or seven score... would that I could join them in your happy country, but I am forced to return to hateful England....

The bearer of this, Daniel Davis, is about to emigrate to your country with his wife and seven children. He is by trade a mason and understands the farming business pretty well.... His wife has had some education and has sometimes kept school.... Two of her brothers are in the ministry in England among the Presbyterians... I am ashamed to trouble you and Dr Rogers so often with the concerns of these poor Emigrants, but what in God's name can I do? ...I cannot describe to you the condition of our poor country, thousands of the poor move about the country begging bread.... Myriads would emigrate if they had money....

The Remaking of Wales in the Eighteenth Century, edited by Trevor Herbert and Gareth Elwyn Jones.

1794 ff.

THOMAS JOHNES OF HAFOD (1748-1816), *was M.P. for Cardigan Boroughs 1774-80; then, after his father's death, for Radnor until 1796; and then for the County of Cardigan until his own death. He was a landowner and creator of a notable house and landscape. He was an avid collector of books and manuscripts, a translator of antiquarian French manuscripts and also set up a private press (the Hafod Press) in 1802.*

JOHNES to his friend George Cumberland.
July 28, 1794. Hafod.

Sir,

You have shown so much partiality to the Country round the Devil's Bridge that I shall make no apology for troubling you with this letter.

It is to inform you that within these few days an apparently valuable mineral spring has been discovered close by the Devil's Bridge. It seems to be a very strong Chalebeat; as you may wish to taste some of it, I have ordered a small bottle of it to be sent by the Coach directed for you to the care of Mr Edwards in Pall Mall, and I shall write to him this post to desire he would forward it to you. If further

Tunbridges or Cheltenhams should arise there, I trust that the beauties of Nature are of features too grand for any ornaments of Art to have other effects than to make the old Lady appear more beautiful....

To James Edward Smith, in London.
March 13, 1796. Hafod.

My dear Sir,
...I wished for you here during the dry and sharp weather to enjoy one of the grandest sights I ever witnessed. I took the opportunity of the great dryness to set fire to some mountains covered with Furze. The wind was very high and the acres of flame as they rapidly ascended must have been something like a grand eruption of Lava, for it ran up in streams of fire and flame. The wind dissipated the Smoke and when you went on the Top of the Hill to the windward side, you appeared as above the Clouds, which every now and then a sudden Gust divided to give you a Glimpse of Paradise below. The Smoke was grand and put one in mind of one of the lines of Virgil's description of Orion; Ingrediturque solo, et caput inter nubila condit (*Aeneid* X, 767).

To Arthur Young (Secretary of the first Board of Agriculture).
April 15, 1799. Hafod.

Dear Sir,
(Johnes apologises for the failure of the Cardiganshire Agricultural Society to send Young their annual report... the society in a poor state because of the death of the secretary. Continues...)
...This has been a very hard Winter upon us Mountain Farmers. The losses among the sheep and lambs are very great indeed. I know not when to expect an end of it, for it snows and hails as fast as if it was the middle of December instead of April.

But in June of the same year Johnes writes in the following vein to a friend:

To James Edward Smith.
June 23, 1799. Hafod.

My dear Sir,
...My sinking fund will be in Larch plantations. I am even more wild about them than my good friend Anderson, and intend every

year after this ensuing season to plant out a million as long as I live and have ground for it....

Our weather has been uncommonly hot and I never saw the foliage so magnificent as this year, nor the Hawthorns nor Crabs in such high beauty. Our woods are like flower gardens, and many have flowered which I never remember before....

A Land of Pure Delight: selections from the letters of Thomas Johnes of Hafod, Cardiganshire (1748-1816), ed. and introduced by Richard J. Moore-Colyer (Gomer: Llandysul, 1992).

In 1807 Johnes suffered a severe blow in that his splendid house was badly damaged by fire and many of his books and manuscripts were lost. The following two letters written to fellow antiquarian and booklover Edward Williams (Iolo Morganwg) from a castle near Aberystwyth interestingly relate to this loss.

To Edward Williams.
November 13, 1807.

Dear Sir,

I have not had the pleasure of seeing or hearing from you this long time. I hope therefore you have enjoyed good health. You will have seen in the papers my accident at Hafod, and the irreparable loss I have in many things sustained. I am, I hope, duly thankful that it was not worse, and that no lives were lost nor anyone the least hurt.

I am now busy rebuilding it and I should be very much obliged to you if you would confirm by an *early post* directed as above whether there be any blocks of marble fit for columns or for paving staircases in your country and the prices they would come to per foot in working and polishing them.... I have not the plans before me and I cannot send you the exact dimensions....

In the second letter he asks for further information about marble and continues:

All the books in the gallery and anti Library have been destroyed but the most part of the four bookcases in the large library have been saved – very luckily a fine library that I purchased at Venice was in London when the fire happened and this escaped. My Mss are gone and I shall not again attempt to collect more – but in regard to printed books I shall be richer than ever – for independent of what has been saved and this Venetian Library I have purchased a fine collection of topography and of early printed works I have now some of Caxton's printing, and all in good condition....

Ever, Dear Sir,

Yours very truly,

T Johnes.

Iolo Morganwg Correspondence, National Library of Wales 21282.

1794 ff.

SAMUEL TAYLOR COLERIDGE (1772-1834). *Poet, critic, philosopher. Coleridge embarked on a walking tour of Wales in July 1794 with his fellow undergraduate Joseph Hucks – 'a man of cultivated tho' not vigorous understanding' was the ambivalent description Coleridge gave of him. (See HUCKS, p. 139). Coleridge had just met Robert Southey in Oxford where they had thought up their scheme for a pantisocratic community. In November 1802 Coleridge visited Wales again with his seriously ill friend, Tom Wedgwood and made some interesting brief comments in his Notebook.*

SAMUEL TAYLOR COLERIDGE to Robert Southey.
Sunday, July 13th, 1794. Wrexham.

...From Llanvilling we penetrated into the interior [of] the Country to Llangunnog, a Village most roman[tica]lly situated – We dined there on hash'd Mutton, Cucumber, Bread & Cheese and Butter, and had two pots of Ale – The sum total of the expence 16 pence for both of us! From Llanvunnog we walked over the mountains to Bala – most sublimely terrible! It was scorchingly hot – I applied my mouth ever and anon to the side of the Rocks and sucked in draughts of Water cold as Ice, and clear as infant Diamonds in their embryo Dew! The rugged and stony Clefts are stupendous – and in winter must form Cataracts most astonishing – At this time of the year there is just water enough dashed down over them to 'soothe not disturb the pensive Traveller's Ear.' I slept by the side of one an hour & more. As we descended down the Mountain the Sun was reflected in the River that winded thro' the valley with insufferable Brightness – it rivalled the Sky. At Bala is nothing remarkable except a Lake of 11 miles in circumference. At the Inn was sore afraid, that I had caught the Itch from a Welch Democrat, who was charmed with my sentiments:

he grasped my hand with flesh-bruising Ardour and I trembled, lest some discontented Citizens of the *animalcular* Republic should have emigrated. Shortly after, into the same room a well drest clergyman and four others – among whom (the Landlady whispers me) was a Justice of Peace and the Doctor of the Parish – I was asked for a Gentleman (i.e. to propose a toast) – I gave General Washington. The parson said in a low voice – (Republicans!) after which the medical man said – damn Toasts! I gives a sentiment – May all Republicans be *gulloteen'd*! – Up starts the Welch Democrat – May all *Fools* by gulloteen'd and then you will be the first! Thereon Rogue, Villain, Traitor flew thick in each other's faces as a hailstorm – This is nothing in Wales – they *make calling one another Liars etc* necessary vent-holes to the sulphurous Fumes of the Temper! At last, I endeavoured to arbitrate by observing that whatever might be our opinions in politics, the appearance of a Clergyman in the Company assured me, we were all *Christians* tho' – (continued I) it is rather difficult to reconcile the last Sentiment with the Spirit of Christianity. Pho!' quoth the Parson – Christianity! Why we an't at *Church* now? Are we? The Gemman's Sentiment was a very good one – 'it shewed, he was *sincere* in his principles!' – Welch Politics could not prevail over Welch Hospitality – they all except the Parson shook me by the hand, and said I was an open-hearted, honest-speaking Fellow, tho' I was a *bit* of a Democrat.

...At Denbigh is a ruined Castle – it surpasses every thing I could have conceived – I wandered there an hour and a half last evening (this Tuesday Morning). Two well drest young men were walking there – Come – says one – I'll play my flute – 'twill be romantic! Bless thee for the thought, Man of Genius & Sensibility! I exclaimed – and preattuned my heartstring to tremulous emotion. He sat adown (the moon just peering) amid the most awful part of the Ruins – and – romantic Youth! struck up the affecting Tune of *Mrs Casey* – 'Tis fact upon my Honor!

To Henry Martin.
July 22, 1794.

Abergeley is a large Village on the Sea Coast – Walking on the sea sands – I was surprized to see a number of fine Women bathing promiscuously with men and boys – *perfectly* naked! Doubtless the citadels of their Chastity are so impregnably strong that they need not the ornamental Outworks of Modesty. But, seriously speaking, where sexual Distinctions are least observed, Men & Women live together in the greatest purity. Concealment sets the Imagination a working, and, as it were, *cantharidizes* our desires.

'Coleridge's Letters Written on the Tour of Wales', see entry for HUCKS pp.138-141. See also *Collected Letters of S.T. Coleridge,* ed. E.L. Griggs (Oxford: 1956-71).

NOTEBOOK

1802.
Wedn. Nov. 17. walked from St. Clear to Larn (or Laughern) the vale on each side of me deep, the Hills high, not unwooded or uncottaged, yet on the whole little impressive / the first view of Larn with its fine richly ivied Castle close upon the sea, & its *white & all white* Houses, interesting; – unfortunately at low Tide – or I should have seen the Castle washed by the sea – The Bay is a great river of Greenish Water taking one Bend among fieldy Hills – the outline sufficiently various, & the whole Breastwork of the Hills sinking & swelling very playfully being low Tide, many Tongues & many Islands of mud-sand (with its little Brooks from the Salt water marshes showing stately Lines) 4, 5 or 6 promontories, like Boars' Heads, some of them with pretty cottages on the slope....
The murmur of the main Sea/ & the Barking, yelping, whining, wailing of the various Sea fowls.
One third of the Furze (Bushes) in plentiful Blossom/Daisies, & Tansy with the white petals fallen off & only lingering a few on the yellow Head- Periwinkle by the Cockleshell Dunghill – the recesses & little Gills of the Promontories....
The Ivy on the Castle I observed to be a beautiful yellow green when it faced the sea/ but a deep dark green on the sheltered sides, & even in the sheltered recesses of the seaward side/
A number of handsome *glassy* Houses in Larn/ never saw such a profusion of tall broad Windows, except in Hamburg – before one of the doors two large Cages with two fine Parrots screaming away – Hen & two or 3 large chicks perching upon one Cage, but unscared/ & a handsome Cock on the other with its bold brave old England face. I waited for him to crow, but he did not –
Cottages favourable only to vegetable Life – Hot bed of wild weeds on their roofs & ivy on their walls but – the shrivelled Shrimps of cold & Hunger swarthied Tenants/
White Church with grey Steeple a furlong or so from the Town near the bottom on a Hillside –

Here
lieth the Body
of Marg. Bevan, who
departed this Life the 9th day of
June 1727. Aged 19 years
Here lie 2 Sisters side by side
They sleep & take their rest,
Till Christ shall raise them up again
To live among the Blest –
...

While I took the copy, the Groundsel showered its white Beard on me/ Groundsel & Fern on the grave, & the Thorns growing that had been bound over it

On a square Tomb as high as half up my Thigh, where the Tom Tits with their black velvet Caps showered down the lovely yewberries on me. Here lyeth the Body of Sara & Hannah Jones the Daughters of Evan Jones & Jane his Wife. Sara Jones died January the 19th, aged 2 years & 3 months/Hannah Jones departed this Life the 8th day of September, 1746, aged 15 years/

What Christ said once he said to all.
Come unto me, ye children small
None shall do you any wrong
For to my Kingdom you belong.

Also the Body of the above Jane Jones who died Feb.13.1753, aged 49 years.

She long in pain & sickness lay
Till Death did carry her away
Her Rest gives me a restless Life
Because she was my dear full Wife
Yet her in time I hope to see
With Christ in blest Eternity.

Also the Body of the above Evan Jones who departed this Life March 22, 1794, aged 96 years – the Tomb stone 6 spans & an inch long no room even for one couplet on the old man/

S.T. Coleridge Notebooks, Vol. I (Routledge and Kegan Paul: 1962).

JOSEPH HUCKS (1772-1800), *became a friend of Coleridge when they were students at Cambridge and they undertook a tour of North Wales together. Hucks became a lawyer but died of consumption at the age of 28. The following are extracts from a series of letters he wrote while on the tour to an unknown friend.*

July 11, 1794. Bala, North Wales.

...In the neighbourhood of Welsh Pool, stands Powis castle, formerly called Pool castle, from its vicinity to Welsh Pool; it was built A.D. 1110 by Cadogan ap Bledhyn, who was not long suffered to enjoy it, before he was murdered by his nephew Madoc.... The castle commands an extensive view of a fertile vale, through which the Severn, yet in its infancy, rolls gently along. The road from thence to Llanvilling is very intricate, and we contrived to lose our way more than once, notwithstanding we had been told it was as straight as an arrow; we wanted about five miles of the latter place, when we met with an honest Cambrian of a very respectable appearance – we did not fail to make some inquiry of him concerning our road; he stopped his horse very politely, and informed us that he was then returning from Llanvilling, the place of his nativity, which he had not seen for more than twenty years before; he added that we should find an excellent inn, and plenty of the best ale in Wales; he then wished us a pleasant walk, assuring us we should meet with princely accommodations, and earnestly recommending the sign of the *goat,* at the same time advising us to make use of his name, for Owen ap Jones ap Evans was as well known as any name in Wales. I relate this little anecdote to you, because I think the character of a people is best delineated by their actions, and their leading features are as completely developed by an action, or an anecdote of themselves, apparently insignificant, as they could possibly be in five hundred philosophical pages upon the nature of the climate, situation, or government, and the physical causes and effects they may have upon the human genius and disposition.... It was late when we arrived, and we were much disappointed with respect to those excellent accommodations our honest friend had hinted at, for we could get nothing but dry bread and bad cheese, poor cheer for two hungry travellers that had scarcely eat any thing since breakfast....

July 14th, 1794. Denbigh.

Llangollen is most delightfully situated, but the place itself has nothing to boast of, except a very good inn which fortunately belies its appearance. We were entertained, upon our arrival, by a celebrated Welsh harper, who tuned his strings to so Orphean a measure, that a crowd soon collected round the door of our little inn, some of whom began to dance after the rustic fashion of their country; the simplicity of former times struck forcibly upon my mind, and brought back the pleasing recollection of those happy ages, when riches and luxury had not corrupted the heart of man; but when all mankind were brothers and the interest of one became the interest of all. It afforded me a satisfaction I had never before experienced, to find myself amongst a people, who act with all the simplicity of nature; totally destitute of the assumed appearance and artificial manners of more modern times. The Welsh musick assimilates to the genius of the people, and is in general wild and irregular, but often plaintive, and always affecting; for the harp is perhaps more calculated to express the extremes of passion than any other instrument; it is astonishing with what skill and execution it is sometimes played upon, and with what enthusiasm the country people listen to it....

July 16, 1794. Abber.

Holywell is a clean built town, surrounded by a most beautiful country. There is a manufacture established at this place, that once gave bread to thousands, but alas! the loom is now forsaken for the sword....

The town and neighbourhood, as might be expected, abound with numbers of poor women and children, who are half starving, whilst their husbands, fathers and brothers, are gloriously signalizing themselves in the service of their country; and if by chance the ruthless sword of war should spare the poor man's life, and send him to his long wished-for home, with the trifling loss of a leg, or an arm, he will at least have the consolation of reflecting that he might have lost them both; and should his starving family, in the bitterness of want, by chance reproach him for his incapacity to relieve them, he will no doubt silence their murmurs and turn their sorrow into joy, by reminding them, that it was in the glorious cause of their king and country that they suffered.... Abergeley is a small watering place, about half a mile from the sea – They have a strange custom there, that has an air of great indelicacy to a stranger; which is, that the inferior orders of people commonly bathe without the usual precautions of machines or dresses; nor is it singular to see ten or a dozen of both sexes promiscuously enjoying themselves in the lucid element, regardless, or rather unconscious, of any indecency. Not being myself accustomed to this mode, I chose to retire farther up; but it is very unpleasant bathing, being a flat level beach, and necesary to wade a quarter of a mile into the sea before one can arrive at any comfortable depth.

July 19, 1794. Caernarvon.
(On copper mines near port of Amlwch)

These mines have an appearance uncommonly grand and striking – a vast, yawning chasm, displaying full to the view of the astonished stranger its sulphurous contents; hundreds of workmen employed in a variety of different occupations; some boring shafts, other selecting the ore, which is slung up to the top, or, if I may use such an expression, ushered into the world in little baskets. In some places the chisel and the pick-axe find room for employment; in others the men are sedulously engaged in blowing up large pieces of the rock by means of gunpowder, the report of which reverberating from side to side, in this immense cavity, occasions such a tremendous explosion, that all nature seems to tremble to its centre.

Upon the whole these mines bear an apt resemblance to the infernal regions, and, like the pestilence from the pit of Acheron, the sulphur which issues from them, spreads desolation around, so that not the slightest vestiges of verdure are to be traced in the neighbouring fields.

July 24, 1794. Tan y Bwlch.
(On castles – seeing Caernarvon)

Thank heaven, these fabricks of despotism are at length either levelled with the ground, or present a memorable lesson to mankind of the futility of human ambition.... Every castle that now remains is a monument of shame to our ancestors, and of the ignoble bondage under which they bent: and hence in part arises that satisfaction, which the mind is conscious of feeling, in contemplating their ruins....

July 29, 1794. Aberistwith.

The country people have no idea that a stranger can be ignorant of their roads; we have not unfrequently asked the way, and received for answer, 'that it was as straight as we could go,' when, in a very few paces, we have been perplexed by two roads, one declining to the right, and the other to the left....

From Barmouth to Dolegelly we were highly gratified; the road wound round along a ridge of rocks, that hang over the Avonvawr, an arm of the sea; which, at full tide, has the appearance of a large lake, surrounded with beautiful woods: The mountains on both sides, but particularly on the opposite shore, were strikingly grand; and above all, Cader Idris reared its head into the clouds, which, together with the sombre aspect of the evening, and the hollow murmurings of the sea gave an awful sublimity to the scene that cannot be described....

August 2, 1794. The Old Passage.

Ragland castle is a very fine ruin, belonging to the duke of Beaufort; the road from thence to Tintern, would gratify the most romantic imagination; the last three miles, or more, being a continual descent through a deep and gloomy wood, till the astonished traveller bursts from the surrounding scenery full upon the Wye, that rolls its muddy waves in rich meanderings through this solitary glen. The lively picture that immediately offers itself to the view, of boats in full sail, of others landing their cargo, with the busy and cheerful cries of the sailors and workmen, was like the effect of enchantment, and almost created in me an imagination, that I had arrived in another world, and had discovered a new order of beings. At some distance stands the abbey, whose holy isles, and melancholy shades, were once devoted to religious fervour and monastic discipline....

In Wales, pride and poverty go hand in hand, and the disposition of the people is strongly blended with superstition. When we were at the top of Cader Idris (the etimology of which signifies the chair of the giant Idris), the guide shewed us the giant's bed, at which we could not help laughing; the honest fellow, however, rebuked us for such levity, and expressed his belief as to the identity and existence of the giant, at the same time justifying himself from the authority of a clergyman, who had lately made a pilgrimage to the same spot; and, immediately falling down on his knees, began to say his prayers in a devout manner, and an audible voice; without doubt to appease the manes of this tremendous giant, and breathe out a pious requiem to his soul.

A Pedestrian Tour through North Wales in a Series of Letters, J. Hucks, ed. by Alun R. Jones and William Tydeman (Cardiff: University of Wales Press, 1979).

EDWARD WILLIAMS (IOLO MORGANWG) (1747-1826).

Poet, antiquarian, scholar, radical, Unitarian, and forger. Edward Williams was a fascinating, controversial character who spent much of his life in the village of Flemingston in the Vale of Glamorgan. It seems that his gifts as a poet in the Welsh language and his wide knowledge of medieval writings enabled him to present his poetic forgeries as authentic documents. He was, in effect, the Welsh Thomas Chatterton and it is somewhat ironic to find, in 1803, Robert Southey sending him a set of Chatterton's works. In 1792 he founded the Gorsedd, or assembly of bards and representatives of the other arts through which he wanted to propound notions of a Druidic civilisation to which Welsh culture owed its being. His correspondence reveals the esteem in which he was held by many of his contemporaries; he seems to have been regarded as an authority in many subjects, not only history and antiquities but new developments in agriculture, manufactures, geology, etc.

The following may provide some little inkling of his personality and the breadth of his interests. What is perhaps surprising, especially in the light of his radical views, is that in the first extract, the journal of a walk into Carmarthenshire, he makes no mention of any agrarian disturbances which were occurring during that time. The succeeding letters show him in various modes.

Journal of an Excursion into Carmarthenshire in June, 1796.

On the 15th June I set out for Carmarthenshire through the very large parish of Langevelach, that abounds in coal and iron... A Glamorgan tradition says that the South Moulton (in Devonshire) breed of cattle originated from four cows and a bull that a Sir Edward Stradling of St. Donat's Castle gave a Devonshire farmer as a fortune with an illegitimate daughter. The reader may vouch for which he pleases either the truth or the falsehood of this anecdote, or if he thinks it better may care nothing about it. Recording facts, anecdotes and observations as they occur I fall into excentricities....

On my journey once more.... Cottages, many of them constructed of large stakes and wattled, then plaistered over with a mixture of loam and cow-dung. Some of them whitewashed.

I come to Llandarog 8 miles from Lannon. A village with a large but rudely built church that has a school in it, a common thing in Wales. The churchyard has many gravestones of excellent black marble found in the neighbourhood.... Women wear whittles, a very old fashion, and bad not for its age, but because the modern rural cloak is much more convenient and comfortable than the whittle, and equally cheap; utility is the only thing that should fix fashions nor should anything but a greater utility be permitted to change them; but let the Carmarthenshire lasses retaining their perfect innocence and pleasing simplicity of manners wear their whittles for ever rather than run like some of the Glamorgan hare-brained wenches into the follies of fashion. Ignorance of the English language guards many parts of Wales from a number of bad habits, from fashions, from party contentions, and from modern honours, of all things in the world the most dishonourable to human nature, the most purely Devil of any thing....

Camarthen Town.

A very good town for Wales, its trade consists chiefly of imports for the supply of the country; they have not many exports. It has a trade by sea with London and Bristol, a London Waggon weekly, a daily mail coach, a great number of good houses, and a very good market. The people are reckoned the politest in Wales, and are very hospitable.... The common people speak much better English than what we hear from those of the same rank in any town of England, London not excepted. The reason is that the English was not introduced into Wales until about the time of Elizabeth, when the language was nearly, if not quite, at its most pure degree of improvement. Whereas the common English retain much of their ancient Saxon words and terminations "housen", "peasen", 'him", "theirn", etc. instead of the wicked innovations of "houses", "peas", "his", "their", etc....

We walked to Abergwily.... The prospects from Abergwily Bridge are some of the most charming that I ever saw, hills, vales, lawns, woods rivers, etc., in all the luxuriance, in all the maze fullness of the wildly beautiful that can possibly be conceived; the most sportive and fertile imagination of landscape painting never equal'd the real nature of this spot.

On the river Towy I saw some fleets of ancient British ships, vulgo Coracles built (I use dignified language) with wickers and bull-hides. Each captain after his voyage, arriving in port with a valuable cargo of salmon and sewin, etc, takes his ship on his back and brings her to moorings in the chimney corner. More than half the inhabitants of Abergwily are Captains of this description, whose cargoes are much more valuable in quantity than the Poorjack of Newfoundland. The Towy is a fine river, navigable for ships of 200 tons up to Carmarthen Town, which is, I think, more than ten miles from the sea....

June 22. After almost a week of rainy weather I leave Brechfa. I set
out for Carmarthen with a friend by a way nearer than that by which
I came. Over pretty high mountains of peaty soil.... Timber, plants
leaves, nuts, acorns, even animals have been found in bogs in a state
of preservation, uncorrupted, at least not to the degree of dissolution;
we never see this, I believe, in clay of any depth. The gentlemen
members of the Snowdon Hunt in North Wales have a custom of
BURYING LEGS OF MUTTON in the Snowdon bogs on the day
of their annual feast, and take up others that have remained there
since the preceding yearly dinner, when they are found perfectly
sound and sweet not the least taint but eat very tender and have a far
more delicious flavour than any other mutton. Let London and Bath
speculators that care not what vicious appetites they gratify, so they
but get money, avail themselves of this anecdote and take leases of
good bogs and firmly and inaccessibly fence them in; then buy up all
the legs of mutton (no matter for the poor) and conserve them for a
whole year in their bog. They will find epicures enough to buy them
at very good price cent. per cent. profit at least.

Carmarthenshire Antiquarian Society Transactions, XIV (1919-21).

EDWARD WILLIAMS to ?
Oct 13th, 1811. Flimston, near Cowbridge, Glamorgan.

Revd Sir,
    Pardon me for not acknowledging long ago your very polite and
friendly letter.
    I am just returned from a visit to my inestimable Friend, the Revd.
Mr Davies of Neath. Amongst other favours he showed me a copy
of his circular letter to the Unitarian Ministers and Congregations,
exhibiting the plan of a Unitarian Academical Institution in this
Country, which he and the Revd James have in contemplation, and
which I warmly hope will meet with success, nothing can be of
greater importance than this to the cause of genuine Xtianity in
Wales; the Carmarthenshire Academy, for the last eight or ten years
has not afforded a competent supply of well-educated Ministers,
many Congregations are obliged to content themselves with unedu-
cated Ministers, and some have none at all.
    Mr Peters, the Head Tutor at Carmarthen is also the Divinity tutor,
he is a rank Calvinist, and as rankly intolerant, in connection with the
Academy; he has a grammar school out of which he continues to fill
the Academy with students well educated in his own Theological

principles, but not half educated in anything else; he appears to use his utmost endeavour to suppress free enquiry, to snip rationality in its very bud; for one year back Unitarian candidates have been frequently almost generally rejected, and, with the exception of two or three at farthest, Welsh is the Language of Religious worship in all our congregates as it is also of 19 in 20 of all the Dissenting Congregations in Wales; we still however wish that all our Ministers might be able to officiate in the English language; this could be well attained by the means of an institution founded and conducted on liberal and enlightened principles. English is not the vernacular of the country but it is to be considered amongst us rather as a learned language which I wish to see cultivated amongst us in all its purity and elegances; nothing can be more conducive to the improvement of our native Welsh Literature with which rational religion must always be almost indispensably connected; it is thus and thus only, that young men destined for the Ministry will be properly taught how to think and *reason correctly*, the paths of literature are the only unencumbered path of free and rational enquiry, and it is only by walking in them that we can hope to combat effectively the sophistries of reasonless opponents....

Correspondence of Iolo Morganwg, National Library of Wales 21286.

To the Rev. David Davis of Neath.
January 15th, 1813. Cardiff.

I understand by your letter to Taliesin that you will be for some little time longer than I had imagined in London; for this reason I have taken the liberty of writing you from this town, where I am now, as I may say it, weather bound. We had last Tuesday a greater fall of snow than has been seen in this country for nearly thirty years: it lies all over the country, even in open ground, more than six inches deep; a depth that is not remembered by any man living in this part of the country. It has not drifted much, for it fell in almost perfect calm. It is now some years since we have seen any snow in this southern part of the Vale of Glamorgan; for what falls in snow, in the upper parts of the county, generally falls in rain in the lower parts of the Vale, along the Bristol Channel; or if a little snow falls, it generally dissolves and disappears in five or six hours.

I have, almost two years ago, drawn up a sketch of the meteorology of Glamorgan (which will do well enough for all the maritime parts of South Wales) for Mr T. Rees, with a sketch also of its geology, &c., but I have not yet finished them. I have turned over my MS documents for historical matter, and though I have bestowed a good deal of time and labour on this subject of my researches, I have done little more than forming an index, or table of references, to the MSS. where such matter may be found: such is the labour and time that must necessarily be employed, in forming collections from MS, documents, where nothing has previously been done. Mr Rees, probably, never experienced what it is to grope about, as it were in the dark, for a little historical knowledge. How many MSS, have I deliberately read over, whence I drew no other information, but that there was nothing to be found in them to my purpose. No collections for the history of Glamorgan have ever yet been made at least they are unknown, or not accessible. The large, thick, and closely written folio, by Rice Meyrick, Esq. of Cotterel, in Glamorgan, was unfortunately burnt in the Havod library. Mr Rees compiles from collections already made, or prepared to his hands, so that I have not been able to keep pace with him – he has slipped like an eel out of my hands.... The compilations of scissors and paste-pot from already formed collections in print, can so far outstrip the pen, and laboriously slow research amongst the miscellaneous confusion of old MSS., as roebuck or greyhound can outstrip the slowly crawling snail....

To his son, Taliesin.
November 6th, 1813. Dunraven Castle.

Dear Tally,

Here I have been for some days, having been sent for by Mrs Wyndham for the purpose of attending the opening of a part of the ancient entrenchment and embankment, which is very high and steep on the outside. The basis for at least three-fourths of its height, consists of stone and clay well rammed together. The top consists of stone and mortar, not formed as a wall, but only heaped together, as the clay and stone had been in the lower parts; that is, the stones thrown together promiscuously, without any other order than that of merely forming a heap along the top of the embankment, and mortar thrown in amongst them. The mortar was well made; it consists of lias lime and sea-sand in very proper proportions, and is not in the least decayed. It is as hard nearly, if not absolutely so, as the stone itself. This is a little wonderful when we consider that it is probably but little less than two thousand years old. *Dindryvan* (*hodie* Dunraven) was the residence of the great *Caractacus* (Caradoc ap Bran) who, at the head of his Silurian warriors, so successfully held out against all the powers of Rome for nine years, defeating them in upwards of seventy battles. The very rude manner exhibited here of using stone and mortar must be of very remote antiquity, and in use before the much better, and what we may term *artistical* method, which the Britons might, indeed must, have learned from the Romans, was known. The whole is covered over with grass and turf, so that no stone or mortar appears until openings are made. Whether it was thus designedly covered or turfed over, or that this kind of surface has been the gradual accumulation of time, may admit of some dispute, or rather of difference of conjecture.

Dunraven is the most ancient house or residence of ascertained date, of any, I believe, in this island. It is mentioned in history as one of the residences or castles of the princes of Glamorgan, through all ages, from *Caractacus* down to Jestyn ap Gwrgan, in whose time it became the property (by an act of royal thievery) of Sir William de Londres, who afterwards gave it to Arnold Butler. From the Butlers it came by marriage to the Vaughans, and from them, by marriage also of an heiress, with a *Wyndham*, to the present family. It is remarkable that Bran, the father of *Caractacus*, who also resided here, should have given land whereon to build a church (Llan) to Ilid Sant, as he was termed – that this church should have given name to the parish of Llanilid, and Llanilid should continue, even to this very day, a part of the *Dindryvan* or Dunraven Estate for 1800 years. We may fairly suppose that *Branfendigaid*, on resigning the functions of government to his son *Caractacus*, retired with *Saint Ilid*, whom he brought with him here from Rome, and that the house called *Trefran*, near Llanilid Church, was the residence of his latter days.

Recollections and Anecdotes of Edward Williams or Iolo Morganwg B.B.D., Elijah Waring (Gilpin: 1850).

The following letter was written by the Rev. Thomas Beynon *of Llandeilo fawr to Edward Williams on October 19th, 1818 inviting him to a meeting in Carmarthen on October 28th. Iolo had already received an invitation from the Bishop of St. David's to dine with him on that occasion.*

REV. THOMAS BEYNON to Edward Williams.

Sir,

As a friend to ancient British Literature, I naturally conclude it will give you much pleasure to find by the inclosed paper, which I suppose you have already seen that it is proposed to hold an 'Eisteddfod' annually in different parts of the Principality for the purposes therein expressed. A meeting of friends to the institution will be held on the 28th of this month at Carmarthen, for the purpose of arranging matters; and as you are possessed of more knowledge relating to Welsh Antiquities than probably any one now alive, it would give me, and many others, much pleasure if you could make it convenient to attend the meeting. I should be happy to defray the expenses of your journey backwards and forwards, either on horseback, or by the Mail coach, or in any other way you choose to travel....

With real respect and regards
Your most obedt. humble servant
Thos. Beynon.

Correspondence of Iolo Morganwg, National Library of Wales 21286.

1797

JOHN HENRY MANNERS *(later fifth Duke of Rutland). This journal of a tour in South Wales by Manners, a scion of a noble family, is of interest on several accounts but perhaps particularly because of his intimate knowledge of the French Republican invasion of Pembrokeshire and its aftermath.*

August 8, 1797.
...Merthur lies in the middle of these desolate hills, rich indeed in their production of ore; and is a large place chiefly occupied by the families of the workmen belonging to the forges. Travellers do not often go there but it is a place as well worth their notice as any in Wales. We dined heartily, and at dusk in the evening, the rain ceasing for half an hour, walked towards the forges. We wandered about for some time, and then went immediately to them, guided by the streams of fire which were bursting forth from the chimnies. The distance of them from the town is about threequarters of a mile, and the rail road along which we walked ran by the side of a canal; as we approached them, the effect was grand and sublime beyond all description. The fires from the furnaces were bursting forth in the darkness of the night, and every moment we saw, as it appeared, a red hot bar of iron walking towards us, the man who carried it not being visible. In the perspective we could see numbers of Vulcans

dragging about pigs of iron just taken from the furnaces, the fires of which would dazzle the strongest eye, and pursuing their different occupations, while their grimy figures and gloomy visages, were visible by the light of the forges... the regular thumps of an immense hammer, which we heard far off before we came near the works, and gradually increasing to a thunderous noise as we approached, completed the grandeur of the scene. I never saw any thing that gave me more the idea of the infernal regions....

Manners and his companion made their way to Pembrokeshire where the notorious attempted invasion by the French revolutionary troops had just taken place. They stayed with Lord Cawdor who was in command of the defending troops. His journal continues:

August 20, 1797.

...By the account the French gave themselves they had three points chalked out for their landing, at one of which (in the Bristol channel) they had been disappointed. Their object was Bristol, and they had been for two days in the channel. The first land they made after Lundy Island, was one extremity of St. Bride's Bay. General Tate, who was commander of the expedition, was an old man, and of Irish birth.... The orders which they brought with them, and which Tate afterwards shewed to Lord Cawdor were curious. They were to do as much mischief as possible, to burn and destroy all towns and villages they came near, to aim their vengeance at the clergy and nobility; to destroy all the chateaux of the latter, and at the same time to hold out liberty and conciliation to the inhabitants of the country. How far the line of conduct which they adopted during the two days they were masters of their own actions tended to ingratiate them with the peasantry I shall not pretend to determine.... Tate, who was standing on a rock near the scene of action, when the skirmish between the five Welsh peasantry and French soldiers took place, told Lord Cawdor afterwards, that he had never seen peasants behave with such resolution, or attempt to oppose regular infantry. All day on Thursday two or three Frenchmen were standing at different distances on the hill, some way from the main body, waving colours, as if to invite the country people to join them. Their standing at a distance from their troops proved they did not wish to frighten the peasants, and several of the latter rode up and conversed with them during the day. Lord Cawdor had on Thursday night about 500 well armed people with him. About nine on Thursday evening the French aide-de-camp and another officer arrived, proposing terms of surrender, owing as was afterwards found out, to the beginning symptoms of disorder in their army. This happened from the following circumstances. A smuggling vessel having been wrecked the day before on the coast, the soldiers without any regard to discipline, took possession of the casks, and drank to intoxication. This combined with the departure of the frigates, [which had brought them over] which was wholly unexpected to the soldiery, created murmurs amongst them, which the officers found would soon increase to open rebellion.... To his proposal of terms Lord Cawdor sent him word, that his force was every instant increasing, that the country people were all in arms, and that under these circumstances he could not think of terms, but if he would consent to an unconditional surrender, he would give every accommodation to the officers and men....

Monday, August 21.

This morning we all paraded before eight o' clock, in order to be present at the embarkation of some of the French prisoners taken in the late expedition.... We rode to the French prison, and went into it. It was a bad place for prisoners; as had the men chosen they might easily have made their escape. As the treatment they experienced there under the eye of Lord Cawdor was such as to satisfy them perfectly, they were rather sorry at their removal, which was to be Portsmouth. They knew the difference of treatment they would experience there, and although they stood a greater chance of a speedy exchange, they were not satisfied with their removal. Thirty of them had some time before broke loose from their prison, and taking a fine large pleasure boat of Lord Cawdor's, escaped to sea....

As soon as all was ready, the gates were thrown open and they began their march. The escort consisted of about 200 men.

...The road was lined with many spectators who were anxious to see the last of their invaders. Women, men and children, crowded to see them, while they marched in the middle of their escort, laughing and singing all the way. It was a pretty sight to see them winding up the hills before us, and along the turnings of the road, while the arms of the troops were glittering in the sun.

J. H. Manners, *Journal of a Tour into Wales* (1805).

The end of the eighteenth century saw the onset of enormous change in South-East Wales. The town of Merthyr Tydvil was at the heart of the revolution: there and in the surrounding region were all the raw materials necessary, coal, iron ore, limestone, water, timber, to supply the needs of an expanding iron industry. A number of men, chiefly it would seem from outside Wales, had perceived the latent possibilities in the area and profited from the cheap leases granted to them by local aristocratic landlords to establish ironworks in Merthyr itself and in the valleys eastwards and westwards. The Guest and Crawshay families became the most prominent and powerful among a number of ironmasters. Richard Crawshay (1739-1810), who took over the Cyfarthfa ironworks in 1794 and established a Crawshay dynasty, died a millionaire; and by the middle of the nineteenth century Josiah John Guest (1785-1852), elected first M.P. for Merthyr Tydfil after the 1832 Reform Act, owned, at Dowlais, the largest iron company in the world. Merthyr, itself, became distinguished by the most iniquitous and brutal marks of the industrial revolution.

Letters drawn from the letter books of the Dowlais Iron Company, throw some light on the variety of human relationships involved in the industry. The quotations here are chiefly about labour conditions the regulation of wages and the ruthless opposition to trade unions matters upon which the owners themselves attempted irregularly to combine. The people quoted include members or associates of the Guest family (Guest, Taitt, Evans etc.) and other ironmasters, Crawshay, Homfray, Thompson, etc.

WILLIAM TAITT to brother-in-law Thomas Guest.
17th January, 1799. Cardiff.

I have had some conversation with Mr Homfray & Mr Richard Hill about the Guineas to the Foundry. The former says he will immediately Stop the payment of them to his Men & the latter says that as soon as the existing Agreements are out with their Founders he also will refuse to Continue it, therefore if it be necessary to temporise with the men we surely have a right to be put on the same footing as the Penydarran Company viz. 60 Tons but there is one Consideration above all, which is, that I take for granted our Founders are under Agreements in which this new demand cannot be. Therefore they must abide by their agreements or be sent to Bridewell [Gaol] by a Magistrate. It is a Rascally demand & must be resisted in the first Instance. The encreased Quantity of Iron made is a Sufficient encrease of Wages to them & especially as it cannot be attributed to any exertions of theirs: but to our having expended £3000 to improve our Blast Discharge or take any men you please only I rely on your close attention to the business that we do not suffer by changing....

Set Daniel Onions to Watch the Brandy Dealers & take them before Mr Homfray & have them punished....

WILLIAM TAITT to brother-in-law Thomas Guest.
3rd February, 1799. Cardiff.

I shall not wonder at more Combinations of the kind you mention, but I differ with you in Opinion as to the Conduct to be pursued; you must Act with firmness, 'tis the want of that hitherto in the Manager which has made the men so unruly. I advise you going to Mr Homfray or Mr Crawshay & get them to commit to Bridewell 2 or 3 of the Ring leaders under the Act 6 Geo 3 Chap 25... they may afterwards be Indicted for the Conspiracy notwithstanding the Commitment. I have Consulted Mr Wood on this, who is so of opinion. Pursuing this Mode now will save us much trouble hereafter....

JOHN GRIFFITHS to William Taitt.
8th February, 1799. Cardiff.

I humbly beg your pardon for taking Liberty to write to you: but I hope you will Condesend to take Some notice of the folowing Lines. About 18 months back I agreed to Come to Dowlais to be a keeper at No.3. So when I went to set on to work I found the furnace in very bad Condition for the hearth would not hold the iron of 3 hours blowing and Mr Onnions tould Me Several times that they Could do no good with her from the first blowing in to that time I Came to her, but however I got the furnace in good Condition Enough in about the Space of 9 days or a fortnight and Sir I Refer you to the truth of what I write to Mr Onnions who I make no doubt will Sertify the same: I did not Expect no reward, but I must confess I thought I should been Placed a Little more in the Confidence of my Employers than if the [furnace] had done well before, all this I Submit to your Consideration: and Now Sir another thing I have to Lay before you is: we had made at No 3 Something above 51 tons of iron: about 3 weeks back and the other two furnaces had made something above 40 tons each. So Dick Davis hapened to go to the office first and the guinea* was refused to him as was Costomary, so he Came and tould the Rest of the keepers and me how it was. Then they all declared that they would not work Except they should have it. So we went all together to the office, and because Dick Davis and me Could Speak english they desiered of us to taugh for them as well as our selves. So Contiquently there was Some dispute but there Was nothing spoke that was vexatious. But however we insisted of haveing the gueneas that was then due, and we did not Look at it to be just to stop this money without any previous Notice and then we where willing to work, for the same as they did in other iron works, or we would Come to aney other agreement that Was reasonable; and now Sir, I am informed by Mr Onnions that I am to be discharged and Dick Davis Likewise because we spoke and the rest did not, when at the same time they were all there and spoke the words in the Welsh tongue to us as we spoke to the masters, and that Saturnday morning, before the dispute happened, there Came Some Smuglers to the work with the intention to sell their brandy: and the men that (worked) the other turn stole it from them and they was all drunk by five or six of the Clock in the morning that they could not work, so I was sent for about 7, and they gave some of it to me, and I must own that I drank rather free, and it Like to intoxicate me as well as the rest, so the strenth of the spirits Caused me to say more than if I had been Sober, and I am to be discharged the 9th instant, and Now Sir, I humble request is to desire of you to use your good offices to effect a reconciliation between my preasant master and me, or at Least to Let me work till I Can find a keeper place in elsewhere, for I have a family to maintain and Cant subsist Long Without work.

Sir, I Remain your most Obedent and Humble Servant, John Griffiths, keeper, and one of the Dowlais Volanteeer Companey.

* *Evidently a bonus.*

JOSIAH JOHN GUEST to uncle William Taitt.
May 21, 1815. Plymouth (Works).

...I had heard on Friday that the Men meant to meet at the Waun tomorrow (being Fair Day) & to proceed to some extremities, but took no notice of it. I have shewn them to Mr Hill who thinks with me that there is nothing serious to be feared, but at the same, as it is well to be on our Guard, we intend to send two or three Men upon whom we can depend to be there (as part of them) & should there be a Meeting, to learn their intentions & to mark the Ring Leaders,

& should they intend to commit immediate Mischief, as I understand they threaten to break our large Pond, to give us immediate Notice, though I repeat we consider it will end in nothing I thought right to apprize you hereof....

Iron in the Making, Dowlais Iron Company Letters, 1782-1860, ed. Madeline Elsas (Glamorgan County Record Office: 1960).

Guest's letter, demonstrating how the ironmasters used spies to keep watch on the workers, was a harbinger of what was to come late in the following year, 1816. With the end of the Napoleonic Wars the market for iron had collapsed, wages were cut, the price of corn rose, and when a further wage cut was announced on October 15th workers from Merthyr and Tredegar determined on a strike and a large number of them set off to ensure the stoppage of all the other ironworks in the area. The following letter from William Crawshay junior to Guest, designating the workers as 'the enemy', describes the situation.

WILLIAM CRAWSHAY JUNIOR to S.J. Guest.

The enemy in too great strength to oppose with any probability of success, have possessed themselves of all our Works & wholly stopped them. They are yet exulting in their victory & are about to proceed to Penydarren & Dowlais. My spies tell me they threaten hard your shop*, for they are hungry. I have been in the midst of them all & found as usual arguments useless.

Though the ironmasters were alarmed – Guest barricaded himself in at Dowlais House and fired on the crowd, wounding several – the recurring pattern of events soon prevailed: the military were called in, the Riot Act was read on several occasions and within a few days all was over – until the next time.

* *The mention of 'your shop' refers in all likelihood to the Company or 'Truck' Shop at Dowlais where, as virtually throughout the whole region, the worker was obliged to exchange tokens, given to him in lieu of wages, for the necessities he required. The practice, which resulted in the ironmaster making a certain profit, was made illegal by the Anti-Truck Act of 1831 but despite this it persisted in various places for some time.*

The Nineteenth Century

1801

LADY CAROLINE CAWDOR to Charles Fulke Greville.
*After his efforts with the French invading force in 1797, it seems that Lord
Cawdor was engaged in a less successful venture in 1801.*

November 18, 1801. Stackpole Court.

I am happy to tell you that Lord Cawdor is considerably better tonight
than he was when I wrote to you yesterday. The feverish symptoms are
much abated and he is in much less pain from his bruises. The history
of the business is this.

He heard last Sunday evening that a smuggling vessel was coming
into Freshwater East to land her cargo of spirits. He and Mat, Dio
and Hand set out after dinner and rode down to the sand. The
people, as soon as they saw them coming, ran off leaving all their
casks on shore. Mat Campbell sent Kenneth to fetch some carts,
thinking there was an end of the business, but in the meantime before
he could return with them, the people on board the vessel, having
discovered how few their numbers were and that they were perfectly
unarmed, returned on shore again in two boats in considerable
numbers, seized all the casks, and took them back to the vessel. Lord
C. and Matt. did not of course attempt to oppose them when the
numbers were so unequal, and were returning home when they were
attacked by some of these horrible desperate villains. Two of them
fell upon Lord C., one armed with a great bludgeon, the other with
a large poker with which he hit Lord C. a violent blow on his arm.
Lord C. jumped off his horse and tried to catch hold of him, when
another came behind and knocked him down with a blow on his
head. In this situation, with both these men thumping him, it is most
fortunate he was so little stunned as to be able to get up and twist
the poker out of the man's hand, with which he hit both of them, and
then they both ran away.

In the meantime Mat. was attacked by two others, and you know
how little able he is to make much resistance. Hand and Dio,

however, came to his assistance. They beat off one of the men and the other they secured and carried him to Rogers' house in Trewent. A short time after the house was surrounded by about thirty of the gang, people of the country armed with bludgeons, who immediately rescued their comrade.

Warrants are out for apprehending those men that are known but none are yet taken. It was, to be sure, a most foolish business to think of going against smugglers without arms, and I trust they will act with more caution in future. I think it most wonderful their escaping with their lives or at least without broken bones. Lord C. has been very ill in consequence: he kept his bed all day yesterday, and was twice blooded but, thank God, he is so much better tonight I feel quite easy about him....

Pembrokeshire Life (1572-1843).

1810

THOMAS LOVE PEACOCK (1785-1866). *Satirical novelist and essayist, friend of Shelley. Peacock wrote the following letters to his friend E.T. Hookham from Maentwrog, Merionethshire on his first visit to Wales.*

January, 1810.

...Maentwrog (pronounced Mantoorog) is eight miles from Tre-Madoc. I have taken a lodging here *pro tempore* while I look about the country for something less expensive....

This is a delightful spot, enchanting even in the gloom of winter: in summer it must be a terrestrial paradise. It is a beautiful narrow vale, several miles in length, extending in one direction to the sea, and totally embosomed in mountains, the sides of which are covered, in many parts, with large woods of oak. My sitting room has a bow window, looking out on a lovely river, which flows through the vale. In the vicinity are many deep glens, – along which copious mountain streams, of inconceivable clearness, roar over rocky channels – and numerous waterfalls of the most romantic character.

There is no other lodging of any description, to be obtained in this part of the world, but that in which I now am, and which suits me admirably in all respects but one. If I could induce mine host to moderate his demands a little, I should feel perfectly happy in casting anchor here. I am in a detached house, called the lodge: there are not above seven houses in the place. The post-office is at Tan-y-Bulch, a solitary inn just by, at which a picturesque tourist lately made a pause of five months being unable to tear himself from so fascinating a scene... Maentwrog, small as it is, contains a lawyer, doctor and parson: the latter is a little dumpy, drunken, mountain-goat.

Pray write me a long letter in the course of a day or two – I do not like to send for my books till I am settled in a permanent residence.

March 22nd, 1810. M. Lodge.

I sit down with a resolution to write a very long letter, so put on your nightcap and compose yourself at full length on the sofa. When your letter arrived last week announcing the departure of my *library* and *wardrobe,* I resolved to devote the whole interval to exploring the vicinity, and have been climbing about the rocks and mountains, by the river and the sea, with indefatigable zeal, carrying in my mind the bardic triad, that a poet should have an eye that can see nature, a heart that can feel nature, and a resolution that dares follow nature; in obedience to which latter injunction I have nearly broken my neck. Now were I to attempt a description of all I have seen, and felt, and followed, I might fill seven sheets of foolscap, and still leave the cream of the tale unskimmed: I shall therefore content myself with promising, when you come here in August (which may no evil genius prohibit!) to show you scenes of such exquisite beauty and of such overpowering sublimity, as once beheld, can never be forgotten.

The other day I prevailed on my new acquaintance, Dr Griffith, to accompany me at midnight to the black *cataract,* a favourite haunt of mine, about 28 miles from hence. Mr Lloyd, whom I believe I have mentioned to you more than once, volunteered to be of the party; and at twenty minutes past eleven, lighted by the full-orbed moon, we sallied forth, to the no small astonishment of mine host, who protested he never expected to see us all again. The effect was truly magnificent. The water descends from a mountainous glen down a winding rock, and then precipitates itself, in one sheet of foam, over its black base, into a capacious basin, the sides of which are all but perpendicular, and covered with hanging oak and hazel. Evans, in the *Cambrian Itinerary,* describes it as an abode of damp and horror, and adds, that the whole cataract cannot be seen in one view, as the sides are too steep and slippery to admit of clambering up, and the top of the upper fall is invisible from below. Mr Evans seems to have laboured under a small degree of alarm, which prevented accurate investigation, for I have repeatedly climbed this *unattemptable* rock and obtained this *impossible* view; as he or any one else might do with little difficulty: though Dr Gryffydh, [sic] the other night, trusting to a rotten branch, had a fall of fifteen feet perpendicular, and but for an intervening hazel, would have infallibly been hurled to the bottom. But a similar mistake is not likely to occur in daylight. – Let me advise you, while I think of it, to provide yourself, for your journey with *nails* in the heels of your shoes which may save you from the misadventures of the jolly miller who lived on the river Dee, who, according to the old song, had a *bump* upon his *rump*.

The Works of Thomas Love Peacock Vol. 8 (Constable: 1934).

1811-12

PERCY BYSSHE SHELLEY (1792-1822). *Poet, essayist and political radical. Shelley first went to Wales in July 1811 several months after he had been sent down from Oxford because of the publication of his* Necessity of Atheism. *He was also at extreme odds with his family but was befriended by his cousins who owned a house near Rhayader, from which the following letter was written to Elizabeth Hitchener, a schoolmistress who shared some of his radical views.*

SHELLEY to Elizabeth Hitchener.
13 July, 1811. Cwm Elan, Rhayader, Radnorshire.

...This county of Wales is excessively grand; rocks piled on each other to tremendous heights, rivers formed into cataracts by their projections and valleys clothed with woods, present an appearance of enchantment but *why* do they enchant, *why* is it more affecting than a plain, it cannot be innate, is it acquired? – Thus does knowledge lose all the pleasure which involuntarily arises, by attempting to arrest the fleeting Phantom as it passes – vain – almost like the chemist's aether it evaporates under our observation; it flies from all but the slaves of passion and sickly sensibility who will not analyse a feeling. I will relate you an anecdote, it is a striking one; the only adventure I have met with here. My window is over the kitchen; in the morning I threw it up, and had nearly finished dressing when 'for Charity's dear sake' met my ear, these words were pronounced with such sweetness that on turning round I was surprised to find them uttered by an old beggar, to whom in a moment the servant brought some meat. I ran down and gave him something: he appeared extremely grateful. I tried to enter into conversation with him – in vain. I followed him a mile asking a thousand questions; at length I quitted him finding by this remarkable observation that perseverance was useless. 'I see by your dress that you are a rich man – they have injured me and mine a million times. You appear to be well intentioned but I have no security of it while you live in such a house as that, or wear such clothes as those. It wd. be charity to quit me.'

Shelley returned to the same district in April, the following year, with his wife Harriet and her sister, after spending some time engaged in political activity in Ireland. The following letter is to William Godwin, philosopher, novelist, author of Political Justice, *later to be Shelley's father-in-law.*

SHELLEY to William Godwin.
April 25, 1812. Nantgwillt, Rhayader, Radnorshire.

My Dear Sir,

At length we are in a manner settled. The difficulty of obtaining a house in Wales (like many other difficulties) is greater than I had imagined. We determined, on quitting Dublin, to settle in Merionethshire, the scene of Fleetwood's early life*, but there we could find not even temporary accommodation. We traversed the whole of North and part of South Wales fruitlessly, and our peregrinations have occupied nearly all the time since the date of my last.

We are no longer in Dublin. Never did I behold in any other spot a contrast so striking as that which grandeur and misery form in that unfortunate country. How forcibly do I feel the remark which you put into the mouth of Fleetwood, that the distress which in the country humanizes the heart by its infrequency, is calculated in a city, by the multiplicity of its demands for relief, to render us callous to the contemplation of wretchedness. Surely the inequality of rank is not felt so oppressively in England. Surely something might be devised for Ireland, even consistent with the present state of politics, to ameliorate its condition....

Nantgwillt, the place where we now reside, is in the neighbourhood of scenes marked deeply on my mind by the thoughts which possessed it when present among them. The ghosts of these old friends have a dim and strange appearance when resuscitated in a situation so altered as mine is, since I felt that they were alive. I have never detailed to you my short, yet eventful life; but when we meet, if my account be not candid, sincere, and full, how unworthy should I be of such a friend and adviser as that whom I now address! We are not yet completely certain of being able to obtain the house where we now are. It has a farm of two hundred acres, and the rent is but ninety-eight pounds per annum. The cheapness, beauty, and retirement make this place in every point of view desirable. Nor can I view this scenery – mountains and rocks seeming to form a barrier round this quiet valley, which the tumult of the world may never overleap; the guileless habits of the Welsh – without associating *your* presence with the idea, that of your wife, your children, and one other friend, to complete the picture which my mind has drawn to itself of felicity. Steal, if possible, my revered friend, one summer from the cold hurry of business, and come to Wales. Adieu!

* *The hero of Godwin's novel* Fleetwood.

After various wanderings, during which Shelley came under surveillance by the Home Office because of his subversive political activities and writings, he and his family found what they thought was an ideal location in the house, Tan-yr-allt, at Tremadoc. Here a scheme to preserve the coastline was being undertaken and Shelley, at first, viewed this with great enthusiasm and offered his services. But his radical views and support of the workers' grievances soon antagonised certain people and there seems little doubt that he suffered a violent attack. The following letter is to Thomas Hookham, his bookseller.

SHELLEY to Thomas Hookham.
Dec 3, 1812. Tanyrallt, Near Tremadoc, Carnarvonshire.

The parcel of books is not yet arrived. I own I am rather anxious concerning it, as the irregularity of the coaches to this solitude among mountains frequently causes mistakes. I have read Mr Peacock's verses. Independently of their poetical merit, they are accurately descriptive of the exquisite souls by whom I am encompassed. Bigotry is so universally pervading, that the best are deeply tainted. I was speaking of Mr Peacock to a lady who knew him during his residence in Wales. In many respects she is a woman of considerable merit, and except in religious matters, a model of toleration. 'Oh,' she said, 'there Mr Peacock lived in a cottage near Tan-y-bwlch, associating with no-one, and hiding his head, like a murderer, but,' she added, altering her voice to a tone of appropriate gravity, 'he was *worse than that,* he was an *atheist!'* I exclaimed much against the intolerance of her remark, without producing the slightest effect. She knows very well that I am an infidel; but perhaps she does not do me justice! There is more philosophy in one square inch of any trades-man's counter than in the whole of Cambria. It is the last stronghold of the most vulgar and commonplace prejudices of aristocracy. Lawyers of unexampled villainy rule and grind the poor, whilst they cheat the rich. The peasants are mere serfs, and are fed and lodged worse than pigs. The gentry have all the ferocity and despotism of the ancient barons, without their dignity and chivalric disdain of shame and danger. The poor are as abject as samoyads, and the rich as tyrannical as bashaws.

SHELLEY to Thomas Jefferson Hogg.
December 3, 1812. Tanyrallt.

...The society in Wales is very stupid. They are all aristocrats and saints: but that, I tell you, I do not mind in the least; the unpleasant part of the business is, that they hunt people to death, who are not so likewise....

SHELLEY to Thomas Hookham.
March 3, 1813. Tanyrallt, Tremadoc.

Dear Sir,
I have just escaped an atrocious assassination. Oh, send £20 if you have it! You will perhaps hear of me no more!
Your friend,
Percy Shelley.

SHELLEY to Thomas Hookham.
March 6, 1813. Bangor Ferry.

My Dear Friend,
In the first stage of our journey towards Dublin we met with your letter. How shall I express to you what I felt of gratitude, surprise, and pleasure not so much that the remittance rescued us from a situation of peculiar perplexity, but that one there was, who, by disinterested and unhesitating confidence, made amends to our feelings, wounded by the suspicion, coldness, and villainy of the world. If the discovery of truth be a pleasure of singular purity, how far surpassing is the discovery of virtue!
I am now recovered from an illness brought on by watching, fatigue, and alarm; and we are proceeding to Dublin to dissipate the unpleasant impressions associated with the scene of our alarm.

We expect to be there on the 8th. You shall then hear the detail of our distresses. The ball of the assassin's pistols (he fired at me twice) penetrated my nightgown and pierced the wainscot. He is yet undiscovered, though not unsuspected, as you will learn from my next....

Yours ever faithfully and affectionately,

Percy B. Shelley.

The Letters of Percy Bysshe Shelley, ed. F.L. Jones (Oxford University Press: 1964).

1819

MICHAEL FARADAY (1791-1867). *Eminent physicist and chemist, discoverer, among other things, of magneto-electricity. The following are extracts from his journal, written on a walking tour in Wales at the age of 27, early in his scientific career.*

Sunday, 18th July, 1819.

I resolved when I left London, to write down every evening that which amused me during the day. But resolutions, Dr Johnson observes will not execute themselves; and it is only now for the first time, I have put pen to paper in the way of journalising, though a full week has elapsed since I began to move about the Country....

Monday, July 19th.

'Tis still very gloomy and heavy, and much like rain this morning, and the tops of the hills are enveloped in clouds and mist. I will write a little more of past non-adventures.

After an early breakfast on the Monday Morning, just a week since today, I took a Post-chaise and proceeded on to Merthyr. We soon left the Vale of Glamorgan, got amongst the hills, and had some very pretty scenery. The rocks were dark gray sandstone, containing mica. There were kilns here and there for the burning of lime, and about 7 miles from Cardiff there were some large beds of water worn pebbles and boulders of an immense size, through which the road had been cut. After the eighth mile, coal works began to appear, and continued at intervals up to Merthyr.

On approaching Merthyr, the great change upon the surface of the earth, indicated the extensive works beneath. Tramways ran in every direction, and every now and then a range of thirty or forty trams laden with coal, or ore, or limestone, illustrated the advantage of this mode of conveyance. On all sides were piled up mountains of slag, cinder and refuse; or sometimes of valuable materials or products as coal, Ironstone, and Iron. Men, black as gnomes, were moving in all directions, taking to and bringing from the furnaces, and works; and as we came into sight of these erections, flame upon flame appeared rising over the country and scorching the air....

In the afternoon I rambled with Mr Wood over the works and saw the various operations. I was much amused by observing the effect the immensity of the works had on me. The operations were all simple enough, but from their extensive nature, the noise which accompanied them, the heat, the vibration, the hum of men, the hiss of engines, the clatter of shears, the fall of masses, I was so puzzled I could not comprehend them, except very imperfectly. The mind was drawn to observe effects, rather for their novelty than their importance; and it was only when by going round two or three times I could neglect to listen to sounds at first strange, or to look at rapid motions, that I could readily trace the process through its essential parts, and compare easily and quickly, one part with another.

Friday Evening, (Devil's Bridge).

The bridge from which this place takes its name is a structure made of slate fragments connecting the sides of two very high slate cliffs which are not however far asunder. The bridge is not more than 13 ft. over but is elevated 114 ft. from the torrent beneath. A new and handsome structure has been erected over the old one so that no access can be had to the latter, but it may be viewed from various spots some of which however rather calculate to alarm the nervous.... On leaving the bridge I followed a path onto the road which descending down the steep sides of a glen brought me after a somewhat dangerous descent to the rocks in the river bed below. After leaping on a few hundred yards from mass to mass over the slate fragments which lay heaped up forming the bottom of the ravine I got opposite to a fall not produced by the stream beneath the bridge but by another opposite the Inn (the Rhydol). It was not high but very beautiful and the ruins of the rocks about were very magnificent. The whole river for some hundred yards was perfectly white with foam from the resistance they gave to it....

Leaving this place after a long rest on the edge of the pool I advanced in another direction through the wood and got a fine view of the first fall or that occasioned by the stream beneath the bridge (The Mynach): this was very hansome. There were several smaller leaps made by the water before it took its grand descent and then it rushed in a strong white torrent down the smooth steep side of the precipice almost to the bottom terminating its descent however in a disturbed rush through a heap of fragments below. This fall is 208 ft. in height. It may be seen from many points of view and is fine in all of them....

Saturday, July 24th. Machynleth.

A journal always contains something monotonous and yet I cannot exactly say what it is ... there is something lingering on the mind which like the drone of a bagpipe though not principal is always present. Now in the way of experiment My Dear Margaret [his sister] I will suppose myself scribbling to you.

...I was up pretty early... we took our meal and departed, the waiter having assured us we should easily find our way over the mountains to Machynleth (pronounced Mach-hune-leth) it not being more than 20 miles distant due north. Now this sounded very smooth and fair but you will perceive that no account was taken of the following circumstances.

1 no roads, 2 no houses, 3 no people, 4 rivers but no bridges, 5 plenty of mountains. However we had got out Nichol's compass and water cup and trusted to chance for the rest and as it happened chance served us very well. We followed the road for about 3 miles and then came to a turnpike as we expected we happened too to find a woman in the toll house but she talked no English so that she was as bad as no woman to us. Taking our chances we struck off at a venture into what we supposed the mountain road leaving the rest to happen as it might. We were not without our pleasures on this droll expedition. The view was beautiful in all directions being enlivened with wood and water and in crossing the river Rheidol one of these which runs to the Devil's Bridge we stopped on its bridge to admire a beautiful cascade made by its stream just before it.

I have said there were no people in our road. In this I erred for we found one here and there but then they as often did us harm as good. They knew no English but 'yes' and as our questions were for simplicity put thus 'right for Machyleth?' pointing at the same time along the road we fancied right we generally got the above word as our answer right or wrong. If we repeated the question pointing another way it was still *yes* and on our still hesitating and wishing to have some other proof that they spoke with understanding it was either 'Yes inteet' or 'Dim Sasnach'. Every now and then in the way of corroboration we referred to our map, made observations on our shadows or marked the compass and in this way we proceeded 7 miles with wonderful success.

We were, however, too wary from past experience to suffer any opportunity of setting ourselves right to slip and happening when thus far on our road to see some tilers and thatchers on a barn top we scampered across the ground to them to ascertain first whether they spoke English and next know where we were. Fortune favoured us wonderfully. One man who had come from a distant place to work there spoke English and informed us we were wrong and going awry over the country. But we were not far wrong as yet and had not more than an extra half mile to do.

Luckily there was an old shepherdess on the spot (not an Arcadian) who had a son somewhere on the hills who knew his way across the mountains to Machynleth and for a certain fee would show it to us acting as guide. After hollering in all directions over the hills the young swain appeared and arriving at last at the place, we bargained with the dame that he should show us 9 miles over the mountains for two shillings. Poor fellow, twas hard earned money but it was a little fortune to him, and it was all the silver we had or could get in these places.... He led us directly North up and down, up and down the whole way, the hot burning sun striking upon our heads and not a breath of wind to refresh us.... When we were within five miles of Machynleth, standing on the edge of a mountain and looking into the immense vale below he said he had done his duty and must return....

The scenery now began to change and I wished you had been with us to enjoy it. On our left we had a fine view of Cardigan Bay. Beneath us was the mouth of the river Dovey or Dyfi opening into it and in the distance the extreme northern points of the Bay in Carnarvonshire. Before us now was Cader Idris rising above a host of mountains assembled at his base and separated from us by a broad deep well cultivated wooded valley.... We descended from our exalted station along a rugged path and the vale beneath and soon entered amongst wood on the sides of the dells. The scenery became more and more enchanting as we proceeded equalling all the cultivated beauties of Hafod and surpassing them in the introduction of peasants huts of the finest form and state for a picture. These huts were very peculiar in their appearance and have a highly romantic air. They are built of slate fragments and are massy and ponderous. The chimney and fireplace from their weight frequently sink a little and depress the end of the house giving the appearance of great age, and the roof is generally covered with vegetation. Sometimes they are thatched and this is often done with green rushes or grass which in the course of a few years is hidden by the foliage of fern and other plants which it nourishes. At other times they are slated but then moss is put under every slate at the edge to exclude wet, and this promotes another kind of vegetation and lichen and stone crop abound on such roofs. The lower part of these cottages are very nicely lime washed and the inside and neighbourhood is always very clean. And now you may easily imagine how beautiful a feature they form in a view when accompanied with wood and water and at times by the very peculiar peasantry of the country.

Today, Monday, July 26th, we have now taken a moderately long march of 28 miles from Dolgelly to this pretty place of Bethgellert....

During one shower we stepped into the shelter of a cottager's doorway. A poor woman was within with her family and seeing us she used all the English in her possession and bade us 'sit down'. Her little boy got us chairs and we entered and rested ourselves. The hut was a little place made of stones and thatch standing on a very few yards of ground. The rooms we were in occupied by far the greater part of it and extended upwards from the foundation to the roof. Still however we almost filled it from side to side and from top to bottom. There were two or three pieces of wonderfully clean and bright oaken furniture about as a clock, a chest of drawers, a dresser and shelves etc., and the crockery ware and other small things arranged in their respective places were in the nicest order. Even simple three legged stools looked respectable from the care taken of them. They were either white as milk or bright as hands could make them. The outsides of the houses are either painted or lime washed and the insides are rubbed and scoured until they surpass anything I have seen in London....

Wednesday, July 28th. [On Anglesey]

On approaching Amlwch we perceived by the country and the roads we were rapidly nearing the copper works for which this place, and indeed the whole island, is so famous. The country before us appeared brown and barren and the roads were mended with slag....

Thursday, July 29th.

...Whilst Captain Leaman arranged his morning affairs and procured us cloaths for the mine, we rambled about among the workmen. The ore is raised from the mine by the whimsey in large heavy masses and is then thrown over a stage onto the ground below where it comes into charge of the cobbers, principally women and boys. We came up to a large group of these, about 8 or 9 women were sitting on the ground in the midst of heaps of ore, their mouths were covered with a cloth to keep the dust of the ore from entering the breath. The fingers and thumb of the left hand were cased in strong iron tubes forming a sort of glove. A large hammer was handled in the right hand and a block of ore placed before them served as an anvil. Thus furnished they were employed in breaking lumps of ore into small pieces and selecting the good from the bad. These, and indeed all who work at the mines, are paid piece-work according to the quantity and quality of what they produce an assay master being employed to ascertain the latter and overseer the former....

We now dressed. I stripped off everything but my stockings and boots and took possession of a miners trousers, shirt and coat all of thick flannel. Then putting on a thick woollen cap, hanging a candle to my breast button and taking another lighted and garnished with clay in my hand I was now ready to descend.... The place we prepared to descend was a small aperture in the earth about 4ft by 3ft wide and a ladder appeared at its mouth which descended into the darkness below. Captain Leaman chose this shaft because it was the most *comfortable*.... Having taken a lesson how to hold our candles we got on to the ladder. It was not long but on reaching its termination we had to swing around it by a little stage on to a second and from that on to a third and so on until I lost count of their number.... At last we began to enter the vein and had to shuffle on in a more irregular manner... our progress was at first through very confined passages but on a sudden we entered a place like a large chamber so large that our light would not reach across it. Here the vein had swelled out into a bunch and had afforded a very rich mass of ore. Here again it became very narrow and we had in one corner to lay down on our backs and wriggle in through a rough slanting opening not more than 12 or 14 inches wide. The whole mountain being above us and threatening to crush us to pieces. You will understand my Dear Girl we were now in those parts of the veins which had been cleared of ore by the workmen.... You will remember we were now in the centre of the mountain and its whole weight resting over us and this weight would long ago have crushed the two sides of the empty veins together if precautions had not been taken to keep the place open and support the mountain....

Proceeding along one of these galleries we came at last to a chasm at the bottom of which we could just see men with lights.... We crossed this place on a plank and a rope loosely put over it and advancing onwards soon after descended again creeping and sliding, tumbling and slipping as before.... Now at times we began to hear explosions which reverberated throughout the mine in grand style and we soon came up to two men who were preparing a blast.... It is astonishing how careless the men become of the peculiar dangers to which they are liable from the frequency with which they meet them.

They go on hammering without the least care at the hole charged with powder and now and then explode it by the attrition they cause before they are out of the way and then men get killed. They put their candles anyhow and anywhere and their powder is treated in the same manner. Magrath, to rest himself whilst the Captain gave directions sat down on a tub and stuck his candle against its side. We found out afterwards it was what they kept the powder in....

Friday, July 30th.
...It was our intention to see the slate quarries about 6 miles from Bangor....

We now began to see the quarries at intervals from amongst the trees like a number of hills of rubbish on the side of the mountain before us and their appearance increased our eagerness to be at them.... We had to make our way round and between several high hills of refuse slate before we got fairly into the works, but when there we were charmed with the novel and strange appearance of things. The splintery character of all about us, the sharp rocky projections above us, the peculiar but here general colour of the rock together made up an appearance unlike anything we had seen before. We pushed on boldly by men and offices and made up inclined ways and along railways towards the explosion we heard a little way off. After having seen two or three very curious places we tempted a man to leave his work and show us the road to the most interesting parts of the quarry and he took us among the cliffs where we almost repented we had asked to go. Smooth perpendicular planes of slate many many feet in height, depth and width, appeared above and below in all directions, chasms yawned, precipices frowned, and the path which conducted amongst and through these strange places was sometimes on the edge of a slate splinter not many inches wide though raised from the cliffs beneath into mid air. We then mounted and at last gained a kind of slate promontory which had been left projecting across the quarry. It was narrow but walled on both edges. From hence we had a kind of bird's eye view of the excavations and workings and saw the men like pygmies below pursuing their various objects. It was certainly a very singular scene and like nothing else I know of....

Michael Faraday in Wales, edited by D. Tomos (Gwasg Gee: 1973).

JOHN FROST (1784-1877), *was a draper, prominent in the munici-
pal politics of Newport, being variously councillor, Mayor and a J.P. His
belief in the radical reform of society also made him one of the leaders of
the Chartist movement as it developed in Wales. For his part in the
Chartist-inspired Newport Rising which took place on 4th November
1839 and in which at least 22 people were killed and many more injured
when troops fired on a crowd of about 20,000, he was transported to
Australia for life. After fourteen years he was pardoned and allowed to
return to England and Wales in 1856 where his activities demonstrated
that his views remained unchanged. In the course of his life he wrote many
open letters, often printed as pamphlets, exposing general injustices and
local malpractice. First, come extracts from a long letter he wrote in 1821
to Sir Charles Morgan, the reactionary local landowner whose dubious
activities he exposes. Following this are extracts from a letter he wrote
while in gaol serving a sentence for libel allegedly committed in the course
of the first letter.*

JOHN FROST to Sir Charles Morgan.

Sir,
    When you, Sir, about fifteen years ago, solicited my vote as a
Freeholder for the County of Monmouth, and, when I with a skein
of thread around my neck, came into your presence, I shook like an
aspen leaf. Not, Sir Charles, that there was anything terrific in your
appearance, for you were, and still are, a handsome little man. But
you were a Baronet, *Sir Charles Morgan*, of *Tredegar*; a man
possessed of great power: a knowledge of this operated on my
nervous system, and produced the effects which I have described.
    In a short time after, Lord *Arthur Somerset* called on me for the
same purpose. This visit was near killing me. I had at that time got
a little higher in the world. I was, when his Lordship came into my
shop, in the act of weighing snuff. The sight of a Lord so overpow-
ered me, that instead of putting snuff into the box of an old woman,
it dropped from my hand, and I became motionless as a statue. My
tongue clave to my mouth. Mr Prothero will probably recollect,
(though I suppose having been since engaged in affairs of great
importance, these little things have escaped his memory) that, when
he introduced his Lordship, I could scarcely reply to the very simple
question he put to me. But, now Sir Charles, I have seen a little more
of the world. I have lived long enough to know, that men may possess
immense wealth, without making use of that wealth to promote the

happiness of their fellow creatures; and that, although men may abound in riches, although men may have in their power, the means of securing the respect of their neighbours; yet, that it is possible, that a man, with all these advantages, may live unrespected, and die unregretted....

A knowledge of these things, has taught me to estimate rank and riches very differently. I believe, were I now to come into the presence of a Lord, or a Baronet, my feelings would be of a very different kind. I should no longer look on the possessor of titles, and riches, as deserving of respect. My enquiry would *now* be, how does this man act? Does he make use of his riches, to promote the happiness of his Countrymen? Is he, on all occasions, ready to help those in distress? And, if I found, that a man was the reverse of this: I should look on him as deserving of the hatred of his fellow creatures, and instead of paying such a man any outward marks of respect, I should view him as a monster, and do all in my power to excite the like feelings in others....

What? to bow before one who has nothing to recommend him but riches? Let those do it who prize wealth. The possession of great wealth is proof presumptive, at least, of great dishonesty. When we enquire how great estates have been, and still are acquired; the mode is not calculated to raise the possessors in the esteem of the public....

You have Sir Charles on various occasions declared, that it would give you pleasure to promote the interest of the inhabitants of Newport. This was a wise determination; for, as the greater part of the town belongs to you, in promoting the welfare of the inhabitants, you serve yourself.

The Gentlemen of Tredegar, were formerly celebrated for the kindness with which they treated their tenants. They were considered as the best of Landlords. They perceived not the propriety only, but also the policy of such conduct; for as they and their families were supported in splendour by the labours of their tenants, it became a duty on the part of your ancestors, to do everything consistent with reason to promote the comfort of those, by whom they were supported....

In order that the public may have clear ideas of the origin of the dispute between the burgesses of *Newport* on the one part, and yourself, the mayor and aldermen of Newport, and your agent on the other; it will be necessary that I refer to transactions which took place about twenty years ago.

When the Agent of his Grace the Duke of Beaufort took possession of property which the burgesses claimed, the late Sir Charles Morgan and yourself, attended at the meetings of the Burgesses which were held for the purpose of obtaining the property, which they considered the Duke had taken possession of illegally. The application to the Duke of Beaufort on the part of the burgesses was successful. The burgesses were restored the property of which they had by mistake been deprived....

What did the burgesses do when the Duke of Beaufort restored the Wharf to them? What did they do? They evinced a spirit not often found among the great.... The Duke of Beaufort had expended a large sum of money on the property of others, many of the burgesses were poor, yet they agreed that the property should be valued, and that his Grace should be repaid nearly the whole of what he had laid out....

But how, Sir Charles has this money been applied? The question to you is a very proper one. You were active in obtaining the property for the burgesses. You declared, that the only object you had in view, was the good of the burgesses. Have you performed your promise? His Grace, the Duke of Beaufort has received nothing of what he expended on the property, the burgesses have received nothing, then what is become of the money? The Wharf has been let at upwards of £100 a year, the rent has been regularly paid, and yet there is no account of the money! Another circumstance occurred at the meetings of the burgesses which does no credit to Sir Charles Morgan. In building the Tredegar Warehouse, an encroachment was made on the property of the burgesses. Those who know the ground, say that nearly three-fourths are built on the land of the Freemen. This Sir Charles was stated to you. You promised to become tenant to the burgesses. Have you performed your promise? Have you become tenant to the burgesses? You have received, I believe, for upwards of twenty years, £150 a year for the Tredegar warehouse and Wharf, a great part of which is built on the land of the Freemen; and while many of the burgesses, and the widows of burgesses have wanted the common necessaries of life: you, Sir Charles have enjoyed their property. Here's a pretty affair! And in a lawmaker too. If I were a tenant of Sir Charles Morgan I would refuse to pay rent, and I should be justified both by the law of nature and the law of the land....

When you, Sir Charles view your extensive estate, and in the pride of your heart, say 'all this is mine', you should consider what it is which makes it valuable? If you ever put this question to yourself, the answer is ready: the labour of my tenants. This it is which makes that valuable, which without, would soon become a desert. You, Sir Charles, neither plow nor sow. You are exposed, neither to the burning rays of the sun by day, nor to the chilling frost by night.

These things are endured by others. And when, with labour of body and of mind, they succeed in preserving the fruits of the earth; they take them to market, they sell the produce, and give you the money. With this money you support yourself and your family. You are clothed in purple and fine linen, you fare sumptuously every day, while many of those who produce all the comforts, all the luxuries of life, are like Lazarus, they would very gladly feed on 'the crumbs which fall from your table'. This is not a highly wrought description, it is the plain and sober language of truth. But say you, the property is mine. It was honestly acquired by my ancestors, it has been left to me, and by virtue of their bequest, I now enjoy it. Very well, Sir Charles, let it be so. This is not the time to talk of the titles by which the great landed estates are held. I will admit what you say to be correct. I will admit (and that is I believe admitting a great deal) that every house and every field belonging to Tredegar estate, were acquired honourably. But, Sir Charles, they can be of no value to you, unless by the labour of others; and surely you will not contend, that the labour or the property of your tenants is less sacred than yours?...

This is I believe clear, that every tenant of yours has a title to his property equally sacred as that of yours to Tredegar estate; this no one will for a moment doubt. But, say you, if I have violated a law; if I have taken possession of property to which I have no claim, the law is open. 'We live in a country whose laws are the envy and admiration of the world. Let the law take its course, and I will abide by its decision.' Very good, Sir Charles. This is the old story about the laws of our country. Fine doctrine this. Very fine in theory, but very deficient in practice. It is well known, that justice cannot be obtained in this country without money; and a great deal of it too. If any one wish to have a clear exemplification of this, let him employ your agent; he will soon teach him what sort of laws we live under. It is notorious, that the rich in this country oppress the poor; we have every day clear proofs of this.

When a poor man suffers from a rich one, and when the rich man, in the pride of his heart, tells the sufferer to seek redress from the law; he adds insult to injury. The wealthy man knows, that he has the means, although his cause be a bad one, of triumphing over him who has no money; and we daily see poor men, placing in the hands of the rich, those things which are made use of to their own injury. If the burgesses of Newport were to commence legal steps to recover the property, of which you have unjustly deprived them, you would fight them with their own weapons. The rent which you receive from the Tredegar warehouse would be employed to injure the real owners of the property....

What a disgraceful circumstance for a man of your estate, to be enjoying property which belongs to the poor. You at a public meeting, declared that you would pay the freemen rent. You have never fulfilled your promise.... Governed by the advice of the most base of mankind, and influenced in too great a degree by your own selfish feelings, you think yourself as secure, as if your own conduct were of the most upright kind.... I shall endeavour to prove to you by events which have taken place within your own recollection, that men placed in situations superior even to yours, have when too late, regretted, that their conduct had not been more conformable to those principles of justice, which, I believe are written on the heart of every man....

Printed by Samuel Etheridge (1821).

JOHN FROST to the Radicals of Monmouthshire.
Sep. 1822. Monmouth Gaol.

Gentlemen,

Here I am. Prothero* has fixed me snugly at last. I am surrounded by a wall twenty feet high. I am under the protection of no less a man than the High Sheriff for the County. I am not permitted to go beyond certain limits; I am not permitted to breathe the impure air of Monmouth town, lest my health should be affected; and in order to render the thing complete, my humble abode has been changed for that of a Castle.

Surely you will say, 'all this care of your person must proceed from the warmest affection'? No doubt of it. No one could have given stronger proofs of regard than Prothero has bestowed on me. He has for the last two years been 'about my path and he has espied out all my ways'. When I went wrong, he soon put me right; and lest I should in the bustle of life forget the many favours which he has conferred on me, I am now secluded from the world, where I have an opportunity of meditating on those virtues which have been the cause of so much happiness to the inhabitants of Newport.

Monmouth jail is pleasantly situated: it is healthy and commodious. The regulations appear to be good. The Governor humane and attentive. On the morning after my arrival, I went with the Turn-key to see the convicts. Here are six under sentence of transportation. Their cells are remarkably clean, and they appear to enjoy as much comfort as men in their situation could expect. What brought you here, said I to one of them? Why for making free with a horse, or said he, rather for selling a horse stolen by another man. Another had found an old copper furnace which he attempted to turn into money, and for these offences these men are to be transported. Thus it is thought I in our blessed country; the little rogues are punished while the great ones escape....

It is a principle laid down by the law, that every man accused of an offence, shall be tried by his peers. If a nobleman were to commit an offence, he would be tried by his Peers. If Sir Charles Morgan were to be tried, he would expect that his judges should be his equals. If Lawyer Prothero were to commit an offence against the law, he would not expect to be tried by a jury of Cobblers! The men who composed my jury were, in the general acceptation of the phrase, my superiors; whether they were so in reality might afford a subject of discussion; they no doubt thought so, and the public believed it, therefore this is evidently a departure from the principle on which the law of the land, and the most material part of the law is founded.

It is evidently more dangerous for a man to be tried FOR SOME OFFENCES by his superiors than by his inferiors. Many men placed in a superior situation of life, really entertain very crude notions of those whom they consider their inferiors. Accustomed to be obeyed from their infancy, possessing that which gives them so much influence in the world, they are inclined to punish with the greatest severity, those who attempt to inculcate the doctrine of equality. In my letter to Sir Charles Morgan, I had made use of language, not pleasing to the pride of the great. I had attempted to ridicule the respect, generally paid to the wealthy. I had attempted to persuade my readers, that not riches, but their proper application only, deserves respect. This language must have been galling to those who have nothing to recommend them but their property; who if they were to be thrown on the world tomorrow would be unfit for the least situation. When the PROPRIETY, of publications of this sort was the point to be decided by a jury composed of wealthy men, what could be expected. Precisely that which has taken place....

Frost went on to detail the iniquities of the trial and to advocate the necessity for change in government and in law.

* *Thomas Prothero was Sir Charles Morgan's lawyer and agent, a man whom Frost abhorred.*

Printed by S. Etheridge, Newport Reference Library (1822).

Another vital cause of popular disturbance was the enclosure of common land which was greatly accelerated in the early decades of the nineteenth century by various Acts of Parliament. One Englishman, AUGUSTUS BRACKENBURY, repeatedly built a house and cottages on land he had purchased in Cardiganshire in 1819 and repeatedly they were burnt or pulled down by the local population until eventually he left the neighbourhood. The struggle became known as 'Rhyfel y sais bach,' 'the war of the little Englishman'. Brackenbury wrote this letter of protest to the authorities in 1821.

To the right honourable
Lord Viscount Sidmouth.
&c &c &c 16th June, 1821.

My Lord,
I take the liberty of submitting to your Lordship a case of peculiar hardship in which the grievances appear to proceed not from individual malice but from the Dispositions of the Body of the People of a considerable District, and in which it seems impracticable to obtain either an adequate remedy for the past or protection for the future from the local Magistracy or in any ordinary manner.

It may be in your Lordships recollection that in the year 1817 His late Majesty's Government on the Application of the Magistrates of Cardiganshire deemed it necessary to send a Detachment of the 38th Regiment of Foot to Aberystwith for the protection of the Commissioners acting under an Act passed in the 55th year of His late Majesty for the Inclosure of Waste Lands in the Lordship of Mevenidd in the County of Cardigan, against the Peasantry of the Neighborhood who resisted the Inclosure with a violent and organized opposition which set the civil powers at defiance.

It is against the same violence rendered more daring by impunity, and more malignant by its being at present directed against an individual Englishman, for that reason stigmatized by the offenders as a Stranger, that I now entreat your Lordships protection.

In the latter end of the year 1819 I purchased about 900 Acres of the Waste Lands from the Commissioners acting in the execution of the above recited Act and in that Purchase acquired a Title which cannot be impeached.

Since I came into possession I have been the object of unceasing persecution. I began to improve my Property by fencing, reducing into cultivation, and building; my fences were thrown down, and in the space of 13 months, five times successively have Buildings been erected by me and destroyed in spite of every precaution, by Mobs riotously assembled and in most instances disguised and armed – I have frequently been assaulted with Stones; my Dwelling has repeatedly been fired at with Ball. I have been informed not in consequence of my own investigation only but from anonymous Threats conveyed to me by Letter, that the injuries which I received were the effects of a general Conspiracy consolidated by an unlawful Oath against me as an Intruder, and that not my Property only but my life would be endangered; Information on Oath which I have been able to obtain has been met by the most unblushing perjury and the peasantry seem to have been encouraged in their Outrages, and in the effrontery with which they defend themselves on any Accusation by an Opinion which it appears impossible to remove from their minds that the Magistrates of the Country are not cordial in their desire to bring the Offenders to Justice. These causes render all my attempts at redress by the ordinary means unavailing; and unless I am entitled in your Lordships consideration to some extraordinary protection from His Majesty's Government, I fear I must submit to be an example in the 19th Century of a Subject of this Realm, without the means of prevention or redress, deprived of a valuable Property by open and lawless force.

I subjoin an Appendix containing a detail of some of the injuries and acts of violence I have suffered.... Respectfully and earnestly entreating your Lordships attention to my case, I have the honor to subscribe myself....

Augustus Brackenbury.

Ceredigion II, David Williams (1952).

Brackenbury evidently received little help from Their Lordships, the conflict continued and in 1826 the local people can be found complaining against him.

The Humble Petition of the INHABITANTS OF THE HUNDRED OF ILAR in the County of Cardigan.

Whereas the following is a true Statement of Augustus Brackenbury and his Men's Barbarity and illegal Proceedings on Mynned bach previous to the demolishing and pulling down his Castle and Fortress on the sd. Mountain, is submitted to your wise Consideration.

On Sunday 23rd of April as Elizabeth Jones was going from her

Service on a Visit to her Parents, passing his Castle, she was drag'd by Brackenbury and one of his Bullies with Imprecations of throwing her into a deep moat which surrounds his Castle. Her Cries being heard by a man who happen'd to be near went to her Assistance, whom they also abus'd in a most barbarous Manner holding a Musket to his Face, threatening to shoot him, but at last struck him with the Muzzle of it and cut a deep Gash on his upper Lip. Had he not been at Hand at the Time most probable they would have committed more Violence and violate her Person. On the 27th April a poor Boy happening to be near was pursued by Brackenbury and the poor Boy in order to escape the Pursuit threw off his wooden Shoes, which he carried to his Castle and never return'd them to the poor fatherless Boy. On Sunday May the 7th and the two following Sundays mangled and destroyd the turf of Elizabeth Morgan, and carried off at the same Time a few dry Bushes which she fix'd near her Dwelling to dry Linen &c upon. May 10th stealing the Turf of Joshua Davies and breaking his Cart.... This is but a short Sketch of Brackenbury and his Bullies's Barbarity and Cruelty on Mynnyd Bach. – No Person could pass and repass without being insulted, assaulted, pursued and shot after; and all the diabolical Practices committed (in particular) on the Sabbath Days – by carrying Fire Arms, Shovels and other Implements suitable for their evil Purposes – such Cruelties and Barbarities irritated the Inhabitants (and no wonder if rightly considered) to demolish and pull down his Castle and his strong Holds – We are sorry to say that our Justices seem to be partial to Brackenbury's Conduct. Had they listen'd to the complaint of the suffering Individuals his Castle might still have been standing.... If some way or another be not contriv'd to put a stop to his Atrocities it is to be feared further Mischief and serious consequences will ensue.

June 12th 1826 We are (Honored Sir) most respectfully
    your obt Servants and Sufferers
    in the Hundred of Ilar.

David Jones, *Before Rebecca* (Allen Lane: 1973).

1824

THOMAS CLARKSON (1760-1846), *was an indefatigable anti-slavery agitator who won a prize for a Latin essay on slavery at Cambridge in 1785 and henceforward devoted his life to its abolition. He travelled constantly in Britain and Europe both on behalf of the abolition of the slave trade and later on behalf of the abolition of slavery in the West Indies. The Bill to abolish the slave trade was passed in 1807 – Wordsworth wrote a sonnet to Clarkson on that occasion, ending:*

The blood-stained Writing is for ever torn;
And thou henceforth will have a good man's calm,
A great man's happiness; thy zeal shall find
Repose at length, firm friend of human kind!

Not so! Despite ill-health, Clarkson soon began to campaign on behalf of the abolition of slavery itself in the West Indies. The following extracts from his diary derive from his tour of Wales in 1824 for the Anti-Slavery Society. The entries dealing with South Wales show him engaging the interest and support of virtually everyone he met for the purpose of pressurising the Government. In North Wales it was a different story: he began to encounter opposition and a desire to leave things to the Government. The Emancipation Act was finally passed in 1833 and upwards of a million slaves were freed.

August 12th, 1824.
Went to Denbigh – Called upon Charles Sankey esq. Banker who promised to go into the Town and try to get half a dozen people to meet to form a committee.

Friday, August 13th.
Mr Sankey had performed his promise and came to me to say that the Gentlemen upon whom he had called thought that matters had better remain as they are i.e. under the hands of the Government, believing that the latter would proceed in the matter as quickly as circumstances would permit but that if they were negligent in fulfilling their pledge they would willingly interfere. I then waited upon the Revd R. Howard, the Rector, for whom I had a letter from the Revd Dr Trevor. He held the same Language – he was not inclined to a Committee. If the Government was found negligent he would be glad to interfere. He was sure *slavery* had received its *Death-Wound* and that it was the Will of Providence that slavery should cease. There was, he said, but one opinion in the *Country upon this* and it would be impudent at the present moment to interfere with the Government, either to suspect them or to go on more quickly than their own judgement. He could not therefore sanction a Committee at Denbigh but if another were formed at Rythyn he would attend the Communications from them – Several about here at the Shrewsbury Assizes. [He finds that possible supporters were away, detrimental to his efforts.]

Went to Rythyn.

...waited upon Edward Jones esq. Solicitor who heard me with the greatest attention and promised all his assistance.

Saturday, August 14.

Today Mr Jones brought the word that he had spoken to seven Gentlemen in the Town who were the principal inhabitants. He found that Mr Newcome, the Warden, had been speaking to them about my coming; but that they had made up their minds to do nothing – Mr Peers, a magistrate had poisoned some of them. He had formerly been a *Slave-Captain* and told them that *no Evils* existed in the Colonies. This *indisposed* them to act. Besides they were all High Churchmen and high Government-Men: they thought that Government having taken up the matter, there ought to be *no meddling with them at all*. They would not consent to do anything, by which their sincerity should ever be suspected – Mr E. Jones said that in Denbighshire, Merionethshire, and all the Country round the People were half a century behind those of *South Wales*, and a *century* behind those of England. They were *ignorant* and *indifferent* about what did not belong to *themselves* and so *subservient,* as to cringe *and to obey* all that their superiors *chose to command them* to do and fearful of *disobliging* them. Hence the Men of fortune, who were Government men and Tories held supreme sway. In this district also *a dissenter was despised.* Nothing *would do but what came from the Church.* I must be *exceedingly cautious, how I suffered dissenters to originate anything.* But here was not only a *Prejudice* against *dissenters* because they *differed from the Church;* but *because they were the lowest of the People* – their *Preachers* too were *very low men like themselves.*

Mr Jones formed a 'private' committee of a few like-minded people. Clarkson found that committees could be formed at Bala and Dolgelly. But at Carnarvon....

Sat, August 21st.

All the Gentry here are *Government-Men* to a Man and *unhappily* some are against us – Capt. Parry of the Navy, a Magistrate and Gentleman of Fortune in the town is one of these. He states that to his Knowledge the *Slaves* are better off than the *British Labourers* – and Mr Pennant, the Heir of Lord Penrhyn, a man of £50,000 a year, living in the neighbourhood, is quite against us in consequence of *being a very large West Indian Proprietor.*

[Clarkson was later warmly welcomed by the Bishop of Bangor but found that people who might support him wanted circumspect action.] ...Poor Mr Wilberforce is very unpopular here....

Thomas Clarkson Diaries, National Library of Wales 14984.

1824

WILLIAM WORDSWORTH (1770-1850). *Poet whose work is a landmark in the history of English Literature. He wrote the following travel letter of a tour in Wales with his wife and daughter to Sir George Beaumont, friend and patron of artists and writers.*

WORDSWORTH to Sir George Beaumont.
September 20th, 1824. Hindwell, Radnor.

...On a beautiful day we took the steam packet at Liverpool, passed the mouth of the Dee, coasted the extremity of the vale of Clwyd, sailed close under Great Orme's Head, had a noble prospect of Penmaenmawr, and having almost touched upon Puffin's Island, we reached the Bangor Ferry a little after six in the afternoon. We admired the stupendous preparations for the bridge over the Menai, and breakfasted next morning at Carnarvon. We employed several hours in exploring the interior of the noble castle, and looking at it from different points of view in the neighbourhood. At half-past four we departed for Llanberis, having fine views, as we looked back, of C. Castle, the sea, and Anglesey. A little before sunset we came in sight of Llanberis Lake, Snowdon, and all the craggy hills and mountains surrounding it; the foreground a beautiful contrast to this grandeur and desolation – a green sloping hollow, furnishing a shelter for one of the most beautiful collections of lowly Welsh cottages, with thatched roofs overgrown with plants, anywhere to be met with; the hamlet is called Cwm-y-Glo. And here we took boat, while the solemn lights of evening were receding towards the tops of the mountains. As we advanced Dolbardin Castle came in view, and Snowdon opened upon our admiration. It was almost dark when we reached the quiet and comfortable inn at Llanberis. Here we passed the morning of the Sabbath in a quiet stroll round the upper lake – Dora *not* being strong enough on that hot day to accompany us, attempted to sketch the Church and some of the Cottages – often wishing, as we all perpetually did, that you would pop up on us.

In the afternoon there being no carriage-road, we undertook to walk by the Pass of Llanberis, eight miles, to Capel Cerig; this proved fatiguing, but it was the only oppressive exertion we made during the course of our tour. We arrived at Capel Cerig in time for a glance at the Snowdonian range, from the garden of the inn in connection with the lake (or rather pool), reflecting the crimson clouds of evening. The outline of Snowdon is perhaps seen nowhere to more advantage than from this place. Next morning, five miles down a beautiful valley to the banks of the Conway, which stream we followed to Llanrwst; but the day was so hot that we could only make use of the morning and evening. Here we were joined, according to previous arrangement, by Bishop Hobart, of New York, who remained with us till two o'clock next day, and left us to complete his hasty tour through North and South Wales. In the afternoon arrived my old college friend and youthful companion among the Alps, the Rev. R. Jones, and in his car we all proceeded to the falls of the Conway, thence up that river to a newly-erected inn on the Irish road, where we lodged; having passed through bold and rocky scenery along the banks of a stream which is a feeder of the Dee. Next morning we turned from the Irish road three or four miles to visit the 'Valley of Meditation' (Glyn Mavyn) where Mr Jones has, at present, a curacy, with a comfortable parsonage. We slept at Corwen, and went down the Dee to Llangollen, which you and dear Lady B. know well. Called upon the celebrated Recluses [The Ladies of Llangollen], who hoped that you and Lady B had not forgotten them; they certainly had not forgotten you, and they begged us to say that they retained a lively remembrance of you both. We drank tea and passed a couple of hours with them in the evening, having visited the acqueduct over the Dee and Chirk Castle in the afternoon. Lady E. has not been well, and has suffered much in her eyes, but she is surprisingly lively for her years. Miss P. is apparently in unimpaired health. Next day I sent them the following sonnet from Ruthin, which was conceived, and in a great measure composed, in their grounds

> A STREAM, to mingle with your favourite Dee,
> Along the VALE OF MEDITATION flows;
> So styled by those fierce Britons, pleased to see
> In Nature's face the expression of repose;
> Or haply there some pious hermit chose
> To live and die, the peace of heaven his aim;
> To whom the wild sequestered region owes,
> At this late day, its sanctifying name.
> GLYN CAFAILLGAROCH, in the Cambrian tongue,
> In ours, the VALE OF FRIENDSHIP, let *this* spot

Be named; where, faithful to a low-roofed-Cot,
On Deva's banks, ye have abode so long;
Sisters in love, a love allowed to climb,
Even on this earth, above the reach of Time!

The allusion to the Vale of Meditation in the above, would recall to the Ladies' minds, as it was meant to do, their own good-natured jokes of the preceding evening, upon my friend Mr Jones, who is very rubicund in Complexion and weighs about 17 stone, and would, as they said, make 3 good hermits for the Vale of which he is Curate. We passed 3 days with Mr J's friends in the vale of Clwyd, looking about us, and on the Tuesday set off again, accompanied by our friend, to complete our tour. We dined at Conway, walked to Benarth, the view from which is a good deal choked up with wood. A small part of the castle has been demolished, for the sake of the new road to communicate with the suspension bridge, which they are about to make to the small island opposite the castle, to be connected by a long embankment with the opposite shore. The bridge will, I think, prove rather ornamental when time has taken off the newness of its supporting masonry; but the mound deplorably impairs the majesty of the water at high-tide; in fact it destroys its lakelike appearance. Our drive to Aber in the evening was charming; sun setting in glory. We had also a delightful walk next morning up the vale of Aber, terminated by a lofty waterfall; not much in itself, but most striking as a closing accompaniment to the secluded valley. Here, in the early morning, I saw an odd sight – fifteen milkmaids together, laden with their brimming pails. How cheerful and happy they appeared! and not a little inclined to joke after the manner of the pastoral persons in Theocritus. That day brought us to Capel Cerig again, after a charming drive up the bank of the Ogwen, having previously had beautiful views of Bangor, the sea and its shipping. From Capel Cerig down the justly celebrated vale of Nant Gwynant to Beddgelert. In this vale are two small lakes, the higher of which is the only Welsh lake which has any pretensions to compare with our own; and it has one great advantage over them, that it remains wholly free from intrusive objects. We saw it early in the morning; and with the greenness of the meadows at its head, the steep rocks on one of its shores, and the bold mountains at *both* extremities, a feature almost peculiar to itself, it appeared to us truly enchanting.

The village of Beddgelert is much altered for the worse; new and formal houses have supplanted the old rugged and tufted cottages; and a smart hotel has taken the place of the lowly public-house in which I took refreshment almost thirty years ago, previous to a midnight ascent to the summit of Snowdon. At B. we were agreeably surprised by the appearance of Mr Hare, of New Col: Oxford. We slept at Tan-y-bwlch, having employed the afternoon in exploring the beauties of the vale of Festiniog. Next day to Barmouth, whence, the following morning, we took boat and rowed up its sublime estuary, which may compare with the finest of Scotland, having the advantage of a superior climate. From Dolgelly we went to Tal-y-llyn, a solitary and very interesting lake under Cader Idris. Next day, being Sunday, we heard service performed in Welsh, and in the afternoon went part of the way down a beautiful valley to Machynlleth, next morning to Aberystwith, and up the Rheidol to the Devil's Bridge, where we passed the following day in exploring those two rivers and Hafod in the neighbourhood.

I had seen these things long ago, but either my memory or my powers of observation had not done them justice. It rained heavily in the night and we saw the waterfalls in perfection. While Dora was attempting to make a sketch from the chasm in the rain, I composed by her side the following address to the torrent:

> How art thou named? In search of what strange land,
> from what huge height, descending? Can such force
> Of waters issue from a British source
> Or hath not Pindus fed thee, where the band
> Of Patriots scoop their freedom out, with hand
> Desperate as thine? Or come the incessant shocks
> From that young Stream, that smites the throbbing rocks
> Of Viamala? There I seem to stand
> As in life's morn; permitted to behold,
> From the dread chasm, woods climbing above woods,
> In pomp that fades not; everlasting snows;
> And skies that ne'er relinquish their repose;
> Such power possess the family of floods
> Over the minds of Poets, young or old!

If the remembrance of 34 years may be trusted, this chasm bears a strong likeness to that of Viamala in the Grisons, thro' which the Rhine has forced its Way. Next day, viz., last Wednesday, we reached this place, and found all our friends well, except our good and valuable friend, Mr Monkhouse, who is here, and in a very alarming state of health....

Now, my dear Sir George, what chance is there of your being in Wales during any part of the autumn? I would strain a point to meet you anywhere, were it only for a couple of days....

Letters of William and Dorothy Wordsworth: The Later Years, Part I, 1821-28, (Oxford University Press: 1978).

FELIX MENDELSSOHN (1809-47). *German composer who made
many visits to Britain on one of which, at the age of 20, he visited Wales
and wrote the following letter.*

To Abraham Mendelssohn Bartholdy [his father].
August 25, 1829. Llangollen.

Anything but national music! May ten thousand devils take all
folklore. Here I am in Wales, and oh how lovely, a harpist sits in the
lobby of every inn of repute playing so-called folk melodies at you –
i.e., dreadful, vulgar, fake stuff, and *simultaneously* a hurdy-gurdy is
tootling out melodies, it's enough to drive one crazy, it's even given
me a toothache. Scottish bagpipes, Swiss cow's horns, Welsh harps –
all playing the Huntsmen's Chorus with ghastly variations or impro-
visations, not to mention the lovely songs in the lobby – it's the only
real music they have! It's beyond comprehension! anyone like myself,
who can't abide Beethoven's Nationallieder, should come here and
hear them howled by shrill nasal voices, accompanied by doltish
bumbling fingers, and then try to hold his tongue. The whole time
I've been writing these lines the fellow out in the hall has been
playing:

and he does variations on this, while the hurdy-gurdy interrupts with
a sacred song in A-flat major. I am going mad and will have to leave
off writing until later. –

August 26. And in so doing I did the right thing; last night in
despair I went to visit the innkeeper's three daughters, who have a
piano, and asked them to play something on it for me; they are quite
pretty and did so – the organ grinder and the harpist fell silent (the
latter is also the barber, it turns out, as I discovered this morning) –
the daughters then started up on the organ, but I was blissful, the
muette de Portici and several contredanses did me good. Afterwards
they asked me to 'favour' them, so I favoured them from my heart,
racing up and down the keyboard and playing away my toothaches;
the evening was quite pleasant, and I returned to my room too late
to resume writing. And yesterday afternoon I had already climbed to
the top of a high mountain, with the ruins of a Roman citadel at the

summit, had looked far out into the blue distance, and down to the dark, lonely valleys below – then climbed right back down into one of these quiet valleys, in which the walls and windows of an old abbey are covered and overgrown with lovely green trees – the abbey is right next to a rushing, babbling brook, mountains and rocky cliffs are spread all around, the choir of the church has been converted into a stable, the altar into a kitchen, above the tops of the gables you can see the tops of the beeches towering in the distance which could be a chapter in themselves, and the sky was serenely gray.... Blue sky and sunshine do so much to warm my heart, and are so indispensable for me! But here they don't exist. This actually grieves me seriously, or almost. The summer is gone, and without having sent a single summer day. Yesterday was a *good* day, i.e. I only got soaked three times, kept my coat over my shoulders the whole day, and saw the sun a few times through the clouds. *Bad* days are beyond imagination; a raging, whistling storm has been blowing for four weeks almost without interruption and in addition the clouds have come cascading down and it would be raining terribly, if the storm would just let it fall in peace; but it snatches it up, tosses it around in the air, whipping the spray against your face – there's nothing to do for it except to sit around quietly indoors.... My trip to Ireland came to naught in Bangor and on the Isle of Anglesey – in spite of all the dampness I was still thinking of making an attempt at it for a few days; but then the steamer came, having taken fifteen hours instead of six, and when I saw all the seasick passengers, wet, weak, and cursing as they tottered around, I signed up for a mainland-bound coach. I have struggled just as hard as one can with the weather, have got myself soaked to the skin almost daily, have seen the mountains looking like furniture, chandeliers, and rugs in some old palace, hidden beneath gray cloth covers, with only a few glorious corners poking out, but now I'm through with it. Tomorrow I'm going to visit my family in the country, and by the middle of next week I'll be back in London.

– In the meantime we have had two bright, cheerful days, like sunshine; and how strange that everything seems so different from how one had pictured it....

Felix Mendelssohn A Life in Letters, ed. by Rudolf Elvers, trans. from the German by Craig Tomlinson (Fromm International Publishing Corporation: New York, 1986).

1831

Letter from ZEPHANIAH WILLIAMS, *one of the leaders of the Chartist movement in South Wales who was transported together with John Frost after the 1839 Newport Rising. The letter is to Benjamin Williams, a Dissenting Minister 'respecting the injustice of the slanderous mode of persecution by which he endeavoured to deprive the writer of the esteem and affection of his friends.' After all the variations in religious belief so far expressed, here is a non-believer stating his moral attitude.*

ZEPHANIAH WILLIAMS to Benjamin Williams.
Newport, 1831.

Sir

...I am given to understand, that you were recently accusing me, at the house of a neighbour whom I esteem a friend, of the most diabolical conduct; from what authority, I do not know; and supposing you to have believed what you said, it is contrary to the faith which you profess.... Your conduct and your doctrine are at variance, for you are holding to your flock that God will have the number which he has decreed, and afterwards going to my neighbours to persuade them, that an impotent mortal, like myself, may be the means of leading an infinite number of those who are already decreed for happiness (for you could not mean that such as are reprobate could be endangered by my heresy), into eternal misery.

...Although I may be considered by you as one that is decreed for eternal misery, I have a right to enjoy that inward satisfaction, which the idea, and the practice of justice, can alone impart; without tamely submitting to such molestation, as our difference of opinion may give you, in your opinion, a right to offer me. While you place your reliance on that religion, which you believe to have been given by God, you are free to enjoy the full benefit of such a belief; but you must grant me, on the other side, an equal right to participate in my full share of that happiness which the practice and love of equity can afford. Think it not strange that I should be ready to exclaim, 'How amiable art thou, O Virtue!' with as much fervour as you can exclaim, 'How great is the merit of the Atoning Blood!' ...The search after truth has cost me many sacrifices; and it will, doubtless, cost you as much. You will pardon me for expressing my doubt of you being possessed of sufficient courage for the experiment. The reflection, that all the doctrines which you have so earnestly inculcated from time to time, and on the preaching of which you have depended for your bread, are but human fabrications, will be intolerably severe....

I am well aware, indeed, that the admission of truth is opposed to the temporal interests of some, and the prejudices of others; it is, however, worth any sacrifice: and though that important word FAITH once sounded in my ears as the only thing needful I am convinced that *that* is but a Will-o'-the-Wisp, which leads men to bogs and fens: but that truth like the regular return of the sun in its gradual progress, exposes both sides of every object for our inspection. O Theologians! Let men's minds be filled with true ideas: let their reason be cultivated and invigorated by frequent exercise: let them be habituated to reflect on the good and bad effects of every action: this will at last so fix them in virtue, that all the allurements of vice can never unroot, though they may shake them. The fear of hellfire may operate, as the kindling of faggots does on the wild beasts of the desert: but domestication can alone subdue that natural hostility, which rages in the heart of wild beasts; and nothing but education can tame the ferocity of uncultivated human nature....

Letter in Newport Museum.

1831 ff.

THE MERTHYR RISING *of June 1831 and its aftermath – called by historian John Davies 'the most ferocious and bloody event in the history of industrial Britain' – was largely provoked by the depression in the iron trade of 1829 and the years following during which wages were substantially cut. To the harsh lives of the workers were added greater poverty and insecurity. Many were driven into debt and through the, to them, nefarious Court of Requests (debtors' court) suffered widespread confiscations of their property. Even the Marquis of Bute, in constant contact with the Home Secretary, Lord Melbourne, wrote on June 8th,* 'I have thought it my duty hitherto in my letters to your Lordship to confine myself entirely to the facts and to avoid alluding to any individuals or to any theory. The Court of Requests, although introduced by benevolent intentions, is no doubt become a real evil....' *Part of the background, too, was the radicals' (predominantly middle class) demand for Parliamentary Reform which prompted echoes among the working class. A number of disturbances broke out during May and at a Reform rally held on May 30th on the Waun, a hill outside Merthyr, a set of radical demands was excitedly approved by the crowd. Next day, the first of the insurrection, the crowd swept around Merthyr and its environs, gathering force all the time, and with the immediate aim of reclaiming goods distrained by the hated Court of Requests. Later, with the Red Flag raised for the first time in Britain, the crowds toured the district putting out furnaces in the works. On June 3rd a crowd of up to ten thousand marched on Merthyr. The ironmasters, the Marquis of Bute and others had been much alarmed by the developments and soldiers from the Argyll and Sutherland Highlanders had been drafted in and stationed at the Castle Inn. Here the magistrates and ironmasters were also waiting. The Riot Act was read but the crowd refused to disperse and fighting broke out in which more than twenty workers were killed and a number of soldiers wounded. For several days the rebellion flared up all over the district but could not be sustained in the face of the military force. In July, 28 people were put on trial, some were imprisoned, others transported and 2 sentenced to death. Lewis Lewis, an undoubted leader, was reprieved and transported for life but Richard Lewis, commonly known as Dic Penderyn, accused of wounding a soldier, was hanged. Petitions and witnesses were advanced on behalf of his innocence; even the trial judge, Judge Bosanquet, became anxious about the execution of the death sentence but the Home Secretary was adamant. Evidently bogus confessions by Penderyn and Lewis Lewis were circulated which caused the following statement to be issued by the Chaplain of Cardiff Gaol and two other ministers.*

From CHAPLAINS OF CARDIFF GAOL.
August 1st. 1831. Cardiff.

We hereby humbly certify that we have respectively attended Richard Lewis now under sentence of death in the Gaol of this place since his conviction, and that he has uniformly and solemnly denied any participation in or knowledge of the act of wounding, or endeavouring to wound the Soldier, for which offence he, the said Richard Lewis, is condemned to die.

Signed Daniel Jones (Chaplain to the Gaol)
William Jones (Baptist Minister)
Lewis Powell (Independent Minister).

HO 17/128 Part 2.

This statement was discovered, among other hitherto unknown papers dealing with the case of Richard Lewis, in the Record Office of the Home Office in 1970.

Letter (translated) from DIC PENDERYN to his sister, August 1831.

I ask you to come at once to fetch my body, since there is no likelihood of anything else at present. Come to Philip Lewis and get him to bring down a cart tonight and as many men as he can manage to bring with him. I believe the Lord has forgiven me my divers sins and transgressions, but since I am accused, I am not guilty, and for that I have reason to be grateful.

Gwyn A. Williams, *The Merthyr Rising* (Croom Helm: 1978).

Translated extracts from the REVEREND EDMUND EVANS'S Diary concerning Dic Penderyn.

Friday, August 12, 1831.
Went to the prison to see the prisoner who was to be hanged for the riot in Merthyr and we found him crying sombre tears.

What was troubling his mind was that he judged that he was being wrongly accused.

Saturday, August 13.
A dark and cloudy day. At 5 am we went to the city to see the prisoner and we found him and a clergyman praying.

Mr D. Williams prayed after me and I have never heard such praying before. After this the jailer brought a cup of tea and a thin piece of bread and butter, but he [Penderyn] did not take any food but drank the tea.

Then his wife came there to say her farewell to him and it was impossible for any heart not to rupture in the sorrow that was felt. I hope that I shall never again experience anything like that.

We went to the place where they take the religious service and we took communion with the prisoner.

Out we went to the court, the hangman tied the prisoner and the jailer placed handcuffs on him.

He [Penderyn] said: 'This is wrongful,' and we went after the prisoner to the top of the place, before thousands of sightseers what a sight!

Then the hangman put the rope over his head and the prisoner gave a piercing shriek that echoed over the city and said: 'Oh, what a transgression. Jesus forgive him and also to me' and then the trapdoor fell and he was released.

We turned our backs and went back to where we had the service and kneeled there praying.

Published in the *South Wales Echo*, August 13th, 1997.

Though the rising at Merthyr was defeated in early June, by August a union of the workers, affiliated to Robert Owen's National Association for the Protection of Labour, had achieved widespread membership in the whole area. Something of the ironmasters' response can be seen in the following letters. In September the ironmaster, Josiah John Guest and other employers dismissed all who refused to leave the union – at least four thousand men – and ensured that they did not receive the poor relief to which by law they were entitled. The virtual lockout was in force until mid-November when the starving workers agreed to forsake the union and go back to work. As one of the following letters reveals a similar struggle was taking place in Flintshire.

GEORGE SMITH KENRICK to Josiah John Guest.
August 30, 1831. Varteg Hill Iron Works [Monmouthshire].

My dear Sir,
   In the absence of my Father I have to acknowledge receipt of yours of the 27th instant and I agree with you that the Miners Union has a most mischievous tendency. If the men are Suffered to establish their union upon a regular System nothing but confusion & violence can be expected, and it is better that the evil should be crushed in the bud.
   The Unions have not spread to such an extent here as at Merthyr, but I found that 30 of the colliers & miners had joined it about a fortnight ago & I gave them notice to leave, and that plan I have continued to pursue with them. I believe not one of our Firemen is yet engaged, and it is my intention to let them know that if they join the Union they will inevitably lose their Situation at these works, and I trust they will keep themselves clear of the contagion. I have called upon Mr Hill & Mr Hunt and their views nearly coincide with my own as to the importance of the subject; and that whatever measures are adopted should be followed up at all events, for any triumph on the part of the men at this moment would cement the Union, so that it would resist all our efforts in future. Mr Hunt and Mr Hill were both willing to concur in any general measure and it was agreed that the latter should see Mr Bailey on the subject as we consider him to belong to our district, by that time Mr Smith whom I found absent

from Abersychan will have returned when we can consult upon the measures to be adopted. Should anything material occur respecting the Union you shall be informed of it.

W.H. BEVAN to Josiah John Guest.
September 1, 1831. Beaufort (Monmouthshire).

...On Monday & again yesterday I saw C. Bailey. C. Harford was from home. The former is disposed to take steps to break up the Union Clubs, but suggests, what I think is necessary for the fully carrying the step into effect, that a rigid system of discharges be established. It is evident the men you are picking out, may & no doubt partly will be employed by other Masters ignorant of their having belonged to these societies. Would not a general form of discharge, such as used to be in force, to which when needed the cause may be added, effectually check the disposition now prevalent among the men of controlling the Masters. C.B. says if this is done they will by degrees pick out all their union men....

(Further letter)
September 2, 1831. Beaufort.

"I hereby certify that the Bearer *William Jones Collier*, 'not being a member of any Union or other Society combined for the purpose of Regulating wages', is this day discharged from the employ of *Messrs Kendall & Bevan*, in pursuance of notice to that effect given *by (or to)* the said *William Jones* on the *2nd of August* last. W.H. Bevan."

Would not the above form answer all purposes? Should the man be a Member of the Union the words between the Commas being drawn through with the pen would be a sufficient hint.

The Notices should be printed in duplicate so that a Register would be Kept of each man's discharge. The Words scored under, to be left blank. Will Mr Guest give it his Consideration.

L. EVANS to J.J. Guest.
September 27th, 1831.

Sir,

Having heard yesterday that your Honor had received a letter accusing me as guilty for Preaching in support of the *Union* to this charge I can only say that I never did, nor never will discuss any

Political subject in the Pulpit, and shall feel happy at any time to confront my accuser in your Presence, in fact any society that would require an oath of me to keep their secrets, I would suspect that there must be something wrong in their Proceedings, – In consequence of a Public notice given I have attended one of their Public meetings but never advocated their cause in Private conversation nor in any Public company.

    I am Sir your ever faithful
and very humble servant
L. Evans Esqr.

Iron in the Making, ed. Madeline Elsas, *Dowlais Iron Company Letters 1782-1860,* (Glamorgan County Record Office: 1960).

J.B. BRUCE (Magistrate) to the Marquis of Bute.
19 October, 1831. Duffryn, Aberdare.

My Lord,
    ...Messrs Guest and Hill begged me not to leave Merthyr on account of a large meeting which was expected to be held on the 17th instant. It was not however held and they are tolerably quiet though I should say in a very unsettled and uncertain state. Very few have returned since my last communication to their work. The large Body of the Men are still standing out and the arrival of Twiss(?), a Bolton delegate who is come avowedly for the purpose of assisting and organising the Unions, will I fear retard their submission. He has brought his wife and family to Merthyr which looks as if he meant to stay there. We are in possession of their *secret* articles, than which nothing can be more subversive of the controul of the Master; or, in my opinion, more injurious to the best interests of the country.... They get supplied with flour from Hirwaun, Cyfarthfa, Penydarren, the Monmouthshire Works, and even from Maesteg but applicants are so very numerous that the supply though large does not above half feed them. How long they will be peacable with stomachs only half filled is problematical. I had an interview of an hour with Guest and Hill yesterday; they appear quite determined to hold out, and most of the Men appear equally resolute. They have committed no excesses but still send their wives to demand parish relief with the usual plea that they are willing to work but cannot get it. I saw a large Coal Merchant from the West yesterday who tells me that the colliers at the Swansea mines got a Guinea a week and confine themselves to

seven Baskets. They could easily cut *ten* if they chose. They have also formed Unions. I am
  My Lord
  Your faithful servant
  J.B. Bruce.

Public Record Office H.O 52/16.

THOMAS REVEL GUEST *now brought religion into the battle with the workers, appealing with outrageous casuistry to 'such Members of the Union Lodges as are in connexion with Christian Churches'.*

November 7, 1831. Cardiff.

  Brethren,... Allow one, who humbly hopes that by the grace of God he is a partaker of the common salvation, to address you in reference to the great absorbing subject which occupies the thoughts of most men in this neighbourhood at the present moment, viz. the Union Lodges. It will not be denied that the Kingdom of God is Righteousness, *Peace* & Joy in the Holy Ghost, we are exhorted to follow *Peace* with all men, to use our best efforts to promote *peace*, this then being an object which must be powerfully influential on every real Christian, let us enquire whether Membership with these Union Societies tends to promote *'Peace on earth, goodwill towards men'* or whether it is not calculated to injure if not destroy that spirituality of mind which Saint Paul refers to, Romans 8.6. 'to be carnally minded is Death, but to be spiritually minded is life & *peace.*' ...But you say that these societies are calculated to advance the good of the men & promote the fear of God, & it is said if... any provide not for his own & especially for those of his own House he hath denied the faith and is worse than an infidel, true, most true, but is it not written 'provide things *honest* in the sight of all men', and again 'take heed and beware of covetousness', so that in providing for your own house you are not to infringe on the providential order of God, by invading the rights of others, by attempting to force upon those whom God has set over you, the adoption of such regulations and the payment of such wages as would be beneficial to yourselves while they would be ruinous to your masters here then the Union Societies completely oppose one branch of that commandment on which hangs all the law & the prophets, viz. 'thou shalt love thy neighbour as thyself....'

The Union, which you have inadvisedly been persuaded to join, does not possesss those marks & characters which denote that it is from above, it follows that you have been overcome by temptation in an unwatchful hour & no matter by what obligation you may have bound yourselves to evil, God requires of you, Isaiah 1.16, 17 'Cease to do evil, learn to do well', come out from among them and be ye separate, return again to those paths, wherein you may be enabled by the divine blessing to provide things honest in the sight of all men, and by the fruit of your labour afford your Wives and your little ones that support which you are called upon to render them, alike by the voice of nature and of God....

Madeline Elsas, *Iron in the Making.*

JOHN MAUGHAM JUNIOR to Josiah John Guest.
November 8, 1831. Mostyn, Holywell (Flintshire).

I hope you will excuse the liberty I am about to take in addressing you but my acquaintance with Merthyr & the honor of a slight acquaintance with yourself have caused me to be deputed by the Magistrates here to ask a question in regard to the State of the *'Unions'* in South Wales, which is, have you or any of the Coal Masters in your District been able to break down the Unions & to persuade the men to disassociate themselves from them?

We have a very stubborn Contest going on here now & one very likely to make much disturbance in the Country, growing out of the overbearing Conduct of the men in the Union belonging to the Mostyn Colliery.... The men have complied with everything required of them, except the abandonment of the Union, & they affirm that their Unwillingness to yield upon this point arises as well from the Solemnity of some oath they have taken, as from an apprehension that, if they were to give way & relinquish the Union, they would never be able to get employment elsewhere. It has been stated to the Magistrates that in South Wales the Unions have been overcome & that the men have for the most part given them up. The men, however, flatly contradict this. If you could affirm the statement it is thought that it would do much towards disposing these men to separate from their Union. They are exceedingly destitute....

Dowlais Folio, Glamorgan Record Office 76/77.

JOHN HARLEY to Thomas Revel Guest.
21st. November 1831.
Iron & Tin Works, Pontypool (Monmouthshire).

...I am truly glad to find your men are gone to work again, the trade generally must be greatly indebted for the resolute stand you have made, and the smaller works will now, I hope, have little difficulty in bringing their people to their senses. It is my firm conviction that the trade would eventually have been destroyed if the combination had succeeeded....

Madeline Elsas, *Iron in the Making*.

The workers' attempt to combine in a Union having been, for the time being, defeated some of them reverted to the practices of previous decades when they had imposed a kind of rough justice by violent means. These bands, known as Scotch Cattle, perhaps because they wore skins as disguise and blacked their faces, attacked the property of owners or informers. Their activities were still to be heard of on occasions of industrial strife upwards of a century later. The following letter to the Marquis of Bute deals with one of their attacks.

JOHN H. MOGGRIDGE to the Marquis of Bute.
May 24, 1833. Woodfield

...Having received information in the evening of Monday 20th inst that one George Squire suspected of being an active leader in the present disturbances was with others in the Greyhound Public house in this parish I suggested Mr Matthew Moggridge to take a sufficient force of constables and endeavour to secure him, which he effected about eleven o'clock the same night, and Squire was sent off under a strong escort by a circuitous route to prison convicted on the most conclusive evidence, under the Act of 6 Geo. 4.

In the night of Tuesday 21 an attack was made upon a dwelling house belonging to me in Blackwood Village, occupied by one of the special constables, and the glass and sash frames demolished. And on Wednesday night three workmen's houses the property of W. Perkins were attacked by a great number of persons assembled, having their faces blacked, and being otherwise disguised, the door of one of them beat down and the windows of all demolished, with the whole of the earthen ware and china in one of them and the furniture greatly damaged to the great terror of the inmates, one of whom saved his life only by rolling himself in the bed and getting underneath the bed stead. The attack was here made with stones, some of then very large – and fire arms repeatedly discharged. These outrages were committed in my absence in Glamorgan. I send this off express to meet the mail that you Sir may have the goodness to bring the same before Viscount Melbourne at the earliest opportunity.

John H. Moggridge.

H.O. 52/23.

1839

CHARTISM

The Reform Act of 1832 did nothing to satisfy the political aspirations of the working class and this, together with the general industrial unrest, fuelled increased engagement with the Chartist Movement. Among its leaders in South Wales were the long committed radicals, John Frost and Zephaniah Williams, the bizarre character, Dr William Price and the solicitor, Hugh Williams, an ardent advocate of reform in Carmarthenshire and subsequently to be associated with the struggles of 'Rebecca'. After a General Assembly of the movement in London early in 1839, attended by delegates from Wales, Frost among them, a petition bearing more than 1¹/₄ million names was presented to Parliament. Nothing of any consequence resulted and more violent action began to be advocated. Certainly in Wales, with the arrest of Henry Vincent, noted orator and editor of the Chartist paper, the Western Vindicator *in May 1839, those who favoured direct action gained more support. It is interesting to see how Lady Charlotte Guest, translator of* The Mabinogion *was seeing matters at this time and how her husband was clearly warning off possible Chartist sympathisers:*

LADY CHARLOTTE GUEST – Journal.

May 13, 1839.

...Merthyr* went to the furnaces and I had a long tête a tête till he came in with Mr Price* of Porth-y-glo, who called in consequence of Merthyr's note to him. He owned being favourable to Chartism, but disclaimed all idea of physical force, which he said had almost determined him to abandon the doctrine altogether. Merthyr warned him of the danger of lending his countenance to any societies of the kind and he seemed grateful for the advice. The idea of such a long interview as mine with a Chartist leader would be sufficient to frighten many of my friends. How much people and things are exaggerated....

1* *Her husband* Josiah John Guest, *owner of Dowlais Ironworks whom she called Merthyr.*
2* *Probably* Dr William Price *who, by some accounts, did favour violent action.*

May 19.
...We were to have gone to town tomorrow but there is to be a very great meeting of Chartists, and the Merthyr people are alarmed at the idea of a riot. Merthyr has accordingly determined to await the result, which both he and I believe will not be at all important. In this population of thirty thousand people and upwards there are only two thousand Chartists and they appear perfectly orderly and say they intend nothing but to petition the Queen, in which, as far as this district is concerned, I really believe them. They seem quite different in tenets, etc, from the rabble of Birmingham. By this time tomorrow I suppose I shall know the result of the much dreaded meeting. It is to be held in Blackwood about ten miles from here....

May 20.
...It was nine o'clock ere we went home and were taking a hasty repast when they came and told us that the Chartists were coming by. We went to look at them from the Lodge. There were only about two hundred in number, they walked in orderly manner having flags and music before them. A good many of our people were on the look out to see them return, but they did not join them, though I believe the hearts of many went with them. And thus ended all the alarm for the much dreaded meeting of Blackwood.

Lady Charlotte Guest, *Journals 1833-52*, ed. Earl of Bessborough, (John Murray: 1950).

Lady Charlotte may have been sanguine but the Chartist orator Henry Vincent was subsequently arrested and taken to gaol in Monmouth on a charge of sedition. He was the editor of the Bristol-based Western Vindicator, *the Chartist newspaper which circulated in Wales and the West Country in which he endeavoured to educate the readership about their rights and duties. After being tried and sentenced to one year in gaol he wrote the following letter in the paper suggesting future conduct to his readers.*

HENRY VINCENT to the People of the West of England and South Wales and to the Radicals of the United Kingdom.

My friends – The attainment of Universal Suffrage is worthy of any sacrifice; and it is impossible for the people to obtain without making sacrifices; but it becomes the people deeply to reflect upon the most practicable mode of action, and to decide upon the sort of sacrifice which can be best adapted to compel the Government to admit the justice of the people's claims. I have frequently shown you the folly of propping up the Government with your money: and have shown you the importance of taking your money out of the savings' banks... I have endeavoured to impress upon you the necessity of sobriety, from a conviction *that no drunkard can be a free man*... I have asked you to abstain, as far as practicable, from the use of taxed articles, such as tea, coffee, sugar, tobacco, and snuff; because these articles pay very heavy duty to our rulers, and non-consumption of these articles will materially cripple their revenue....

I am led a little further in my thinking, and come, at once, to the 'Holiday' recommended by the Convention.

I am of opinion, that, if but one-half of the working population suspended their labours, for only one week, the present state of things would be at an end....

THINK ABOUT THE HOLIDAY, PEOPLE!

And mind, if you resolve to have it, let it be as general as possible. Nearly all Wales can strike; the colliers in the North will all strike; it behoves the men and women of the West of England to decide immediately upon the line of conduct they intend to adopt....

My advice to you is to hold district meetings of men, women, and children, in every city, town and village. Let them be held immediately. Explain the importance of the holiday; and take the general opinion of the people thereon....

I am as ever,

Your very faithful friend,

Henry Vincent.

Western Vindicator, August 10th, 1839.

John Frost seems to have made valiant attempts to secure Vincent's release as the following letter from him to the then Home Secretary, the Marquis of Normanby, after submitting a resolution concerning Vincent, passed at what he said was 'one of the largest meetings ever assembled in Wales', illustrates.

JOHN FROST to Marquis of Normanby.

My Lord – I have much reason to complain of the treatment which I have received at the hands of your Lordship. At a public meeting held in Breconshire on the 12th of August a resolution was passed; that resolution was transmitted to your lordship for presentation to the Queen. Your lordship says that it is not usual to lay a resolution of a meeting before the Queen; and if an address adopting the language of the resolution, had been transmitted for presentation, your lordship would have declined laying it before Her Majesty. Why my lord? ...It begins by laying down a principle 'that when oppression exists, it is the duty of every honest man to endeavour to remove the evils, and, if possible, by peacable means?' Is this my Lord erroneous? The resolution says 'the working classes are un-justly treated'. Is this not true, my Lord? It says that the prisoners in Monmouth gaol did no more than their duty in exposing to their industrious countrymen the abuses of the present system.... Shall no petition, no address, from the people to the Queen be laid before her Majesty, if the language be displeasing to the Secretary of State?...

It is notorious to the whole country that the jury who tried the prisoners was highly prejudiced against the Chartists.... Is it consistent with your lordship's notions of justice to keep men in prison who have been found guilty by such means?

What does your lordship mean by 'indulgences consistent with the regulations of the prison?' The regulations of the prison are 'That the prisoners shall be deprived of pen, ink, books, newspapers; that they shall not see their relatives and friends; that they shall be shut up in their cells at eight in the summer and four in the winter; that their food shall be bread, skilly and potatoes'. Your lordship is asked to remove these regulations and substitute better....

I am your lordship's obedient servant,
John Frost.

Western Vindicator, September 10th, 1839.

By November Josiah John Guest was aware that alarm on the owners' part was justified. The following letter to the Marquis of Bute, who wielded patrician influence over Glamorgan, and Lady Charlotte's journals of the same time, witness the fear of the Chartist movement.

JOSIAH JOHN GUEST to Marquis of Bute.
Sunday evening, 3 Nov, 1839. Dowlais.

Dear Lord Bute,

I am sorry to inform you that the opinion which I had formed respecting the Chartists in this neighbourhood has not been confirmed. I have been very much on the look out but all the information which I received up to this day led me to suppose that Chartism was quietly subsiding.

About 6 o'clock this evening however I received intelligence that groups of men, many of them armed with pikes and bludgeons were then going over this mountain towards Nantyglo – that the Chartists of this place had been collected together and taken over in the same direction. Great alarm prevailed in the neighhourhood of Tredegar Works where they were expected to meet at midnight and it was generally reported here that a simultaneous rising of all the Chartists was to take place this evening.

At 8 o'clock I dispatched a messenger to watch their movements – On his return he reported that he saw a very large assemblage of persons near Mr Harford's house at the Sirhowy Works. He would not proceed through the crowds and was attempted to be detained but made his escape – No violence had taken place – and everything has been perfectly quiet in Dowlais and Merthyr – It is commonly rumoured that they are going over to Monmouth to release Vincent from Gaol. I shall receive further accounts before the night is over and will add any thing more that I may hear before I close this letter. 1 o'clock a.m. Every thing remains quiet and the person I have sent out reports that the Chartists are returning homewards peacably although there is great excitement in some of the Monmouthshire Works. I trust no disturbance of the peace will occur. I am
Your very faithful servant
J. John Guest.

Bute Papers, Letter Books 13 and 14, Cardiff City Library.

LADY CHARLOTTE records her impressions of the Chartist rising.

November 3, 1839.

...I have not been long returned and was sitting reading by the Library fire when Thos. Evans sent in to say he wished to speak to Merthyr. He went to him in the Hall. They talked earnestly, and – without having the slightest intention of listening, for I really thought he had merely something to say respecting the Works – my extremely quick ears caught the words 'They were making pikes all night'. This was quite enough to convince me there was some Chartist mischief going forward. I jumped up from where I sat and joined the council. It appeared that Mr Wayne, his brother and Mr Williams, of Garth Hall, had gone over in the morning to the Victoria Works; while they stopped there, several persons came in and warned Mr Wayne senr., the Manager, to go out of the way as there was going to be a general rising of the Chartists immediately. He treated it all very lightly and so did the gentleman and his sons above named. But as they were returning along this road they met many groups going over the hill, amongst whom were a number of individuals armed with guns and pikes and bludgeons. They then of course became alarmed and hastened to come and communicate here what they had heard and observed. Merthyr, immediately on hearing these particulars, sent over to acquaint other Iron Masters of this most singular and mysterious movement among the people, which had been kept so secret as not to have been even suspected until they were seen fairly upon the road. The report was that they were all hurrying to a rendezvous over the hills whence they were to proceed to Monmouth to release Vincent from gaol. The pikes above alluded to have been made in the Victoria Works.... Scouts were sent out during the rest of the evening and the ensuing night. Their reports were vague and sometimes contradictory but it seemed pretty certain that the men turned off from Beaufort towards Newbury....

November 4.

We were all up early and having breakfasted Merthyr and Mr Divett went down to the Works and thence to the village to meet the Magistrates. There were different reports arriving here all day, brought by the different people who had been sent over the Hills to reconnoitre. The only certain thing was that some had proceeded to Newport and others to Abergavenny. There were absurd rumours that the bridge was to be broken down at the latter place and all the coaches stopped... It appears that at Tredegar something of this kind had been expected. The crowds yesterday at Ebbw Vale were so large that all Mr Harford's family are said to have left the house . A public house was broken into by the mob and the landlord and his wife compelled to accompany the party some short way after which they were released. At a tradesman's house they asked for admittance which they obtained, and then expressed a wish for provisions and tobacco, having partaken of which they thanked him and went on... we had numerous messengers here with news. The substance of it was that the mob, to the number of two thousand, had attacked the military in the Westgate Inn at Newport in order to release some prisoners. The soldiers did not fire upon them until they had received one or two volleys from them, and until they had broken into the Inn ...When they came into the passage the soldiers fired, and nine men were killed on the spot and many were wounded*, three of whom died almost immediately. The Mayor of Newport and two other gentlemen were slightly wounded with the pikes of the mob. After this firing had taken place the whole of these poor deluded creatures took to flight. It appears they had buoyed themselves up with the idea that the military were favourable to them and would give up their arms into their hands the moment they appeared. It is said to have been lamentable to see the droves of these poor tired and defeated men returning from their ill-fated expedition, and the scene at Tredegar was equally distressing owing to the wailing of the women, among whom were many Irish, all ignorant of who had suffered, and fearful lest some of their friends should have been among the number of victims....

* *22 were killed and about fifty wounded.*

November 5.

...Since I began writing this long gossip about Riots Merthyr has left his sofa and gone down to the village with Mr Divett. It was reported today that there was to be a large Chartist Meeting tonight on Aberdare Hill, as I before mentioned. Merthyr, as one of the Magistrates, is gone to attend it. The Newport business appears to have been a complete rout. The poor fellows, as they fled, threw away their arms, and 200 stand of arms including pikes were picked up. There are troops at Abergavenny, Newport and Nant-y-glo....

November 9.

...There was a fresh alarm of Chartists this evening and many persons expected a rising, but thank God the night passed over quietly. Mr Jenkins was here giving us a curious account of the compulsion used by these desperate men for others to accompany them. They forced them out of their beds, and those of their party who were too tired to walk to Newport and broke down on the road, it is said, they beat and wounded with their pikes before leaving them. Some of the professors of Religion have joined them. They set off from their chapels last Sunday and I am told they pray there that God will give them the spirit of Chartism. It does seem an extraordinary infatuation. I do not believe that any but Welshmen could be brought up to such a pitch of enthusiasm....

Lady Charlotte Guest, *Journals 1833-52*, ed. Earl of Bessborough.

Lady Charlotte Guest's account reflects only her personal, narrow view. But the whole episode remains debatable. John Frost and Zephaniah Williams were made culpable – first sentenced to death and then the sentence commuted to one of transportation for fifteen years. Dr William Price is said to have escaped to France dressed in women's clothing. The evidence seems to indicate that Frost, at least, was against the proposal to march on Newport involving the possibility of a violent and uncertain encounter; but, unwilling though he may have been, he could not desert his comrades. Exasperated men, like those who wrote the missive quoted below, seem more likely candidates as instigators of the plan. Chartist activity was not confined to south-east Wales; outbreaks had already occurred in Montgomeryshire and Carmarthenshire and the following inflammatory letter is addressed to another district. Perhaps, given the brackets, duplicated to several other districts also.

CHARLES BREWE, JOHN NIBBS and THOMAS BLAND to Chartist Sympathisers in South Pembrokeshire.
November 2, 1839. The Hills near Monmouth.

Chartists and Patriots of Wales!
Hereditary bondmen know ye not
Who would free themselves must strike the blow. (Byron)
    Chartists and patriots of Wales. That time is now approaching that will give us liberty and our rights or death and destruction. No time is more momentous than the present, and under that conviction we deem it our duty to appoint a day for the discussion of the rights and liberties that we will maintain to the last hour of our existence.
    Fellow patriots and Chartists, it is your duty, a duty you owe to the welfare and preservation of your country and to the glorious liberty of the subject and that subject a Chartist, to assemble on Thursday, November 14th 1839, at Tenby on the Castle Hill at 12 at noon when we shall discuss the merits of our cause. And

    If words with argument do not succeed
    They must to Chartist arms in terror yield.

And yield they must when Liberty calls forth brave men to the field of action. Remember, patriots and Chartists, to die in such a cause will ensure your glorious immortality and you will be handed down to posterity as martyrs to the well being of your country.

Remember countrymen, fellow countrymen no longer, that to desert at such an hour you will justly deserve and will merit the hatred of the enlightened individuals composing the great mass of the British public, and an ignominious death will be your portion. With the full conviction of meeting a numerous armed assemblage of our own partisans we be to subscribe ourselves as the officiating members of the Chartist Lodge.

Pembrokeshire Life.

1839 ff.

ALFRED, LORD TENNYSON (1809-92). *Lyrical and narrative poet, appointed Poet Laureate in 1850. Tennyson had a Welsh motto in encaustic tiles on the pavement of the entrance hall to his house: Y Gwir yn erbyn y byd (The Truth against the world). The following letter was written to his future wife, Emily Sellwood, in (July?) 1839.*

ALFRED TENNYSON to Emily Sellwood.

Aberystwith.

I cannot say I have seen much worth the trouble of the journey, always excepting the Welsh-women's hats which look very comical to an English eye, being in truth men's hats, beavers, with the brim a little broad, and tied under the chin with a black ribband. Some faces look very pretty in them. It is remarkable how fluently the little boys and girls can speak Welsh, but I have seen no leeks yet, nor shot any cheeses. This place, the Cambrian Brighton, pleases me not... a sea certainly today of a most lovely blue, but with scarce a ripple. Anything more unlike the old Homeric 'much-sounding' sea I never saw. Yet the bay is said to be tempestuous. O for a good Mablethorpe breaker! I took up this morning an unhappy book of verse by a Welshman, and read therein that all which lies at present swamp and fathom-deep under the bay of Caernarvon was long ago in the twilight of history a lovely lowland, rich in woods, thick with cities. One wild night a drunken man who was a sort of clerk of the drains and sewers in his time, opened the dam-gates and let in the sea, and heaven knows how many stately palaces have ever since been filled with polyps and sea-tangle. How many gentlemen discussing after-dinner politics of that day were surprised by the precocious entrance of lobster before supper! How many young ladies playing at their prehistoric pianos ended some warm love-song of life in a quavering swan-song of death!

Barmouth.
Barmouth is a good deal prettier place than Aberystwith, a flat sand shore, a sea with breakers, looking Mablethorpelike, and sand hills, and close behind them huge crags and a long estuary with cloud-capt hills running up as far as Dolgelly, with Cader Idris on one side.

A Memoir by his son Hallam Tennyson, (Macmillan: 1897).

The following are extracts from his wife, EMILY SELLWOOD TENNYSON's *Journal and letters written when they made a long trip to Wales with their children in the summer of 1856.*

July 28th.
We drove to Bala and admired the valley beyond Llangollen, The lake a beautiful violet colour with white breakers....

August 4th.
Dolgelly. We walked into the field near the Golden Lion. A lovely field it is, encircled by bright streams, mountains beyond, a bridge and church tower in foreground covered with ivy, and Cader Idris towering with its woods over the church and the town.

Aug. 6th.
His birthday. We went to the 'Torrent Walk', a glorious view of Cader Idris over wooded hills at an opening of the road. 'His high rejoicing lines' he said of Cader Idris, he particularly liked the still pools of the torrent. Masses of willow herb and meadowsweet. The Welsh women were very demonstrative, one woman seized on little Lionel and hugged and kissed him as if she were crazy. A.T. bathed in the torrent and delighted in the clearness and in seeing the 'bottom agates' far below.

Aug.12th.
Barmouth. He said that the drive here is beautiful when the tide is in and Cader Idris not veiled in clouds. I admired the place as much as he could wish me to do, I thought I never saw anything more beautiful in its way than the mountain bank with exquisite lights and

shadows on crags and dark groves and fields. The sea and sandhills radiant with sunlight. We had a delightful walk over the cliffs. Heath gorgeous.

Aug. 20th.

...Raining all our drive to Harlech, still we could see something of the grand view of Harlech coming into the town. The castle above the marsh backed by dark wild mountains. I admired Harlech more than any other place I have yet seen in Wales.

Aug. 30th.

Drove through the misty rain to Ffestiniog. Found the poor blind harper sitting with his head on his hands resting on his harp. He played airs to the delight of the children, and afterwards floating Welsh melodies, very sad.

Sept. 2nd.

He set off with Mr Edwards over the mountains to Mr Lloyd's and saw the priceless old Welsh MSS., a Druid's egg (round and half purplish half whitish), some Bards' beads, a stone inscribed with the name of Geraint ap Erbin, a spear head like a Greek spear and three daggers found together split into a hole of rock.

Sept. 5th.

He went up Cader Idris. Pouring rain came on. We waited a long time for him. I heard the voice of waters, streams and cataracts, and I never saw anything more awful than the great veil of rain drawn straight over Cader Idris, pale light at the lower edge. It looked as if death were behind it and made me shudder when I thought he was there. A message came from him through the guide that he had gone to Dolgelly. He admired Tal-y-Llyn and saw some grand effects in going up Cader Idris but the rain spoilt his view.

CAERLEON, September 16, 1856 from a letter from TENNYSON *to his wife.*

The Usk murmurs by the windows and I sit like King Arthur in Caerleon. I came here last night from Newport. This is a most quiet half ruined village of about 1500 inhabitants with little museum of Roman tombstones and other things.

The Letters of Alfred, Lord Tennyson, Vol. II, edited by Cecil Y. Lang and Edgar F. Shannon Jr. (Clarendon Press: Oxford, 1987).

CHARLES CAVENDISH FULKE GREVILLE (1794-1865).

Politician and diarist, he was for many years Clerk to the Privy Council.
His diaries are a noted source of information about the politics of the time.

June 24th 1841. Chester.

Parliament having been dissolved yesterday, all the world are off to their elections, and I resolved to start upon an excursion to N. Wales, which I have long been desirous of seeing, and which I now do with great facility and convenience in consequence of Lord Anglesey's having established himself for a short time at Plas Newydd; so there I am bound. I was induced to make this expedition partly by my wish to see the scenery of N. Wales and the Menai Bridge, and partly from a desire to stimulate my dull and jaded mind by the exertion and the object....

Sunday, June 27th. Plas Newydd.

Left Chester at half-past eleven on Friday morning, having stopt to hear service at the Cathedral, a poor building very Ancient Saxon fine chanting, which I particularly like. A rainy day, nothing particular in the road till Conway, where the Castle is very fine, a most noble ruin, and the old walls of the town with their numerous towers, so perfect, that I doubt if there is anything like them to be seen anywhere. It presents a perfect fortress of those times (the end of the thirteenth century) and Conway is so well worth seeing, that it alone would repay the trouble of the journey. The Castle appears to have been habitable and defensible till after the Civil Wars, the great epoch of the ruin of most of these Ancient edifices. From Conway fine and striking road along the seashore, and round the base of Penmaen Mawr, a mountain nearly as high as Snowdon, crossed the Menai Bridge at dusk, but with light enough to see the wonderful work, and arrived at the place between ten and eleven o'clock. A most delightful place in the margin of the Menai Strait, with the mountains in full view, presenting as the clouds sweep round and over them, and as they are ever and anon lit up by the sun, glorious combinations and varieties of light and shade....

Tuesday, 29th.

Sunday we all went down today in the boats of Lord Anglesey's cutter to Bangor to attend the service in the Cathedral, under the Menai Bridge, which I had not been able to see on my way to Plas Newydd. A poor church at Bangor, Cathedral service, but moderate musick. The Church is divided into two, half for the English and half for the Welsh; the Nave is made the Parish church, and there the service is done in Welsh. There were very few, if any, of the common people at the English afternoon service; in fact, few of them speak anything but Welsh. It has an odd effect to see the women with their high-crowned, round hats on in Church; the dress is not unbecoming. After Church we were followed by a mob to our boats, and they cheered Lord A. when he embarked.

Monday – we walked to the Menai Bridge, where we got into a car and drove to Penrhyn Castle, a vast pile of building, and certainly very grand, but altogether, though there are fine things and some good rooms in the house, the most gloomy place I ever saw, and I could not live there if they would make me a present of the Castle. It is built of a sort of grey stone polishable into a kind of black marble, of which there are several specimens within. It is blocked up with trees, and pitch dark, but it never can be otherwise than gloomy. We then went to the ferry, and got a boat in which we sailed over to Beaumaris and went up Baron's Hill [Sir Richard Bulkeley's], with which I was delighted. The house is unfinished and ugly, but the situation and prospect over the bay of Beaumaris are quite beautiful. Nothing can be more chearful, and the whole scene around, sea, coast and mountains, indescribably beautiful. They compare this bay to the bay of Naples, and I do not know that there is any presumption in the comparison. Just below the house is the Old Castle of Beaumaris, a very remarkable ruin, in great preservation, both the Castle and the surrounding wall. Drove home in another car; which are most convenient conveyances and in general use in these parts.

Tuesday – this morning at eight o'clock went with Lord Anglesey in the 'Pearl' to Carnarvon, where he was, as Constable of the Castle, to receive an address. All the town assembled to receive him, and he was vociferously cheered and saluted with musick, firing of guns, procession of societies, and all the honours the Carnarvonites could show him. After the ceremony went to see the Castle, which is much finer and larger, as well as in better preservation, than Conway, but not in so grand a situation.... We then sailed about in the cutter and saw Snowdon and the other Snowdonian mountains very advantageously.

Friday, July 2nd.
On Wednesday went on an excursion to see the country.... We then went all round Snowdon; but the weather got so bad in the afternoon

that ascending the mountain was out of the question. Nothing can be finer than the scenery between Beddgelert and Llanberis, and the latter is very wild and picturesque, though I was a little disappointed with the lakes... I have never travelled in any country which appeared more completely foreign. The road from Beddgelert is perfectly Alpine in character, and the peasantry neither speak nor understand anything but Welsh, so that it is impossible to hold any communication with them. The women, in point of costume, have no resemblance to English women. Besides the round hats which they almost all wear, and which, though not unbecoming, give them a peculiar air, a great many, though not all of them, wear a sort of sandal on their feet, without soles I believe, but with something bound round their naked feet, the nature and purpose of which I could not exactly make out. The women are generally good-looking, with a vigorous frame, and a healthy chearful aspect; and all the common people are decent in their appearance and particularly civil and respectful in their manner. The cars, which have in great measure taken the place of postchaises, are very convenient, though, being totally uncovered, are only fit for fine weather. The horses which draw them – one horse – are excellent, and they go very fast; but the charge for them is enormous – a shilling a mile.

It is really extraordinary that the English language has not made its way more among the mass of the people. It is spoken at all the inns, but, with the exception of people employed about the house or grounds of a proprietor, very few speak it, and many of those in his employment are wholly ignorant of it.... The country seems to be very ill-provided with schools, nor is English taught at all in those which do exist. Nothing can be less advanced than education in these parts. The Welsh are generally poor and wages are low; their food consists principally of potatoes and butter-milk; the average wage of labour is about nine shillings a week. The people, however, are industrious, sober, contented, and well-behaved; they do not like either change or locomotion, and this makes them indifferent about learning English. They would rather remain where they have been accustomed to work, and live upon smaller wages, than go a few miles off to Carnarvon, where they might earn a couple of shillings a week more. The new Poor Law is only in partial operation here. There is a workhouse at Pwlhelly, and there are Boards of Guardians and all the machinery requisite; but the law is unpopular, and it has never been rigidly and universally enforced. The people are extremely averse to its establishment, and the old system works well enough, for which reasons its operation has not been much meddled with, and they hope that some expedient will be found to prevent its being carried into effect here.

The Greville Memoirs 1840-1860, eds. Lytton Strachey and Roger Fulford (Macmillan: 1938).

1842

CHARLES DARWIN (1809-82), *author of the* Origin of the Species *and the* Descent of Man.

To W.H. Fitton.
c. June 28, 1842. Capel Curig, N. Wales.

Yesterday (and the previous days) I had some most interesting work in examining the marks left by extinct glaciers – I assure you no extinct volcano could hardly leave more evidence of its activity and vast powers. I found one with the lateral moraine quite perfect, which Dr. Buckland did not see. Pray, if you have any comunication with Dr. Buckland, give him my warmest thanks for having guided me, through the published extract of his memoir, to scenes, and made me understand them, which have given me more delight, than I almost ever remember to have experienced, since I first saw an extinct Crater – The valley about here, and the Inn, at which I am now writing, must once have been covered by at least 800 or 1000 ft in thickness of solid Ice! – Eleven years ago, I spent a whole day in the valley, where yesterday every thing but the ice of the Glacier was palpably clear to me, and then I saw nothing but plain water, and bare Rock. These glaciers have been grand agencies; I am the more pleased with what I have seen in N. Wales, as it convinces me that my views, of the distribution of the boulders on the S. American *plains* having been effected by floating Ice, are correct. I am also more convinced that the valleys of Glen Roy & the neighbouring parts of Scotland have been occupied by arms of the Sea, & very likely, (for on that point I cannot *of course* doubt Agassiz & Buckland) by glaciers also.

The Correspondence of Charles Darwin, Vol. II, 1837-43, (Cambridge University Press: 1986).

The REBECCA RIOTS, *whose causes and course have been exhaustively and fascinatingly described by historians in recent years, occurred, for the most part, during the years 1839-43. Several grievances provoked them: in part, the accumulated effects of the depressed state of the agricultural community in West Wales; in part, the implementation of the Poor Law Act of 1834 which forbade the giving of home relief to the needy, substituting instead the universally loathed workhouses; and, more particularly, the insufferable burden caused by the extensive building of many toll gates along the roads. The purpose of the tolls was the maintenance of the highways but numerous companies were involved in the scheme and it seems to have been wide open to mismanagement or corruption. It became the objective of the rioters, often dressed in women's clothes, (traditionally worn with the Ceffyl Pren – an old form of dispensing rough justice which involved a wooden horse or some substitute for it) to destroy the gates. The protesters are thought to have possibly derived their name from Genesis 24:60: 'And they blessed Rebekah and said unto her... let thy seed possess the gate of those who hate them.' Despite attempts to identify a particular leader of the Rebeccaites over the years, it seems there may only have been key figures at certain times and places who adopted the sobriquet. The following letter is from a solicitor, not without sympathy for the Rebeccaites but who was also concerned that the Home Office should understand the seriousness of the situation.*

Letter to the Home Secretary from EDWARD CROMPTON LLOYD HALL, Newcastle Emlyn attorney.
June 15th, 1843.

On my return home this afternoon I found a deputation of about twenty farmers, residing in six or seven different parishes in this neighbourhood, waiting to consult me on ye steps I should deem it most advisable for them and those whom they represented to pursue in consequence of a number of letters having been sent in by or in ye name of ye organised band known as Rebecca and her daughters, commanding them to appear at Carmarthen on Monday next, the 19th of June with their servants and under-tenants, on pain of having their houses pulled down if they dare to absent themselves.

The men appeared quite terrified at ye threat, and with reason, as 'Rebecca' is almost nightly at work pulling down ye turnpike houses, and one house belonging I believe to Mr Saunders Davies, M.P. with all ye furniture was burnt to ye ground three or four nights ago in consequence of ye tenant having done something to give offence to Rebecca.

If her Majesty's Ministers think there is nothing more in these disturbances than a mere local impatience of Turnpike Tolls, they are deceived.

To judge of all ye Welsh and their feelings and modes of thought and action by anything by which an Englishman is acquainted would only lead to error. That they have had great local injustices in many things is too apparent, and unfortunately there is no middle class in the country districts to bind society together. Ye few gentlemen resident here are widely scattered, their homes being in but few instances less than four miles from each others. Ye consequence is that each among his own tenantry is a petty prince, whose word, be it right or wrong, has hitherto been law; and there being hardly any distinction between ye farmers and their labourers, and their language isolating them from the rest of ye Kingdom, they have scarcely emerged from ye state of comparative barbarism and poverty induced by ye internal troubles of this part of ye country.

This being ye case, and ye unfortunate measures of ye Government having fallen upon us with a severity unknown to ye rest of England, ye farmers are pinched in their means, and as ye Turnpike tolls are most extraordinarily heavy and ye gates placed upon ye most catching system throughout this country, they naturally endeavour to relieve themselves of that burden. There being a custom in this part of ye country called 'Ceffil Prens' (derived from ye old Welsh law abolished by ye introduction of ye English law in ye latter part of ye reign of Henry ye 8th), ye mode of getting rid of such a grievance by nocturnal violence is perfectly familiar to their minds.

As to getting evidence against them, that is hopeless. In ye best of times it is difficult to make a Welshman speak ye truth, either with or without an oath, no doubt attributable to ye curious provisions of ye old Welsh laws, traditionary reminiscences of which still remain. Ye offer of a reward, however great, has I believe never been known to produce any effect in this country.

If this state of things is not repressed very shortly, ye effects of Rebecca will, I have no doubt, be directed to other matters; for ye dissatisfaction with ye mode of administering justice and ye laying on of taxation of all kinds is such throughout ye whole of this part of ye country that it is quite palpable they only want leaders to effect a thorough revolution. The people have thus discovered their immense power without knowing how to use it constitutionally.

Letter to Home Secretary, 15 June, 1843. Public Record Office HO 45/454.

Colonel Love who had been in command of the troops who put down the Merthyr Rising and who had also suppressed riots in Bristol, was commanded to go to Carmarthen and assess the turbulent situation there. On 21st June, 1843, he wrote:

COLONEL LOVE to the Home Office.

...sufficient has transpired to convince me that the whole affair of the Trusts demands a strict enquiry. That in general there has been great maladministration is evident, and in very many instances double the toll authorised by Law has been levied by the collectors. It is not for me to suggest what should be done, although I am strongly of the opinion that a strict enquiry would be beneficial to the public and tend perhaps more anxiously than anything else to allay the discontent so generally felt by the farmers.

COLONEL LOVE to the Home Office.
11 July, 1843.

The hostile feeling of the farmers to the payment of the tolls (exorbitant in many instances) was materially increased by the distress of the farmers themselves caused by the high rents, poor and church rates, which together with the very great depreciation in the agricultural produce of the country left them in many instances unable to meet the demands against them, or leaving them without any money after having done so. The increased tolls therefore became a greater hardship as, from the want of money, instances occurred where the farmer having purchased lime could not transport it to his farm from the expense of the tolls....

It is contended that from the improved state of the roads, two horses can now do the work of three, and one horse the work of two, which brings the toll charges nearly to what they were before. But this is very difficult to make the Welshman understand, particularly those who have only one horse....

This made the people reckless and from the destroying gates with impunity they proceeded to acts of greater violence and mixed up what had only in the first instance been a simple case of complaint (which if taken in time might easily have been settled) with the poor laws, tithes and rents, and there is now I regret to say a spirit abroad ready for any mischief – one which nothing at present but the presence of a military force can suppress or keep down.

Nearly the whole of the agricultural inhabitants of the surrounding country sympathise with the rioters, even those who do not join them. Under these circumstances the magistrates, from finding great difficulty in obtaining special constables, are naturally less energetic than we could wish, and rely too much on the military.... The accounts from the Monmouth hills are by no means satisfactory, and if the Ebbw Vale works which have lately failed should be suddenly stopped, great distress and consequent disturbance may be anticipated.

I have ascertained for certain that people connected with the Rebeccaites have been to Merthyr Tydfil and that some Chartists from that place have been into north Wales as well as here, also that people from Ireland connected with agitators in that country have been to Merthyr and the Neighbourhood. There are some Chartists in this town but I do not believe that the farmers have as yet anything to do with them.

There is a report prevalent amongst the people both in this and the Mining Districts (but possibly without foundation) that a general rising is to take place in the middle of August, when it is supposed that the state of Ireland will give more than sufficient occupation for the Troops, and all the speeches of the Chartists tend to this belief....

Pat Molloy, *And They Blessed Rebecca* (Llandysul: Gomer, 1983).

Letter left secretly in the office of the Welshman *and published in its issue of September 1st, 1843.*

The people, the masses to a man throughout the three counties of Carmarthen, Cardigan, and Pembroke are with me. Oh yes, they are all my children. When I meet the lime-men on the road covered with sweat and dust, I know they are Rebeccaites. When I see the coalmen coming to town clothed in rags, hard worked and hard fed, I know they are mine, these are Rebecca's children. When I see the farmers' wives carrying loaded baskets to market, bending under the weight, I know well that these are my daughters. If I turn into a farmer's house and see them eating barley bread and drinking whey, surely, say I, these are members of my family, these are the oppressed sons and daughters of Rebecca.

David Williams, *The Rebecca Riots* (Cardiff: University of Wales Press, 1971).

In the following letter to a friend, the BISHOP OF ST. DAVID'S *advanced his views of the situation.*

September 16th, 1843. Abergwili.

...The well-known road to Abergwili presented only one object to attract any particular attention and that a very melancholy one: a turnpike and toll-house close to Abergwili, recently demolished by Rebecca. One or two articles of furniture were still remaining in a corner of the ruins. Such is the spirit of the times that after the destruction of the house, the collector who also carried on the business of a bookbinder at Carmarthen, could not prevail on any of his neighbours to help him to remove his furniture. At last a stranger consented to let him have the use of his cart for that purpose. But when they arrived at Carmarthen, a mob assembled round the cart, cut the traces, threw the furniture into the street, and were with difficulty withheld from maltreating the owner of the cart. Not content with this they broke open the collector's house, and scattered the books they found there about the street,... Since that the appearance of things has been growing worse and worse. You may judge of it by one specimen. A few days ago Rebecca's emissaries set fire to the cottage of a poor old woman who received the toll at a gate. None of her neighbours would help her to put out the fire, though she assured them "it was not much". But hearing her say this the incendiaries returned to complete the work. It seems that she then gave them to understand that she knew them upon which they instantly lodged the contents of several guns in her head, and she expired almost immediately. A coroner's inquest sat on her body which presented a shocking spectacle, the head being dreadfully shattered. The verdict they returned was to the effect that she died a natural death, through a suffusion of blood in the chest. It was previously believed that no Welsh jury would venture to give a verdict unfavourable to Rebecca, and now the fact is placed beyond a doubt. There is on the one side perfect impunity from the law, on the other no protection from outrages. In fact, nobody who has anything to lose considers either his property or his life secure.... There has been much speculation about the causes of this deplorable state of things and a general disposition to refer it to certain alleged abuses. But I believe I may venture to say, on the concurrent authority of all the persons I have met with who possess the best means of information, that the real cause is very different. Abuses there certainly have been in the management of the turnpike trusts, and perhaps in other matters as the administration of the new poor Law. But it is clear that they have been nothing more than the occasion or often the pretext of the outbreak, and in a different state of things would hardly have excited anything but a slight feeling of discontent which would probably in the end have found some lawful and peacable way of venting itself. The real cause of the present evil is to be sought in the weather of the years 1839-40, in the first of which the crops in this part of Wales were utterly destroyed, and in the second very nearly so, by the rain and floods. The farmers, originally poor, have never recovered from the blow; their distress has rendered them almost reckless and desperate. Believing themselves aggrieved in some points, they resort to illegal combinations at first with a specific object, but now, it would seem, with a general indefinite view of mending their condition by means of a system of intimidation, which up to the moment, they have pursued, notwithstanding the presence of a large military force, with complete success....

Letters Literary and Theological, Connop Thirlwall (Late Lord Bishop of St. David's), ed. J.J. Stewart and Louis Stokes (1881).

But the military force did, not surprisingly, have the upper hand in the end. In early September a riot at Pontarddulais resulted in the capture of several Rebeccaites whose trial in Cardiff took place at the end of October and resulted in their transportation to Australia. Two more suffered the same fate but others who were arraigned were treated with surprising lenience. The Goverment had set up investigations into the disturbances which revealed the many abuses in the turnpike trusts and the widespread hatred of the tithes and the new Poor Law. Rebecca had had an effect and things improved – but not for all as the following comments from Lady Charlotte Guest, writing in her journal, reveal.

LADY CHARLOTTE GUEST – Journal.

December 6, 1843. Sully.

In going up to town Merthyr had crossed over in the packet with the Rebecca Convicts. The personifyer of Rebecca himself was among them. Hearing that Merthyr was on board he asked leave to speak with him, and they had an interesting conversation in which he begged advice as to his best course. Merthyr recommends his being as quiet and giving as little trouble as possible, and above all this, being careful to confine himself as strictly to the truth in any communication he might make as to the transactions which had terminated so fatally for him. The poor man entered into a long statement of the agricultural grievances of his neighbourhood which appeared to be very great.... His astonishment at first seeing a ship, or steamer, is said to have been very great, and his perplexities on the Railway at the train moving without horses quite unassuagable. 'Steam?' asked he. 'What is steam?' Under all this excitement his spirits kept up bravely until he arrived in town and was shown the place of his confinement. 'What, in that little narrow hole? Why, it was impossible to live in that!' And his heart seemed at once to be crushed within him and every hope extinguished. Well might the free child of the mountain shudder and sicken at the sight of that cold and narrow cell!

December 11.
On Monday Merthyr went into Cardiff to meet the Commissioners appointed to enquire into the grievances through which this poor Rebeccaite is transported for one and twenty years!...

The following is a letter from Lady Charlotte Guest's 'personifyer of Rebecca', JOHN HUGHES, written, together with his fellow prisoners, from Cardiff Gaol on November 1st., 1843. Their hope must have been that it would mitigate their sentences; the hope of the authorities that it would deter others as it was issued as a handbill in Welsh and English.

To the Public generally, and to our Neighbours in particular.

We, John Hughes, David Jones, and John Hugh, now lying in Cardiff gaol, convicted of the attack on Pontardulais turnpike gate, and the police stationed there to protect it – being now sentenced to transportation, beg and earnestly call on others to take warning by our fate, and to stop in their mad course, before they fall into our condemnation.

We are guilty and doomed to suffer, while hundreds have escaped. Let them, and every one, take care not to be deluded again to attack public or private property, and resist the power of the law, for it will overtake them with vengeance, and bring them down to destruction.

We are only in prison now, but in a week or two shall be banished as rogues – to be slaves to strangers in a strange land. We must go, in the prime of life, from our dear homes, to live and labour with the worst of villains – looked upon as thieves.

Friends – neighbours – all – but especially young men – keep from night meetings! Fear to do wrong, and dread the terrors of the judge.

Think of what we *must*, and you *may suffer* before you *dare* to do as we have done.

If you will be peaceable, and live again like honest men, by the blessing of God, you may expect to prosper; and we, poor outcast wretches, may have to thank you for the mercy of the Crown – for on no other terms than your good conduct will any pity be shewn to us, or others who fall into our almost hopeless situation.

These Rebeccaites and others suffered but not wholly in vain. A commission was set up in the autumn to examine the situation, the law on the turnpikes was changed and further ameliorative legislation was passed.

1843 ff.

THOMAS CARLYLE (1795-1881). *Historian, biographer and social critic, Carlyle was one of the most eminent Victorian writers. His sojourns in Wales produced some lively letters to his wife, Jane Welsh Carlyle.*

THOMAS CARLYLE to his wife.
Llandough, Cowbridge.
Thursday Night, 6th July, 1843.

Dearest,
...I got down in good time to my Cardiff Steamer; a brisk breezy morning promising well: and again after endless ringing of bells and loading of hampers, and bullying and jumbling, in which I took part only as a distant onlooker, we got off down the muddy Avon once more. I passed a most silent day, remembrances of all kinds and these only my occupation. On the Somersetshire shore we passed a bathing-establishment: hapless Mothers of families sitting on the folding-stools by the beach of muddy tide-streams, Ach Gott! It is a solitary sea the Severn one; we passed near only one ship, and in that there lay a cabin boy sound asleep amid ropes, and a black-visaged sailor had raised his shock-head only half awake, thro' the hatches, to see what we were: they lay there waiting for a wind. I smoked 2 cigars and a half; I hummed all manner of tunes, sang even portions of Psalms in a humming tone for my own behoof, reclining on my elbow; and so the day wore on, and at three o'clock we got into Cardiff Dock; and I, sharp on the outlook, descried the good Redwood waiting there. He had a *tub gig,* a most indescribable thin-bodied semi-articulate but altogether helpful kind of factotum man-servant, who stept on board for my luggage, and so in a few

minutes, after giving a glance at Cardiff Castle, and buying a few cigars, we got eagerly to the road, and not long after five, had done our twelve miles and were safe here. It was the beautifullest day; a green pleasant country full of shrubby knolls and white thatched cottages: altogether a very reasonable drive. Unexpectedly in a totally solitary spot I was bidden dismount, and looking to the right, saw close by the Redwood Mansion. A house about the capacity of Craigenputtock tho' in Welsh style, all trim-shaven, covered with roses, hedged off from the Parish-road by invisible fences and a park of very pretty lawn. The old Lady an innocent native old Quakeress received me with much kind simplicity, asked for *you* etc.: our dinner which she had carefully cooked, and kept hot for an hour and a half consisted of VEAL! Nay I heard of a veal-pie for future use; I suppose they have killed a fatted calf for me, knowing my tastes! There was good *ham* and a dish of good boiled peas and a pudding: I did very well. And then we have been to *walk* since; and the place on the whole is the loveliest and most *silent* in all the Earth, and I think I shall learn to do very well. But here in the meanwhile are tidings of a *dish of hot milk*.... Keep well, and dream of me.

Llandough, 8th July, 1843.

...Yesterday and today have been showery, unfavourable for excursions or making acquaintance with a new country; neither have I slept well, or till today got anything but *veal to dine on*: nevertheless I get along tolerably well, and shall make out my visit, I think, in a reasonable manner... they are very kind to me, very quiet with me: the whole country is of a totally *somnolent* nature, not ill fitted for a man that has come out to see if he can find any sleep!

Yesterday, the breezy morning soon settled down into dim showers of rain: Redwood, at his fixed hour (for he goes like an eight-day clock) returned duly from his office at Cowbridge, and took me off to St. Donat's shores for a bathe, and dinner in his lodging at that village. He has a most lively cantering pony for me: he seems to keep a kind of farm, and has several horses and nondescript serving men not a few. Our road was an inextricable series of lanes, with which the whole country seems to be covered; some two yards wide, of precipitous steepness and the *worst* macadamization I ever experienced in this Planet. My brave pony did not stumble at all; nay seemed entirely indifferent to road, and gallops much at its ease over mere stone-heaps mud-gullies or wherever the direction may be. We passed thro' several hamlets, all littery, unswept, bestrewn with chance stones and pieces of old carts; yet whitened, slated on the *ends*, or well thatched – an air of picturesqueness and sluttish beauty about them; *laziness* and sleep their chief feature. Old castles were not wanting; all grown with ivy, patched sometimes into a kind of farm houses; the people, tho' were many houses, did not appear anywhere: perhaps they were asleep. Devonshire hills lay across the sea, somewhat as Lothian does from Fife. The sea itself when we arrived at it was moaning hoarse, loud and far, over an endless *cairn* of big boulder stones, without a bit of sand or flat ground visible anywhere: a baddish outlook for bathing, unless you meant to play the Leander there! I did step cautiously in, however, then knelt and the big wave of a respectable drab-colour swashed satisfactorily over me, and again over me (filling my very mouth that second time), whereupon I withdrew. My clothes were in a cavern screened from the rain; then, after dressing, I sat perfectly dry, and smoked a cigar not without comfort. One ship was visible in the distance, making out for Ilfracombe or God knows whither: living creature or trace of living creature was none: one of the loneliest wastes in all her Majesty's dominions. Thro' rain we picked our way up again over the cliffs; got into R's lodgings and found spread out for dinner the prophecied *veal-pie* and nothing more! I ate some of it, under spoken protest, and drank three glasses of excellent wine. This and the gallop home again jumbled me considerably; and today I have had to go upon diet, pill-box and teetotalism. No more veal will be presented me here.

Llandough, 11th July, 1843.

...Yesternight in my gallop I came, about a mile to the west or north west of this, upon a beautiful little hamlet or village, all hanging in a straggle on the two sides of a green chasm or ravine, with a white Church-tower atop; the name of it Llanblethian: here, as R. cursorily informed me after my return 'a Mr Star*l*ing once lived, who wrote afterwards, as was said, in the *Times*!' By heaven, I believe it is a fact; for John Sterling* once described the place of his boyhood to me exactly as this is! A new interest is added to Llanblethian; I will go and see it another time before all is done. But now two o'clock being near, I will smoke and wait for Letter. A bathe I suppose comes next. The weather is grey but warm tho' windy. *Before* dinner *I will ride*, not after....

* John Sterling (1806-44). *Carlyle wrote a* Life *of Sterling who was his close friend.*

Llandough, 15th July, Saturday, 1843.

About the time you read this on Monday (that is, towards noon). I shall, it may be hoped, be getting myself planted on the outside of the mail for Carmarthen, about to bid adieu to these *inanaia regna*. The distance before me is some sixty miles: the direction as you may see by turning up the maps of Wales in that Atlas of mine, is north by west; we are to get thither it seems about nine o'clock at night; the Bishop's place, Abergwili, seems to be some mile or two farther. You will bid me good speed! You will have a Letter swiftly under way for me 'Care of the Lord Bishop of St. David's, Carmarthen'; will you not? Swift, swift! I will write you next day from that place; that is to say, on Tuesday, and you will get it on Thursday....

Nothing can be better than my mornings; perfectly alone under the shade of big trees; looking out over the Earth, seeing 'Nature budding, Percy!', and a few Welsh bodies of both sexes, in brown discoloured and indeed quite ruinous hats and costumes, straddling about assiduous at haymaking. I read even Lyell with the 'same relish'! But then indeed comes the afternoon and dinner, or some St. Donat's or the like: such a life is too good to last forever.

Yesterday passed as the brightest beautifullest day in the whole year might do in these circumstances. I had an excellent four hours till two o'clock; then an excellent solitary gallop to a solitary sea-shore, a dip in the eternal element there, and gallop back again. The world was all bright as a jewel set in polished silver and sunshine; the sky so purified by the past day's thunder. The little hamlet of Aberdaw, a poor grey clachan crouched under the shelter of a kind of knoll the half of which was eaten sheer off by the sea, 'poor Aberdaw'! I said to myself, 'thou sittest there ill enough bested, God help thee!' The bits of Welsh women with their cuddies, lugging small merchandise about, a very scrubby kind of figures, seemed highly praiseworthy, humanly pitiable to me. The wood is beautiful when you see it from the knoll-tops, soft, green, yet shaggy and bushy, and sunshine kisses all things: and the upper Moors themselves (dull blunt hilly regions) look sapphire in the distance, and I am *not* to go thither with R!...

Llandough, 16th July, 1843 (Sunday-Night, 10 o' clock).

Yet a few last words before quitting this place! I have had, as usual, a divine forenoon, lying under shady trees in the most exquisite summer atmosphere; and then a most laborious afternoon, bathing, galloping, dining, talking; till now when I ought to proceed to pack and arrange if I did not prefer scribbling to Goody, still a word or two....

But I must not scribble and babble in this manner; at such an hour. Tomorrow at noon I have to be on the roof of the Mail at Cowbridge. A day of hot travel. I shall certainly not be lodged so quietly anywhere. There will be rapid spiritual conversation in the Bishop's; and no green tree with Book and Tobacco to lodge under... Redwood has been entirely hospitable to me; is sorry that I should go; speculates on my coming back etc. as a proximate event: ah me! The old Mother too is very venerable to me. Poor old woman, with her *yearly Monitors*, with her suet dumplings, and all her innocent household good!...

Abergwili, Carmarthen, 18th July, 1843.

My Dearest,

I have been in many 'new positions'; but this of finding myself in a Bishop's Palace so-called, and close by the Chapel founded by old Scarecrow LAUD* of famous memory, is one of the newest! Expect no connected account of the thing, nor of anything whatever today: I have not yet learned the *airts* of the place in the least; and it is a morning of pouring rain; and in one hour (at noon) the brave Bishop, be the weather what it may, decides on riding with me 'four hours and a half' thro' the wildest scenery of the country, that *it* may not suffer by the tempestuous nature of the elements.... Heavens, do but think, I was awoke before seven o'clock, after a short sleep, by a lackey coming in haste, to indicate that I must come and say my prayers in Laud's Chapel of St. John! I did go accordingly, and looked at it and myself with wonder and amazement....

Abergwili is a village of pitiful dimension, all daubed as usual with whitewash and yellow-ochre; it is built however like a common village, on both sides of the public road: at the farther end of it, you come to solemn large closed gates of wood; on your shout they open, and you enter upon a considerable glebe-land *pleasance*, with the usual trees, turf, walks, peacocks etc., and see at fifty yards distance a long irregular (perhaps *cross* shaped) edifice, the porch of it surmounted by a stone *mitre*: ach Gott I was warmly welcomed; tho' my Bishop did seem a little uneasy too, but how could he help it!...

* Bishop of St. David's, *later Archbishop of Canterbury; beheaded by the Puritans in 1644.*

Abergwili, 19th July, 1843 (Wednesday).

My dearest,

...We sallied out yesterday in the midst of thick rain, on two horses, mine was the highest I ever rode.... We rode for four mortal hours; no trotting permitted, except when I contrary to all politeness, went off into a *voluntario,* and then had soon to lie-to for my Host, who rides somewhat ecclesiastically. What was worse too, my high horse was in the fiercest humour for riding, and I longed immensely to take the temper out of him; but no, we plodded along, and saw a circle of views. Views very good; vallies, scrubby or woody hills, old churches, and ragged Welsh characters in torn hats; all very good; but tho' the rain abated, and finally subsided into mud, and soapy dimness, I was glad enough to get home! And today again, while the weather is bright we are to renew the operation at 3 o'clock. Well, and I am very glad I came by this establishment, even at the expense of sleep. Nothing similar had ever before fallen in my way; and it was worth seeing once. Do but think of a wretched scarecrow face of Laud looking down on us, from Laud's own house that once was, as we sit at meat! And there is so much good in all that I see; a *perfection of Form*, which is not without its value. With the Bishop himself, I, keeping a strict guard on my mode of utterance, not mode of thinking, get on extremely well... on the whole right good company, and so we fare along, in all manner of discourse, and even laugh a good deal together. Could I but sleep; but then I never can!

Second Visit to Wales,
Boverton, Cowbridge, S. Wales.

Friday, 2nd August, 1850
[written after visiting Walter Savage Landor at Bath on his way to Wales.]

...Landor was in his room, in a fine quiet street like a New Town Edinburgh one, waiting for me, attended only by a nice Bologna dog. Dinner not far from ready; his apartments all hung round with queer old Italian pictures; the very doors had pictures on them. Dinner was elaborately simple. The brave Landor forced me to talk too much, and we did very near a bottle of claret, besides two glasses of sherry; far too much liquor and excitement for a poor fellow like me. However he was really stirring company: a proud, irascible, trenchant, yet generous, veracious, and very dignified old man, quite a ducal or royal man in the temper of him....

Boverton, 7th August, 1850.

Thanks, Dearest, you are very good and punctual! I got your long Letter yesterday, with its manifold inclosures, and here today, about the same hour (12½ p.m.) comes the magnificent bathing cap, which, please Heaven, I will try in the Bristol Channel tomorrow morning. Today I *have* bathed very early indeed, between 6 and 7, I should say; for my sleep was broken: subsidiary cocks here come to the onslaught (I think), beside swine, oxen, asses, carts: add to which I *had a pill in me*; and this house seems absolutely incapable of ventilation, my poor bedroom with the window open all day has still a close smell: on the whole, I woke wretched about half past 4; and after vain efforts for another hour and a half, gave it up; went into the blessed sunshine (one of the loveliest mornings), and had a beautiful bathe, looking over into Devonshire.... Poor Redwood is kind to a degree, but also fussy and *fiky* (Sc. fidgety) beyond measure; and of a dulness – *ach Gott*, quite gaunt, and as it were approaching the sublime. He waits even now with horses; having decided to give me this *whole* day (bless him), and take me to 'Dunraven Castle' and I know not what....

Boverton, 16th August, 1850.

We accomplished our expedition yesterday; saw the Valley of the Taff in all its beauty, and the foul sulphurous Purgatorio of Merthyr Tydvil in all its ugliness: a laborious business, from six in the morning till 11 at night, hard work without interval; it is in this way that mortal creatures seek 'diversions' for themselves! But it was not of my doing; nay, I find, after all, it will be well worth while to have seen Merthyr, for surely under the canopy there are few stranger things in the way of human town than it is. In 1755, Merthyr Tydvil was a mountain Hamlet of 5 or 6 houses, stagnant and silent as it has been ever since Tydvil (the King's or *Laird's* daughter) was *martyred* there, say 1300 years before: but about that time a certain Mr Bacon, a cunning Yorkshireman, passing that way, discovered there was iron in the ground, iron and coal; he took a 99 years lease in consequence: and in brief there are now about 50,000 grimy mortals, black and clammy with soot and sweat, screwing out a livelihood for themselves in that spot of the Taff Valley. Such a set of unguided, hardworked, fierce and miserable-looking sons and daughters of Adam as I never saw before. Ah me, it is like a vision of *Hell*, and will never leave me, that of those poor creatures broiling, all in sweat and dirt, amid their furnaces, pits and rolling mills. For here is absolutely *no* 'aristocracy', or guiding class; nothing but one or two huge Ironmasters, and the rest are operatives, petty shopkeepers, Scotch hawkers etc. etc. Our Innkeeper (a Bath man) was the most like a gentleman I saw. The Town might be (and will be) one of the prettiest places in the world; and it is one of the sootiest, squalidest and ugliest, all cinders and dust-mounds and soot; their very greens they bring from Bristol, tho' the ground is excellent all round: nobody thinks of *gardening* in such a locality, all devoted to metallic gambling.

Letters to his Wife, ed. Trudy Bliss (Gollancz: 1953).

1844 ff.

FRANCES WILLIAMS WYNN *(daughter of Sir Watkins Williams Wynn one of the long succession of baronets who, at one time, gained the appellation 'the Uncrowned Kings of North Wales').*
An extract from her diary.

Bodryddan: August 1844.
 From Angharad Lloyd★ I have heard a story which is worth recording. Her sister, Helen Lloyd, was (through the interest of Lady Crewe, I believe) governess to the younger daughter of the Duke of Clarence [later William IV]. He, as was his custom, lived with her on terms of familiar intimacy and friendship from the time of her first presentation to the day of his death. He had expressed a strong preference for his second name of Henry, which he liked much better than that of William. The day after the death of George IV, Miss Helen Lloyd met the king at the house of Lady Sophia Sydney; she asked him familiarly whether he was to be proclaimed as King William or King Henry. 'Helen Lloyd,' he replied, 'that question has been discussed in the Privy Council and it has been decided in favour of King William'. He added that the decision had been mainly influenced by the idea of an old prophecy of which he had never heard before, nor had he any evidence that it had ever been made. The drift of the prophecy was that as Henry VIII 'had pulled down monks and cells, Henry IX would pull down bishops and bells'. Helen exclaimed, 'I have seen that in an old book at home'. The King was astonished and pleased; he desired her to send for the book as soon as possible. Diligent search was made for it, but unhappily it was not discovered till after the King's death. "It was found by me, A.L."
 Thus far Angharad; she sent me the book to look at.

A Briefe View of the State of the Church of England as it stood in Queen Elizabeth's and King James his Reigne, to the Yeare 1608. Being a Character and History of the Bishops of those Times, and may serve as an additional Supply to Dr Goodwin's Catalogue of Bishops. Written for the use of Prince Henry upon the occasion of that Proverb –

Herny VIII pulled down Monks and their Cells,
Henry IX should pull down Bishops and their Bells.

By Sir John Harrington of Kilston, near Bath, Knight London, printed for J. Keston, St. Paul's Churchyard, 1653.

In the life of Dr Underhill, in this book, I find, 'I should go from Rochester to St. David's in Wales, save I must bait a little out of my way at four new bishoprics erected by King Henry VIII, of famous memory, and therefore I hope not ordained to be dissolved of a Henry IX, of future and fortunate expectation....'

* Angharad Lloyd – *a Welsh lady from Rhyl, celebrated for her knowledge of the Welsh language and antiquities.*

Diaries of a Lady of Quality, Frances Williams Wynn (1864).

1850

In March and April, 1850, a remarkable series of Letters on the Mining and Manufacturating Districts of South Wales *from a Special Correspondent appeared in the* Morning Chronicle. *They were part of a group of articles dealing with the situation of Labour and the Poor in many parts of the British Isles. The correspondents from all the other districts have been identified but the identity of the visitor to Wales has never been discovered. He produced a detailed and fascinating survey for the readers of the newspaper. South Wales particularly engaged his attention and there it was the conditions of life in Merthyr Tydfil which appalled him as, indeed, they shocked other investigators. He was at pains to declare his impartiality but his human sympathies are clear from the outset. He made his visit some months after a virulent outbreak of cholera and his first letter was published on March 4th, 1850.*

Charged with the duty of reporting upon the condition of the labouring classes and the poor throughout the Principality of Wales,

I direct my attention, in the first instance, to the great ironworks and collieries of South Wales because these occupy by far the most important and interesting division of this country, as regards the purposes of my inquiry, and also because, as will be seen in the course of my Letters, they stand most in need of an early investigation....

There are now employed in the works at Merthyr and Dowlais, under and above ground, about 20,000 hands. The labour of these classes, from the highest to the lowest, is of the heaviest kind; often it is highly dangerous. To 'win' and 'get' the minerals at prodigious depths in the bowels of the earth, surrounded by a sulphurous and explosive atmosphere, and subject to accidents which no human sagacity can foresee nor any precaution avert; to convey the rough treasures to the surface; to break, cleanse, and calcine, to smelt, refine and manufacture them are the duties of the workman. For the successful accomplishment of these tasks, the requirements are physical courage, strength and endurance, and above all, a fair degree of practical skill; these qualities are combined in him. Although capital is the motive power, it is upon the rude virtues of the workman that the entire system of manufacture of iron practically rules. If our coal and iron form the substantial basis of our national opulence and power, he by whose skills and labour those minerals are provided ought at least to be well clothed and well fed, to have the means afforded him of educating and advancing his children and of providing for his old age out of the produce of his labour whilst he is capable of work. It is my duty to inquire and ascertain if opportunity for all this is afforded him by the remuneration which he receives at the present time; and to show, as far as I may be able, the relation subsisting in these districts between the price of labour and the profits of capital....

The first impression of a stranger who visits Merthyr is that it is a town of workmen's houses.... The style of building is of the rudest and least commodious kind, and is one cause of the low state of health.... The main streets have a road sound at bottom, which is all the praise that can be awarded them, for they are rarely cleansed. It is, however, in the streets and courts which branch off on the right and left, that the filthy state of the town is most apparent. There is not a public sewer or drain throughout the town of Merthyr a place, be it remembered, having upwards of 40,000 inhabitants.... The houses, those of the tradesmen excepted, have no privies, nor any receptacle whatsoever for house refuse, nor have they except in a few instances any outlet behind. The consequences, as regards public decency and health, are absolutely shocking. In the district between

High Street and the river in Pen-y-Darran, and particularly in Dowlais, where, though the highest part of the town, cholera raged with the most deadly malignity, the heaps of putrefying and fermenting refuse are as astonishing as they are pernicious.... No wonder, with such a state of things, that disease is rife and life precarious. Looking at a gigantic heap of this refuse, stretching along the bank of the river, I was forcibly reminded of those mounds of rubbish which travellers describe as existing in Cairo and other cities of the east, and to which is attributed much of the severity of the plague....

The next, and a still more serious evil, is the scarcity of water.... Carefully examining every quarter of the town, I found but three pumps and one shallow draw-well which, being without apparatus for raising water, I conclude was of no service. In Dowlais and Pen-y-Darran there are a few 'spouts' fed by landsprings, from the mountains above, which afford streams insufficient in quantity and of uncertain supply. To these the women and children resort in crowds, often waiting hours before their turn comes round.... The evil is felt the more acutely, because the occupation of the colliers and miners is of so filthy a nature that they are compelled to wash themselves all over on their return from their day's work.... This scarcity of water was pointed out to me by the Rev. Mr. Campbell as the most crying grievance which the people have to endure. Yet water is abundant in the mountains above, and the traveller who on his way to the town passes fine reservoirs kept up apparently regardless of expense, and with extreme care, might suppose that at least the houses, if not the streets, were kept well supplied. But the water in these reservoirs, and the copious streams of the rivers Taff and Morlais, are absorbed entirely in the works. The ironmasters have a long-vested and absolute right in them, and the only question affecting them in this particular is whether, knowing the condition of the town, they ought not to have assisted the inhabitants in procuring a supply from a quarter which would not affect their own interests. There is a point in the mountains not far from the town where water might be obtained from a rivulet called Taff Vachan; the ravines below it, which are nevertheless much higher than the town, might at small expense be dammed up so as to form natural reservoirs, from which a supply of pure and good water might be had at a comparatively trifling expense. But in this place the working classes and the poor are almost entirely unrepresented; they are from their circumstances and position utterly helpless as regards the improvement of the town, and although they have the sympathy of the clergy, professional men and tradesmen, amongst whom there exists a great degree of public spirit, hitherto nothing has been done.

After his thorough investigations in Merthyr the Morning Chronicle *Correspondent continued with his letters describing conditions of labour in many other parts in Wales, including a strike in Aberdare, the Truck shops in Rhymney and Ebbw Vale, the copper works at Swansea and the lead mines in North Wales. These Letters, edited and reorganised by J. Ginswick, appeared in Vol. III of* Labour and the Poor in England and Wales 1849-1851, Frank Cass (1983).

The following letter from the manager at Dowlais to Lady Charlotte Guest who, after her husband's death now owned the works, shows the continuing prevalence of cholera outbreaks in Merthyr.

JOHN EVANS to Lady Charlotte Guest.
20th September, 1854. Dowlais.

...We have had twenty one deaths since Saturday and the disease [cholera] is spreading. The people are so frightened that they are leaving the place in droves, especially the Irish, amongst whom so far it has been most fatal.

It attacks all the dirty courts and gulleys and the over crowded houses. There are very few that survive many hours when once attacked. God grant that in his mercy to us that the heavy scourge may soon pass away. All that can be done for them to alleviate their distress shall be strictly attended to. We shall remove a lot up to the Barn today, and further provision is being made for the reception of a large number. It is very distressing to see the state of excitement which prevails amongst the men. It is with the greatest difficulty that we can carry on the Mills & other departments. The men are leaving the place altogether....

Madeline Elsas, *Iron in the Making.*

1854

GEORGE BORROW (1803-81). *The English writer George Borrow's* Wild Wales *is an account of a walking tour he took through Wales in 1854. Unlike most travellers in Wales he was well acquainted with the Welsh language and he has numerous anecdotes to recount particularly those having connection with Welsh literature.*

...My curiosity having been rather excited with respect to the country beyond the Berwyn, by what my friend, the flannel worker, had told me about it, I determined to go and see it. Accordingly on Friday morning I set out. Having passed by Pengwern Hall I presently arrived at a small farm-house standing on the left with a little yard before it. Seeing a woman at the door I asked her in English if the road in which I was would take me across the mountain – she said it would, and forthwith cried to a man working in a field who left his work and came towards us. "That is my husband," said she; "he has more English than I."

The man came up and addressed me in very good English; he had a brisk intelligent look, and was about sixty.... He told me that the little farm in which he lived belonged to the person who had bought Pengwern Hall. He said that he was a good kind of gentleman, but he did not like the Welsh. I asked him if the gentleman did not like the Welsh, why he came to live among them. He smiled, and I then said that I liked the Welsh very much, and was particularly fond of their language. He asked me whether I could read Welsh... and I entered into discourse with the man about Welsh poetry and repeated the famous prophecy of Taliesin about the Coiling Serpent. I asked him if the Welsh had any poets at the present day. "Plenty," said he, "and good ones – Wales can never be without a poet." Then after a pause he said that he was the grandson of a great poet.

"Do you bear his name?" said I.

"I do," he replied.

"What may it be?"

"Hughes," he answered.

"Two of the name of Hughes have been poets," said I – "One was Huw Hughes, generally termed the Bardd Coch, or red bard; he was an Anglesea man, and the friend of Lewis Morris and Goronwy Owen – the other was Jonathan Hughes, where he lived I know not."

"He lived here, in this very house," said the man. "Jonathan Hughes was my grandfather!" and as he spoke his eyes flashed fire.

"Dear me!" said I; "I read some of his pieces thirty-two years ago when I was a lad in England. I think I can repeat some of the lines." I then repeated a quarter which I chanced to remember.

"Ah!" said the man, "I see you know his poetry. Come into the next room and I will show you his chair." He led me into a sleeping room on the right hand where in a corner he showed me an antique three cornered arm chair. "That chair," he said, "grandsire won at Llangollen, at an Eisteddfod of Bards. Various bards recited their poetry, but my grandfather won the prize. Ah, he was a good poet. He also won a prize of fifteen guineas at a meeting of Bards in London."

...So John Jones and myself set off across the Berwyn to visit the birthplace of the great poet Huw Morris.... We passed over the top of the mountain and... in a little time entered the valley of Ceiriog.... At the entrance of this valley is an enormous crag. After I had looked at the place for some time with considerable interest we proceded towards the south, and in about twenty minutes reached a neat kind of house, on our right hand, which John Jones told me stood on the house of Huw Morris. Telling me to wait, he went to the house, and asked some questions. After a little time I followed him and found him discoursing at the door with a stout dame of about fifty-five years of age, and a stout, buxom damsel of about seventeen, very short of stature.

"This is the gentleman," said he, "who wishes to see anything there may be here connected with Huw Morris."

The old dame made me a curtsey, and said in very distinct Welsh, "We have some things in the house which belonged to him, and we will show them to the gentleman willingly."

"We first of all wish to see his chair," said John Jones.

"The chair is in a wall in what is called the hen ffordd (old road)," said the old gentlewoman; "it is cut out of the stone wall, you will have maybe some difficulty in getting to it, but the girl shall show it to you." The girl now motioned us to follow her, and conducted us across the road to some stone steps, over a wall to a place which looked like a plantation.

"This was the old road," said Jones; "but the place has been enclosed. The new road is above us on our right hand behind the wall."

We were in a maze of tangled shrubs, the boughs of which, very wet from the rain which was still falling, struck our faces, as we attempted to make our way between them; the girl led the way, bare-headed and bare-armed, and soon brought us to the wall, the boundary of the new road. Along this she went with considerable difficulty, owing to the tangled shrubs, and the nature of the ground, which was very precipitous, shelving down to the other side of the enclosure. In a little time we were wet to the skin, and covered with the dirt of birds, which they had left while roosting in the trees; on went the girl, sometimes creeping and trying to keep herself from falling by holding against the young trees; once or twice she fell and we after her, for there was no path, and the ground, as I said before, very shelvy; still as she went her eyes were directed towards the wall, which was not always very easy to be seen, for thorns, tall nettles and shrubs, were growing up against it. Here and there she stopped, and said something, which I could not always make out, for her Welsh was anything but clear; at length I heard her say that she was afraid we had passed the chair, and indeed presently we came to a place where the enclosure terminated in a sharp corner.

"Let us go back," said I; "we must have passed it."

I now went first, breaking down with my weight the shrubs nearest to the wall.

"Is not this the place?" said I, pointing to a kind of hollow in the wall, which looked something like the shape of a chair.

"Hardly," said the girl, "for there should be a slab on the back, with letters, but there's neither slab nor letters here."

...We had now been, as I imagined, half an hour in the enclosure, and we had nearly got back to the place from which we set out, when we suddenly heard the voice of the old lady exclaiming, "What are you doing there, the chair is on the other side of the field; wait a bit, and I will come and show it to you"; getting over the stone stile, which led into the wilderness, she came to us, and we now went along the wall at the other end; we had quite as much difficulty here as on the other side, and in some places more, for the nettles were higher, the shrubs more tangled, and the thorns more terrible. The ground, however, was rather more level. I pitied the poor girl who led the way, and whose fat naked arms were both stung and torn. She at last stopped amidst a huge grove of nettles, doing the best she could to shelter her arms from the stinging leaves....

"Is the chair really here?" said I, "or has it been destroyed? If such a thing has been done it is a disgrace to Wales."

"The chair is really here," said the old lady, "and though Huw Morus was no prophet, we love and reverence everything belonging to him. Get on Llances, the chair can't be far off;" the girl moved on, and presently the old lady exclaimed, 'There's the chair, Diolch i Duw!"

I was the last of the file, but I now rushed past John Jones, who was before me, and next to the old lady, and sure enough there was the chair, in the wall, of him who was called in his day, and still is called by the mountaineers of Wales, though his body has been below the earth in the quiet churchyard one hundred and forty years, Eos Ceiriog, the Nightingale of Ceiriog, the sweet caroller Huw Morus, the enthusiastic partizan of Charles and the Church of England, and the never-tiring lampooner of Oliver and the Independents. There it was, a kind of hollow in the stone wall, in the hen ffordd, fronting to the west, just above the gorge at the bottom of which murmurs the brook Ceiriog, there it was, something like half a barrel chair in the garden, a mouldering stone slab forming the seat, and a large slate stone, the back, on which were cut these letters

H.M.B.

signifying Huw Morris Bard.

"Sit down in the chair, Gwr Boneddig," said John Jones, "you have taken trouble enough to get to it."

"Do gentleman," said the old lady; "but first let me wipe it with my apron, for it is very wet and dirty."

"Let it be," said I; then taking off my hat I stood uncovered before the chair, and said in the best Welsh I could command, "Shade of Huw Morus, supposing your shade haunts the place which you loved so well when alive – a Saxon, one of the seed of the Coiling Serpent, – has come to this place to pay that respect to true genius, the Dawn Duw, which he is ever ready to pay. He read the songs of the Nightingale of Ceiriog in the more distant part of Lloegr, when he was a brown-haired boy, and now that he is a grey-haired man he has come to say in this place that they frequently made his eyes overflow with tears of rapture."

I then sat down in the chair, and commenced repeating verses of Huw Morris. All which I did in the presence of the stout old lady, the short, buxom and bare-armed damsel, and of John Jones the Calvinistic weaver of Llangollen, all of whom listened patiently and approvingly, though the rain was pouring down upon them, and the branches of the trees and the tops of the tall nettles, agitated by the gusts from the mountain hollows, were beating in their faces, for enthusiasm is never scoffed at by the noble simple-minded, genuine Welsh, whatever treatment it may receive from the coarse-hearted, sensual, selfish Saxon.

1854

NATHANIEL HAWTHORNE (1804-64). *American novelist and short story writer. Hawthorne's* English Notebooks *were largely written in the years 1853-57 when Hawthorne was American Consul in Liverpool. In the course of his stay in Liverpool he made several visits to North Wales.*

July 19. A week ago I made a little tour in North Wales with Mr. Bright. We left Birkenhead by railway for Chester at two o'clock; thence for Bangor; thence by carriage over the Menai Bridge to Beaumaris. At Beaumaris, a fine old castle, – quite coming up to my idea of what an old castle should be... the outer wall is so thick that a passage runs all around the castle, which covers a space of three acres.... The main castle is entirely roofless, but the hall and other rooms are pointed out by the guide, and the whole is tapestried with abundant ivy, so that my impression is of grey walls, with here and there a vast green curtain; a carpet of green over the floors of halls and apartments; and festoons around all the outer battlement, with an uneven and rather perilous footpath running along the top....

At Bangor we went to a handsome hotel, and hired a carriage and two horses for some Welsh place, the name of which I forget; neither can I remember a single name of the places through which we posted that day, nor could I spell them if I heard them pronounced, nor pronounce them if saw them spelt. It was a circuit of about forty miles, bringing us to Conway at last. I remember a great slate quarry; and also that many of the cottages, in the first part of our journey, were built of blocks of slate. The mountains were very bold, thrusting themselves up abruptly in peaks, – not of the dumpling formation which is sometimes too prevalent among New England mountains. At one point we saw Snowdon, with its bifold summit... there were one or two lakes which the guidebook greatly admired, but which to me, who remembered a hundred sheets of blue water in New England, seemed nothing more than sullen and dreary puddles, with bare banks, and wholly destitute of beauty. I think they were nowhere more than a good hundred yards across. But the hills were certainly very good, and though generally bare of trees, their outlines thereby were rendered the stronger and more striking.

Many of the Welsh women, particularly the elder ones, wear black beaver hats, high crowned and almost precisely like men's. It makes them look ugly and witch-like. Welsh is still the prevalent language, and the only one spoken by a great many of the inhabitants....

At some unutterable village we went into a little church, where we saw an old stone image of a warrior, lying on his back, with his hands clasped. It was the natural son (if I remember rightly) of David, Prince of Wales, and was doubtless the better part of a thousand years old. There was likewise a stone coffin of still greater age; some person of rank and renown had mouldered to dust within it, but it was now open and empty. Also, there were monumental brasses on the walls, engraved with portraits of a gentleman and a lady in the costumes of Elizabeth's time. Also, on one of the pews, a brass record of some persons who slept in the vault beneath; so that, every Sunday, the survivors and descendants kneel and worship directly over their dead ancestors....

September 13. My family went to Rhyl last Thursday, and on Saturday I joined them there.... Rhyl is a most uninteresting place, – a collection of new lodging houses and hotels, on a long sand beach, which the tide leaves bare almost to the horizon. The sand is by no means a marble pavement, but sinks under the foot, and makes very heavy walking; but there is a promenade in front of the principal range of houses, looking on the sea, whereon we have rather better footing. Almost all the houses were full, and Sophia had taken a parlour and two bedrooms, and is living after the English fashion, providing her own table, lights, fuel and everything. It is very awkward to our American notions; but there is an independence about it, which I think must make it agreeable on better acquaintance. But the place is certainly destitute of attraction, and life seems to pass very heavily. The English do not appear to have a turn for amusing themselves....

On Monday we went to Conway by rail. Certainly this must be the most perfect specimen of a ruinous old castle in the whole world; it quite fills up one's idea. We first walked round the exterior of the wall, at the base of which are hovels, with dirty children playing about them, and pigs rambling along, and squalid women visible in the doorways; but all these things melt into the picturesqueness of the scene, and do not harm it. The whole town of Conway was built in what was once the castle yard, and the whole circuit of the wall is still standing in a delightful state of decay.... I think it added to the impressiveness of the old castle, to see the streets and the kitchen gardens and the homely dwellings that had grown up within the precincts of this feudal fortress, and the people of today following their little businesses about it. This does not destroy the charm; but tourists and idle visitors do impair it. The earnest life of today, however, petty and homely as it may be, has a right to its place alongside of what is left of the life of other days; and if it be vulgar itself, it does not vulgarize the scene. But tourists do vulgarize it; and I suppose we did so, just like the others.

September 20. I went back to Rhyl last Friday in the steamer.... The next morning I made an excursion in the omnibus as far as Ruthin, passing through Rhyddlan, St. Asaph, Denbigh, and reaching Ruthin at one o'clock.... All these villages were very lively, as the omnibus drove in; and I rather imagine it was market day in each of them, – there being quite a bustle of Welsh people. The old women came around the omnibus courtseying and intimating their willingness to receive alms, – witch-like women, such as one sees in pictures or reads of in romances, and very unlike anything feminine in America. Their style of dress cannot have changed for centuries. It was quite unexpected to me to hear Welsh so universally and familiarly spoken. Everybody spoke it. The omnibus driver could speak but imperfect English; there was a jabber of Welsh all through the streets and market-places; and it flowed out with a freedom quite different from the way in which they expressed themselves in English. I had had an idea that Welsh was spoken rather as a freak and in fun than as a native language; it was so strange to find another language the people's actual and earnest medium of thought within so short a distance of England. But English is scarcely more known to the body of Welsh people than to the peasantry of France. Moreover, they sometimes pretend to ignorance, when they might speak it fairly enough.

Two days later Hawthorne and his family made an excursion to Rhyddlan where they visited the castle ruins. In their walk over the moor back to Rhyl they were overtaken by rain and strong winds and forced to take shelter.

...We took refuge in a little bit of stone cottage, which, small as it was, had a greater antiquity than any mansion in America. The door was open, and as we approached, we saw several children gazing at us; and their mother, a pleasant looking woman, who seemed rather astounded at the visit that was to befall her, tried to draw a tattered curtain over part of her interior, which she fancied less fit to be seen than the rest. To say the truth, the house was not at all better than a pigsty; and while we sat there, a pig came familiarly to the door, thrust in his snout, and seemed surprised that he should be driven away, instead of being admitted as one of the family. The floor was of brick; there was no ceiling, but only the peaked gable overhead. The room was kitchen, parlour, and, I suppose, bedroom for the whole family; at all events, there was only the tattered curtain between us and the sleeping accommodations. The good woman could not or would not speak a word of English, only laughing when Sophia said, "Dim Sassenach?" but she was kind and hospitable, and found a chair for each of us. She had been making some bread and the dough was on the dresser. Life with these people is reduced to its simplest elements. It is only a pity that they cannot or do not choose to keep themselves cleaner. Poverty, except in cities, need not be squalid. When the shower abated a little, we gave all the pennies we had to the children and set forth again. By the bye, there were several coloured prints stuck up against the walls, and there was a clock ticking in the corner, and some paper-hangings pinned upon the slanted roof....

Nathaniel Hawthorne, *Notes of Travel, Vol. I* (Houghton, Mifflin & Co.: 1870).

WILLIAM EWART GLADSTONE (1809-98). *The great liberal statesman and Prime Minister had a home in Wales, Hawarden Castle, to which he frequently returned. He came into possession of Hawarden through his wife and the misfortunes (or rather the mismanagement of their fortunes) of her brothers and the fact that none of them had any descendants. His voluminous but, for the most part, briefly factual diaries, and the copious amount of letters he wrote there, reveal the extent of his reading and writing but little of it refers to Wales. The following extracts from his diary find him on a tour of North Wales in September, 1855.*

10. M. (Llanrwst)
Started at 3.25 for Llanrwst 16 miles over the hills: a beautiful walk: took 3hr 30m. reached at dusk.... Four miles with a self sufficient but straightforward and intelligent pedlar: most warlike. Read two short books of Odyssey in evg. Eagles Inn, good eating: not dear: not clean.

11. T.(Dolgelly)
Off with Willy at 9: forty miles (one astray) to Bettys-y-Coed, Penmachno Festiniog, Transfynnydd and Dolgelly. The first eight and last ten miles lovely.... Read Odyssey – Inn Golden Lion: Good.

12. Wed (Barmouth)
After a good night we gave up Machynelleth but tried Cader Idris: saw a grand precipice and beautiful views but the clouds prevented our reaching the top. We went in the afternoon down to Barmouth where we found the Inn excellent. Read Odyssey.

13. Th. (Beddgelert)
An early bathe at Barmouth. 10 long miles (north) to Harlech: where we saw a grand old castle nobly situated. Our weather was at first doubtful and wet; as we went on to Tanybwlch, a most beautiful drive, it became fair and even fine. I walked over to Beddgelert; Willy riding with me, Pont Aber Glaslyn surpassed all my expectations....

14. Fr. (Capel Curig)
Goat at Beddgelert very good. We drove to Llanberris through the grand base & beneath the base of Snowdon, which was an approach to the sublime in character far exceeding its dimensions. We did not like the Llanberris Inn (Victoria) overmuch but the situation at the mouth of the deep vale is pretty. We saw the Fall & Dolbadern Castle

wh is curious. I then walked up the pass & we drove down to Capel Curig: a bad approach though between high mountains.

15. Sat. (Penmaenmawr)

Capel Curig Hotel: good. C's urgency took us backwards on our line for Snowdon: the view of wh was grand but from the masses of rolling clouds which circled round the peaks. We started at $10^1/2$. I took (walking) 1h.12m. to the point of leaving the road. We went slowly to the top by the two Llyns and arrived (some of the last part both steep and giddy) at 1.55. We could not see beyond arms length; & waited for the chance of better things till 3.15, employing ourselves upon luncheon, the materials of wh at the hut were good. (They made a charge of 5/- for bed supper and breakfast: moderate enough). We came down by the highest route: I took 1h.20.m to the road and then walked $8^1/2$. along the road by Capel Curig towards Llyn Ogwyn. The two basins are very grand. In Scotland they would I think be called Corries: the upper one is the finest as a whole, the lower one has the grander precipice. Lake Ogwyn and Nant Ffrangon below it are quite worthy of the Snowdon group. In the midst of the Cabinet – mountain scenery wh makes these counties so beautiful, Snowdon & its family form an island of real grandeur in character. We baited & had tea in a tolerable Inn at Bethesda: & reached home at 11 p.m. I reckon it 10m. from C.C. to the top: two fives.

The Gladstone Diaries, Vol. V, ed. M.R.D. Foot and H.C.G. Matthew (Oxford: Clarendon Press, 1974-1994).

A letter from GLADSTONE *of 28 December, 1882 – written at Hawarden during his third premiership to the then Bishop of Durham – concerned the appointment of a Bishop of Llandaff.*

I welcome cordially your intervention in the matter of the Llandaff see. Indeed I was just about to write to you to ask the following question. 1. Does Archdeacon Watkins know Welsh: & if so is it as a native or as an acquired language? 2. What does your Lordship think of his general qualifications for the See?

A vacancy in a Welsh see costs me more trouble than six English vacancies. I feel it is my duty to ascertain if possible by a process of exhaustion whether there is any completely fit person to be had among men of the Welsh mother tongue. In the main it is a business of constantly examining likely or plausible cases & finding they break down. The Welsh are to be got at through the pulpit: & yet here is a special danger, for among the more stirring Welsh clergy there is as much wordy & windy preaching as among the Irish.

I have not yet finally abandoned the notion of a Welshman, having certain cases still under examination. In the meantime I have been reminded of Archdeacon Watkins hence my enquiries to your Lordship. I want to know whether he will do as a pure Welshman; & if not, then whether as semi Welshman he is the best man available....

In June 1887 Gladstone visited Swansea to rally the liberal cause there – part of his visit was devoted to opening the new Town Library; he received such a warm reception that he abandoned soon afterwards his half-hearted opposition to the establishment of the Welsh Church. His diary notes of June 5 contain the following brief remarks.

The astonishing procession. Sixty thousand? Then spoke for near an hour. Dinner at 8, near an hundred: arrangements perfect. Spoke for nearly another hour....

The Gladstone Diaries, Volume XII.

1856 and 1859

GEORGE ELIOT (1819-90). *Great British novelist, author of* Middlemarch, Daniel Deronda *etc. The following two letters, written while she was holidaying in Wales with G.H. Lewes, were to one of her greatest friends.*

Letter to Sara Hennell.
June 29, 1856. Tenby.

...Yes, indeed, I do remember old Tenby days, and had set my heart on being in the very same house again. We saw a ticket in the window and turned in, but alas! it had just been let. It is immensely smartened up, like the place generally, since those old times, and is proportionately less desirable for quiet people who have no flounces and do not subscribe to new churches. Tenby looks insignificant in picturesqueness after Ilfracombe; but the two objects that draw us hither, zoology and health, will flourish none the worse for the absence of tall precipices and many-tinted rocks. The air is delicious – soft but not sultry – and the sands and bathing such as to be found nowhere else. St. Catherine's Rock with its caverns is our paradise.

We go there with baskets, hammers and chisels, and jars and phials, and come home laden with spoils. Then there is Monkstone point, where we mean to go and explore pools and crevices, and Caldy Island, where Gosse tells us there are treasures to be found. Altogether, we are contented to have been driven away from Ilfracombe by the cold wind, since a new place is a new experience, and Mr Lewes has never been here before. To me there is an additional pleasure – half melancholy – of recalling all the old impressions and comparing them with the new. We went into the market yesterday, but the Fish-women with whom Mr Bray was an especial favourite are no longer there. The Fish market is moved to a subterranean place near the quay. Everywhere new houses and smarter shops – everywhere signs that we are twelve years (or more?) older than when we all landed from the Bristol Packet, feeling rather nauseabondes, and thinking the town looked rather dingy.

We have a project of going into St. Catherine's caverns with lanterns, some night when the tide is low, about eleven, for the sake of seeing the zoophytes preparing for their midnight revels. The Actiniae, like other belles, put on their best faces for such an occasion.

Letter to Sara Hennell.
August 29, 1859. Conway.

Dear Sara,

I got your letter only this morning almost too late, I fear, for my answer to be of any use. We set off on Thursday night from London....

I cannot give you our permanent address at present, for we have been so unfortunate as to be obliged to take temporary lodgings here – a sad disappointment. You did not – *could* not over-rate the beauty of Penmaenmawr, but you underrated the difficulty of getting lodgings there, for we could get absolutely *none*. I never turned my back on a place with more regret. There is a lone house on the beach near Abergile that we are now in suspense about; if we don't get that we shall try Penmaenmawr again after the lapse of these few days....

Letters of George Eliot, ed. G.S. Haight (Yale: 1954-78).

CHARLES KINGSLEY (1819-75). *Novelist, poet, clergyman, Christian Socialist. The following letters were written to his wife while Kingsley was on a trip to North Wales with his friends, Tom Taylor and Tom Hughes.*

12 August, 1856. Capel Curig.

We are sleeping here, being too tired to get an inch further. We never slept forty winks last night in the train; started from Bangor at 5, and were on our legs till 5 p.m. We went up Nant Francon, then up to Idwal. Fish would not rise; but the rivers are flooded and, therefore, we shall have noble sport. But the glory was what I never saw before, all those grand mountains, 'silver-veined with rills,' cataracts of *snow-white cotton threads,* if you will, zigzagging down every rock-face – sometimes 1000 feet – and the whole air alive with the roar of waters. The greenness and richness of the mountains after our dusty burnt-up plains, is most refreshing.

All day we had steaming gleams; but the clouds on Glydyr Vawr only broke to form again, and we had twenty showers, shrouding the cliffs with long grey veils of lace. I wish I could tell you what the mountains are. Not pink, not purple, not brown, but a sort of pale pink madder, with vast downs of bright green grass interspersed. And oh, as we walked past Colonel Pennant's cyclopean walls at Bangor, and saw that great gap high up in the air ten miles off, and knew that we should be in it ere noon, it was like a dream; and all the more dreamy for the sleeplessness of the past night. We found a noble fountain, which Colonel Pennant has built by the road side, and there washed ourselves into our senses, and went on. At Bethesda we tried for breakfast at six a.m., and were refused by all the few houses that were open, till we found a nice little woman, who gave us infinite broiled ham, tea, and porter, to carry up the hills. We tried Ogwen River for salmon peel, amid those exquisite parks and woods; but it was too much flooded. By night I had picked my first Saxifraga stellaris, and I knew that I was in the *former world.* The parsley fern is growing between every stone, and the beech fern too, but the latter very poor. I have dried for the children the waterlobelia, and Sparganium natans, to do which I walked up to my knees on Idwal. I had not pluck to go up to the Fwll Du. Tell my mother I am going there shortly. Snowdon is now looking like a great grey ghost with seven heads, and as soon as one head is cut off a fresh one grows; but more are cut off than grow, and the clouds which stream up from the S.W. fall lower and lower, and have now canopied the whole head of Moel Siabod, who is looking in at our window 2000 feet down, the impudent fellow, though I am 1000 feet high. Wherefore we shall have more rain....

Tomorrow up at six; walk to Pen-y-gwryd, and then up to Edno!

Pen-y-Gwyrd.

I have had, as far as scenery is concerned, the finest day I ever had. We started for Edno at 10, but did not find it till 2, because we mistook the directions, and walked from 10 till 1.30 over a Steinerer Maar, a sea of syenite and metamorphic slate which baffles all description, 2000ft. above Gwynant, ribs and peaks and walls of rocks leaping up and rushing down, average 50 to 100 ft., covered with fir, club moss, crowberry and barberry, and ling, of course. Over these we had to scramble up and down, beating for Edno lake as you would beat for a partridge, but in vain. All we found was one old cock grouse, who went off hollowing "Cock-cock-what-a-shame-cock-cock" till we were fairly beat. In despair we made, not a dash, but a crawl, at Moel Meirch ('Margaret's Peak', some pathetic story I suppose), which rises about 100 ft. above the stony sea, a smooth pyramid of sandy-pink syenite. Hughes got up first, by a crack, for the walls are like china, and gave a who-whoop; there was Edno half a mile beyond, and only a valley as deep as from Finchampstead church to the river to cross, beside a few climbs of 50 ft. So there we got and ate our hard boiled eggs and drank our beer, and then set to, and caught just nothing. The fish, always sulky and capricious, would not stir. But the delight of being there again, 2200ft. up, out of the sound of aught but the rush of wind and water and the whistle of the sheep (which is just like a penny whistle ill-blown), and finding oneself *at home* there! Every rock, even the steps of slate and footholds of grass which – and I used to use, just the same. Unchanged for ever. It is an awful thought. Soon we found out why the fish wouldn't rise. The cloud which had been hanging on Snowdon, lowered. Hebog and Cnicht caught it. It began to roll up from the sea in great cabbage-headed masses, grew as dark as twilight. The wind rolled the lake into foam; we staggered back to an old cave, where we shall sleep, please God, ere we come home, and then the cloud lowered, the lake racing along in fantastic flakes and heaps of white steam hiding everything 50 yards off one minute, then leaving all clear and sharp-cut pink and green. While out of it came a rain of marbles and Minniè bullets – a rain which searches and drenches, and drills. Luckily I had on a flannel shirt. We waited as long as we dared, and then steered home by compass, for we could not see 50 yards, except great rows of giants in the fog, sitting humped up side by side, like the ghosts of the sons of Anak staring into the bogs. So home we went, floundering through morass and scrambling up and down the giants, which were crags 50 to 100 ft. high, for we dared not pick our road for fear of losing our bearings by compass. And we were wet – oh, were we not wet? but, as a make-weight, we found the "Grass of Parnassus" in plenty, and as we coasted the vale of Gwynant, 1500ft. up, the sight of Snowdon, sometimes through great gaps of cloud, sometimes altogether hidden, the lights upon that glorious vista of Gwynant and Dinas, right down to Hebog – the flakes of cloud rising up the vale of Gwynant far below us – no tongue can describe it. I could see Froude's fir-wood, and home close, quite plain from Moel Meirch. It looked as if you could have sent a stone into it, but it was four miles off. I have got for you grass of Parnassus; Alpine club-moss; ladies mantle; ivy-leaved campanula; beech fern; A. Oreopteris (sweet fern).

The great butterwort is out of flower (as is the globe flower), but it starts every bog with its shiny yellow-green stars of leaves. Good bye. I am up at half past 3 for Gwynant, which is full of salmon....

Charles Kingsley: his letters and memories of his life, (Henry S. King & Co: London, 1877).

1860s

REV. MICHAEL D. JONES. *This letter is from the Reverend Michael D. Jones, a professor at the Independent College, Bala. It concerns the feudalistic behaviour of the great landlords during the election of 1859 when Liberal candidates stood in Tory seats regarded by landlords as part of their fiefdom. Evictions, such as he describes also took place after the 1868 election which followed on the Reform Act of 1867. Many farmers voted Liberal and subsequently were evicted. All this contributed to the achievement of the secret ballot.*

The people of Merionethshire have been brought to feel the neccessity of secret voting, as the landlords, after the last election, have made those electors who refused to become their tools to smart in their material interests. The late Mr Price, of Rhiwlas, made several tenants the object of his wrath, by turning them out of their farms. Sir Watkin* in the same way, raised the rents of eleven of his tenants who had remained neutral, and ejected five that voted against the candidate he aided. Two of Mr Price's tenants have died in consequence of this persecution, namely, Mr Roberts, of Frongoch, the father of six children, one of which was born since his death, and his sister, who was also the head of a family. The ill-feeling that followed the election no doubt affected the health of Mr Price, so that he also is dead. I was no elector at the time; but I did my best to support the Liberal candidate by public speaking, canvassing, etc. My mother, aged seventy-six, was a tenant of Sir Watkin, and she lost her farm, and in January 1861, she died. I had a chapel built upon a common, which common Sir Watkin bought off the Crown, and then sold my chapel to the highest bidder.

* Sir Watkin Williams Wynn – *one of the long succession in the great landed family of that name.*

Letter published in *The Elector* and quoted in *Letters and Essays on Wales* by Henry Richard.

1864 ff.

MATTHEW ARNOLD (1822-1888). *Poet, critic, educationalist and inspector of schools who expressed in his* Lectures on Celtic Literature *his profound conviction of the value of Celtic literature and culture. The following letters show him on holiday in North Wales.*

August 7, 1864. Llandudno.

My Dearest Mother,
...Yesterday morning, instead of writing to you, as I had intended, I started with dear old Tom for the interior of the country, being sick of lodging-houses and sea-side. We got by rail some four or five miles on the Llanrwst road, and then struck up a gorge to the right, where there is a waterfall. After this drought the waterfall was not much, but we continued up the valley, which was very austere and wild, till we got to Llyn Eigiau, or the Lake of Shallows, lying under very fine precipices, and stretching up the roots of Carnedd Llewellyn, the second highest mountain in Wales, some three or four hundred feet higher than Scafell. After sitting a long while by the lake, in loneliness itself, we came back by another valley, that of the river Dulyn, which flows from two small lakes, which we hope to explore on Tuesday. This mountain mass in which Carnedd Llewellyn stands is very little visited, except the hills just over Aber, and yesterday we saw not a single tourist, though here and on all the great lines they

swarm. The charm of Wales is the extent of the country, which gives you untouched masses which the tourists do not reach; and then the new race, language and literature give it a charm and novelty which the Lake country can never have. Wales is as full of traditions and associations as Cumberland and Westmorland are devoid of them. The very sands we can see from this house, the Lavan Sands, or Sands of Waiting, between this and Beaumaris, have more story about them than all the Lake Country.... The bathing in the sea is spoilt by the vile jelly-fish, which sting frightfully, and both Budge* and I caught it the first day we were here. They used, I remember, to torment me at Abergele in old days. But it is the river and lakes of fresh water which my heart desires, and to these I shall get as much as I can while I am here.

* his son.

August 20, 1864 [to his mother].

...We have just returned from a delightful little excursion.... Flue* had never seem Llanberis, so the day before yesterday she, I, Dicky, and Lucy started by train for Caernarvon.... At Caernarvon the children dined at the Uxbridge Arms, and then began, for me, the real pleasure. We started in a car, for the railroad ends at Caernarvon, and drove that beautiful eight miles to Llanberis. I don't know whether you remember the sudden change at the half-way house from the dull fertile flat which borders the sea to Llyn Padarn and the mountains. And such a mountain as Snowdon is! We have nothing that comes within a hundred miles of him.... The day was perfectly fine and clear, and having ordered dinner at seven, we went to that beautiful waterfall on the way up Snowdon, about half a mile from the hotel. The fall was beautiful even in this weather, and indeed the green at Llanberis was fresh and bright as in Switzerland, in spite of the drought. The children had their tea at one end of the table, while we had dinner at the other; and then, while Flue put them to bed, I strolled to the Dolbadarn tower, and had a long look at the two beautiful lakes and the pass in the moonlight. Next morning we started at eleven in a carriage and pair for Llanrwst. A soft grey morning with a little mist passing on and off the tops of the highest hills. Flue enjoyed the pass as much as I could have desired, and indeed it is most impressive; my recollection by no means did it justice. Then by Capel Curig and the Fall of Llugwy to that beautiful Bettws y Coed and Llanrwst. At Llanrwst we dined, and got back here by the train a little after eight o'clock. The people travelling about in Wales, and their quality, beggar description. It is a social revolution which is taking place. And to observe it may well fill one with reflexion....

* *Arnold's wife.*

To Miss Arnold [his sister Fan].
Saturday, August 1864. Llandudno.

My Dearest Fan,
...Yesterday, however, I was for three hours and a half on the Great Orme and this evening I shall manage to get an hour or two there. But what is this when I see Carnedd Llewellyn opposite to me, and all the hills steeped in an ethereal Italian atmosphere that makes one long to be among them? Till yesterday I have thought this place bleak and harsh; and still I miss rivers and green fields, and would rather be at a Welsh farm among the mountains. However, this suits the children best. But yesterday brought an air and sun which perfectly transfigured the place. The poetry of the Celtic race and its names of places quite overpowers me, and it will be long before Tom forgets the line, 'Hear from thy grave, great Taliesin, hear!' from Gray's Bard, of which I gave him the benefit some hundred times a day on our excursions.... All interests are here – Celts, Romans, Saxons, Druidism, Middle Age, Caer, Castle, Cromlech, Abbey, – and this glorious sea and mountains with it all.

To M.E. Grant Duff, M.P.
August 22, 1879. Fairy Hill, Swansea.

...You have been much in my mind lately, for you first turned to me to try and know the names and history of the plants I met with, instead of being content with simply taking pleasure in the look of them; and you have at least doubled my enjoyment of them by doing so. I send you two things which grow beautifully here, on the south-western peninsula of Gower, fifteen miles from Swansea, the St John's wort and the Oenothera. The Oenothera is a beautiful sight, covering every grassy spot in the sand, by Oxwich Bay, where we were yesterday.

To his wife.
August 25, 1885. Duffryn, Mountain Ash, South Wales.

...There is nothing on the journey more beautiful than the passage at Church Stretton between Caer Caradoc and the Long Mynd, which you have seen; but it is a pleasing country all the way, and Welsh valleys and rivers, with the high viaducts spanning them, very interesting. There were traces of rain from Abergavenny onwards; they had a little rain yesterday morning, and much the day before; today it is beautiful. This valley is beautiful, and the house and grounds so placed that the mines and houses of miners do it no harm; but the population swarms, it is really one street from here to Aberdare, four miles.... This morning we all drove into the Eisteddfod and heard Sir G. Elliot's address; it was all rather dull, but I got off speaking by saying I would only speak once, and *that* they wished should be on Thursday, the chief day....

August 26, 1885.

...I send Fan the ivy-leaved campanula, which grows in quantities on the mountains where we walked yesterday. All the country has a softness and foreignness which are not English, and the plants would be very interesting if one had but more time to look for them.... We have been again at the Eisteddfod this morning; I had to make a little speech to second the vote of thanks to the president, because, it appeared, he wished it. The people here receive me so well that it wonderfully takes off from the difficulty of speaking. The audience is certainly a wonderful sight and, I shall always think, does credit to the country which can produce it. It was much fuller today than yesterday, and will be much fuller tomorrow than today because the shops in Aberdare are to be closed early....

Letters 1848-1888, collected by G.W.E. Russell (Macmillan: 1895).

1864

GERARD MANLEY HOPKINS (1844-89). *English poet who, after his studies at Oxford, decided to become a Jesuit priest. The last three years of his training for the priesthood were spent at St. Bueno's College, near St. Asaph. There he not only resumed the writing of poetry but also studied Welsh.*

Letter XXXIV.
20 July – 14 August 1864.

GERARD MANLEY HOPKINS to Alexander Baillie.
...From the top of this page has been written at Pen-y-lan, Maentwrog, Merionethshire, where I arrived last Monday, August 1st. I have had adventures. I was lost in storms of rain on the mountains between Bala and Ffestiniog. It really happened what is related in novels and allegories 'the dry beds of the morning were now turned into the channels of swollen torrents,' etc. At last a river ran across the road and cut me off entirely. I took refuge in a shepherd's hut and slept among the Corinthians. They, I mean the shepherd and family, gorged me with eggs and bacon and oaten cake and curds and whey. Thus I did what old gentlemen tell you with a sort of selfish satisfaction that you must learn to do.

ROUGHED IT:

I believe it means irritating the skin on sharp-textured blankets. These old gentlemen have always had to do it when they were your age....

Further Letters of Gerald Manley Hopkins, ed. C.C. Abbott (Oxford University Press: 1938).

To his mother, Kate Hopkins, senior.
Sept 20, 1874. St. Beuno's, St. Asaph, North Wales.

My dearest Mother,
...I have got a yearning for the Welsh people and could find it in my heart to work for their conversion. However on consideration it seems best to turn my thoughts elsewhere. I say this because, though I am not my own master, yet if people among us show a zeal and aptitude for a particular work, say foreign missions, they can commonly get employed on them. The Welsh round here are very civil and respectful but do not much come to us and those who are converted are for the most part not very staunch. They are much swayed by ridicule. Wesleyanism is the popular religion. They are said to have a turn for religion, especially what excites outward fervour, and more refinement and pious feeling than the English peasantry but less steadfastness and sincerity. I have always looked on myself as half Welsh and so I warm to them. The Welsh

landscape has a great charm and when I see Snowdon and the mountains in its neighbourhood, as I can now, with the clouds lifting, it gives me a rise of the heart. I ought to say that the Welsh have the reputation also of being covetous and immoral: I add this to forestall your saying it, for, as I say, I warm to them and in different degrees to all the Celts.

Selected Letters, ed. Catherine Phillips (Oxford University Press: 1990).

From GERARD MANLEY HOPKINS' Journal, 1874.

Sept. 6.

With Wm. Kerr, who took me up a hill behind ours (ours is Mynefyr), a furze-grown and healthy hill, from which I could look round the whole country, up the valley towards Ruthin and down to the sea. The cleave in which Bodfari and Caerwys lie was close below. It was a leaden sky, braided and roped with cloud, and the earth in dead colours, grave but distinct. The heights by Snowdon were hidden by the clouds but not from distance or dimness. The nearer hills, the other side of the valley, shewed a hard and beautifully detached and glimmering brim against the light, which was lifting there. All the length of the valley the skyline of the hills was flowingly written all along upon the sky. A blue bloom, a sort of meal, seemed to have spread upon the distant south, enclosed by a basin of hills. Looking all round but most in looking far up the valley I felt an instress and charm of Wales. Indeed in coming here I began to feel a desire to do something for the conversion of Wales. I began to learn Welsh too but not with very pure intentions perhaps. However on consulting the Rector on this, the first day of the retreat, he discouraged it unless it were purely for the sake of labouring among the Welsh. Now it was not and so I saw I must give it up. At the same time my music seemed to come to an end. Yet, rather strangely... I had no sooner given up the Welsh than my desire seemed to be for the conversion of Wales and I had it in mind to give up everything else for that; nevertheless weighing this by St. Ignatius' rules of election I decided not to do so....

Oct. 8.

Bright and beautiful day. Crests of snow could be seen on the mountains. Barraud and I walked over to Holywell and bathed at the well and returned very joyously. The sight of the water in the well as clear as glass, greenish like beryl or aquamarine, trembling at the surface with the force of the springs, and shaping out the five foils of the well quite drew and held my eyes to it.... The strong unfailing flow of the water and the chain of cures from year to year all these centuries took hold of my mind with wonder at the bounty of God in one of His saints....

Nov. 8.

Walking with Wm. Splaine we saw a vast multitude of starlings making an unspeakable jangle. They would settle in a row of trees; then, one tree after another, rising at a signal they looked like a cloud of specks of black snuff or powder struck up from a brush or broom or shaken from a wig; then they would sweep round in whirlwinds – you could see the nearer and farther bow of the rings by the size and blackness; many would be in one phase at once, all narrow black flakes hurling round, then in another; then they would fall upon a field and so on. Splaine wanted a gun: then "there it would rain meat" he said. I thought they must be full of enthusiasm and delight hearing their cries and stirring and cheering one another.

1875
Feb. 7.
I asked Miss Jones in my Welsh lesson the Welsh for *fairy,* for we were translating Cinderella. She told me *cipenaper* (or perhaps *cipernaper, Anglice kippernapper*)*: the word is nothing but *kidnapper,* moulded, accorded to their fashion to give it a Welsh etymology, as she said, from cipio/to snatch, to whisk away. However in coming to an understanding between ourselves what fairies (she says *fairess* by the way for a she-fairy) and kippernappers were, on my describing them as little people 'that high', she told me quite simply that she had seen them. It was on or near the Holywell road (she indicated the spot). She was going to her grandfather's farm on the hill, not far from where Justice Williams lived, on the slope of the Rhuallt. It was a busy time, haymaking I think. She was going up at five o'clock in the morning, when she saw three little boys of about four years old, wearing little frock coats*[2] and odd little caps running and dancing before her, taking hands and going round, then going further, still dancing and always coming together, she said. She would take no notice of them but went on to the house and there told them what she had seen and wondered that children could be out so early. "Why she has seen the kippernappers," her grandmother said to her son, Susannah Jones' father.

* She afterwards told me the true Welsh word *tolwyth-teg.*

*² She afterwards called the coats long (*llaes,* that is/trailing; perhaps unconfined by a girdle) and black. The caps or hats were round and black.

The Journals and Papers of Gerard Manley Hopkins, ed. Humphrey House and Graham Storey (Oxford University Press: 1959).

1870 ff.

FRANCIS KILVERT (1840-1879). *In 1865 Kilvert went as curate to Clyro in Radnorshire and the core of the diary for which he is now famous and from which the following extracts have been taken was written there between 1870 and 1872. A large number of his notebooks containing his diaries appear, however, to have been censored or destroyed by his widow and niece.*

Septuagesima Sunday, St. Valentine's Eve (1870).
  Preached at Clyro in the morning (Matthew xiv, 30). Very few people in Church, the weather fearful, violent deadly E. wind and the hardest frost we have had yet. Went to Bettws in the afternoon wrapped in two waistcoats, two coats, a muffler and a mackintosh, and was not at all too warm. Heard the Chapel bell pealing strongly for the second time since I have been here and when I got to the Chapel my beard moustaches and whiskers were so stiff with ice that I could hardly open my mouth and my beard was frozen on to my mackintosh. There was a large christening party from Llwyn Gwilym.... The baby was baptized in ice which was broken and swimming about in the Font. A sad day for mother and child to come out.

Thursday, 17 March.
  On leaving the school at 11, I went up to Cae Mawr to see Morell and he proposed a walk to Aber Edw as the morning was so lovely.... We went on till we came to a brow of a hill which fell away abruptly from our feet. Then we saw the Begwns behind us looking very near, much too near, and directly afterwards we spied a whitewashed church perched on a tump and shaded by a huge yew in the valley below. I took the Church to be Aber Edw Church, but coming to a shoemaker's house with a small farm yard we found it was Llandeilo, and we looked blankly at each other having completely lost our way. The handsome black-haired and bearded shoemaker... volunteered to show us the way... he led us over the shoulder of another great rolling hill till we saw Aber Edw lying below us, the famous rocky wooded

gorge, the Edw and the Wye and the meeting of the sweet waters. The turf was firm dry and elastic, splendid walking.

About a hundred yards from the road amongst the rocks and bushes was Llewellyn's Cave* with a door. We went in. There was a step down into it and the Cave was a square dark small chamber just high enough to stand upright in, and at the further dark end a hole or shaft probably a chink in the rocks up which we could thrust our arms and sticks without feeling the end. Names were carved on the walls. The shoemaker said his parents used to talk a great deal about Llewellyn but he had forgotten all the stories except that Llewellyn came down a steep bank called the Henallt above Aber Edw, nearly the same way as we came. English maiden hair fern was growing plentifully about the rocks and I brought away a plant from the rock exactly over the Cave mouth....

* *The cave where Llywellyn, 'The Last Prince' is supposed to have taken refuge before his death in 1282.*

Sunday, Christmas Day.
As I lay awake praying in the early morning I thought I heard a sound of distant bells. It was an intense frost. I sat down in my bath upon a sheet of thick ice which broke in the middle into large pieces whilst sharp points and jagged edges stuck all round the sides of the tub like chevaux de frise, not particularly comforting to the naked thighs and loins, for the keen ice cut like broken glass. The icewater stung and scorched like fire. I had to collect the floating pieces of ice and pile them on a chair before I could use the sponge in my hands for it was a mass of ice. The morning was most brilliant. Walked to the Sunday School with Gibbins and the road sparkled with millions of rainbows, the seven colours gleaming in every glittering point of hoar frost. The Church was very cold in spite of two roaring stove fires.

Tuesday, March 14, 1871.
The afternoon had been stormy but it cleared towards sunset. Gradually the heavy rain clouds rolled across the valley to the foot of the opposite mountains and began climbing up their sides wreathing in rolling masses of vapour. One solitary cloud still hung above the brilliant sunlit town, and that whole cloud was a rainbow. Gradually it lost its bright prismatic hues and moved away up the Cusop Dingle in the shape of a pillar and of the colour of golden dark smoke. The Black Mountains were invisible, being wrapped in clouds, and I saw one very bright dazzling cloud where the mountains ought to have

been. This cloud grew more white and dazzling every moment, till a clearer burst of sunlight scattered the mists and revealed the truth. This brilliant white cloud that I had been looking and wondering at was the mountain in snow. The last cloud and mist rolled over the mountain tops and the mountains stood up in the clear blue heaven, a long rampart line of dazzling glittering snow so as no fuller on earth can white them. I stood rooted to the ground, struck with amazement and overwhelmed at the extraordinary splendour of this marvellous spectacle. I never saw anything to equal it I think, even among the high Alps. One's first involuntary thought in the presence of these magnificent sights is to lift up the heart to God and humbly thank Him for having made the earth so beautiful. An intense glare of primrose light streamed from the west deepening into rose and crimson. There was not a flake of snow anywhere but on the mountains and they stood up, the great white range rising high into the blue sky, while all the rest of the world lay at their feet ruddy rosy brown. The sudden contrast was tremendous, electrifying. I could have cried with excitement of the overwhelming spectacle. I wanted someone to admire the sight with me. A man came whistling along the road riding upon a cart horse. I would have stopped him and drawn his attention to the mountains but I thought he would probably consider me mad. He did not seem to be the least struck by or to be taking the smallest notice of the great sight. but it seemed to me as if one might never see such a sight again. The brilliant yellow light gradually deepened with the sky to the indescribable red tinge that snowfields assume in sunset light, and then the grey cold tint crept up the great slopes quenching the rosy warmth which lingered still a few minutes on the summits. Soon all was cold and grey and all that was left of the brilliant gleaming range was the dim ghostly phantom of the mountain rampart scarce distinguishable from the greying sky.

Tuesday, 17 October, 1871. [Kilvert visits St. David's.]

We intended to have taken a dogcart to St. David's but the morning was rainy and the roads bad, so the landlady, Mrs Philpotts, persuaded us to have a pair of horses and a carriage with a head, and we found she was right. We started at 8 o'clock in a warm drizzle. People were pouring into Haverford West Fair from all the country-side on foot and horseback, in traps, carts and waggons and a 4-horse biweekly omnibus from St. David's. Droves of black cattle and sheep were pouring along the muddy roads. Most of the men wore blue coats and the women long blue cloaks.

At last we rattled into the village city, the Cathedral City of St. David's. And so we came to the end of the world where the patron saint of Wales sleeps by the Western sea.... The village stands on the brow of the deep steep-sided glen in which the Cathedral is buried and from which the Tower is seen emerging. Like most of the houses in these parts the village roofs were all whitewashed and I kept on fancying that snow had fallen and whitened the roofs. At a little distance this peculiarity gave the village city a strange appearance. It looked like a snowy city, a city in the snow....

...We sallied out again and descended upon the South side of the Cathedral. It was melancholy to see the devastation made by time and neglect and execrable taste and Churchwarden's Gothic. But when we entered the Church by the South door I was astonished at the magnificence of what was left, the grand rich Norman arches, the massive round pillars enriched by pilasters and their wealth of mould-ings in the nave and the splendour of the piers which support the Tower, the four lofty arches and the glory of the roof, the solemn grandeur of the silent Choir and the rich dark purple of the stone....

Then the old Canon put on his black fur cloak and came with us across the little quaint short bridge over the little river to the Cathedral to show us the curiosities. We saw St. David's Shrine on the North side of the Choir with its simple low arcading and the small holes for hands to pass through to deposit offerings to the Shrine of the great Welsh Saint. The tomb is simple and humble like the spirit of the man who sleeps below. In the middle of the Choir, in front of the high altar, stands the tomb of the Earl of Richmond, father to Henry VII. The tomb is dilapidated and the Dean and Chapter are hoping that the Queen will restore the tomb, so they have done nothing to it. There was a huge rent in the East End of the tomb through which we inserted our umbrellas and stirred the kingly dust. It felt much like common earth....

Kilvert's Diary, Chosen and edited by William Plomer (Jonathan Cape: 1960).

1875

WILLIAM MORRIS (1834-96). *Artist, poet, socialist and visionary. Morris's paternal ancestors on both sides were Welsh and he seems to have retained a romantic attachment to Wales although it appears he only visited it at the time when the following letter was written to his daughters.*

To Jane Alice and May Morris.
5 April, 1875. Bull Hotel, Bala.

Dearest Jenny and May,

...'Tis a queer dull little grey town is Bala: but we are resting the horses here for a day. This morning I went out fishing in the rain up a very pretty river, the Welsh name of which will not stick in my head: I caught but two trouts which we had for dinner.

The little town lies at the head of a lake some 5 miles long which the Welsh call Llynn Taged: I don't know what that means: indeed I am but an ignorant person in Wales. The country is pretty about the lake but not so fine as some we have been through. We had a beautiful ride yesterday from Dinas Mawddwy up the valley of the Dyfi (a river) till it came to an end, and then over the mountain-necks into another valley, and so here. The Dyfi valley was most beautiful, and I thought it would be so nice to have a little house and a cow there, and a Welsh pony or two. The little houses are very rough outside but cleaner and trimmer inside than one might imagine. We had our lunch in one (a pot-house) yesterday, and they brought us the biggest loaf I ever saw: the Italian cakebread was a mere joke to it: it was very good to eat....

The Letters of William Morris, ed. Philip Henderson (Longmans, Green & Co.: 1950).

1876

JOHN RUSKIN (1819-1900). *Critic and explainer of art, architecture and literature, Ruskin became the most vehement critic in the nineteenth century of industrialism and its effect on human life. In his autobiography,* Praeterita, *he wrote of Wales:*

...My first sight of bolder scenery was in Wales; and I have written, – more than it would be wise to print, – about the drive from Hereford to Rhaiadyr, and under Plynlimmon to Pont-y-Monach: the joy of a walk with my father in the Sunday afternoon towards Hafod, dashed only with some alarmed sense of the sin of being so happy among the hills, instead of writing out a sermon at home; – my father's presence and countenance not wholly comforting me, for we both of us had alike a subdued consciousness of being profane and rebellious characters, compared to my mother.

From Pont-y-Monach we went north, gathering pebbles on the beach at Aberystwith, and getting up Cader Idris with help of ponies: – it remained, and rightly, for many a year after, a king of mountains to me. Followed Harlech and its sands, Festiniog, the pass of Aberglaslyn, and marvel of Menai Straits and Bridge, which I looked at, then, as Miss Edgeworth had taught me, with reverence for the mechanical skill of man, little thinking, poor innocent, what use I should see the creature putting his skill to, in the half century to come.

The Menai *Bridge* it was, remember, good reader, not *tube*; but the trim plank roadway, swinging smooth between its iron cobwebs from tower to tower.

And so on to Llanberis and up Snowdon, of which ascent I remember, as the most exciting event, the finding for the first time in my life a real 'mineral' for myself, a piece of copper pyrites! But the general impression of Welsh mountain form was so true and clear that subsequent journeys little changed or deepened it....

In the early 1870s, attempting to put into practice the ideas which he had come to believe about human activities and their misapplication, he founded the Guild of St. George (at first called the Company) which was to be devoted to the cultivation of the land and of manufacturing with as limited use of mechanical means as possible. Believing also in the right education of the workman and the educative power of art, he founded a museum and began the publication of selected books. Certain people helped him in these ventures and one of them was a wealthy widow, Mrs Fanny Talbot, who donated some land and eight cottages at Barmouth in North Wales to the Guild. In August 1876, Ruskin visited Barmouth, made some brief comments in his diary and wrote an Open Letter, one of a series he addressed to the Workers and Labourers of Great Britain under the title of Fors Clavigera, *an extract from which follows.*

Letter LXIX.

I have just been down to Barmouth to see the tenants on the first bit of ground, – noble crystalline rock, I am thankful to say, – possessed by St. George in the island.

I find the rain coming through roofs, and the wind through walls, more than I think proper, and have ordered repairs; and for some time to come, the little rents of these cottages will be spent entirely in the bettering of them, or in extending some garden ground, fenced with furze hedge against the west wind by the most ingenious of our tenants.

And in connection with this first – however small – beginning under my own eyes of St. George's work, – (already some repairs had been made under my direction, under the superintendence of the donor of the land, Mrs Talbot, before I could go to see the place) – I must state again clearly our St. George's principle of rent. It is taken first as the acknowledgement of the authority of the Society over the land, and in the amount judged by the Master to be just, according to the circumstances of the person and place, for the tenant to pay as contribution to the funds of the Society. The tenant has no claim to the return of the rent in improvements on his ground or his house; and I order the repairs at Barmouth as part of the Company's general action, not as return of the rent to the tenant. The reader will thus see that our so-called 'rents' are in fact taxes laid on the tenants for the advancement of the work of the Company. And all so-called rents are, in like manner, taxes laid on the labourer for the advancement of the work of his landlord. If that work be beneficial, on the whole, to the estate, and of all who live on it, the rents are on a right footing; but if they are abstracted by the landlord to his own private uses, he is merely another form of the old medieval Knight of Evilstone, living as hawk in eyrie....

John Ruskin, *Collected Works, Vols. XXVII and XXXV,* ed. E.T. Cook and A. Wedderburn (London: George Allen, 1903-1912).

1882

LLOYD GEORGE (1863-1945). *Politician and statesman, first elected to Parliament in 1890 where for some years he espoused the cause of Disestablishment and Welsh nationalism. From 1905 he held ministerial posts in the Liberal government and, as Chancellor of the Exchequer, introduced social reforms which were a foretaste of the later Welfare State. He became Prime Minister in 1916 and held the post until 1922. He remained an M.P. until 1945 when he was given an earldom but he died soon afterwards. The following few extracts from his diaries and letters give some insight into his youthful views and ambitions in Wales.*

Sat. 19 Aug, 1882.
Reading *Democracy* the popular novel which exposes American politics. My poor studies!... Idea struck me that it would not be a bad 'spec' some time to write a novel demonstrating how the poor are

neglected in religion and politics, and inculcating a principle of 'religion & politics' for the poor. Bravo! A really *brave* (Oh!) design.

Sun. 2 March, 1884.

Believe in my heart of hearts – and I told my brother William today – that a good walk on such a beautiful day would have shown far greater appreciation of the Blessing than sticking in a musty hovel to listen to the mumbling of musty prayers and practice.

Sun. 2 October, 1884.

Got up 7. Fine morning – Took a walk – far as Dwyfor. Nothing convinced me more than this walk of the scandalous waste of opportunities involved in a chapel huddling a religion of pseudos – the calm and beauty of the scenery breathes far more divinity than all the psalmodies and prayers of a million congregated churches.

Feb. 1886. After a meeting at Blaenau Ffestiniog where Michael Davitt, the Irish Land League leader was the main speaker L.G. also spoke – diary entry runs:

Regarding Davitt, I am favourably impressed by his presence. He appears to be very earnest and sincere – tho he spoke for about an hour he was listened to with unflagging interest. He highly complimented me – told me that I aroused by far the most enthusiasm – that it was quite evident that I touched the heart of the audience. Although he could not understand me, he knew very well I was eloquent [L.G. spoke in Welsh].... My speech gone like wild-fire through Ffestiniog they're going to make me an M.P. ...*I feel like I am in it now.*

To his future wife [undated probably 1887) from Criccieth.
He clears himself of any charge of impropriety arising from his visiting a girl, the daughter of a fishmonger, who was implicated in a breach of promise case.

One of the few religious dogmas of our creed I believe in is – fraternity with which you may couple equality. My God never decreed that farmers & their race should be esteemed beyond the progeny of a fishmonger & strange to say Christ – the founder of our creed selected the missionaries of his noble teaching from amongst the fishmongers. Do you really think that the Christ who honoured & made friendship with Zebedee the fishmonger's son would disdain the acquaintaince of a poor toiling fishmonger's daughter? And who are lawyers & farmers daughters that they should presume to despise that class from amongst which the prince of eternity selected his friends. If proof was required of the utter hollowness of what is known as respectable Christianity let him but study the silly scorn of classes for their supposed inferiors. The barbarous castes of the Heathen Hindoo are but a faint imitation.... You seem to think that the supreme function of a wife is to *amuse* her husband – to be to him a kind of twin or plaything to enable him to while away with enjoyment his leisure hours. Frankly, that is simply prostituting marriage. My ideas are very different – if not superior – to yours. I am of opinion that woman's function is to soothe & sympathize & not to amuse. Men's lives are a perpetual conflict. The life I have mapped out will be so especially – as lawyer and politician. Woman's function is to pour oil on the wounds – to heal the bruises of spirit received in past conflicts & to stimulate to renewed exertion. Am I not right? If I am then you are pre-eminently the girl for me. I have a thorough belief in your kindliness and affection.

As to setting you free, that is a matter for your choice & not mine. I have many times impressed upon you that the only bond by which I have any desire to hold you is that of love. If that be lost then I would snap any other bond with my own hand. Hitherto my feelings are those of unflinching love for you & that feeling is a growing one.

You ask me to choose – I have made my choice deliberately & solemnly. I must now ask you to make your choice. I know my slanderers – those whom you allow to poison your mind against me. Choose between them & me – there can be no other alternative.

May I see you at 7 tomorrow?

The following letters to his wife contain reports of L.G.'s triumphant meetings in 1893-95 when he was espousing Welsh disestablishment and subsequently formed the Cymru Fydd [Young Wales] League designing it to be the spearhead of the North and South Wales Liberal Federations whose objective should be home rule for Wales. His plan was soundly defeated at a meeting of the South Wales Liberal Federation on January 16 1896. (See the final letter below).

17 May, 1894. Caernarvon.

Mag – nificent meetings. Immense – swept all before us. Made many converts by my speech last night. I was in fine form and carried them step by step completely with me. This afternoon we had also the same measure of success attendant on our efforts. Bryn candidly confesses that the meeting last night was a great surprise to him. He thought all along that I would get a vote but he thought also that the opposition would be much more formidable than it has turned out to be. But it was simply a pitiable collapse....

18 May, 1894. Rhyl.
Well we are winning hands down. Last night we had a magnificent meeting at Conway. I never spoke better in my life. The Conway people were completely carried away. It was I think one of the finest things I have ever done. They were perfectly unanimous & enthusiastic....

19 May, 1894.
We had a first rate meeting last night – altho' barely a few hours' notice had been given we had a full house – scores were even standing at the end of the hall. I had the very amusing experience of receiving an encore. I had spoken for about three quarters of an hour & then sat down but the audience insisted on my getting up again - cheered & cheered again until I got up and went on for another quarter. Resolution – strong – carried with but four dissensions. Daily Post admits today we have carried North Wales.

23 May, 1894. Rhyl.
After breakfast this morning in came Miss Gee with a story that the Welsh M.P.'s had met & condemned us. We got the papers at once & discovered that about a dozen of them had met 'informally' & after censuring us determined upon summoning a meeting of the Welsh Party for Friday afternoon to discuss our conduct. I then decided at once that my place was in London to face the cowards who would not even criticise our action in our presence when we challenged them but who condemn us when our backs are turned....

We had a magnificent meeting yesterday. Denbigh was very striking & at Mold the meeting was most enthusiastic. Gee is with us *heart & soul*. He is not in favour of giving in whether we get assurances or not. Go on with the formation of an independent party – that is his & my idea....

4 June. Cardiff.
Been engaged all day with the editor & subsequently with the proprietor of the S.W.D. News. They have as you know been fiercely opposed to us. Of course I couldn't expect them to confess that they have been wrong but I tried to induce them to drop the past & go in on general grounds for the formation of a Welsh National Party. *I have succeeded* with Alfred's help.

They intended boycotting our meeting tonight but after my talk it has been arranged to send up the chief reporter & the editor up to the meeting tonight. Now what do you think of that for a triumph?

5 June. Aberdare.

We had a magnificent meeting last night – about 4,000 people in all. The South Wales Daily News editor & chief reporter were there & were very much impressed. They give my speech an exceedingly prominent position & type – dividing it into sections with flaming head-lines. They refer to it in the leading article as 'the eloquent speech etc'. Their articles today are very different in their tone. They go in for a Welsh party. We are winning hands down....

19 November, 1895. Tredegar.

You have more brains than you give yourself credit for. Mrs Freeman was telling Towyn Jones on Monday that you were the very essence of common sense. She never met anyone so thoroughly sensible. That is exactly my opinion. You have the most valuable intellectual faculty – sound judgement & if you have transmitted it to the children I shall be more content than if they have inherited all the troublesome powers I may be endowed with. Got a capital meeting last night altho' the audience in these semi-English districts are not comparable to those I get in the Welsh districts. Here the people have sunk into a morbid footballism.

21 November, 1895. Swansea.

Last night's demonstration was simply *immense* – that is the word. Nothing like it in the Rhondda – not in the memory of the oldest inhabitant has anything to equal it been seen. Crowds from all parts of the Rhondda came down. Hundreds of D.A. Thomas' own colliers amongst them. Mabon★ looked blue. I talked Home Rule for Wales & all the Nationalist stuff which the Mabon crew so detest – but the people cheered to the echo. The Rhondda has been captured.

★ Mabon – William Abraham – *Miners' leader and M.P. for the Rhondda; Radical Liberal at this time but later a member of the Labour Party.*

16 January, 1896. Newport.

The meeting of the Federation was a packed one. Associations supposed to be favourable to us were refused representation & men not elected at all received tickets. There were two points of dispute between us. By some oversight they allowed me to speak on one &

we carried it – as it turned out not because the majority of the meeting was with us but becuase they went to the vote immediately after my speech & I can assure you the impression made could be felt. I simply danced upon them. So they refused to allow me to speak on the second point. The majority present were Englishmen from the Newport district. The next step is that we mean to summon a Conference of South Wales & to fight it out. I am in bellicose form & don't know when I can get home.

The Making of Lloyd George, W.R.P. George (Faber: 1976).
Lloyd George Family Letters 1885-1936, ed. Kenneth O. Morgan (Oxford University Press, University of Wales Press: 1973).

1885

BEATRIX POTTER (1866-1943). *The well-known writer of animal stories for children, in her youth wrote a journal in code. The following describes a visit to Wales.*

Wednesday, 13 May. [1885].

Went with papa and mama to Machynlleth in Merioneth. From Euston to Stafford by Holyhead Mail all very well, but the Welsh railways are past description. Four hours to go sixty miles between Shrewsbury and Machynlleth. When mushrooms are in season the guard gets out to pick them.

Machynlleth, wretched town, hardly a person could speak English. Wynnstay Arms to which we were directed, closed since two years. Lion, only other, a singular place. Country most beautiful, but on rather an awkwardly large scale for getting about. House we went to see, *Pennal Power*, in a wilderness. Widow, Mrs Thruston, alarming result, and warning of living in the wilds.

Village of Pennal consisted of three large Chapels and about twelve other houses. Welsh seem a pleasant intelligent race, but I should think awkward to live with. The children exceedingly pretty, black or red, with pink complexions and clear blue eyes. The middle-aged are very plain, but the old people are better. The language is past description.

Journal of Beatrix Potter from 1881 to 1897, transcribed from her code writing by Leslie Linder (Frederick Warne & Co., 1966).

1886

THOMAS ELLIS (1859-99). *The following is the election address of Thomas Ellis in 1886 which led to his election to Parliament as a Liberal Member. He was the first to include self-government for Wales in an election manifesto but, as can be seen, it also embraced social, economic and religious reform. After his early death he joined the legion of 'lost leaders.'*

To the Electors of Merionethshire.

Gentlemen,

I ask for your votes as the chosen candidate of the Liberal party in Merionethshire.

Mr Gladstone is ready to listen to the voice and entreaty of Ireland for the right to run her own affairs, by her own sons, on her own land. I give him my warmest support.

It is time for Parliament to listen to the voice of Wales. It is demanding the Disestablishment of the Church of England in Wales, and the use of its endowments for the good of the nation generally.

It is desirous of perfection in its educational system – the poor like the rich to have the same opportunities to take advantage of all the educational resources of the nation.

It is demanding a thorough reform in the Land Acts, in order to guarantee security of home, fair rents and the security of the fruits of the labours of the worker, the farmer, and the merchant.

It is demanding Home Rule, so that the control of the drink trade, public appointments, and the means of national development are in the hands of the Welsh people.

From complete conviction I will do what is in me to support these measures and every measure for the improvement of the people of Wales.

I am, gentlemen,

Your obedient servant,

Thomas Edward Ellis.

1887

LETTERS FROM WALES – *a series of Letters was published in the* Times *in 1887 dealing with the state of Wales in especial relation to the Land, the Church and the Tithe by a Special Correspondent. The anonymous Correspondent was J.E. VINCENT, a defender of the landed class, solicitor of the North Wales Property Defence Association and the chancellor of the diocese of Bangor. Here he is writing about Welsh nationalism, adducing arguments which could indubitably be echoed today over one hundred years later.*

Oct, 28, 1887.

...Thoughtful men cannot shut their eyes so firmly as not to see that ever since Mr Gladstone's ill-advised speech at Swansea (in June 1887) a vigorous appeal has been made to the Welsh people with the object of rousing in them a struggle for independence. The time was cleverly chosen. No man, living or dead, ... has ever exercised so much influence over Welsh minds as Mr Gladstone possesses. His eloquence charms a people who delight in oratory; his cunning of phrase is congenial to their habits of thought; his apt allusions to their history fascinate them. And the Swansea speech – every line of which is capable of being explained away – was delivered at an opportune moment. It was spoken at a time when Welshmen, in common with the rest of their fellow-subjects, had grown weary of the endless wranglings of a House of Commons condemned to ceaseless attention to Ireland, when the efficiency of the Parliamentary machine seemed almost to be irretrievably lost....

Now the writer of these "Letters from Wales", in spite of abuse which has been poured upon him by the Welsh press, in spite of the fact that he has been dubbed Balaam and Munchausen, and has been described as tainted with the priesthood and full of the savour of the tithe, is, as a matter of fact, an ardent Welshman. He yields to none in an almost passionate love for the traditions of his country or in admiration of that taste for culture, for poetry, for literature and for music of which Welshmen are justly proud. It is, however, possible to indulge and to foster all these feelings and at the same time to deplore and regard as omens of calamity to come the methods which are now in use to stir up nationalistic aspirations in the Principality. Let me beseech my fellow-countrymen to look at the matter with practical eyes. Many centuries ago the ancestors of our fellow-subjects in England conquered us, and the constant tendency has been towards real, no less than nominal, amalgamation. We are citizens of that State which stands first in the world as the champion of absolute freedom; Englishmen have no advantage over us in point of citizenship; we are placed on a footing of perfect equality with them. It is true that in times past an attempt has been made to Anglicize us – in passing I may pause to say that this failure is a matter of triumph to me – but it has failed. Our language is full of vitality and of the power of expansion; we are not Anglicized in that matter, and we never shall be. Moreover, the Anglicizing policy has been deliberately relinquished and condemned as a blunder. Our national institutions have the patronage of Royalty; no attempt is now made to discourage our language or to discredit our traditions. Cannot we be content to look facts in the face, and to see that it is out of the question, for obvious geographical reasons, that we should be divorced from England?

...We desire, it seems, to keep Wales, Welsh appointments, Welsh emoluments for Welshmen. Would it not be well to pause and consider whether we should be gainers or losers if a similar policy were pursued across the border? Would it not also be wise to reflect upon the nature and the extent of this unity which we boast? We are one in language, in literary and musical taste, but it may well be doubted whether the unity goes further than this. In old times we were constantly embroiled in petty quarrels, and signs have not been wanting of late to show that the ancient spirit is still alive.

"Caernarvon, the capital of Wales!" I can fancy a series of enthusiasts saying, "Denbigh is the place; Aberystwyth is more central, Wrexham more influential; Cardiff, Newport, Swansea have infinitely stronger claims for the honour...."

The small towns with which I am best acquainted are full, as every candid man who knows them will immediately confess, of mutual jealousies.... Nor as far as one can judge, have North and South Wales that warmth of friendly affection for one another which would justify us in expecting a minute assembly representing the two to be characterized by orderly and quiet attention to public business.

A republication of Letters from Wales (W.H. Allen: 1889).

1889

QUEEN VICTORIA (1819-1901). *Extract from the Queen's Journal.*

August 26th, 1889. Pale – Llanderfel.

After luncheon we all started for Llangollen, going by rail, and had a beautiful afternoon. In three-quarters of an hour we reached Llangollen, where it seems I had passed the night with Mama, in a small inn, overlooking the river, which is still standing. The station was very prettily decorated. We at once entered our carriages, Beatrice, Alicky, and Liko driving with me. We turned sharp to the left above the station, where there was a Guard of Honour of the

Volunteer Battalion of the Welsh Fusiliers, with their band and goat, with its gilt horns (my gift), and drove up the beautiful, wooded, mountain-girt, deep valley, dotted with villas and cottages, to Bryntysilio, the well-known residence of Sir Theodore Martin, who with Lady Martin received us at the door. The place is beautifully situated, and the house is furnished and arranged with the greatest taste. They showed us all their rooms and his study, with the table at which he wrote dearest Albert's life. Had tea in the Drawing-room, during which a selected number of Llangollen choirs sang Welsh songs, in the pretty sloping garden. It is wonderful how well these choirs sing, being composed merely of shopkeepers and flannel weavers.

QUEEN VICTORIA to Sir Henry Ponsonby.
27 Aug, 1889. Pale – Llanderfel.

Would Sir Henry write fully to the Prince of Wales of the excellent and enthusiastic reception we have all met with here and to Sir F. Knollys to tell him *how* much this naturally *sensitive* and warmhearted people *feel* the neglect shown them by the Prince of Wales and his family, and that really it is very wrong of him not to come here. It is only five hours from London, and as the Prince of Wales takes his title from this country, which is so beautiful, it does seem very wrong that neither he nor his children have come here often, and indeed, the Princess and the children not at all....

Letters of Queen Victoria, ed. G.E. Buckle (John Murray: 1930).

1898 ff.

EDWARD THOMAS (1878-1917). *Poet and prose writer whose parents came from Wales to which he himself felt a strong attachment although he was born and brought up in London. He married his wife, Helen, when he was very young and subsequently earned a precarious living by writing prose books – among them was* Beautiful Wales *– although his true gift was for poetry which he did not begin to write seriously until he met Robert Frost in 1913. He was killed in the First World War and most of his very fine poems were only published posthumously. The first letters here were to Helen before their marriage written from the house of Welsh relatives where he was staying.*

EDWARD THOMAS to his future wife.
Sunday, August, 1898. 7 Woodville Street, Pontardulais.

I have spent half another day in the usual Way, – a little better –
for I heard a Welsh service, – Church of England it is true, – at a
small ancient church in a pretty place four miles off at Llanedig –
Edwy's Church. My thoughts were too satiric and cynical to record
here – all those angular, awkward, grim Welsh people – and the insin-
cere, fox-hunting parson; the nailed boots clattering ill-manneredly
on the harsh floor – We had a delightful walk afterwards along the
riverside, I and a cousin and Gwili*. We were near the home of the
otter; kingfishers were there; flowers, too, that you and I know, lovely
one, – buttercup, bramble, meadowsweet, honeysuckle and some we
have not seen together....
I wrote one goodish sentence about the young poplars in the rain
yesterday, that is all....

* Gwili – John Jenkins – *poet, theologian, winner of the Crown at the
National Eisteddfod in 1901.*

August 19th, 1898.
...I can look back contentedly upon the full-packed hours I have
just spent in Caermarthenshire – contentedly! – more than that!
Do not expect from me a close and orderly account of what I did.
That would mean such labour that I should describe things which
really did not make a powerful impression on me. Instead I will just
babble to you the tones that are still vibrating loudly in my brain. –
No, do not ask for a record, for that would remind me of how tiring
a human being I am, how little sensitive to loveliness and greatness.
Loveliness and greatness – I have seen them both in these two days.
I have seen the vale of Towy and its river, – a flat wealthy plain
framed by sudden wooded hills on every side all peaceful, glowing,
and peopled by folk of quite ideal sweetness; that was the loveliness.
The greatness was all the greatness of the past; for as yet these quiet
valleys have no new greatness, however much people so earnest and
intelligent may do. Greatness of the past! The castles of Wales! I saw
several of them; one was actually in the grounds of the farm at which
I stayed, its name was Dryslwyn Castle. The farm is called Dryslwyn,
and means Tangled Brakes. Well, these castles called up very few
feelings in me, except such as I fear have been stolen from reading
of matters like this; still, even so, I felt a positive pleasure in seeing
at last what I had only heard of before. This particular castle was very
ruinous, fragmentary, standing on the edge of a steep hill remarkable
for its compactness and shapeliness – in shape like a Noah's ark, and

very regular though natural. Fancy attacking it up such a slope! I ran up – and nearly died in my panting – I stood actually in the window cut out of the 3 foot thick wall, where the knights aimed their arrows and mangonels (great wooden slings); they were now adorned with the daintiest of pale tufted ferns; near them were the flowers you love, red campion, harebells, mallow and wild thyme. The perfect strength of the building was touching; even overhanging parts were quite firm, so skilful was the architecture, *so good the mortar.* Yet it must soon perish; and then there will be no voice with which these cruel ambitious Norman knights can speak to us. They built sincerely and well but they have been overtaken by Time, and will soon be beaten by it. We nowadays cannot – or do not build – so nobly.

Then we went to Grongar, which is not naturally remarkable; but of course it is world famous on account of the poem of Dyer, which you shall see when I come back. In the distance we saw De Nevers* Castle among woods; as the name shows it is Norman – Some other day I hope to see this and another castle – Castle Carrig Cennen, which we did see but only at a distance....

* *In a later letter he corrects this to Dynevor.*

Sunday.

I gave you last night some idea of what we *saw* but I did not say anything about the people. Nevertheless except repeating what I have said of other Welsh people, I will say little. They were pious, decent, clean and passionately happy, and this, too, though they were all orphans, though they have seen many troubles, though Mr Harris ... the only son there is delicate and painfully deformed, a hunchback. Besides him there were his three sisters, sharp featured, somewhat refined, spare natured... when they spoke English, they spoke it well evidently with some knowledge of English literature. Their Welsh I could not follow, but it was evidently humorous within comely bounds; and to this was added that great enthusiasm which is exclusively Welsh, – the enthusiasm for Welsh poetry; when they sing it is the songs of men who have lived near them, who still live there, or who have known and loved them. There is this about Welsh poetry so different to English; it is entirely Welsh, it refers constantly to Welsh men, traditions, places, by name, and is proud of all; whereas English poetry has no such character, – except Wordsworth's perhaps. The poetry too, is all made to be sung and is sung. Why! when we were out, two or three of my companions were always singing a Welsh hymn or song, and sang so heartily and seriously; moreover all know the songs the others know and the tunes! Those songs of Watcyn Wyn's* were all sung to the tunes of old Welsh airs which have a common but inexpressible charm; they are just a little melancholy yet sprightly like a pattering dance. When I come back I shall bring with me a copy of this book, containing the music also. 'The Maids of Caermarthen' and 'The Girl of Llandybie' are delightful; and I mutter all day the tune of 'Tra bo clochty yr y pentre'*[2] which is 'while the belfry in the village' then I forget the rest but the substance is while the belfry in the village charms the countryside I will love the maid of Llandybie. In this too he talks of the 'Lwchion lacher', the bright Loughor which is the river that flows a quarter mile from here pronounced Loo-choore (guttural ch). You see the character of them. They are simple and truly homely, since they are all about the home of the poet. Yet I daresay this poetic value is not greater than English poetry nowadays; only it is simple, less ambitious; and of course sounds stranger (and more striking to me) in a strange tongue; then also it has the advantage of music which few English verses have. These men, too, Helen, something like you are living lives exactly in accordance with their powers Yes! and with their desires, probably. Or is it that I know more of Welshmen than English and have passed over the successes of the latter. Certainly, I think a poet, especially a lyric poet, has an infinitely greater chance here than in England, a greater chance of perfection in his art and in his fame. I myself, if only I were greater, might lament I came to London to be born....

* Watkin Hezekiah Williams (1844-1905). *Principal of a school in Ammanford where young men prepared to become Nonconformist ministers. He published several volumes of poetry and won the Bardic Chair and Crown. Edward Thomas quotes the two poems in his book* Beautiful Wales.

*[2] *Corrects this in a later letter to* 'Tra bo'r clochdy yn y pentre'.

26/viii/98.
...I have again been away from Pontardulais.... Early on Tuesday I went off to Amanford to the bard Watcyn Wynn.... Again I had an entirely delightful time....

We drove in a wagonette several miles in the afternoon to a village called Trapp and thence walked to Castle Carreg Cennen, the object of the expedition.

On our way we saw the 'Llygard y Llwchwr', the 'eye of the Llwchwr' that is the fountain spring – It is very small and tranquil; above it is a cave without end; really without end; for it is quite safe and people have advanced hour after hour without being stopped; it is in limestone and may be leagues long. On the way the hedges, which are steep and turfy, ferny walls topped by hazels, cut off our view; then we saw the castle. It is plain and ugly, upon the edge of a perpendicular grey cliff, softened each side by a green ascent through oaks, hazels, fern and gorse by which we approached the castle. The climb must have given me years of life, or made the years I shall live more intense than before! To feel the keen sweet air pumped in intrepidly! to be a more healthy flower under the puissance of the winds! every breath was full of all the potent odours of flowers and green things; it was magical also with delicious poisons – from purple flowers. My thoughts in the castle and in its presence were tumultuous, and upset partly by my puny terror at the steep rock and the threatening ruins. I was awed by the vigour and perseverance of an age that could produce such work; by the cruelty of time and of succeeding generations of men. My own littleness was never so clear; I seemed less than the pebbles which we sent spinning over the abyss; my value and beauty seemed incomparable to that of the harebell which I picked from the ruined walls. They were not melancholy thoughts yet too stormy and strange to leave me laughing joy; though I laughed loud and happily all day. I wish I could sing my feelings....

Much remains of this castle, but it is almost tottering; the elder tree is in its walls, the grass on its floors....

Correspondence of Edward and Helen Thomas, National Library of Wales 22914C.

The Twentieth Century

EDWARD THOMAS to Ian MacAlister from Tiry Vail, Amanford.
August 30th, 1900.

After all Wales is good for me. In spite of my accidentally cockney
nativity, the air here seems to hold some virtue essential to my well-
being, and I always feel in the profoundest sense, at home. Anyhow
I am vastly better, though still unable to walk the two or three miles
necessary to reach the nearest waterfall among trees, or the nearest
Castle – Careg Cennen, which has a site as imposing as Edinburgh
Castle, as I hear from those who know both. But the castle is a fearful
place, and glimpses through its shooting-gaps on to a plain about 400
feet sheer below, leave my body like a telegraph wire in a high wind.
I still wait for a visit from my prosaic Muse; and have to fill up my
hours of solitude with writing distasteful scraps of a novel....

EDWARD THOMAS to Gordon Bottomley.
November 23rd, 1905. Swansea.

On Tuesday I came here and I have been fiercely bored ever since.
Swansea is a big rather notably ugly town and what with my not very
intimate acquaintance with my host I am being reduced to inaction.
Everything is against me. A mile off lives an old Aunt whom I
remember seeing when I was 4; two miles off is an old Lincoln friend
whom I have not seen since 1900. I have seen them both and they
have plunged me into languid and unpleasant reminiscence, and
altho' the Welsh mutton is good my food is thus not altogether
bracing. Also the merriest man I ever knew – Watcyn Wyn – the
bard who wrote The Maid of Llandebie and The Maids of
Caermarthenshire – is to be buried today: and on Sunday I am to be
taken in my bowler hat and collar to a Welsh chapel in the town. And
I have still a lame foot and cannot confidently start a long walk. Of
all these blessings my temperament makes the best as you know it
would. So how can I write?...

My host is a schoolmaster. The school is adjacent and now I hear
a master's whistle assembling a crowd of ragged children, and see

him with miniature ferocity giving silly little cuts with the cane to the boys who are healthy enough to ignore his commands. So I end.

The Life and Letters of Edward Thomas, John Moore (Heinemann: 1939).

To Helen Thomas.
5 ix 10, [1910].

Dearest one,
    ...Arthur with difficulty decided not to fish after so many black days and we both took train to Aberystwyth and got there by 11 in a carriage crowded with young farmers' wives and their babies taking butter into town.... Aberystwyth is a Welsh town with a sea-front of nothing but tall lodging houses ending in a castle at one end and a steep hill at the other. There is a pier in the middle. The sky was perfect with white cloud and the sea shimmering away to very distant hills along the coast north and south. We had meant to take the light railway to the Devil's Bridge 12 miles up the river Rheiddol but Arthur began to think possibly this was the day of days for fishing [and] decided not to go. The light railway went winding with the river which ran in a beautiful valley with oakwoods half way down and then green fields and corn below and a few farms. Gradually the valley narrowed, the hills grew steeper and the fields smaller and smaller, and the railway ran on a terrace above steeper and steeper slopes and round sharper and sharper corners which I did not like at all. I felt so foolish in such a train on such an expedition that I fully expected a calamity as punishment. For miles you could almost touch the tops of trees growing below the carriage. The smoke was wafted continually into our eyes in the open carriage and it stank horribly. A father of a family in front with large ears, very confident manner, loud voice and facetious temper talked most of the time to his obedient family. When we got out I just went down towards the Devil's Bridge – where the opposite hillside's trees almost meet and hide the river a hundred feet below – and saw 'Tea 6d 9d and 1/- Falls 1/- and all sorts of people parading about off into the hotel which owns the falls, a solitary young man looking romantic and the confident man coming along, his son carrying the camera. So I fled without seeing the falls or bridge and set out walking for Tregaron 15 miles away. I did not see anything quite so extraordinary as the Devil's Bridge but crossed a very beautiful valley and steep oak woods with sheep farms and wild bare hills beyond and above and had many glimpses of wild valleys with a farm every half mile or so half hidden under a small

clump of trees half way up the hillside.... I had tea at 6 and then
about 7 miles back – the wind south and the sky clouded over and
some of the mountains were half lost in misty cloud.... I enjoyed
walking along a solitary road with the heather peat and the Leirg(?)
valley below me all the time – robins singing here and there – The
only person I passed was an old old woman with a great bunch of
black curls sprouting under a beaver hat of the old Welsh type only
not very tall....

Correspondence of Edward and Helen Thomas, National Library of Wales
22914C.

1904 ff.

VIRGINIA WOOLF (1882-1941). *Novelist and essayist, famed for her
innovations in the art of fiction. The following are extracts from letters she
wrote while staying at Manorbier in Pembrokeshire: the first two were
written to her close friend, Violet Dickinson, a few days after the death of
her father, the writer Leslie Stephen, in February, 1904; the third to her
sister, the painter Vanessa Bell, when she was staying in Manorbier alone
in August 1908.*

VIRGINIA WOOLF to Violet Dickinson.
28 February, 1904. Manorbier, Pembrokeshire.

...We have come to the right place. Never were people so lucky as
we are in practical things. The house holds us perfectly, and is warm
and comfortable, and I haven't seen such splendid wild country since
St. Ives – indeed one thinks of St. Ives in many ways. We have
already spent an astonishing amount of time walking about on the
cliffs. Even lying in the sun. We live almost under the shadow of a
great feudal castle, which stands on a cliff over the sea. Nessa and I
have walked right along the coast already, never meeting anyone.
  There are about 3 houses here, and a wild queer Church on the
hill. It is cold, but very clear and bright, and no sound but wind and
sea....

March, 1904.

...We saw Choughs and Ravens the other day, climbing up rocks
to get at them, and rolling about in the maddest way.

Our only excitement has been the death of the washerwoman! As she stood at her tub. The village thought there ought to be an inquest, but didn't know how to begin; the doctor and policeman arrived separately from neighbouring villages, and refused to do anything without the other. So finally the village determined on its own account that death was due to natural causes, and have just buried her, going past the window in the oddest way. The first 6 rows of mourners held black edged handkerchiefs to their eyes, or mouths: they weren't crying; and the rest look fairly cheerful. Aint it barbaric? As you can imagine the whole village turned out to watch, and last night the young men who have nice soft voices sang a hymn under our windows....

VIRGINIA WOOLF to her sister, Vanessa Bell.
Thursday, 20 August, 1908. Manorbier.

...I walked along the Cliff yesterday and found myself slipping on a little ridge just at the edge of a red fissure. I did not remember that they came so near the path; I have no wish to perish. I can imagine sticking out one's arms on the way down, and feeling them tear, and finally whirling over and cracking ones head. I think I should feel as though I saw a china vase fall from the table; a useless thing to happen and without any reason or good in it. But numbers of people do fall over; my good landlady tells me stories. Her son-in-law was found dead in the road, his horses coming home before him, and no one knew how it happened. She is full of saws, and wisdom about making the best of things, and "here we are, and we must grin and bear it." She offered me a horn cup, made from an ancestral cow, which I had to refuse as well as I could: and then said that I was like the gentleman she had just had – a true lady.

I don't think the Cliffs are as fine as Cornish cliffs, and the land is certainly tamer, but then Manorbier is practically in the 40ties; there was a school treat on the beach yesterday, and for some reason it seemed to me exactly the kind of thing that happened in the year 1845. They drove off in a two horse waggon, with little bonnets, and side whiskers....

The Flight of the Mind: The Letters of Virginia Woolf, Vol. I 1888-1912, eds. Nigel Nicolson and Joanne Trautmann (The Hogarth Press: 1975).

WILFRED OWEN (1893-1918). *Renowned poet, killed in action during the First World War. He was of Welsh extraction though born and brought up in Oswestry. When a child he spent occasional holidays with relatives in Wales, the following letter being written on one of those occasions.*

22 August, 1905. Rhewl, near Ruthin.

Dear Mother,

I hope you are all quite well, I am eating tremendously. We went gathering nuts this morning I have got altogether, 113. I am going to bring them home for the children you must not tell them please. Mr Jones has bought 120 sheep today. They are so tired after walking 3 days that some will let me stroke them. I can count up to 10 in Welsh, and have learnt a few expressions. It will soon be time to milk the cows now. I can milk a bit. I drink buttermilk for dinner, a have cream on the stewed fruit. Indeed I fare very sumptuously, & wish Mary was here to eat the plums we get off the tree every day.

There are nine little piggies. You would be amused if you saw them. Their heads are too large for their bodies & their tails are like curly bits of string. [Drawing of pigs]

We are having fine weather now. I am very glad of the boots, because in the morning the grass is wet. I have not been to Ruthin yet. When I go I mean to buy a little tiny boat to sail down the Clwyd. It is nearly time for the post now.

With love and kisses always from Wilfred.

Wilfred Owen Collected Letters, ed. by Harold Owen and John Bell (Oxford University Press: 1967).

1912

KEIR HARDIE (1856-1915). *Socialist, Scotsman, miners' leader, one of the founders in 1893 of the Independent Labour Party, was elected as one of the members of Parliament for the two-member constituency of Merthyr Tydvil in 1890. He was the first Socialist M.P. to be elected in Wales. The following open letter, written by Hardie, appeared in the local paper of the I.L.P. the* Merthyr Pioneer, *on Saturday, June 15th, 1912. It was addressed to 'His Most Gracious Majesty King George the Fifth on his proposed Visit to Dowlais Ironworks.'*

Your Majesty,

I gather from the public press that you, accompanied by the Queen, are about to pay a visit to Merthyr. It is being reported that the object of the visit is to enable you to become better acquainted with your people – a most laudable object. You will find the people of the Merthyr and Aberdare Valleys well worthy of a better acquaintance, and were it possible for you both to spend a few days in social converse with them they would be able to tell you many things which your exalted position precludes you from knowing. For myself, however, I must say that the ostensible object of your visit does not seem very convincing. I do not know what reasons were advanced to induce you to single out Merthyr for this special honour, although probably you had no real say in the matter and I should certainly not have intervened were it not that there are certain facts which, in fairness to yourself, you should know before giving final assent to the arrangement.

The lesser of the facts is that a very large proportion of the electors of the Merthyr Boroughs are good sound Labour men and Socialists. This, of course, is an evidence of their intelligence which I hope you will fully appreciate. For some time past, however, there has been a movement on foot amongst the reactionary elements in the constituency to check the growth of the working class movement, and, particularly, to oust me from the Parliamentary seat... it is hoped that you will succeed where all else has failed, and that your presence may be taken as a hint that an advanced Socialist and Republican like myself is not the sort of member whom the workers should send to represent them in Parliament. No effort will be spared to make your visit as imposing and impressive as possible with this end in view, and those members of public bodies who most bitterly oppose any expenditure of money in improving the town or relieving destitution will be in the forefront of those who will clamour for expenditure upon decorations and the like on the occasion of your visit... Let me add, that I view these efforts to use you as a political agent with perfect composure, and merely mention the matter as a preliminary to something else of far greater importance.

That something else is this. The arrangements contemplated, I understand, include a visit to Dowlais where you are to be shown over a part of the Iron Works and to be entertained there to lunch. It is this fact which has led to this letter being written. The Dowlais Iron Works, with those of Cyfarthfa which are now blended with Dowlais, have been in existence for over a century. During that period these works have yielded scores of millions of pounds in dividends and profits to their owners who have thus become wealthy to an amazing degree. The profits and dividends have enabled them to become great landed proprietors who now rank with the county aristocracy of more than one shire in England. Even now the public balance sheets prove that the profits exceed £500,000 a year. It would naturally be assumed that a firm so prosperous would have been noted for a fair, if not generous, treatment of its working people, and also for its benefactions to the town in which its wealth was being made. The very opposite of this is the case. The whole of Merthyr and Dowlais will be searched in vain for any evidence of public spirit on the part of the Guests, the Crawshays, or (as the firm is now named) the Guests, Keens and Nettlefolds. There are no public buildings, monuments, public parks or public institutions due to their generosity or civic patriotism....

That of itself, would be a serious indictment, but there is a much graver one to follow. From the days of its earliest inception down to a few months ago this firm had the unsavoury notoriety of being the worst sweaters of labour in the whole of Wales.... No thought, care or consideration for the comfort, safety or convenience of the workers was ever given by the firm.

In March, 1911, between 40 and 50 Dowlais moulders came out on strike because of an insidious attempt on the part of the firm to still further reduce the miserable pittance they were receiving in the form of wages. You will be driven through the main street from Merthyr Station up through Penydarren to the Dowlais Works. There will be gay buntings and great crowds to watch you pass. Look at them closely, especially from the upper end of Penydarren to Dowlais. I have no doubt they will do their best to make themselves look respectable, but even then you will find evidences of deep poverty to which you will not be able to close your eyes. Were it possible for you to leave your carriage and walk round the purlieus, the back closes, the slums, the horrible hovels in which hundreds of the workers of Messrs. Guest, Keen and Nettlefolds are herded together and for which they pay extortionate rents in Cyfarthfa, Penydarren and Dowlais, Your Majesty would be shocked. And these disgraceful conditions are the direct outcome of the low wages reduced still further by broken time paid by the firm....

I mentioned above that the moulders came out on strike in March of last year. In process of time their example affected other bodies of workmen in Dowlais, and the agitation for improvement became general. The firm, however, turned a deaf ear to every appeal until the Government, convinced by the facts and figures which I put before them, and which they properly tested by their own investigators informed Messrs Guest, Keen and Nettlefolds that no further

Government contracts would be given the firm until they paid their workers the Trade Union rates of pay. This example was followed by every one of the self-governing Dominions overseas and, thus brought to bay, the firm had, of dire necessity, to grant the workmen Trade Union conditions. But the matter did not end there. The striking moulders, with the exception of the few the firm could not do without, were, on one pretext after another, refused employment; and even now, fifteen months from the date of their coming out on strike some of these men are still on the street....

The reason why the astute gentlemen who are arranging this trip for you have decided to take you to Dowlais and to have you entertained by the firm may now be clear to you. It is that the principal shareholders of the firm who are leading lights in the social world of London, Birmingham and elsewhere may be rehabilitated, whitewashed and once more made to appear respectable members of society. This does not appear to me to be a very kingly office. I respectfully ask Your Majesty, therefore, before consenting to visit Dowlais Works or to be entertained there, to make enquiries concerning these facts; and if you find – as you must find if you inquire – that they are true both in substance and in fact – to refuse to be a party to the arrangement of either visiting the works or being entertained there to lunch. From a people so kindly as the Welsh, you are bound in any case, as the head of the State to receive a warm welcome, but that warmth will he turned to enthusiasm if you boldly take your stand on the side of the workers and refuse to lend the countenance of your presence to a firm whose whole record is bad... Go to Dowlais by all means. See the people and their homes, but shun the works as you would a plague spot....

Yours respectfully,

J. Keir Hardie.

1915 ff.

SAUNDERS LEWIS (1893-1985). *Playwright, essayist, critic and in 1925 one of the founders of the Welsh Nationalist Party, of which he was President from 1926 until 1939. He was born in Liverpool of Welsh parentage, his commitment to Welsh nationalism springing from his profound commitment to the Welsh language. The following letters were written to his future wife in the early part of his life.*

SAUNDERS LEWIS to his future wife.
July 2nd, 1915, 6 a.m. Queen's Hotel, Newport, Mon.

My dear Margaret,

...Do you know that Caerleon where King Arthur and Launcelot and the Knights of the Round Table lived is quite close to here? When I went through it first in the train I remember feeling a thrill at the thought of being on the central ground of all the old romances. I was through there last night on a bicycle. It was dark and a lovely sky and the roads and fields were beautiful. There was an enchanting smell of mown hay and the village was quiet with only a light here and there in a cottage window. I felt distinctly that those old knights and ladies still haunted the place at night. I could almost feel them there. A field there is called the Round Table field, where excavations are being made and some old Celtic relics found and these have been put in a local museum....

July 16th, 1919. 1 Fyfone Villas Swansea.

...We live very quietly at Swansea. It is not a town that grows pleasanter....

On Saturday, however, my uncle took me motoring to Carmarthen, a beautiful old country town twenty-eight miles from here in the dip of the Towy valley, the town you would fall in love with at first sight, not big, but quiet, quaint, with good bookshops, and engravings in the windows, the office of a Welsh newspaper, a market square and some impossible statues of an old Welsh General of Wellington's time or of South African soldiers, an old yew-hidden church and churchyard with memories of Peter Williams and Jeremy Taylor and seventeenth century Wales, and memories many hundred years older than those; then the quaint low parlours of sedate Welsh inns, the country around of low and high hills, the winding salmon-haunted river with its wooded valleys and the whole green countryside and white cottages and farms nestling in every hollow and hillside. You could imagine life being continuous there throughout the centuries, decently, placidly, with no great changes, but with traditions of grace and beauty and seriousness, old families occupying old homesteads and moving in quiet ways towards quiet resting places. I've vowed to go there for two days or three before returning to Liverpool. Penrith, of course had a similar charm, but they talk Welsh in the narrow streets of Carmarthen....

Swansea, July 21st, 1919. 1 Fyfone Villas.

...Briefly, I meant that Wells was not serious enough; there are problems that matter but 'Empire' is not one of those. For Empire is a myth, and like all myths a tyranny and bad religion, and men wage war and destruction for imperial juggernauts of their own pride, destroy life for a bubble's sake. And that's why I dislike Kipling (genius as he truly is); but he's raised men's passions and whipped men's fury and written canting verses, like 'Recessional' and 'If' and the 'Seven Seas' to make men hoarse, a foul high priest in a filthy temple where the Union Jack is an obscene God....

On Saturday we had a great drive from Swansea to Carmarthen and then up the Towy Valley nearly to Llandovery and with the Black Mountains on our right. There was no real rain and the view of the Towy Valley was beyond description; we stayed in one little village for tea and at the inn we had to serve ourselves. For everyone had gone to the village peace-day sports, and there we went also after eating. It was the very heart of Wales; not an English word on the sports field from grown-up or child, but racing and shouting and prize-giving and picnicking, and all in great spirit, and some of the most original and humorous characters I've ever met. We passed Dynevor which is the old capital of south Wales and the royal seat of the Dyfed kings before the conquest of Edward I. Carmarthen is a county of the most splendid thatched roof anywhere....

Swansea, Aug. 6, 1920. 1 Fyfone Villas.

Yesterday I spent at the National Eisteddfod at Barry. A fairly pleasant little town gay and beflagged for the great week of its life, then an enormous pavilion for 15,000 people and that full, and musical and literary competitions the long day through, and a concert at night. And gradually, spite that I constantly whipped my flagging patriotism, a headache grew on me, and I grew tired and tireder, and the whole thing struck me not as the splendid symbol of lofty national culture it is supposed, but a very blatant and philistine exhibition of second-rate talent riding the high horse and making an unconscionable fuss of itself. One of the romantic figures there was an Irish lord, Lord Ashbourne, in native old Irish costume, kilts etc, and he wore the dress quite well, quite unconscious of any strangeness about it. He contrasted queerly with the Welsh bards in their ridiculous white shrouds straddling grotesquely in the mud and rain. This letter is a fearful breach of loyalty, I see, so it shall stop....

Oct. 5, 1920. Dolauhirion, 14 Cambrian Place, Aberystwyth.

...On Saturday I had a delighful pilgrimage to the home of an eighteenth century Welsh poet and antiquary at 'Allt Fadog' (Madog's wood or hill), some five miles from here along the Rheidol river. The house, an old farmhouse stands as it stood when Lewis Morris lived in it. Have you ever seen one of these genuine old farm kitchens – the oak beams of the ceilings, the settle by the hearth, the great hearth itself stone-paved beneath its chimney, the chain-swung cauldron over the fire of coal and wood, the hams hanging from the ceiling, the dressers and delf....

This old Welsh civilisation grips me by the roots. I went to Llanbadarn Fawr church on Sunday evening to the Welsh service, and I felt jealous of the curate whose work it is to administer in that church, to be familiar with it daily and to go in and out among the farms and cottages of the village. An old woman said to me 'There's only one Llanbadarn Fawr in all Wales', the sense of pride in your village is almost like the sense of ancestry in its effects. I hardly talk English at all in this life, so if my letters reflect it, you know why....

Monday evening, 17.10.21. 10 Hamilton St, Cardiff.

Last week I addressed the Cardiff Welsh Societies on the question of forming a Welsh repertory company here and they proposed doing something. A committee has been appointed to consider my scheme. So I have some hope – though not too much. These Welsh folk have so little sense of what is good in art and literature that to hope over much is foolish. You've no idea how I envy Ireland and the Irish their sense of beauty in art, literature and religion. It's dead in us; Nonconformity and English landlordism have made us what we are and it will take many generations, a century perhaps, to recover it....

Friday, 17.3.22. 10 Hamilton St, Cardiff.

...The play presents great difficulties. I really don't know how I'll get to rehearsals, and there are heaps of other problems getting a hall (would you believe a city like Cardiff hasn't a public hall that can be hired?), and worse yet, getting good actors. Our crowd are terribly amateurish. I suppose however there must be a beginning. But it drives me to voluble oaths when the only good actress and a pretty one too has poor Welsh, and she has to be taught pronunciations; yet her parents know more Welsh than English. The rest are perfect in their speech but they have devilish hands which can't find rest, and hopeless stage manners. Altogether we're a funny crowd, and Lord knows how we'll shape.

This week has brought us spring with a bound and celandines and daisies are in every field. Last Sunday I walked over the fields to Llandaff Cathedral for the evening service. I had not been there before. The church is not one of the seven wonders of Wales but yet it has qualities, and is old. It looked very well outside under the full moon. But I always wish every time I enter a church, that people would drop the vicious habit of preaching in churches. It turns every service into buffoonery. I am always astounded at the vandal daring of men who shout such commonplace twaddle into the grey beauty of great cathedrals. Queer they don't die at the sound of their own voices....

Letters to Margaret Gilchrist, eds. Mair Saunders Jones, Ned Thomas and Harri Pritchard Jones (Cardiff: University of Wales Press, 1993).

1916

BERTRAND RUSSELL (1872-1970). *Philosopher and author of many important philosophical works, Russell was also an advocate of many advanced political and social causes. His active opposition to the First World War finally resulted in his imprisonment. These extracts from letters to Lady Ottoline Morrell, with whom he had an affair, were written in July 1916 when he was campaigning against the war in South Wales. In his later years he made his home in North Wales.*

BETRAND RUSSELL to Lady Ottoline Morrell.
Central Hotel, Merthyr, Sunday evg.

My Darling – I found your letter when I arrived this morning....
    We had another terrible Comm[ee] yesterday. I don't know how it will work out. I came down as far as Cardiff late last night & on here this morning. I spoke here at 2.30 a *wonderful* meeting, as they had promised. The Chief Constable even is friendly here – I had some talk with him afterwards. I find the police short-hand writer who takes down every word I say is getting his orders from London, not the local police. There were between 2000 & 3000 people, quite unanimous – it was very inspiring.
    I want a *great* fuss made about my not being allowed to go to America. I left it to Allen to arrange the fuss. Probably he will have

spoken to you about it. Trinity* is going to consider on Tuesday whether to dismiss me for 'grave moral obloquy' but no doubt I have incurred that.

I did have hopes the war would end this year but now I have practically none. Apparently Kitchener's 3 years will be right.

* *Trinity College, Cambridge.*

Tuesday mg. Port Talbot.

...The state of feeling here is quite astonishing. This town subsists on one enormous steel works, the largest in S. Wales; the men are starred, & earning very good wages. They are not suffering from the war in any way. Yet they seem all to be against it. On Sunday afternoon I had an open-air meeting on a green: there were two Chapels on the green, & their congregations came out just before I began. They stayed to listen. A crowd of about 400 came – not like open-air meetings in the South where people stay a few minutes out of curiosity & then go away – they all stayed the whole time, listened with the closest attention, & seemed unanimously sympathetic. The man who has been organizing for me here works 12 hours every day except Sunday in the steel works. Their energy is wonderful.

Sunday evening I spoke at Briton Ferry – a really wonderful meeting – the hall was packed, they were all at the highest point of enthusiasm – they inspired me & I spoke as I have never spoken before. We put a resolution in favour of immediate peace negotiations, which was carried unanimously. (I did not notice any abstentions, tho' presumably the two plainclothes men who had come to take notes must have abstained). Those who had not already signed the peace petition signed it in large numbers. One needs no prudent reticences – no humbug of any sort – one can just speak out one's whole mind. I thought the great offensive would have excited them but it hasn't.

Yesterday evening I spoke at Ystradgynlais, a mining town of 16,000 inhabitants. The meeting was smaller & my impression was that a good many people at it were undecided in their minds – that sort of meeting is really more useful than an enthusiastic one. The audience were almost all miners – they seemed intelligent and hopeful.

I enclose a little leaflet which is distributed at my meetings. If you don't burn it at once, you are liable to imprisonment....

Merthyr, Wed. evg.

The Rev. Morgan Jones is a *splendid* man – I go to lunch with him in the hills near here every day. He is a *real* saint, full of simple courage. He has preached against the war from the start, & is being turned out – probably to starve. But he is so loved in Merthyr that something is sure to be done for him. The I.L.P. have taken to going to his Chapel, 'tho many of them are not Xtians. The C.O.s* are producing a new religion which I fully share. The difference of Xtian & agnostic has become insignificant among them. Wherever one goes one finds it & everywhere one finds the C.O.s the happiest men imaginable.

* *Conscientious Objectors.*

Harry Ransom Humanities Research Centre, The University of Texas at Austin.

1916

ROBERT GRAVES (1895-1985). *Poet, novelist, essayist, interpreter of mythologies. Graves owned a house in Harlech when he was a young man and wrote of the area, 'above Harlech I felt a personal peace independent of history or geography.' The following letter was written from there soon after he had been badly wounded in France during World War I.*

ROBERT GRAVES to Siegfried Sassoon.
2 May, 1916. Erinfa, Harlech, N.Wales.

My dear Sassoon,
This is the first day that I have felt really strong enough to write you the letter you deserve, being now more or less recovered from the amazing lot of blood I lost last month.
Well, old thing, I'm really desolated at having deserted you and the battalion but I couldn't help it. My people forced me before a specialist who ordered an immediate operation which he said would only take three weeks, which would have meant that having got a three weeks' extension to my leave I would have gone straight back to the battalion. As it was, it proved much more serious and I am on a month's back leave after which bloody Litherland, I suppose. But I swear I'm not skrimming my shanks: though I can't pretend I like

284

Fricourt better than this heavenly place I honestly would go back tonight if I could.

I can't do purple patches well, but Merioneth now is nothing but bright sun and misty mountains and hazy seas and sloe blossoms and wild cherry and grey rocks and young green grass. I am writing in my small, white-walled cottage of which I must have told you – the one that once belonged to a consumptive coachman, then to a drunken carpenter, then became a brothel, then a Sunday school and now serves as pleasaunce for me and my two sisters....

There is a peculiar cuckoo in the woods just outside with a bad stammer. It says cu-cuckoo and sometimes even cu-cu-cuckoo. I must tell the *Spectator* about it....

In Broken Images: Selected Letters of Robert Graves 1914-1946, ed. Paul O'Prey (London: Hutchinson, 1982).

1916

DORA CARRINGTON (1893-1932). *Carrington left home in her teens to study painting at the Slade School of Art and there became acquainted with many budding artists of that time. More importantly her friendships extended into literary and intellectual circles in which such figures as Virginia Woolf, E.M. Forster, Lady Ottoline Morrell etc. were prominent. She became the close companion of Lytton Strachey and stricken by his death in 1932 she shot herself some weeks later. In recent years her merits as a painter have been belatedly recognised.*

The following letter was written to the painter, Mark Gertler, from North Wales where Carrington was spending a short holiday with Lytton Strachey and other friends.

Monday. August, 1916.
c/o Mrs Hiles, Llanbedr, Taly-cafn S.O. N.Wales.

I arrived here on Saturday evening. After a terrible, one of the most terrible, journeys I have ever undergone. Crowds of horribly sticky sweating people.

I am most happy here. Just Lytton, Barbara and Nicholas. We go out most of the day for long walks, and bathe in a wonderful pool with waterfalls. The mountains are quite high, and one gets Cézanne landscapes of mountains with dull green trees, and ugly white cottages with Slate roofs.... Barbara's cottage is very small, all white outside with a small garden filled with flowers. And all round these huge mountains and a big river in a flat valley below.... The Weather is wet here and quite cold.... This country is really very fine. But so different from Hampshire that I find it hard to get my eye ranged properly. It is all so big, and there is no crisis like one has in England. By a big hill and the rest of the country flat and one sees everything planed out so as to speak, leading up to the centre. Here it [is] vastly big and no order.... The people all speak Welsh here and But little English....

Carrington: Letters and Extracts from her Diaries, ed. David Garnett (Oxford University Press: 1979).

1925

EVELYN WAUGH (1903-66). *English novelist – for a time Waugh was a dissatisfied schoolmaster at Arnold House, Llanddulas, Denbighshire.*

Sunday, 25 January, 1925.

Yesterday morning the bell rang for school and everyone went up in a great shouting crowd, the masters in the midst. Soon Banks arrived with a list and started directing them into various rooms under various masters.... I bored myself and the Fourth Form with some Latin verbs for fifty minutes. Then I went next door and tried to make the Fifth understand what 'Metre' meant with some little success.

In the afternoon I went for a walk and discovered that besides the sea, the railway and the quarry there are some mountains. It is a highly geological country. Everyone in Wales has black spittle and whenever he meets you he says 'borra-da' and spits. Also I discovered that everyone's manners are so good that when you say 'Am I going the right way to Llanddulas?' they always say 'yes.' This courtesy led me many miles astray.

EVELYN WAUGH to Harold Acton.
18 February, 1925. Arnold House.

An Indian Ass which I had been eagerly awaiting arrived two days ago. You must think that I have, with all else, left my manners and friendship behind that I have taken so long to thank you for it. But indeed you cannot imagine what a time I am having. There is a woeful imposition called 'a week on duty' which has at last fallen to my turn. It means that from eight in the morning until eight at night one has literally no minute to spare in which to read a postcard or visit a *cabinet*. From eight at night until ten I sit with a blue pencil correcting history essays. Last night a boy had written 'at this time it was reported that James II gave birth to a son but others supposed that it was conveyed to his bed in a hot water bottle'....

I got very very drunk all alone a little time back and was sick among some gooseberry bushes. I also found a hairdresser in a tiny town called Rhyl who collected Austin Spare's drawings and was writing a book about Cabbalism. I am growing a moustache and learning to smoke a pipe and ride a horse and am altogether quite becoming a man. De profundis E.

Letters of Evelyn Waugh, ed. M. Amory (Weidenfeld & Nicolson: 1980).

1925 ff.

DAVID JONES (1895-1974). *Poet and artist, born in Kent, was Welsh on his father's side and lived for short periods in Wales at Capel-y-ffin in the community set up by Eric Gill, and with the monks on Caldey Island from where he wrote the following letters.*

DAVID JONES to Philip Hagreen.
26 March 1925. The Abbey, Caldey.

...I have done a good deal of drawing since my arrival. The weather has been so good that I simply felt that Gulliver or no Gulliver I must take the opportunity and do some outdoor work, as it would be absurd to leave here without having done some work.... I wish I could bring the results of my labours to show you – not that they are at all good – but merely rather interesting. I like the stone walls and the murderously sharp rocks... only I find the *form* most infernally diffi-cult to correlate – if you follow. I have never before drawn the sea – it is difficult not to be led up various impressionistic and realistic and otherwise dangerous paths when faced with sea – or – even worse, to fall back upon some dead convention.

There is also a superb plantation of new trees here, which is thrilling, very thrilling – like the Garden of Gethsemane and the Garden of the Tomb and the Garden of – well – the other sort of garden, where Venus disports herself. In fact it is as 'B' [Belloc] would say, 'a garden universal, a garden Catholic' – not that it is a flower garden, but a garden of small trees and winding paths – but oh! so difficult to seize hold of when one tries to draw it....

To H.S.E.
Sunday, 2 October, 1927. Coburg Hotel Tenby.

Here I am a prisoner not being able to say to the sea be still – I cannot reach Caldey until the weather changes! It's very depressing – anyway being alone in a hotel always really drives me mad! Tenby is rather charming of course but it is fiendishly windy and a beastly drizzle.... There are very few people in this hotel and no one of my kind. I mean, you know, no one to talk to. Well, there is a parson of some sort who told me all about red sandstone before breakfast.

Dai Greatcoat: A self-portrait of David Jones in his Letters, ed. René Hague (Faber: 1980).

1931

THOMAS JONES (1870-1955). *Frequently known by his initials TJ, Thomas Jones was a distinguished civil servant, appointed Deputy Secretary to the Cabinet by Lloyd George and subsequently working for Bonar Law, Ramsay Macdonald and Stanley Baldwin. He was instrumental in the foundation of the Gregynog Press and Coleg Harlech. The letter to him from George M.L. Davies provides a vivid description of conditions in Wales in the 1930s.*

Letter to his daughter Eirene (White).
October 20 [1931]. Gregynog Hall, Newtown.

10 p.m. and a tempting fire in my room so I thought I would scribble you a line, chiefly in order to tell you one of Dean Inge's stories at dinner before I forget it. He is on his way to deliver an inaugural lecture at Aberystwyth.... M. [Mussolini] was having an interview with the King of Italy when the latter dropped his handkerchief; M. picked it up and the King thanked him rather effusively.
M. 'But that is what any one of your subjects would be proud to do.'
King. 'Well, it is true I do rather treasure this handkerchief. It is

about the only thing into which I am allowed to put my nose!'
Another –

Where five economists are gathered together there will be six conflicting opinions and two of them will be held by Keynes!

Letter to Thomas Jones (TJ) from GEORGE M.L. DAVIES.
April 21, [1937]. Maes-yr-leaf, Educational Settlement, Rhondda.

The exodus goes on here at an accelerating pace and parents are following their children to England. In the absence of any new industries here there seems to be no economic alternative; but the uprooting is a distressing business for the older people who miss all their warm neighbourliness and social or religious interests of these valleys when they go to some atomic suburb like Dagenham. In Birmingham they have formed an association for the migrants who meet once a month and try to look after the newcomers. I met a couple of hundred of them.... Last night I was at a gathering of representatives of the churches at Tylorstown which has been very hard hit. Several of the older men spoke in an almost desperate way. And yet there is intimacy, frankness, kindness; and courage in these chaps that makes one glad to be near them.

All they could think of in the way of external aid was that the Churches should press the Government to bring in some industries and that the P.D.C. (Powell Duffryn Coal Company) should be petitioned to sell coal to unemployed men at pit-head prices. So far it has been difficult to get the P.D. people to budge, either in furthering cooperative levels for voluntary work and free distribution of coal or in concessions of cheap coal. To see swarms of men picking the tips, in the weather we had last winter was a horrible sight.

None the less this is a wonderful place, with nearly all the talents.

THOMAS JONES to Violet Markham.
August 31, [1940]. Brynawelon, Criccieth.

L.G., Dame Margot, Olwen and two sons, and Megan here apart from visitors. L.G. brimful of energy and talk from breakfast to bedtime, canvassing every phase of this war and the last, and what Cromwell did and Marlborough and Napoleon and Soult and Ney and Massena and Scipio Africanus. He is terribly realistic and critical, especially of John Anderson.* We are going in a moment off to Ffestiniog with some expert from Beaverbrook to see what can be done with the big quarries as possible sites for factories and shelters. He has already persuaded Beaverbrook to use the Port Dinorvir quarries, but only last week. It is a thousand pities he is not inside the Cabinet. I find him far more alive and stimulating than any Cabinet Minister I meet and he would be so much better inside instead of chafing and stamping among his family in impotent futility. Like many others of great imaginative gifts and public courage, he is physically a coward and obsessed with safety problems.

* *Lord President of the Council in the War Cabinet, with responsibility for overall economic planning.*

Thomas Jones, *A Diary with Letters* (Oxford University Press: 1954).

1933 ff.

DYLAN THOMAS (1914-53). *Poet, short story writer, born and educated in Swansea. His first book of poems,* 18 Poems, *was published when he was only twenty years old and the majority of the following letters were written in his early youth.*

To Pamela Hansford Johnson.
[late October 1933] Blaen-Cwm, Llangain, near Carmarthen.

...I am staying, as you see, in a country cottage, eight miles from a town and a hundred miles from anyone to whom I can speak on any subjects but the prospect of rain and the quickest way to snare rabbits. It is raining as I write, a thin, purposeless rain hiding the long miles of desolate fields and scattered farmhouses. I can smell the river, and hear the beastly little brook that goes gurgle-gurgle past this room. I am facing an uncomfortable fire, a row of china dogs, and a bureau bearing the photograph of myself aged seven – thick-lipped, Fauntleroy-haired, wide-eyed and empty as the bureau itself. There are a few books on the floor beside me – an anthology of poetry from Jonson to Dryden the prose of Donne, a Psychology of Insanity. There are a few books in the case behind me – Bible, From Jest to Earnest, a History of Welsh Castles. Some hours ago a man came into the kitchen, opened the bag he was carrying and dropped the riddled bodies of eight rabbits on the floor. He said it was a good sport, showed me their torn bellies and opened heads, brought out the ferret from his pocket for me to see. The ferret might have been his own child, he fondled it so. His own eyes were as close-set as the eyes of the terrible thing he held in his hand. He called it, 'Billy fach.'

Later, when I have finished this letter, I'll walk down the lane. It will be dark then, lamps will be lit in the farmhouses and the farmers will be sitting at their fires, looking into the blazing wood and thinking of God knows what littlenesses, or thinking of nothing at all but their own animal warmth.

But even this, grey as it is, and full of the noise of sanitating water, and full of the sight of miserably wet fields, is better than the industrial small towns. I passed them in the bus coming down here, each town a festering sore on the body of a dead country, half a mile of main street with its Prudential, its Co-op, its Star, its cinema and pub. On the pavements I saw nothing but hideously pretty young girls with cheap berets on their heads and paint smudged over their cheeks, thin youths with caps and stained fingers holding their cigarettes, women all breast and bottom, hugging their purses to them and staring in at the shop windows, little colliers diseased in mind and body as only the Welsh can be, standing in groups outside the Welfare Hall. I passed the rows of colliers' houses, hundreds of them, each with a pot of ferns in the window, a hundred jerry-built huts built by a charitable corporation for the men of the town to breed and eat in.

All Wales is like this. I have a friend who writes long and entirely unprintable verses beginning, 'What are you, Wales, but a tired old bitch?' and 'Wales my country, Wales my cow.'

To Pamela Hansford Johnson.
[early December 1933]

...My Life ,The Touching Autobiography Continued From the Last Letter But Three (or Four).

Gower is a very beautiful peninsula, some miles from this blowsy town, and so far the Tea-Shop philistines have not spoilt the more beautiful of its bays. Gower, as a matter of fact, is one of the loveliest sea-coast stretches in the whole of Britain and some of its tiny villages are as obscure, as little inhabited, and as lovely as they were a hundred years ago.* [*In the margin:* * this sounds like a passage from a Tourist Guide.]

I often go down in the mornings to the furthest point of Gower – the village of Rhossilli – and stay there until evening. The bay is the wildest, bleakest, and barrenest I know – four or five miles of yellow coldness going away into the distance of the sea. And the Worm* [*In the margin:* * Perhaps this accounts for my Complex], a seaworm of rock pointing into the channel, is the very promontory of depression.

291

Nothing lives on it but gulls and rats, the millionth generation of the winged and tailed families that screamed in the air and ran through the grass when the first sea thudded on the Rhossilli beach. There is one table of rock on the Worm's back that is covered with long yellow grass, and, walking on it, one [feels] like something out of the *Tales of Mystery and Imagination* treading, for a terrible eternity, on the long hairs of rats. Going over that grass is one of the strangest experiences, it gives under one's feet, it makes little sucking noises, & smells – and this is to me the most grisly smell in the world – like the fur of rabbits after rain.

When the tide comes in, the reef of needle rocks that leads to the base of the Worm, is covered under the water. I was trapped on the Worm once. I had gone on it early in the afternoon with a book & a bag of food, and, going to the very, very end, had slept in the sun, with the gulls crying like mad over me. And when I woke the sun was going down. I ran over the rocks, over the abominable grass, and on to the ridge overlooking the little reef. The tide had come in. I stayed on that Worm from dusk till midnight, sitting on the top grass, frightened to go further in because of the rats and because of things I am ashamed to be frightened of. Then the tips of the reef began to poke out of the water, &, perilously, I climbed along them onto the shore, with an 18 mile walk in front of me. It was a dark, entirely silent, entirely [empty?] road. I saw everything on that walk – from snails, lizards, glow worms & hares to diaphonous young ladies in white who vanished as I approached them.

To Pamela Hansford Johnson.
Sunday, April 15th, [1934].

The worms are doing very nicely today. Sunday in Wales. The Sunday-walkers have slunk out of the warrens in which they sleep and breed all the unholy week, have put on their black suits, reddest eyes & meanest expressions, and are now marching up the hill past my window. Fathers are pointing out the view to their stiff-collared whelps. I'd like a big green stick with a pike on the end. Mothers are resting their bellies on pram-handles; little girls are telling each other their harmless stories of affectionate Sunday School mistresses, boys with pomaded scalps are thinking of picture shows and lingerie, and all the starch, the thin pink blood, the hot salty longings, and the respectable cream on the top of the suburban scum, run down the stones, like a river end up in the Sabbath well where the corpses of strangled preachers, promising all their days a heaven they don't believe in to people who won't go there, float and hide truth. Life passes the windows, and I hate it more minute by minute....

To Pamela Hansford Johnson.
May [about 21, 1934]. Laugharne.

I am spending Whitsun in the strangest town in Wales. Laugharne, with a population of four hundred, has a townhall, a castle, and a portreeve. The people speak with a broad English accent, although on all sides they are surrounded by hundreds of miles of Welsh country. The neutral sea lies at the foot of the town, and Richard Hughes writes his cosmopolitan stories in the castle....

I wish I could describe what I am looking on. But no words could tell you what a hopeless, fallen angel of a day it is. In the very far distance, near the line of the sky, three women & a man are gathering cockles. The oyster-catchers are protesting in hundreds around them. Quite near me, too, a crowd of silent women are scraping the damp, gray sand with the torn-off handles of jugs, & cleaning the cockles in the drab little pools of water that stare up out the weeds & long for the sun. But you see that I am making it a literary day again. I can never do justice (*the words* in my precious prose *are deleted*) to the miles and miles and miles of mud and gray sand, to the unnerving silence of the fisherwomen, & the mean-souled cries of the gulls & the herons, to the shapes of the fisherwomen's breasts that drop, big as barrels, over the stained tops of their overalls as they bend over the sand, to the cows in the fields that lie north of the sea, and to the near breaking of the heart as the sun comes out for a minute from its cloud & lights up the ragged sails of a fisherman's boat. These things look ordinary enough on paper. One sees them as shapeless, literary things, & the sea is a sea of words, and the little fishing boat lies still on a tenth rate canvas. I can't give actuality to these things. Yet they are as alive as I. Each muscle in the cocklers' legs is as big as a hill, and each crude footstep in the wretchedly tinted sand as deep as hell....

It's getting cold, too cold to write. I haven't got a vest on, and the wind is blowing around the Bristol Channel. I agree with Buddha that the essence of life is evil. Apart from not being born at all, it is best to die young. I agree with Schopenhauer (he, in his philosophic dust, would turn with pleasure at my agreement) that life has no pattern & no purpose, but that a twisted vein of evil, like the poison in a drinker's glass, coils up from the pit to the top of the hemlocked world. Or at least I might do. But some things there are that are better than others. The tiny, scarlet ants that crawl from the holes in the rock on to my busy hand. The shapes of the rocks, carved in the chaos by a tiddly sea. The three broken masts like three nails in the breast of a wooden Messiah, that stick-up in the far distance from a stranded ship. The voice of a snotty-nostrilled child sitting in a pool and putting shellfish in her drawers. The hundreds and hundreds of rabbits I saw last night as I lay, incorrigibly romantic, in a field of buttercups & wrote of death. The jawbone of a sheep that I wish would fit into my pocket. The tiny lives that go slowly & languidly on in the cold pools near my hands. The brown worms in the beer. All these, like Rupert Brooke, I love because they remind me of you. Yes even the red ants, the dead jawbone & the hapless chemical. Even the rabbits, buttercups & sailing masts....

Darling, I love you.

XX

To Oscar Williams.
October 30, 1945.

...It is hysterical weather where I am writing, Blaen Cwm, Llangain, Carmarthenshire, Wales, in a breeding box, in a cabbage valley, in a parlour with a preserved sheepdog, where mothballs fly at night, not moths, where the Bible opens itself at Revelations; and is there money still for tea? My son, in the nonstop, probably frog-filled rain, is performing what seems, from this distance, to be an unnatural act with a beaver. Looking closer, I see he is only destroying his sister's doll – the little pixie. I can hear, from far off, my Uncle Bob drinking tea and methylated spirits through eighty years of nicotine-brown fern. My father, opposite, is reading about Hannibal through a magnifying glass so small he can only see one word at a time. I could lie down and live with Hannibals. And my wife is washing an old opera....

Dylan Thomas, *The Collected Letters of Dylan Thomas*, ed. Paul Ferris, (Dent: 1985)

1935 ff.

JOHN COWPER POWYS (1872-1963). *Prolific writer of novels, poetry, essays, autobiography and letters. Having spent his youth in the West Country, he lived in the U.S.A. for many years but in July 1935 he and Phyllis Playter moved to Wales, living in Corwen until 1955 when they moved to Blaenau Ffestiniog. During those years he wrote his Welsh historical novels* Owen Glendower *and* Porius. *The following are, first, extracts from his diaries and then from his letters.*

Wednesday, 10 July [1935].

[We] set out in the Rain to visit the Hanleys.* We have decided that when people say that Wales has such a large *rain-fall* they forget to make any mention of the particular *kind* of rain that this rain fall consists of – namely misty rain, mountain-mist rain, soft vaporous rain, rain that is *really entering into a cloud,* which has *not* burst into ordinary rain yet, but just holds its rain in a diffusion of soft warm cloudiness.... Rain in Dorset drenches you to the skin very soon whereas after walking to the Hanleys in pouring rain, only it is not 'pouring' – that is the point – but *diffused* we sat there talking without thinking of wet & I even put on my wet coat to keep me warm after tea ere they lit the fire....

* *The novelist* James Hanley.

Wednesday, 9th December, [1936].

A Magical Morning! very low opalescent clouds full of fostering milk as it were from the very breasts of Demeter, risen from the earth under the wooing of the air-children & ready to fall with fecund nourishment on all living things. The sun making *vignettes,* suspended in mid-air between earth and clouds. Here an emerald-green field, here a supernaturally large tree or a group of *brown* trees, here a column of smoke rising straight up like an enchanted lily-stalk & expanding as it rises, here a single gate, there a church-spire, here train-smoke, *wandering and lost,* not knowing which is the misty sun-sprinkled earth & which the opalescent sky! & the whole earth & sky held up as they are thus mingled together as if by the hands of an invisible Atlas! I have never known such a *WELSH DAY.*

Sunday, 20th June, [1937].

[Eben] walked down the hill with me & told me that 200 years ago the Greatest Welsh Bard – this was concerning my having to compose an 'Englyn' – was a young woman called Gwenwil *Bychan* or *Fychan* to whom came competing & rivalling & contending bards from all over the mountains & two of these put their heads together to fool her & composed a bawdy Rabelaisian poem (referring to her chief difference from a man) but instead of being reduced to shyness or confusion she replied in a poem even more shameless & a good deal more witty. The gist of which I found it hard however exactly to follow as Eben spoke it but (...) note that it is *wit* & *art* & intellectual *deftness* rather than *inspiration* that is the mark of Welsh poetry....

Friday, 25th June.

The day has been still, hushed, calm & full of hot sunshine from *Dawn to Eve!* We drove or rather old Littleton* drove us on Highway A5 past the *Viaduct* & past my imaginary *Tassel Inn* & past the route taken by young Rhisiart ap Griffin from *Chirk* towards Valle Crucis through Gobowen & thro' Oswestry to *Meifod* where we had lunch near or even *in* the churchyard where the school children were having their lessons. It was a beautiful church with Norman arches & Norman font & one ancient sarcophagus-lid of the old Celtic Design of some ancient chieftain with a little naked man on it and strange starfish & most heathenish & mystical ornamentation.... Then we drove on, Littleton with the great Church-Key forgotten in his pocket, thro' honeysuckle hedges, thro' roses & wild roses, thro' hay-fields, oh so *many hay-fields* & the incredibly beautiful hills & woods in the valley of the Vyrnwy & of the *Severn* of the County of Montgomeryshire the old Land of Powys.... The Sexton had told us there were *three Maen y Meifods* one of which we believed was our ancestors' abode but we saw none of these but ... we finally arrived at the grand & supreme *point of our Journey.* This culmination of our pilgrimage was *MATHRAFAL* the palace of the Princes, built by none other than King *ELISEG.* I cannot describe to you the romance of this place. It was more than magic, more than mystery – like a thousand years of high reveries of an intense imagination of lonely thoughts separated from everything – alone – an airy castle above tree-tops.

* *One of his brothers.*

Petrushka and the Dancer: The diaries of John Cowper Powys 1929-1939, selected and edited by Morine Krissdottir (Carcanet Press: 1995).

The following letters are chiefly, in the first place, to his brother, the novelist and essayist, Llewellyn Powys (1884-1939), and those following to his friend, Louis Wilkinson, biographer of the Powys brothers.

14 July, 1935.
7 Cae Coed, Corwen, North Wales.

...I have found a heavenly walk along the opposite bank of the Dee. I can go very agreeably to the little town of Corwen by the Dee, for the river bends away from the town and then sweeps round again towards it – but the walk I found today was much pleasanter still, for it was in the opposite direction from this small town and save for the cattle I had no interruption to my peace, and today in thundery weather through soaking-wet long grass I met not a soul save a solitary swan in the centre of the dark water. What a river it is! It is making a deep impression on my mind – the swirl of the water, its dark-brown colour, the tall alder trees and foxgloves – I've never seen such foxgloves as grow everywhere here....

There's a prehistoric camp, 'Y Gaer', beyond the town and I climbed it and walked round it – it has a ruined stone wall and the remains of ruined towers, the like of which I've never seen or knew existed!

10 August, 1935.
...We went to Carnarvon by bus and passed thro' Bettws-y-Coed and thro' Llanberis Pass and thro' Cerrig-y-Druidion and thro' Bangor to Carnarvon. The Eisteddfod Pavilion called in Welsh by the significant syllables ye Babbel had 8,000 people in it and could not contain two more, but by paying 2/- apiece we got into the enclosure round 'ye Babbel' and stood by an entrance just behind the white head of Lloyd George (drawing). And Phyllis thought he had a *ribala* air and I thought he looked like a sly, sleek, drunk old Lion chanting a passage out of Rabelais! Then we rambled about Carnarvon Castle, which we both thought the best castle we have ever seen....

6 September, 1935.
I am now always followed by a Swan. Whether it is hungry or whether, to the reverse of Leda, it wishes to be embraced by the aged 'Iolo Goch', I do not know. But the bird followed the Black and me for a quarter of a mile down stream yesterday, as we tracked the Dee our usual way – and as it went it uttered the syllable "Nep!" very unmistakably, again and again, in a funny snappy sort of tone. I have 'fed it bread' (as Americans say) but it took not the faintest notice of what I threw in, but as soon as I went on it followed again – and on that occasion it was up-stream it went after the Black and myself, and just as fast as down-stream (well, not *quite,* but nearly) crying, as I glimpsed it between the Alders (which here grow as tall as big trees), Nep! Nep! Nep! in its querulous petulance.

I saw a big Salmon floating down dead, that had evidently been killed and partly devoured by an otter. These animals, as Bewick's *History of Quadrupeds* or Goldsmith's *Animated Nature* say, are very plentiful in this river. I wish you could hear Hanley's sardonically indignant and savage humorous description of the fine ladies and gentlemen (followed by local stationmasters in Sunday clothes) who hunt the otter in the Dee about here. So far I've not *ever* seen an otter, but the number of moorhens that the Black Dog disturbs are amazing.

12 February, 1936.

...Such a hard frost has gone on here without pause for about two weeks! But I felt the sun thro' my old bones up the mountain this morning, and not a cloud in the sky today. Down by the Dee I saw a tiny little unknown bird of brown, not blue, feathers and with a black head like a marsh-tit or cole-tit, desperately and distractedly digging with its infinitesimal beak in the iron-bound river bank for I know not what. I called to the Old (the dog) but it took no notice – was it a frozen lobworm's tail? It almost stood on its head as it tugged frantic for bits of something for its minute crop, and it took no notice of the Old or the man. I saw its back feathers rumpled up as it pulled and tugged. And great greenish blocks of ice came floating down the swift black waters of the Dee. The black cattle are penned in barns and enclosures. Only the sheep, these alert Byzantine-looking lambs of God, left afield and ready to follow any Homo Sapiens they catch sight of, running after him in hope he comes with provender more nourishing than this frost-bitten grass....

To Alyse Gregory, wife of his brother.
15 March, 1936.

Alyse dear, dear Alyse, You were so sweet and good to me that day by Bertie's* grave.... Yes, it was queer, as I tried to explain to Lulu, how I reacted completely away, away from that tender, reverent, early christian piety of tenderly devout, sweetly unctuous holy respect for the body – the bodily 'remains' of the dead – *Remains, Remains.* I felt almost hostile to them as if 'they' were an enemy to Bertie as if they were, these poor 'remains', and what an ugly, what a hideously revolting word! and why plural? Why not 'body' or 'cadaver' as Lulu loves to call it – in conspiracy (or had been) with those fatal excretions that had caused his death. I longed to be able to repeat some of the great rolling lines of *Hydriotaphia*, or *Urn-Burial*. I did think of the white bones in Homer, purged and liberated by fire. *White bones,* that's the thing to be. And after cremation you know it's not 'ashes' as we think; it is little bits of white bones. White bones, white bones, that's the cure for groans and moans! But I didn't feel like the last rites of supreme unction at all! Not at all, I felt almost more grim than a Homeric. I felt like a –

But the second that kind clergyman did start off on those familiar verses of the Revelations, all casual and wayside as it was to us three there behind Bertie's coffin with those grate-black handles, automatically John's lips drew down all shaky and quivery, and that up-bubbling lump grew, dissolved – grew, dissolved grew – turned into Salt water! Such is the power of the Word, the Logos! Maybe the incantation of such mythic poetry – 'the incantation of my verse' - is deeper in us than the grimmer, calmer mood? Not just Sentiment, but a jetting up, a spouting up, of the melting, flowing together of many waters, the subterranean super-personal river of all human souls in one accumulated PROTEST against Annihilation!...

⋆ *One of the six Powys brothers.*

Maundy Thursday, [9 April], 1936.
...I like going before breakfast up the narrow lane between high un-mortared stone walls behind our group of little new houses, until (quite a fair way up) I debouch into a large, sloping, rough field of thorns and mountain-ashes and birches and rocks and tiny rivulets, and a little flock with a black sheep, and walk clear round this field, listening to crowing of cocks, the whistling of trains, the baaing of sheep, and the lovely mediaeval brazen sound, harsh-sweet, of the Corwen Church tower clock, out of sight behind the hill where the Gorsedd stones do lie in a circle, put there round a natural great one in centre for the bards at a competition. It is here and it is thro' this field, which might be called Corwen Great Field, that we shall reach it, without passing house or road that they will announce on 16 May (when Katie is with us, D.V., D.V.) with swords and staves and dragon-banners and Eleusinian Mysteries, the coming in August of the Powys Eisteddfod....

11 June, 1936.
The Town-crier here, and a roadmender too he is, is my favourite Welshman round here. I stand and listen – *not* pretending my absorbed interest as he talks in English like an elfin orator, for he is a little eldritch red man, 'dyn bach goch', passing eloquent, and I hear spellbound his tales of one thing and another....

11 October, 1937.
...Our present Worry (immediate and present) is this singular Drought – this lack of water that has befallen this county of Merioneth. Up above us a mile up the Berwyn Mountain is a Reservoir all depends on, and last night when coming home with a neighbouring farmer to show us an as yet undiscovered sheep-track

and a secret way into the Colonel's Grouse Preserves, we peered down into this Reservoir. Behold! all but a small portion was empty of water. The Council are worried, and we only get water through our pipes at rare daily times; announced by John David (the Town-Crier) in Both Languages, like a Herald in the time of King John.

Saturday, 10 June, 1939.

Lulu Darling, Let me hear ere so very long how your HEALTH is ...And I also want to hear very very much and so does P.P. Phyllis Playter or Phyllis Powys (a happy Signature for a Girl without Lines) what your final opinion carefully weighed is as to the Press notices of your Book. The Best by far as far as I've seen – and you may be sure all your Welsh readers in Corwen are alive-O in these matters except brother John – is the great Welsh South-Welsh Metropolitan Paper, the *Western Mail* of Cartdydd or Cardiff. This Reviewer could hardly write from the stress of his appreciation. It was from this *Western Mail* that I got the best (by far) praise I've ever had of my master-piece, namely *Glastonbury*.

Both for me and for you our Horoscopes are very favourable to South Wales!...

There's the Town Crier's Bell! announcing in Welsh a Great Pacifist Meeting in Corwen of the Peace Pledge Union, of which R. Heron Ward is a secretary. I must now put on my new black overcoat not paid for yet, but the money is there....

1 November, 1939. Corwen.

We gaze with awe at the great artist Mr Jones the Black, our Ca Coed neighbour, who cuts letters on tombstones.... We've got him to make a stone for our dead dog. How queer looks Born Poughkeepsie upon a slab of Welsh slate!

I have got to page 1950 and I shall compose D.V. Touch-wood, Touch Wood D.V., the last page of my *Owen,* taking the pen and paper to the Chapter House there in Valle Crucis Ruins, because there are buried Princess Myfanwy of Dinas Bran; and Iolo Goch; 'Iolo the Red' – Owen's only close intimate and friend (a bard whose works are still printed) – so the ghost of Iolo Goch will, if any could, inspire my Ciceronian Peroration at the finis!...

Well! Who can tell anything these days, but I trust when you read this your chest will be firmer and your legs stronger,

Your devoted John.

Llewelyn Powys died at Clavadel, Switzerland, 2 December 1939.

Letters of John Cowper Powys to his brother Llewellyn 1925-1939, Vol. II, edited and selected by Malcolm Elwin (Village Press: London, 1975).

To Louis Wilkinson.
November 8th, 1938.

Yes, I've felt those extremely disagreeable feelings wh. you describe. But I think the best defence of Chamberlain is the awful & incredible but we still must say not *impossible* chance that in our unpreparedness we'd have been *Defeated!*...

...My own personal *worry* is my Financial Situation just now. But I've been out of the Blue offered a lecture by the Welsh Miners in South Wales at Bridgend & they are putting me up & giving me the amazing & most royal fee of Ten Guineas! Think of that – & the old gentleman without teeth too! These Welsh Miners are the ones to do things in that Grand Style upon which I used to lecture. My weekly bulletin for old Emma Goldman's Catalans says that the Welsh Miners have given to Spain – & in spite of their own Depressed Areas – a larger sum of money than any other Proletarians in the world & only a few are orthodox communists. They *are* what I've lectured so often about, 'Titanic Celts' – born 'Annibynniwrs' – Independents – Ho! Ha! Ho! But when I tell you that I'm to lecture on *Welsh Mythology* you can believe, teeth or no teeth, these great musical Rugger-lads will get their money's worth!

December 9th, 1938.
...Well, I gave those South Wales people the longest lecture I've ever given in my life. I acted, as Lola wd. say, "like a crazy man." 'Twas of course the old Circus Clown smelling the saw-dust of the arena again! But I said in my lecture what you say about Welsh women until my chairman, an English gentleman of the upper middle class – the class that *doesn't exist* in Wales & whose ways & values I had clean forgotten – looked so "funny" that it began to tickle the audience & they said afterwards "Your chairman didn't understand". But I had the whole-hearted support of the maddest Welsh & they applauded like the devil when I launched out into frantic praise & eulogy of the famous Welsh Cagliostro of the 18th Century & beginning of the 19th, a friend of Tom Paine & the one who started – some say *Invented* – all these elaborate druidic 'eisteddfod' ceremonials – Iolo Morgannwg or Iolo of Glamorganshire who called himself the "Bard of Liberty."

April 12th, 1949.
...Yes sure I did get that 2nd letter of yours quick after the 1st about Queensberry wherein you discussed further the subtle nature of psychological snobbishness and connected this Fear I have for

what Mr de Kantzow used to call "Magnates" – 'Powys we must propitiate Magnates!' – with – and correctly so, no doubt – the Johnson side of our family rather than the Powys side. On the other hand there is a terrific tendency in the Welsh to propitiate; but their propitiation is coherent, subtle, cunning & deliberate – a *policy*, in fact! a deep and ineradicable one, the result of being forced to be "collaborators" "beneath the drums" and I forget what* – of 4 or 5 conquests. It's rather like M. Arnold's Hindus or Indians: "The East bowed low before the blast in patient deep disdain & let the legions thunder past, and plunged in thought again." Except that the last thing the Welsh plunge into is "thought." *They* plunge into the intricacies of very stiff & formal Mandarin-like (extremely technical, not always inspired, & rarely philosophical or metaphysical) verse competition and musical competition in the Eisteddfods.

* 'Drums and Tramplings of three conquests.' *Religio Medici.*

Early in 1955 John Cowper Powys moved to Blaenau-Ffestiniog, Merionethshire.

June 1st, 1955.
...This cloud-cuckoo town pleases us more & more! There's no place like it! This morn I went for a walk from 8 a.m. to 10 a.m. & found myself in an Elysian Meadow (larger than any field) already surrounded by high mountain except in one little gap to the South. It was a grassy meadow in the centre of a long-exploded crater – the centre of Etna or Vesuvius (10 times bigger) after an explosion of some 10,000 years ago. And here I laid down with marsh marigolds on one side & meadow orchids on the other, & with my back to a Granite Rock or that stuff volcanoes produce whose name escapes me....

July 22nd, 1955.
...Yes, there *are* aspects of this place that are 'grim' but there are also small grassy valleys with streams of water running thro' them from which to look up at the grim mountain precipices all round towering above you as you lie on some sun-warmed rock listening to the water, & watching white sea-gulls and hay-fields and reedy marshes gives you the feeling you get from a poem like Keats's.

"Mother of Hermes & still youthful Maia – or may I woo thee in earlier Sicilian or thy smiles seek as they once were sought in Grecian isles by bards who died content... rounded by thee my song shall die away content as theirs

Rich in the simple worship of a day."

...What is so specially amazing here is to see the way the sheep &
lambs walk gravely down the street.

Letters of John Cowper Powys to Louis Wilkinson 1935-1956, (Macdonald:
1958).

1936

*On the occasion of King Edward VIII's famed visit to South Wales, he
spent the first night in the Royal train at Boverton near Llantwit Major.
Here a farming scheme had been started on behalf of unemployed miners
and next morning he was greeted by an arch made of leeks. Later he went
to Dowlais and visited the deserted furnaces overgrown with grass and
weeds. Asking various men how long they had been out of work, he
received the brief replies, "Five years," "Seven years" "Nine years," upon
which he turned to the accompanying party and said "Terrible" and
subsequently added the words, "These works brought all these people here.
Something should be done to get them at work again."*

    *Next day printed copies of 'an Open Letter to His Majesty King
Edward the Eighth' (reminiscent of Keir Hardie's 'Open Letter to King
George V') were distributed in the streets of Pontypool, signed by men
from Monmouthshire Eastern Valley who took part in the recent
unemployed march to London. It was enclosed in a loyal address to the
King from Blaenavon inhabitants. The King asked to see it and read it.
As partly reproduced in the* Western Mail *it ran as follows:*

Today you will be visiting the towns and villages of our valleys and
a valley blighted by the dead hand of poverty.

We regret your tour has been planned in such a way that the terrible effects of this poverty will not be seen by your Majesty.

*It then went on to describe the plight of the unemployed, to criticise the
means test and* 'the puny efforts of various voluntary social centres'
and declared, 'As unemployed men we say that our economic and
social plight is the result of the policy pursued by your Ministers and
Government.'

Western Mail, November 20th, 1936.

JACK JONES (b.1898-?), *began work in the mines in 1912. He was a founder member of the Communist Party of Great Britain and during the 1926 General Strike was imprisoned for selling the 'Daily Worker' on colliery premises. In the following years he was victimised and out of work until 1934 when he obtained employment as checkweigher at the Cross Hands Colliery. The following letter to the Miners' Lodge there tells of his intention to join the International Brigade fighting on behalf of the Republican government in the Spanish Civil War. He was captured and imprisoned in Spain but released in 1939 and returned home to become Miners' agent for the Rhondda district in 1940.*

JACK JONES to the Miners' Lodge, Cross Hands.
March, 1938.

...The events of last week and the crisis in the Cabinet confirms to the full the correctness of my decision to go to Spain. It is clear the National Government is prepared to surrender to the Fascist Powers, to give endorsement to the Nazi aggression in Austria and to give support to the Italian-German invasion of Spain....

The world is at the crossroads, and the battle is being fought in Spain. I am convinced if the working class forces of this country permit the present policy of Fascism to continue in Spain it will seal the fate of the workers of this and every other country for many decades.

I accept the policy being pursued by the National Council of Labour, and the steps being taken by the E.C. of the S.W.M.F. [South Wales Miners Federation] to do all possible to bring about the defeat of the National Government, and change the policy of this country towards foreign affairs and particularly Spain.

It is absolutely correct to fight for the ending of the Non-Intervention farce in Spain, that the Spanish Government be granted full rights to purchase arms, that we do all possible to help the Spanish Democratic people with food and milk, but I am more convinced that we should help Democratic Spain with men to strengthen the International Brigade....

Brailsford has stated in last Sunday's *Reynolds' News* that the future of European democracy is being fought out in Spain and that the fight is not going to be won for Democracy on condensed milk. I can go further and translate his statement to mean that more men are wanted for the International Brigade.

...May I draw to a close with a personal note. I am thankful for the experiences I have gained in Cross Hands, for the help and courtesy I have received in general. It will be encouragement in my new activities....

My decision to go to Spain is in accord with all ideals and ideas I hold. It is my proud claim to be one of the oldest members of the South Wales Communist Party, being one of its foundation members, and in going to Spain, I believe I am carrying out a fundamental tradition of the Party to serve the Working Class....

With Warmest Greetings and Salud,

Jack Jones.

South Wales Coalfield Archive, Library of University of Wales, Swansea.

1942

GRAHAM SUTHERLAND (1903-1980). *British landscape and portrait painter. This letter is a remarkably illuminating account of an artist's feeling for certain aspects of landscape, in particular in Pembrokeshire.*

Letter to Sir Colin Anderson.

Dear Colin,

You ask about the places which have started me off – which have started ideas for my paintings. Certainly I would rather write to you about such places than about the paintings themselves; for how can a painter explain his paintings.... But in describing the sort of things that start one off – the country that one likes, perhaps, and its peculiarities, it may be possible to give some kind of hint as to the genesis of the paintings....

I expect that you may have noticed that for the last few years I have been preoccupied with a particular aspect of landscape – and not only that, but, for the most part, with a particular area of country.

It was in 1934 that I first visited Pembrokeshire. I was visiting a country, a part of which, at least, spoke a foreign tongue and it certainly seemed very foreign to me, though sufficiently accessible for me to feel that I could claim it as my own.

After a good deal of wandering about, I came upon two very remarkable passages of country situated in the arms of land which embrace the great area of St. Bride's Bay. The arm towards the north is like an isosceles triangle on its side, the narrowest angle forming St. David's Head to the west. One approaches across a wide plain from the north, its emptiness relieved by the interlocking of tightly-packed strips of field and their bounding walls of turf-covered rocks. One soon notices an irregularity of contour on the horizon which resolves itself into what appears to be two mountains. As one approaches still closer one sees that these masses of rock scarcely attain a height of more than seven hundred feet. But so classically perfect is their form, and so majestic is their command of the smoothly-rising ground below, that the mind comfortably corrects the measurement of the eye and holds their essential mountain significance. A rocky path leads round the slopes of the nearer mountain, where, to the west the escarpment precipitates itself to a rock-strewn strip of marsh, marked out with the crazy calligraphy of the foundations of primitive hut dwellings: from here the ground rises to a vast congregation of rocks, fallen cromlechs, and goats' caves, which continue their undulating and bewildering disorder until they plunge, in the terraces of St. David's Head, into the table of the sea. The southern slopes yield to the plain again: but here the land gradually sloping to the sea, is studded with rocky cairns of every size. Between these are fields, each with a spear of rock at its centre. It is as if the solid rock foundation of the earth had thrown up these spears to transfix and hold the scanty carth of the fields upon it. Farms and cottages – glistening white, pink and blue-grey – give scale and quicken by their implications our apprehension of the scene.

In this direction, nearer the sea, the earth is comparatively flat, but this flatness is deceiving and makes the discovery of little steep valleys more surprising. These valleys possess a bud-like intricacy of form and contain streams, often of indescribable beauty, which run to the sea. The astonishing fertility of these valleys and the complexity of the roads running through them is a delight to the eye. The roads form strong and mysterious arabesques as they rise in terraces, in sight, hidden, turning and splitting as they finally disappear into the sky. To see a solitary human figure descending such a road at the solemn moment of sunset is to realise the enveloping quality of the earth which can create, as it does here, a mysterious space limit – a womb-like enclosure – which gives the human form an extraordinary focus and significance.

At the risk of talking like a guide-book, I must tell you of the area to the south. I shall never forget my first visit. We approached by a flat winding road and had slipped into one of the little valleys I have attempted to describe. To the left this opened out to reveal what appeared to be a watery inlet narrowing to its upper end. As the road progressed we caught further glimpses of this and curiosity was roused. We had intended making for a village called Dale, marked on the map as lying to the north side of the mouth of Milford Haven. Fortunately, we missed the road and found ourselves descending a green lane buried in trees, which, quite unexpectedly, led to a little cove and beach by the banks of a narrow estuary.

Here is a hamlet – three cottages and an inn crouch under the low cliffs. A man is burning brushwood cut from a tree bleached and washed by the sea. The flame looks incandescent in the evening light. The tide in the estuary (or pill, as such inlets are called here) is out, and we walk across the sandy bed of the opening and look down its winding length to the place where it narrows to the upper end.

I wish I could give you some idea of the exultant strangeness of this place – for strange it certainly is, many people whom I know hate it, and I cannot but admit that it possesses an element of disquiet. The left bank as we see it is all dark – an impenetrable damp green gloom of woods which run down to the edge of low blackish moss-covered cliffs – it is all dark, save where the mossy lanes (two each side) which dive down to the opening, admit the sun, hinged, as it were, to the top of the trees, from where its rays, precipitating new colours, turn the red cliffs of the right-hand bank to tones of fire. Do you remember the rocks in Blake's 'Newton' drawing? The form and scale of the rocks here, and the minutiae on them is very similar.

The whole setting is one of exuberance – of darkness and light – of decay and life. Rarely have I been so conscious of the contrasting of these elements in so small a compass.

...It is no uncommon sight to see a horse's skull or horns of cattle lying bleached on the sand. Neither do we feel that the black-green ribs of half-buried wrecks and the phantom tree-roots, bleached and washed by the waves, exist but to emphasize the extraordinary completeness of the scene. Complete, too, is the life of the few inhabitants – almost biblical in its sober dignity. The people in this part appear quite incurious of the activities of a foreigner. The immense soft-voiced innkeeper and his wife, small as he is big, sit, when they are not working, bolt upright, on a hard bench in the cool gloom of the parlour which forms the only 'bar' of the inn, or they sit – for he is ferry-man and fisherman, as well as innkeeper – gazing across the ferry.

The quality of light here is magical and transforming – as indeed it is in all this country. Watching from the gloom as the sun's rays strike the further bank, one had the sensation of the after tranquillity of an *explosion* of light; or as if one had looked into the sun and had turned suddenly away.

Herons gather. They fly majestically towards the sea. Most moving is the sound of snipe which flicker in their lightning dash down the inlet, to and from the sea.

These and other things have delighted me. The twisted gorse on the cliff edge, such as suggested the picture 'Gorse on Sea Wall' – twigs like snakes, lying on the path, the bare rock worn, and showing through the path, heath fires, gorse burnt and blackened after fire, a tin school in an exuberant landscape, the high overhanging hedges by the steep roads which pinch the setting sun, mantling clouds against a black sky and the thunder, the flowers and damp hollows, the farmer galloping on his horse down the estuary, the deep green valleys and the rounded hills and the whole structure, simple and complex.

It was in this country that I began to learn painting. It seemed impossible here for me to sit down and make finished paintings 'from nature'. Indeed, there were no 'ready made' subjects to paint. The spaces and concentrations of this clearly constructed land were for storing in the mind. Their essence was intellectual and emotional, if I may say so. I found that I could express what I felt only by para-phrasing what I saw. Moreover, such country did not seem to make man appear little as does some country of the grander sort. I felt just as much part of the earth as my features were part of me. I did not feel that my imagination was in conflict with the real, but that reality was a dispersed and disintegrated form of imagination.

At first I attempted to make pictures on the spot. But soon I gave this up. It became my habit to walk through and soak myself in the country. At times I would make small sketches of ideas on the backs of envelopes and in a small sketch book, or I would make drawings from nature of forms which interested me and which I might other-wise forget. The latter practice helped to nourish my ideas and to keep me on good terms with nature. Sometimes, through sheer laziness, I would lie on the warm shore, until my eye, becoming riveted to some sea-eroded rocks, would notice that they were precisely repro-ducing, in miniature, the form of the inland hills....

I have confined myself to writing about a particular area and I do this because it was in this area that I learned that landscape was not necessarily scenic but that its parts have an individual figurative detachment. I found this was equally true of other places which I visited later; but the clear, yet intricate construction of the landscape of the earlier experience, coupled with an emotional feeling of being on the brink of some drama, taught me a lesson and had an unmis-takable message that has influenced me profoundly....

Horizon, 1942.

CARADOC EVANS (1878-1945). *Short story writer, novelist and general scourge of the Welsh, Caradoc Evans presented a jaundiced view of Welsh life and people which he believed earned him the sobriquet of 'the best-hated man in Wales.' His journal, from which these extracts are taken, was written during World War II when he was somewhat less combative.*

God never meant me to live in the country. Here you see the same persons every day. You hear the same war grumbles although the war has not touched the farmers except to put more money in their pockets and to exempt their sons. One never hears a word about the sacrifices of other people. The war is being fought for certain persons who are not in it, for certain persons who truly believe that their flesh is more precious than the flesh of the fighter, that the fighting men were born to hew a path for them....

Mari Lewis, the wife of a farmer on the other side of the valley, tells me about two women who quarrelled. One used to change the other into a cow and chase her all over the place. She says she knew the two women. She often used to see the bad woman at a farm when as a fact she was miles away. Mari Lewis says witches are able to transport themselves.

A man prayed in Capel Horeb for fine weather. He said: "God bach, you are up to your old tricks again. Why don't you stop having jokes with us now my hay is down and rotting?" Another man prayed in Horeb. He said: "Yesterday was a grand day, Big Man and I cocked my oats, and last night you sent a storm and blew all the cocks down. What a one you are!"

I said to James Bwlch, a farmer, last evening, that there are many people I would see going to hell. "Of course," he said, "you don't believe there is a hell or you wouldn't talk like that. As sure as there is a heaven there is a hell. Did you ever hear the story about a tom-cat? A druggist in Corwen had a tom-cat that was a big nuisance in the neighbourhood and he had him castrated. A day or two later the cat was seen mooning about Corwen. A lady was concerned about it and found its owner and said to him that the cat looked very sad. 'Yes,' said the druggist, 'it's going about cancelling engagements....' "

I do not know why I am alive. But of course no one knows that. But why am I on earth when so many very useful men are being removed?

The servant here, a German Jewess refugee, went for a walk yesterday and she met a man. The man said to her: "I have five cows, seven pigs, and so on. Will you marry me? Let me know next Sunday. You will know me by my dog."

Last Sunday afternoon preacher Methodist said: "If you are sleepy, people, sleep. If I was not here very likely and most probably I would be in a big chair sleeping. Sleep, people. I will not say anything to startle you awake."

Mrs Pugh who keeps the pub brings you your beer, takes your money, finds the key of her cash drawer, unlocks it, gives you the change, locks the drawer, and hides the key. Buying a beer is a long ceremony. By the time she has locked the drawer you call for more beer. Mrs Pugh is 83. Yesterday she spent in bed very weak and without appetite. The weakness must have come upon her suddenly. One day last week she was giving me her views on Capel Horeb and some of Horeb's members, especially Horeb's big heads. She hates Horeb. "Church am I, Mr Evans bach. Capel and beer do not mix...."

The favourite broadcaster is Winston Churchill. He was favourite even when Chamberlain was P.M. We like him because he casts out devils with energy and vigour. We like him for his sound English; every Welshman knows good English and likes it. When an eloquential preacher denounces sinners we are glad we are not sinners. When Winston Churchill denounces Germans we are glad we are not Germans. Faint hearts he strengthens and the timid man he makes into a warrior....

I rise at about 7.30. I have my bath and dress and switch on the radio. Every morning I am subjected to the most futile and unctuous smug thing in religion. I suppose he has his fans. He must have otherwise the BBC would not employ him. The servant in this house listens in with me, and throughout she says:

"Well-well-well. Dear-dear-dear." She says that all day at the things that please her and the things that don't....

Mary Tycannol tells me that Hitler was in college in Aberystwyth. This much is certain. Miss Arnold corroborates. O yes, everyone knows that Hitler was college Aberystwyth. He liked the old town so much that he gave special orders that though London be razed Aberystwyth must be saved....

Preachers in Welsh capels never preach practical workable livable Christianity. They denounce the Egyptians of the Bible and other biblical bad men. They tell you to pray for the heathen and for Hitler, never to pray for yourself. Of course they pray for people who don't go to capel. They never denounce watered milk or dirty milk, cruelty to animals, cheatery and so on. I asked a farmer if he would take up his cross and follow Christ. He said he would. He said he was doing so. Would he give up his money for Christ's sake? This is what he said. "Christ is not a twp. He does not want money. He wants no more than your heart and He has got mine"....

Last Sunday evening preacher Methodist preached on the Hebrew law which ordains that a man should keep a corner of his cornfield for the poor and strangers. He said: "How many of you farmers would keep a corner of your corn for the poor?" A very indiscreet question and the sermon was bad. So they said. There were two preachers last Sunday evening. One was from South Wales. He said: "Prayer will not break the will of God." Boys, bach, what nonsense. If prayer will not break the will of God, then prayer is no good at all. A man said to me: "I pray hard against my enemy and suppose God loved my enemy – O dam'."

'Caradoc's Journal', *Welsh Review*, June and September, 1945.

1956

ABERFAN. *On the 21st. of October 1966 occurred the greatest tragedy in the history of the South Wales coalfield, an area sadly familiar with tragedy, when the waste from a coal tip in the village of Aberfan slid down the valley onto the local Junior school killing 116 children and 28 adults. The dismay and anger of the people of Wales were immediately encapsulated in the following letter from the* BISHOP OF LLANDAFF *which was printed in the* Western Mail *of October 22nd:*

Sir – I write with a full heart (which I share with countlesss thousands) face to face with this terrible tragedy as I try to prepare myself to go today to give what help I can to stricken families. Very many will feel embittered and enraged at a disaster the causes of which some will ascribe to the reckless exploitations of the past, others to the procrastinations or carelessness of the present.

Bitterness will not bring back the dead nor perpetuate their memory. All over South Wales are coal tips full of potential and deadly danger. The task of removing them or making them safe is vast far beyond the means of any local authority.

I call upon all to support me by every means in their power to have this terrible problem faced *at once* by the Government which alone has the resources to deal with it. All political and other differences must be put on one side, survey made, protective measures taken *and the finance made available now* before further disaster takes place.

At any time, given certain conditions of weather, such disasters may occur as is well known to everybody who lives there, in various parts of South Wales.

As the first step I hope that all will write at once in tens of thousands to the Prime Minister, the Secretary of State for Wales, and their own Members of Parliament demanding action *now* to survey and make safe the coal tips of South Wales. In this way, though we cannot bring back the dead nor heal the sorrows of the bereaved we can at least secure that those who have died shall not have died in vain.

In the next few days it was announced that an inquiry into the disaster had been set up with a Welsh Judge in charge. The government also reported that many coal tips had already been secured but that 500 had still to be given treatment. It also appeared that the Bishop of Llandaff's letter had upset a number of Welsh Labour M.P.s in that it implied they needed prodding. The BISHOP *replied to this in a letter to the* Western Mail *on October 27th.*

Sir – I am happy to think that I have many friends amongst the Welsh Members of Parliament, but if the report in your paper today correctly represents the attitude of some of them I am deeply disappointed.

Of course, no one doubts their grief and concern over this terrible disaster. But I believe that the consequences of it will be very great and may well involve controversial and costly measures, both to ensure that it never happens again and to change our whole attitude to existing tips and the disposal of colliery refuse in the future.

In such a position, if I were an M.P., I hope I would not be worrying about my personal feelings, but would be deeply grateful for a great volume of support behind me for the sternest and most far-reaching measures thought necessary.

It is to assure our M.P.s of this that I am asking that letters and petitions to them should be as numerous as possible and should continue over a long time.

Of course, such letters are not being confined to Welsh Members of Parliament.
    Yours faithfully
    Glyn Landav

Many letters supporting him, from leaders of other churches were soon published in the newspaper.

1972

DIARY: *a daily record – from which I have taken excerpts – kept – by an unknown miner, clearly a leading figure among South Wales miners during the miners' strike of early 1972. The strike was called after a demand for an increase in wages, particularly for the lower paid miners, was refused by the National Coal Board. Miners' pay had fallen behind that of many other industrial workers and a large number of them could only obtain a living wage by working excessive overtime. The strike caused widespread disruption in the power industries but the miners finally settled for less than they had hoped. Dai Francis, the Secretary of the South Wales National Union of Miners, is proposed as the possible author of the diary by the South Wales Coalfield Archives but this seems unlikely as Dai Francis is mentioned occasionally in the manuscript.*

Day 1, 9th Jan. Sunday. Official Date.
Little effect because of overtime ban. Miracle C.O.S.A.!* What about C.A.W.U.?

> Whether 'tis nobler in the mind to suffer
> The slings and arrows of outrageous fortune,
> Or to take arms against a sea of troubles
> And by opposing end them....

* *Colliery Officers' Staff Association.*

Day 2, 10th Jan. Monday.
Wheels stopped! Now for it!
Picketing – Good turn out.
Weather – Cold drizzle – no shelter.
Our picketing problem – At the pit – concerned mainly with Ryan's site at the tip and coal in yard.

...when the blast of war blows in our ears
then imitate the action of the tiger;
stiffen the sinews, summon up the blood,
disguise fair nature with hard-favour'd rage....

Good list of pickets to cover the pit and on call to go elsewhere as required.

Day 3, 11th Jan. Tuesday.
Weather – cold as a toad in a frozen pond – Feeling amongst boys – 'none so mean and base that hath not noble lustre in your eye....' We got perished at Dowd's(?) yard but stopped the wagons moving except those who could produce genuine authorisation papers for deliveries to hospitals.

Day 6, 14th Jan. Friday.
Last pay for the boys. Once this is gone the hardship will begin, but they all stand firm that they will stick it as long as necessary.

Day 18, 26th Jan.
...Coal for old people – No progress, only talks and bits of paper. While old 'uns starve, Coal Board bureaucrats quibble about procedures. We'll get coal to them ourselves soon if the Board doesn't budge.

Day 19, 27th Jan. Thursday.
Demonstration, Cardiff.
10,000 marching
Sophia Gardens pavilion – Crammed
Unqualified solidarity
Laurence Daly – Emotive. Full claim?
George Thomas – brushed aside – Memories of Closures! When he was Minister.

Day 21 29th Jan. Saturday
Can't wait for N.C.B. any longer. Great new spirit.
Coal to old people organisation 80 deliveries today.

Day 22, 30th Jan. Sunday.
Lodge distribution organisation continues....
Between six and half past in the winter darkness, with flurries of snow running before the cutting East wind, the cars begin to turn up on the outskirts of the colliery. Already the pickets have a beacon of a fire going in the half oil-drum. Shale from washing the coal has

been tipped here to make a car park and small mountains of the stuff still lie at the edge of the car park, still unlevelled.

We back the cars up to the dumps, switch off the lights and open up the boots. Out come the plastic bags and operation (daily) 'Coal for O.A.Ps' begins. With little talk the lookouts go up and down, stamping their feet, their breath like smoke in the frigid morning air. The 'fitters,' the younger and stronger men, slip quietly off down the black bank from the car park to where eight coal wagons stand. Noiselessly they slip into action. Empty plastic bags are passed up to the men in the wagons and full bags are passed down.

A low whistle and everybody freezes. A soft call and the work goes on. The fuel bags now begin to come up the slippery steep bank, men gasping and snorting as they struggle up the slope with hundredweights of coal on their backs. A group of lads still circle the fire for the benefit of the police patrol cars and the cars bringing the manager and others into the pit. They see only men carrying on the routine picketing. Cigarettes glow in the dark. Albert has begun to share around the daily ration of fags provided by the Lodge.

Off we go up to Graham's smallholding to dump the coal in a central stockpile in the garage. Then back to the pit for more. Change the route on the next trip. Go up through Penybryn, Gelligaer and Pengan first time, then along around Ystrad Mynach and Helgoed on the next trip.

And so like this till the first streaks of light creep into the sky above the Graig and Cefyn Hengoed. The last lot of bags of coal into the boot and we are ready to begin the day's deliveries. Too risky to go on filling from the wagons when the light comes. If we got caught by the police taking coal from the wagons that would destroy the whole operation and the old people would go cold and some would die. Once the coal is away from the pit they have no real evidence.

Boots locked on the first deliveries we join the group at the fire. Albert doles out the fags and we puff and drag and cough partly from tobacco smoke, partly from the sulphur fumes from the fire and some because of coal dust in their lungs. But we feel good! Eighty bags we took out yesterday, quietly slipping them into the coalhouses of the needy ones. One old lady was 97 and without a bit of coal for over a week. The coal merchants are not interested in the problem; there's little profit in it for them, although they've been 'upping' the prices and taking tips too from those who can least afford it. We wasted three weeks trying to get the Coal Board to supply lorries and make it legal for us to get coal to people for whom coal meant life or death. We've offered that volunteers from the Lodge would drive the lorries, fill the coal and carry and deliver it but they were worried about the documentation, weighing and payment. We couldn't waste time on this red tape any longer. We took it into our own hands and we saved many from suffering and some from death.... Illegal? Essential? 'Whatever is in the interest of our people is ethical.'

Day 23, 31st. Jan. Monday.
Thick white frost everywhere. Punishing! The stockpile building up nicely. District meeting this morning at Bargoed Institute. On the news this morning 3 Power Stations closed down – 1 in Doncaster – 2 in South Wales – partly picketing, partly the extra cold weather.

Day 24, 1st. Feb.
...Paid out pickets for last 3 weeks. The rate agreed by the district is 75p for 6 hour stint. Most of our chaps settled for 2 hrs per day. In some cases this amounted to 20x25p=£5.00. There was also a payment of 50p for the demonstration on Thursday 27th January....

Guppy, the butcher, called at the hut this morning and dropped off a pile of meat pies, sausage rolls etc...

'Power abdicates only in the face of superior power'

Day 31, 8th Feb. Tuesday.
News today that Robert Carr will meet the Union and the Board separately tomorrow. Reactions are that expectations are not high that this will bring a settlement.

We have been patient too long. The reward of cooperation is a starving wage.

The squeaking wheel gets the oil.

Cabinet committee on the strike takes emergency powers.

Day 34, 11th Feb. Friday.
On the bench at Bargoed today. Day of the Great Discovery. They still need us badly! Proud to be a miner. We were too patient for too long. Now, they say, in five weeks we have come near to bringing the country to a stop. Power cuts from 10-2 and 9-12 in our area. Different times in different areas. Millions will be laid off from work next week. Robert Carr has set up a court of enquiry.

Day 35, 12th Feb. Saturday.
...Nero fiddled while Rome burned. Mr Heath was on the continent conducting madrigals. He appealed to the miners to return to work. He should set the example by returning to work himself.

At least Nero did something about heating Rome.

Where this crew is eventually going there will be no shortage of heat.

Day 37, 14th Feb. Monday.
Graham and me asked by Dai Francis to go to Bedford College
(London University) to address the students.... Grand time with the
students. Some real Socialists among them. Also one or two
Conservatives to give the meeting flavour....

I shall never forget the spectacle of London 'blacked out' by a
power cut. It was like something from a film based on invasion from
outer space – even worse than war blackouts.

The students had invited a Board spokesman to attend. There was
an amendment to this because some of them felt it unfair to impose
this burden upon two 'inarticulate' miners. After we had spoken and
had answered questions they said we were more articulate than their
lecturers.

Day 41, 18th Feb. Friday.
Findings of Wilberforce enquiry – £5, £6 & £4.50 retro to Nov 1st
and to cover up to next February – 16 months. BBC TV to the pit.
Solid No! from the boys.

Some reactions of leadership not promising. They think this is a
good offer.

Day 43, 20th Feb. Sunday.
...committee meeting – unanimous mandate to reject....
Joe Gormley said last night, 'The miners will accept.'

Day 44, 21st. Feb. Monday.
Area Conference – Labour Club Bridgend.
I was the only one to speak against the recommendation.

My speech was based on the following facts.

1. We started the strike as a crusade for the lowest paid men. We
finish with 90% of our target for the higher paid men i.e. £4.50 of
the £5. We have 62.5% for the lowest paid men i.e. £5 of the £8.

2. These increases are paid over 16 months i.e. $1^{1}/_{4}$ years so it is £4
we have gained not £5.

3. The increases run until 28th Feb, 1973. Our next wage claim
cannot be fought till then.

That is the end of winter strikes. If we ever come on strike again it
will be in the Spring and Summer months.

Nobody could contradict me!

Only slang and criticise.

We shall see who was right.
The final vote was 78-2 in favour.

South Wales Coalfield Archive, University of Wales Library, Swansea.

JONAH JONES (1919-). *Born near Durham of Welsh descent he moved to North Wales after the war to work as printer and sculptor. Famed for his lettering on stone he has also written novels in more recent years. The following are extracts from a journal written while he was Arts Fellow at Gregynog, the house now owned by the University of Wales.*

November 2nd 1981.

A lovely autumn day, all changing lights, the mountain flanks copper and verdigris, dead bracken and green pasture washed clean by all the October rains. Motored to Aberllefni in morning to pick up Wakefield slate panel. The quarry is at the top of a side valley with a bluff right before you at its head. Aberllefni village is a row or two of quarrymen's cottages, trim, well-kept, neighbourly.... Definitely autumn – clear, crisp, a chill in the air, leaves like a million pound-notes underfoot.

Talked to a Nigerian student over Lunch. He was dreading the coming winter, particularly snow. "I wouldn't say Cardiff was world famous for its precipitation," I comforted him.

"When does it start?" he asked. "January? February? I'm really dreading it."

"Sometimes it doesn't start at all." Clearly he didn't believe this. "And when it does, it may not last overnight," I continued. "If it's a bad winter, which isn't often, it may last a few days. Longer than that is phenomenal in Cardiff." But he was determined not to be convinced and clung to his dread of what might never happen.

Met an old farm-hand, retired, who wanted to talk. I was sketching, or trying to. He had worked on Gregynog Home Farm. He wanted a bit of a grouse, I could tell.

"That must have been a privilege," I said.

"Well, no," he replied rather sharply. "It wasn't all er... what d'you call it now? It wasn't all, you know what I mean...."

I tried to help. "Cakes and ale?" I ventured.

"Milk an' 'oney!" he declared, delighted to have found *le mot juste....*

"Twould a' been all right if you coulda gone straight to the fountain head, like," he said, flicking a bent old thumb in the direction of the Hall. "But there was allus the manager, like between you and them. They was right..." and he paused to assess if swear words would be appropriate in my presence (after all, I was sketching Welsh/Hereford crosses and one was even a full Welsh Black).

"...they was right...." But I was not going to help this time, being curious to see if he found the right word for his retrospective indignation... "right – er sort of a bit of a blackguard, you might say, especially that...." I was disappointed.

"Bit of a bugger, was he?" I interposed for his benefit. "Ay, now, there you have it, bit of a bugger, you might say...." and on and on he went with his beefing. The only way I was going to stop him was to admire his stick.

"Holly?" I asked. "No, not light enough colour."

"Na," he replied, again looking for the right word.

"Not blackthorn either," I went on.

"That's right," he replied, but clearly not satisfied, "bit of a thorn to it."

"Very nice, very nice indeed," I blathered on.

"Ah!" It had arrived. "Prunus!" he said with obvious relief.

I was surprised that a good Latin name had lodged itself among the grumbles and rambles of his old country mind. He then mourned the passing of the old Welsh Black, horns and all, and parted, he satisfied with his grouse, I dissatisfied with my sketching.

January 9th, 1982.

By now we are so thoroughly immured from the world by snow that I was even out of touch with this sketchbook. While I was just managing, with the help of the gardeners to get to the Tearoom where I'm dealing with the Dylan★ stone (it was too heavy to get up to the studio), the rest of my things are across the yard. Between them and me are 4-foot drifts of wind-blown snow. Yes, we are cut off. The world is outside, somewhere across the silence. We hear from it occasionally by wireless, TV and telephone. I am imprisoned with about 18 students and staff who should have gone home yesterday. One student walked down the drive which has been partially cleared by the estate's own little tractor snowplough. He reported that 'outside,' the only indication of a road was a level of snow 4 or 5 feet deep and even higher between what were evidently hedges. I recall that Nigerian with guilt.

★ *Stone commemorating Dylan Thomas on which Jonah Jones was carving the lettering. It was installed in Westminster Abbey some weeks later.*

The Gallipoli Diary, Jonah Jones (Seren: Bridgend, 1989).

THE MINERS' STRIKE of 1984-5. *The journal and letters following provide a glimpse into that devastating strike in Wales, particularly with regard to the role of women who played a more overt role than ever before in industrial conflict.*

Women's support group at Maerdy.
Journal by BARBARA BLOOMFIELD, a student at Ruskin College, Oxford, who was writing a thesis about the strike.

Maerdy, Rhondda Valley, South Wales, January 1985....
The coal owners built the workers' homes too. They threw up the small uniform terraces after the first strikes of coal, to attract in workers from other parts of the country. When one miner said, "My house is over 100 years old" it didn't connect for a moment until I looked it up and found that the first strike in Maerdy was in 1875.

Maerdy is the last village in the Rhondda, ringed with a semi-circle of hills to the north which forces the road to peter out as it approaches the pit, sitting alone in a bowl of hills, old, redbrick and squat.

The social centre of Maerdy is the Workmen's Institute, a square, unlovely, apparently semi-derelict, building with graffiti on the blackened outside walls, which started life in 1881 as a coffee tavern. Within twenty-five years it had become the Workmen's Institute and Hall, capable of fitting up to 1,200 people.... During the strike it's been the men who spend much of their time around the Hall although they are not all miners by any means. There are plenty of teenage boys and older men in their fifties and sixties. They're mostly out of work like 32.4 per cent of men in the Rhondda (Rhondda Borough Council figures) and 84 per cent of men over 44 years old (NUM figures). This is a place for early death of 'the dust' as pneumoconiosis is called and it is a place for early retirement so that the younger ones can have a go and for golden handshakes that say a man is finished at the pit at 45 years of age....

The butties, that is, the men from Ferndale who work together in the pit at Maerdy and socialise together after their shift, tend to meet in the back room of the Con. (Conservative Club run by the Communists) where there is a billiard table and separate bar – men only again. The women tend to gather around a big table in the front bar although occasionally their husbands will come through....

It is in these situations that the burning issues get discussed.... The strike is number one of course, and feminism, and Greenham

Common and food, the Labour Party and fuel and the family. There is not much that doesn't lead back to the strike or relate to it.... It didn't take long to realise that it was silly to try to pigeonhole the Maerdy women into some perfect socialist/feminist theory and that they were trying to find a way forward as a group which suited (rather than threatened) their existing way of life. At the same time there was a balance to be struck between home and 'activism'. I'd read countless books about mining life in which women hardly appeared at all except as the invisible labourers who propped up the whole filthy business of being a miner. Always I remembered the words of the author who claimed that the single most revolutionary act for women's liberation in Wales was the installing of pithead baths.

Almost every striking family relies on the generation above for fresh food like vegetables and fruit and for financial help to keep them going... Doris, whose mother was a pitbrow lass (though not at Maerdy where women were never employed in coal mining work) was one of the generation of women who were driven out of the Rhondda during the mining slump of the late 1920s and 1930s and went to become a domestic servant in England. She is violently anti-Thatcher, referring to the Prime Minister at all times as "SHE." Everyone in Maerdy knows who "SHE" is. When Doris made this remark: "I think what SHE'd like to do with the Rhondda is build a big wall around us," I couldn't help but think of the Tory minister who admitted that pit villages are "Socially useful if economically unviable." After all, they embody so many 'virtues' which Tories would claim as much as socialists to be their own: self-sufficiency, help-your-neighbour, family, tradition, and, above all, a pride in hard work.

...It is one of the ironies of the strike that the resistance movement, which has kept, according to Hywel Francis, about half a million people going in the Welsh valleys during the strike, has worked up such a head of steam that the women feel it could go on forever. For all the images of fiery Welsh Communists which history provides, it was the South Wales miners who quietly suggested to the rest of the NUM that there should be a return to work without a settlement.... When this plan became public knowledge, the women were shocked. They had taken over the voice of militancy and were still using phrases like, "I've never let myself think for a moment that we're not going to win".... But while the women, around Christmas time, were organising pickets and planning the occupation of the Furnacite Plant at Abercwmboi, the majority of the Communist miners at Maerdy pit were talking about 'broad alliances' and about the possibility of an orderly return to work with 'dignity and honour.'

Postscript 5 March, 1985. Thousands of Maerdy people and their supporters from Oxford, Birmingham and other places walked up the single road to the pit in the chilly dawn to see the miners go back to work in that 'dignified and orderly fashion'. As they neared the pit, the lights with the television cameras were switched on and, almost by instinct, it seemed, two dozen miners at the front of the procession raised their fists into the air and shouted slogans like 'here we go' and 'we will win.' When the camera lights went out, they stopped immediately and soon filed into the pithead baths to start work. On the television, later that day, it looked a heroic ending to their strike. At the time it had seemed merely a sad one.

Letters to Barbara Bloomfield from BARBARA WALTERS, *'lynchpin' of the Maerdy Women's Group despite being confined to a wheelchair.*

Tuesday, April 2nd, [1985]. Glyncorrwg.

...Losing the strike means the closing of the only pit that's part of their village. The fifty-six miners in this village will be halved by the end. There's much bitterness and depression, the factory recently opened at Cymmer – $2^1/2$ miles from Glyncorrwg – is a German one making black plastic bags, conditions deplorable. NO UNION, eight hours' work, ten minute break, £50 for seven days. If that's the kind of work we'll be accepting you can guess the feeling.

I think cooperatives are the answer. We have many gifted artistic people in these villages. Those women in the support group could turn their hand to anything from cooking to craft and entertaining. They showed they could work as a team. If only all these energies could be used to sustain some kind of livelihood before the rot really sets in. There are rows of houses to be rebuilt. Our men and sons are good at turning their hand to anything, they are survivors, after all, damn, why should money be the answer to everything. Sorry, but I just came back from a meeting now, they're accepting, not fighting....

Tuesday, October 1985. Glyncorrwg.

Dear Barbara and Raphael,
...Looking back on that year's conflict, knowing now the axe has fallen on St. John's in spite of the sustained effort of the Lodge officials, those same good companions who gave so much of

322

themselves to sustain the strength of those around them during that year long struggle. Those of us who helped during that period were wrapped in it, we ate, drunk and slept it, for us nothing outside the good fight existed.

The time wasn't chosen (not by us anyway) for the conflict, it was there as it was there in 1926. In 1984 we linked hands with our past.

We avoided the conflict in 1970 and let our own village pit and railway slip away under our noses, without anything taking its place.

Just like after 1926 when there was the Thirties and there was poverty, it sat amongst us. And here it is now, but you don't talk about being poor, pride takes cover and pretending plays a big part when one is hard up....

Yesterday, a beautiful autumn afternoon, the mellow sun rays coloured the earth as if it was its birthday. I walked over the sites of old levels and pits knowing that under my feet were rich seams of coal sufficient to last into the next century. Some day perhaps when it pleases the world markets they'll come back for it but at what cost then? While walking I met a young mother who had been taking a flask of tea to her young husband. He was picking coal where the striking miners had been picking in 1984, only he'd been filling his coalshed that way now for four years. "It's lonely up here," she said. "Yes," I answered. Yes, and it's bloody lonely on the dole too, I thought.

This year we at Glyncorrwg celebrate the centenary of our school. Now my grandchildren go there and my mother-in-law's great grandchildren. My great grandfather came to Glyncorrwg as a stone mason. He brought his skill with him to this village and helped to build the Viaduct tunnels for the railways. What skills will our children be able to pass on? What will their future be? There is nothing here for them now, losing the battle has meant just that. The fight has been worth fighting for, we paid our debt to the past, we have no shame as we face the future....

Sincerely yours,
Babs & David Walters.

The Enemy Within, Pit Villages and the Miners' Strike of 1984-5, eds. Raphael Samuel, Barbara Bloomfield, Guy Boanas (Routledge & Kegan Paul: 1986).

1986

DANNIE ABSE (1923-). *Poet, playwright, novelist and doctor. Born in Cardiff. The following are extracts from his* Intermittent Journals.

This morning [May 4th] an East wind was blowing so vigorously in Ogmore that our wooden gate had been thrust open. From the bedroom window I could see that a ewe with two lambs had trespassed into our garden. They were munching the daffodils and narcissi, a nice, forbidden, wicked breakfast. I rushed downstairs, still in my pyjamas, to shoo them out.

As I closed the gate behind them I thought more of the East wind than the sheep. Probably it was bearing invisible death-seeds from Chernobyl. Perhaps radioactive raindrops were sipped from the daffodil cups by the ewe and the lambs. Information so far is meagre. In any case, who can believe the complacent stealthy reassuring voices of experts and politicians? How much has been covered up before, how much will be told to us now? Will radioactive iodine be taken up by small thirsty thyroid glands? What about my new grand-daughter and all those like her from Ogmore-by-sea to the Ukraine and beyond where Prometheus is still chained to his rock while the vulture eats his liver?

Last Friday in Cardiff, I visited Llandaff Cathedral. I just happened to be nearby, so popped in as I used to as a boy, passing the yellow celandines beneath the yew tree. Inside soaring spaces of worship – Jewish, Moslem or Christian – I feel not just secular but utterly estranged like one without history or memory. Once more, numb, I observed Epstein's dominating aluminium Resurrected Christ. And it was springtime, springtime in the real world and all seemingly dead things were coming alive again though a cancer sailed in from Chernobyl.

Inside the Cathedral, I ambled towards the Lady Chapel reredos where, on either side of the sculpted Madonna, six niches are filled with gold-leafed wreaths of wildflowers. In Welsh, dozens of flowers are named after the Virgin, as is proper in a nation that reveres the Mam of the family. The marigold is called Gold Mair – Mary's Gold; the buttercup, Mary's sweat; the briar rose, Mary's briar; the foxglove, Mary's thimble; the monkshood, Mary's slipper; the cowslip, Mary's primrose; and the snowdrop, Mary's taper. Tapr Mair.

If a man believed in a deity, any deity, goddess, god or God, he would in that Cathedral have prayed in English or Welsh or no language at all, for the neutralization of the death wind. And in

Ogmore, this morning, as I stood in my pyjamas, while the opera-dramatic clouds, grey, cream or frowning darker tracked so visibly westwards, my own lips moved.

And I wonder now, once again, in the name of the God others believe in, how much longer will so-called civilized nations absurdly pile up unusable nuclear weapons and to what hell will man be consigned if, accidentally or purposefully, radioactive winds sail in from places other than Chernobyl.

December, 1993.

The wind has gone mad. An hour ago, as I bent forward into the blinding wind to the village Post Office store, the sun, indifferent, keeping its own obsessional time, sank lower towards the small quivering shore-hills of Somerset. Some minutes later, carrying the *South Wales Echo* and a bottle of refrigerator-cold milk, I walked back, my fingers freezing, my eyes still watering, in this lunatic gale. The telegraph wires howled like B.B.C. radio sound-effects for a play about a havoc storm at sea.

Looking out towards Somerset I thought how I would dread being out there on a bucking ship in that fairground switch-back, elephant-grey Bristol Channel. Not that one single boat was visible. Indeed, nobody appeared to inhabit the numb, land-locked afternoon either. Ogmore seemed nerveless, deserted. Some sheep huddled behind a stone-armoured wall, a few separate silhouettes of seagulls were flung off course, lifted giddily wide and high against the sky, and an idiot tin can, animated by the relentless wind, scraped the macadam as it bucketed past me, its sound diminishing with every step I took.

Though it was still afternoon, the lamp-posts began to glow. Soon it will be the shortest day of the year. Tomorrow we return to London. This will be our last sojourn in Ogmore this 1993. And, somehow, when I opened our wooden gate, I had that old familiar sense of something ending, 1993 going out as I was coming in. Perhaps it was something to do with the impending early darkness and the fury of the wind – something like a regretful au revoir, a smileless valediction and an end of a book also which, however, possesses a few blank pages after the print has run out. The coalhouse door was flapping and I bolted it tight. Inside the safe house the wind was defeated despite the rattling windows.

It is night now outside. The river, unseen, drifts into the glutted sea, the scarce ghost-stars wheel about the dark poles of the sky.

Dannie Abse, *Intermittent Journals* (Seren: 1994).

ALAN SILLITOE (1928-). *Novelist, short story writer and poet. The following letter was written to the editor of this anthology when Alan Sillitoe was in Wales in search of evidence of his grandfather's life there at the end of the 1880s.*

Rose Cottage Guest House
Blackwood
Gwent.
June 6th, 1997.

Dear Joan,

Thank you for your letter. I'm writing a reply from Wales, staying overnight with my brother Brian. This is our second visit to this area, and we came with a purpose. The first time, ten months ago, there were three Sillitoe brothers and we stayed at Rose Cottage under the name of Burton – as our common grandfather was called. It was raining continually then and fairly miserable in trying to get about, but today the clouds are drifting a bit higher over the hills, and at the moment it's dry.

Our approach was from the M5 and the M50 by Ross on Wye, and the green forests on the border seemed to roll on forever, promising paradise, not forthcoming when we got to the environs of Newport and Cardiff. But things improved when I drove inland towards Risca and Abercarn, then turned west to Pontllanfraith and through Blackwood to get here.

You may well ask why we came to this particular area and I'll tell you. Some years ago we found a family photograph of a blacksmith's forge, a carthorse being shoed by George, our grandfather's brother, while the grandfather, a very tall youth of twenty, looks on from the doorway. On the back of the photograph was written PONTLLAN-FRAITH – which intrigued us all. In my childhood I'd hear that Grandfather Burton used to work in Wales as a journeyman black-smith when he was a young man, but we never knew where until we found the photograph quite recently. We wondered why Wales, whether he had any family there, and in any case how he got to know about work. His brother George must have gone first, but how did he know about it?

Last time we explored the valley north and south from Pontllanfraith, trying to find the forge of the photograph. We talked to local people, who were very kind and did what they could to be helpful. We went into the library at Blackwood to see if they had the name of any photographer at Pontllanfraith who was working in 1888. But we found nothing, and after a couple of days gave up, glad to get no more soakings from the rain, and went back to Nottingham, but intending to come back and do another reconnaissance some time.

One eighty year old man near the end of our search thought the photograph might be of a building in the valley of Abercarn, so that is where we're going to look today. Of course, the chance of finding the place is near to nil, though on the photograph the brickwork looks fairly new. But so many new buildings have been put up in all places since the war around these parts that it must have disappeared by now. Anyway, it's a good reason to take a few days off from my novel, even though I'm near the end of the first draft and thought I couldn't bear to leave it.

I've not been much to Wales, maybe a dozen times to various places, but each time it somehow seems familiar, as if I did indeed have some ancestors connected with the country. It feels even more so in the environs of Pontllanfraith and I'm sure my grandfather had a good time while he was here. Every old pub we go in we wonder whether one of us isn't sitting in a seat he occupied while coating his throat with pints of strong ale. Or we wonder in what cottage he lodged. It's a pleasant game to play. In the Rock Inn – opposite Rose Cottage – where we have lunch, there's a framed photograph on the wall of a blacksmith's forge, but it isn't the one we're looking for – though the poses suggest it might well have been taken by the same person.

Our lunch here was a long time coming and when I told them at the bar that we'd been waiting half an hour the barmaid went into the kitchen and found that our order had been 'lost on the machine' – the lunch machine, presumably. Then it came quickly and all was well. When we asked for more drinks they wouldn't let us pay – said it was on the house – a kindness indeed, because the waiting hadn't bothered me at all since I was writing this letter. There were more apologies when we were leaving, and more thanks from us for the gift of the drinks.

Rain began, as if the Burtons had brought it from Nottingham, though I supposed that there must be far more of that commodity in Wales than there ever was in that town. But rain, however soft and warm (and it was both) alters the picture from quaint to fairly squalid, unless eyes are turned to the hills only dimly seen in the mist, and not to be seen at all when driving around wet bends with impatient traffic behind, nervous to get by. Green lanes take you far from houses and shop fronts, the trees making a sleeve or tunnel for hundreds of yards, and when you get out of the car, as I did several times to look at a likely spot for an old forge, you hear birds, in spite of drumming rain, singing with all the warmth of their little Welsh hearts.

But my cap and mac soon gets decorated with patches of wet after wandering up and down a railway line to no purpose, and I get disconsolately back in the car to pull out the maps and look for another likely locality.

So it goes on, futile plods in the rain, but I'm enjoying the walks and explorations until four o'clock when the idea is taken up that we should go back to Mary's and lie down for an hour. Maybe later there'll be no rain.

I wonder why we're looking for Burton's old forge, but can only see it as an excuse to come to Wales which was so much enjoyed last year. It also occurs to me that alpinists say they climb mountains 'because they're there." Well, maybe we're looking for that forge because 'it's not there,' which for me has always been as valid a reason for searching for something as any.

After a sleep we set off again, no rain this time, trawling around the area and ending up in Cross Keys and Risca, but we found nothing there either. To find the place would mean settling here for a month and walking every neighbouring valley, a not unpleasant prospect if one had the time because it's a beautiful area – as is nearly all of Wales I've been to. But we were discouraged and decided not to bother any more.

Just out of Newbridge we called in a pub for a glass of Welsh bitter and Brian showed the photograph to a man at the bar asking if he knew where the place was.

"Oh yes," he said, "it's just across the road, down the lane, only two minutes away."

On my asking whether one could drive there he said: "You don't need to. Just follow me." So I left Brian and was led fifty yards down a lane, and he said, "The forge has gone now, but it was just behind that barbed wire fence and the houses on the photograph are just above those trees." As indeed they were. Back in the pub this was confirmed by an eighty year old man who said Tommy Marsh was the last man to own the forge and that he the – eighty year old – can remember taking a horse to be shoed for a pound. So by a fluke we had found the place, but we're still mystified as to why our grand-father and his brother came to be working near Pontllanfraith in 1888. What brought them from Nottingham? Was it lack of work there, or did they have family in Wales? And if for the first reason, how did they hear about it?

We'll never know but at least the query brought us to Wales and we should be grateful to Burton for that, as we must be grateful for many other of his traits that came through to us.

By now it was 8.30 and time for supper at the Rock Inn – chops for me and steak for Brian, washed down effectively with more pints of delicious Welsh bitter. Now we have a room with two beds at Mary's place where we also stayed last year. But I see from boards outside that she's put the place up for sale, so where shall we stay when we come again? She's a wonderfully humorous and alive woman of about fifty, amused by these Nottingham men looking for Grandad's forge!

So that's why we came to Wales. The sun made the hills glisten tonight, as if God's special light of benediction was spread on them, and later the clouds were tinted pink and red so I'm sure it won't rain tomorrow. Unfortunately we won't be here to enjoy it. But we're bound to come back to Wales whatever it does.

Love to you both,
Alan.

Acknowledgements

In the task of compiling this book I have been aided by the following institutions and their staffs to whom I owe many thanks: the British Library; the University of London Library; the National Library of Wales; Cardiff City Library; Newport Library; South Wales Miners' Library; the South Wales Coalfield Archives section in the University Library at Swansea; Glamorgan Record Office; the Public Record Office. I am grateful to the National Library of Wales, the South Wales Coalfield Archives (Swansea), Newport Library and the Harry Ransom Humanities Research Center of the University of Texas at Austin for their permission to quote from manuscripts in their possession. I owe the letter from Morgan Llwyd to the kindness of Professor M. Wynn Thomas and the extracts from Coleridge's notebooks to a hint from Professor James Davies. Among other helpful remarks, Cary Archard brought the letter from Carrington to my attention and reminded me of Virginia Woolf's letters from Wales. I am indeed grateful to Alan Sillitoe for permission to use his letter. Acknowledgements of books etc. used are made throughout the text but besides these I have sought and received information and enlightenment from many other volumes too numerous to name. I cannot refrain from mentioning, however, that the *Oxford Companion to the Literature of Wales,* compiled and edited by Meic Stephens has certainly been my constant companion and John Davies's *History of Wales* a touchstone to remind me of the complexity as well as the fascination of Welsh history. Most of all I must thank my husband, not only for my closer introduction to Wales, but also for his affectionate encouragement and advice.

J.A.

Select Bibliography

Dannie Abse, *Intermittent Journals* (Bridgend: Seren, 1994).

Matthew Arnold, *Letters 1848-1888,* collected G.W. Russell (London: 1895).

J. Ballinger (ed.), *Calendar of Wynn Papers 1515-1690* (Cardiff: 1926).

G.H. Bell (ed.), *The Harmwood Papers of the Ladies of Llangollen* (Macmillan: 1930).

Barbara Bloomfield, Raphael Samuel and Guy Boanas (eds.), *The Enemy Within – Pit Villages and the Miners' Strike of 1984-5* (Routledge & Kegan Paul: 1986).

George Borrow, *Wild Wales* (John Murray: 1862).

William Bulkeley, *Diary of William Bulkeley* (Transactions of the Anglesey Antiquarian Society and Field Club: 1931).

H.E. Butler (ed., trans.), *The Autobiography of Giraldus Cambrensis* (Jonathan Cape: 1937).

Calendar of Ancient Correspondence concerning Wales, ed. J. Goronwy Edwards, Board of Celtic Studies, University of Wales History & Law Series, No. II (University Press Board: Cardiff, 1915).

Thomas Carlyle, *Letters to his Wife,* ed. Trudy Bliss (Gollancz: 1953).

Dora Carrington, *Letters and Extracts from her Diaries,* ed. David Garnett (Oxford University Press: 1979).

Thomas Carte (ed.), *A Collection of Original Letters and Papers concerning the affairs of England* (1739).

Catalogue of Manuscripts relating to Wales in the British Museum, compiled and edited by Edward Owen (Honourable Society Of Cymmrodorion: 1922).

Thomas Clarkson, *Diaries* (National Library of Wales, MS 14984).

Samuel Taylor Coleridge, *Collected Letters of S.T. Coleridge,* ed. E.L. Griggs (Oxford University Press: 1956-71); *Notebooks, Vol. I,* ed. Kathleen Coburn (Princeton University Press and Routledge: 1962).

Alexander Cordell, *The Fire People* (Hodder and Stoughton: 1962).

Charles Darwin, *The Correspondence of Charles Darwin, Vol. II, 1837-43,* (Cambridge University Press: 1986).

Daniel Defoe, *A Tour through the Whole Island of Great Britain,* Vol. 2.

J. Goronwy Edwards – see *Calendar.*

George Eliot, *Letters of George Eliot,* ed. G.S. Haight (Yale University Press: 1954-78).

Sir Henry Ellis, *Original Letters Illustrative of English History,* Vol. I, 1st and 2nd series; Vol. III, 2nd and 3rd series (State Paper Office: 1969).

T.E. Ellis (ed.), *Gweithiau Morgan Llwyd o Wynedd, Vol. I* (Jarvis & Foster: Bangor & Dent: London, 1899).

Madeline Elsas (ed.), *Iron in the Making,* Dowlais Iron Company Letters 1782-1860 (Glamorgan County Record Office: 1960).

A.O. Evans, *A Memorandum on the legality of the Welsh Bible,* William Lewis (Cardiff: 1925).

Caradoc Evans, 'Caradoc's Journal', *Welsh Review,* June and September, 1945.

G. Eyre Evans (ed.), *Lloyd Letters* (Aberystwyth: 1908).

J.G. Evans (ed.), *Report on Manuscripts in the Welsh Language,* 2 Vols. (London: 1898-1910).

Theophilus Evans, *The History of Modern Enthusiasm* (London: 1752).

Michael Faraday, *Michael Faraday in Wales,* ed. D. Tomos (Gwasg Gee: 1973).

Celia Fiennes, *The Journeys of Celia Fiennes,* ed. Christopher Morris (Cresset Press: 1949).

George Fox, *Journals* (1694).

John Frost, 'Letter to Sir Charles Morgan', [Newport, 1821], 'Letter to the Radicals of Monmouthshire', [Newport, 1822].

James Gairdner, *Calendar of Letters and Papers, Foreign and Domestic* (London, 1868-1932).

W.R.P. George, *The Making of Lloyd George* (Faber: 1976).

J. Ginswick, *Labour and the Poor in England and Wales 1849-51* (Frank Cass: 1983).

W.E. Gladstone, *The Gladstone Diaries,* ed. M.R.D. Foot and H.C.G. Matthews (Oxford: Clarendon Press, 1974-94).

Robert Graves, *In Broken Images, Selected Letters of Robert Graves 1914-46,* ed. Paul O'Prey (Hutchinson: 1982).

Charles Fulke Greville, *The Greville Memoirs 1840-60,* ed. Lytton Strachey and Roger Fulford (Macmillan: 1938).

Lady Charlotte Guest, *Journals 1833-52,* ed. Earl of Bessborough (John Murray: 1950).

R.T. Gunther, *The Life and Letters of Edward Lhuyd,* (1945).

A.W. Haddan and W. Stubbs (eds.), *Councils and Ecclesiastical Documents relating to Great Britain and Ireland* (Oxford: Clarendon Press, 1869-78).

Howell Harris, *Selected Trevecka Letters 1742-1747,* transcribed and annotated by G.M. Roberts, Calvinistic Methodist Historical Society, 1956; *Howell Harris's visits to Pembrokeshire,* transcribed by Rev. Tom Beynon (Aberystwyth: 1966).

Sir Nicholas Harris (ed.), *Proceedings and Ordinances of the Privy Council, Vol. I* (1834).

Nathaniel Hawthorne, *Notes of Travel* (Houghton, Mifflin & Co.: 1870).

Trevor Herbert and Gareth Elwyn Jones, *Edward I and Wales* (Cardiff: University of Wales Press, 1988).

F.C. Hingeston (ed.), *Lett. Henry IV. Royal and Historical Letters during the reign of Henry the Fourth*, Rolls Series (London: 1860).

Gerard Manley Hopkins, *Further Letters of G.M. Hopkins,* ed. C.C. Abbott (Oxford University Press: 1938); *Journals and Papers of G.M. Hopkins,* ed. Humphrey House and Graham Storey (Oxford University Press: 1959). *Selected Letters,* ed. Catherine Phillips (Oxford University Press: 1990).

B.E. and K.A Howells, *Pembrokeshire Life,* Pembrokeshire Record Society, 1972.

J. Hucks, *A Pedestrian Tour through North Wales in a Series of Letters,* ed. A.R. Jones and W. Tydeman (Cardiff: University of Wales Press, 1979).

William Hughes, *Life and Times of Bishop William Morgan* (S.P.C.K: 1891).

Geraint H. Jenkins, *Protestant Dissenters in Wales 1639-89* (Cardiff: University of Wales Press, 1992).

Arthur Johnes, *Essay on the Causes which have produced Dissent from the Established Church in the Principality of Wales* (Llanidloes: 1870).

Thomas Johnes, *A Land of Pure Delight,* ed. R.J. Moore-Colyer (Llandysul: Gomer, 1992).

Samuel Johnson, *Welsh Diary: Diaries, Prayers and Annals, Vol. I: The Works of Samuel Johnson,* ed. E.L. McAdam, with Donald and Mary Hyde (Yale University Press: 1958).

David Jones, *Dai Greatcoat, a self-portrait of David Jones in his letters,* ed. Rene Hague (Faber: 1980).

David J.V. Jones, *Before Rebecca* (Allen Lane: 1973).

Griffith Jones, *Welsh Piety* (London: 1755).

Jack Jones, *Letter from South Wales Coalfield Archive,* Library of University of Wales, Swansea.

Jonah Jones, *The Gallipoli Diary* (Bridgend: Seren, 1989).

J. Gwynfor Jones, *Wales and the Tudor State* (University of Wales Press, 1989).

Thomas Jones, *Memoirs,* Walpole Society, Vol. 32 (1951).

Thomas Jones, *A Diary with Letters* (Oxford University Press: 1954).

Francis Kilvert, *Kilvert's Diary,* chosen and ed. by William Plomer, (Jonathan Cape: 1960).

Charles Kingsley, *Charles Kingsley, his letters and memories of his life* (Henry S. King & Co.: London, 1877).

Aneirin Lewis (ed.), *The Correspondence of Thomas Percy and Evan Evans* (Louisiana State University Press: 1944).

Saunders Lewis, *Letters to Margaret Gilchrist,* ed. Mair Saunders Jones, Harri Pritchard Jones and Ned Thomas (Cardiff: University of Wales Press, 1993).

John H. Manners, *Journal of a Tour into Wales 1797* (J. Brettell: London, 1805).

T. Matthews, *Welsh Records in Paris* (Carmarthen: 1910).

Felix Mendelssohn: *A Life in Letters,* ed. Rudolf Elvers (Fromm International Publishing Company: New York, 1986).

Pat Molloy, *And They Blessed Rebecca* (Llandysul: Gomer, 1983).

Kenneth O. Morgan, *Lloyd George Family Letters, 1885-1936* (University of Wales Press & Oxford University Press: 1973).

J.E. Morris, 'Two Documents relating to the Conquest of Wales', *English Historical Review,* XIV, July 1899.

Lewis Morris, *Letters of Lewis, Richard, William and John Morris of Anglesey,* ed. J.H. Davies, Aberystwyth (1907-09); *Additional Letters of the Morrises of Anglesey (1735-86),* ed. Hugh Owen, Transactions of the Anglesey Antiquarian Society (Parts 1-2, 1947-49).

William Morris, *Letters of William Morris,* ed. Philip Henderson (Longmans, Green & Co: 1950).

Wilfred Owen, *Collected Letters,* ed. Harold Owen and John Bell (Oxford University Press: 1967).

Matthew Paris, *English History from 1235-1273,* trans. from Latin by Rev. J.A. Giles (1847).

Thomas Love Peacock, *Works* (Constable: 1934).

Thomas Pennant, *Tours in Wales, Vol. I* (1810).

J.R. Phillips (ed.), *Memoirs of the Civil War in Wales* (Longmans, Green & Co: 1874).

T. Jones Pierce (ed.), *Calendar of the Clenennau Letters and Papers in the Brogyntyn Collection,* (National Library of Wales Journal. Supp. Series IV pt.1, 1947).

Beatrix Potter, *Journal of Beatrix Potter,* transcribed by Leslie Linder (Frederick Warne & Co: 1966).

John Cowper Powys, *Petrushka and the Dancer: the Diaries of J.C. Powys 1929-1939,* selected and edited by Morine Krissdottir (Carcanet Press: 1995); *Letters of J.C. Powys to his brother Llewellyn 1925-39, Vol. II,* edited and selected by Malcolm Elwin (Village Press: London, 1975); *Letters of J.C. Powys to Louis Wilkinson 1935-56* (Macdonald: 1958).

Queen Victoria, *Letters of Queen Victoria,* ed. G.E. Buckle (John Murray: 1930).

Henry Richard, *Letters and Essays on Wales* (London: J. Clarke & Co.: 1884).

John Ruskin, *Collected Works, Vols. XXVII and XXXV,* ed. E.T. Cook and A. Wedderburn (London: George Allen, 1903-1912).

Bertrand Russell, *Manuscript Letters to Lady Ottoline Morrell,* Harry Ransom Humanities Research Center, The University of Texas at Austin.

Mary Salmon, *A Source Book of Welsh History* (Oxford University Press: 1927).

P.B. Shelley, *The Letters of Percy Bysshe Shelley,* ed. F.L. Jones (Oxford University Press: 1964).

Graham Sutherland, *Horizon*, 1942.

Jonathan Swift, *The Holyhead Journal*, 1727.

Dylan Thomas, *The Collected Letters of Dylan Thomas*, ed. Paul Ferris (Dent: 1985).

Edward Thomas, *Life and Letters of Edward Thomas*, John Moore (Heinemann: 1939); *Correspondence of Edward and Helen Thomas*, (National Library of Wales, 22914C).

Connop Thirlwall, *Letters Literary and Theological* (1881).

J.M. Traherne (ed.), *Stradling Correspondence – a Series of letters written in the reign of Queen Elizabeth* (Longman, Orme, Brown, Green & Longmans and William Bird: Cardiff, 1840).

Henry Vaughan, *The Works of Henry Vaughan*, ed. L.C. Martin (Oxford University Press: 1957).

J.E. Vincent, *Letters from Wales*, (W.H. Allen: 1889).

Elijah Waring, *Recollections and Anecdotes of Edward Williams or Iolo Morganwg, B.B.D.* (Gilpin: 1850).

Evelyn Waugh, *Letters of Evelyn Waugh*, ed. M. Amory (Weidenfeld & Nicolson: 1980).

John Wesley, *Journal of the Rev. John Wesley*, ed. Nehemiah Curnock (London: 1909).

David Williams, *The Rebecca Riots* (University of Wales Press: 1971).

Edward Williams (Iolo Morganwg), *Journal of an Excursion into Carmarthenshire in June, 1796*, Carmarthenshire Antiquarian Society, Transactions XIV 1919-21. *Correspondence of Iolo Morganwg,* (National Library of Wales 21286).

Gwyn A. Williams, *The Merthyr Rising* (Croom Helm: 1978).

J. Gwyn Williams, *The Quakers of Merioneth during the 17th Century*, Journal of the Merioneth History and Records Society 8, 1978-9.

Virginia Woolf, *The Flight of the Mind: The Letters of Virginia Woolf, Vol. I 1888-1912*, ed. Nigel Nicolson and Joanne Trautmann (The Hogarth Press: 1975).

William Wordsworth, *The Letters of William and Dorothy Wordsworth, The Later Years Part I, 1821-28* (Oxford University Press: 1978).

Frances Williams Wynn, *The Diary of a Lady of Quality* (1864).

Thomas Wright, *The History of Ludlow* (1852).

Thomas Wright (ed.), *Letters relating to the Suppression of the Monasteries* (Camden Society: 1843).

Arthur Young, *Six Weeks Tour through the Southern Counties of England and Wales* (1772).

Acknowledgements are due to the following for permission to reprint work in this collection. Every attempt has been made to contact the copyright holders of the work.

Barbara Bloomfield, Barbara and David Walters: extracts from Raphael Samuel, Barbara Bloomfield, Guy Boanas [eds.] *The Enemy Within – Pit Villages and the Miners' Strike of 1984-5* (Routledge & Kegan Paul: 1986). **Dora Carrington:** extracts from *Letters and Extracts from her Diaries,* ed. David Garnett (Jonathan Cape). **John Cowper Powys:** extracts from *Petrushka and the Dancer: the Diaries of J.C. Powys 1929-1939,* selected and edited by Morine Krissdottir (Carcanet Press: 1995); *Letters of J.C. Powys to his brother Llewellyn 1925-39, Vol. II,* edited and selected by Malcolm Elwin (Village Press: 1975); *Letters of J.C. Powys to Louis Wilkinson 1935-56* (Macdonald: 1958) © Christopher Sinclair-Stevenson as executor of the Cowper Powys Estate. **Caradoc Evans:** 'Caradoc's Journal' extracted from *Welsh Review,* June and September, 1945 © John Harris. **Robert Graves:** extracts from *In Broken Images, Selected Letters of Robert Graves 1914-46,* ed. Paul O'Prey (Hutchinson: 1982) by permission of A.P. Watt Ltd © The Trustees of the Robert Graves Copyright Trust. **David Jones:** extracts from *Dai Greatcoat, a self-portrait of David Jones in his letters,* ed. Rene Hague (Faber: 1980). **Jonah Jones:** extracts from *The Gallipoli Diary* (Seren: 1989) reprinted with the permission of the author © Jonah Jones. **Dylan Thomas:** extracts from *The Collected Letters of Dylan Thomas,* ed. Paul Ferris (J M Dent: 1985). **Evelyn Waugh:** extracts from *Letters of Evelyn Waugh,* ed. M. Amory (Weidenfeld & Nicolson: 1980) reprinted by permission of PFD on behalf of the Estate of Evelyn Waugh © Evelyn Waugh 1925.